D1601375

Aristocratic Life in
Medieval France

————————

· ✧ ·

JOHN W. BALDWIN

Aristocratic Life in Medieval France

The Romances of Jean Renart and Gerbert de Montreuil, 1190–1230

The Johns Hopkins University Press
Baltimore & London

© 2000 The Johns Hopkins University Press
All rights reserved. Published 2000
Printed in the United States of America on
acid-free paper

9 8 7 6 5 4 3 2 1

The Johns Hopkins University Press
2715 North Charles Street
Baltimore, Maryland 21218-4363
www.press.jhu.edu

ISBN 0-8018-6188-8

For Jenny

Il conte d'armes et d'amors
et chante d'ambedeus ensamble . . .

It tells of arms and of love
and sings of both together . . .

JEAN RENART, *Roman de la rose*

Contents

Preface

———

MEDIEVAL history has been based on Latin sources, largely consisting of chronicles and charters. As the official language of the Church, Latin was written by and most often preserved for the clergy. Such texts are an excellent source of information about the ideals and institutions of churchmen and are reasonably satisfactory as regards the activities of kings, barons, and even local lords, all of whom employed clerics to record their affairs, but they are saturated with a clerical point of view that renders them less revealing of the mundane activities of the laity, particularly those about which the clergy were apprehensive. Yet because little else was available until the twelfth century, modern historians have continued to rely on Latin documentation and have found the clerical bias unproblematic.

In twelfth-century France, however, fictional literature appeared written in the vernacular, the language of the laity. Whether the authors and scribes were clerics or laymen, it was nonetheless composed for the direct enjoyment of aristocratic audiences. Depicting the world of warriors, the chansons de geste emerged first, followed by romances that expanded these masculine adventures to encompass themes of women and love as well. The *Chanson de Roland* is the earliest and the best-known example of the first genre, and Chrétien de Troyes's romances about King Arthur's world eventually came to dominate the second, more complex field. By the second half of the century, romances began to treat subjects that had been avoided by clerics writing in Latin—among them the patronizing of jongleurs, fighting in tournaments, making love, appreciating feminine beauty, and celebrating festive occasions—topics that are portrayed in vivid detail and sharp colors, in contrast to the gray, shadowy sketches of the Latin chroniclers.

Former generations of historians have usually hesitated to include this literature among their sources, preferring the putative if somber *veritas* of medieval Latin texts to the imaginative brilliance of the vernacular. Not all, however, because each generation has seen a few who have dared to include fiction in their purview. A century ago, Léon Gautier sought to write about French chivalry exclusively based on the chansons de geste. Among my teachers, Sidney Painter included romance in his evocative essay on the subject, *French Chivalry: Chivalric Ideas and Practices in Medieval France* (1940). More recently, in his *Chivalry* (1984), Maurice Keen has expressed doubts about the historical relevance of the romances, but Jean Flori has been equally at home in Latin and vernacular literature in his numerous fundamental contributions to the field.[1] With the advent of poststructuralism, moreover, literary critics have sought to read historical documents as susceptible to issues of representation common to literature, blurring the boundaries between it and history. This move, in its most extreme form, proposes to reduce historical truth to the status of literary fiction, but it also dismantles the barriers between the two realms and opens literature to historians. If other historians have hesitated, I do not, and I propose unabashedly to read vernacular literary texts as historical sources on the activities of the laity hitherto obscured in clerical Latin.

Unlike my forerunners, who encompass several centuries in their studies, I shall—as has become my habit—focus on a discrete place, northern France, and a limited timespan, the four decades surrounding the year 1200 (1190–1230), the place and time in the Middle Ages with which I am best acquainted. I have chosen two writers, each the author of two romances: Jean Renart of the *Escoufle* (1200–1202) and the *Roman de la rose* (c. 1209), also known as *Guillaume de Dole*, and Gerbert de Montreuil of a *Continuation* (1226–30) to Chrétien de Troye's influential *Conte du graal* (dating from before 1191) and the *Roman de la violette* (1227–29).[2]

The *Escoufle, Rose,* and *Violette,* which make up my central bouquet, have affinities that unite them as a textual corpus and distinguish them from earlier such works.[3] Prominent among their distinctive traits is an acute consciousness of the contemporary context, which enhances them for my historical appetites. The position of Gerbert's *Continuation* is more nuanced. Although it has features in common with the others, its narrative is directly attached to Chrétien's previous romance, with which it shares literary properties. For purposes of my study, it stands to the side of the other three and serves as a key witness to the religious sentiment of its time. As writers of romance, Jean and Gerbert were indebted to the Tristan legend, to Marie de France, and especially to Chrétien, but they sought to distance themselves from their predecessors through their distinctive approach.

To highlight the laicity of these vernacular texts and to reinforce their historical status, I shall keep them in constant dialogue with the Latin writings of contemporary theologians who taught in the cathedral school of Notre-Dame at Paris, known to me from my earlier work. The latter include Master Pierre the Chanter (d. 1197) and a selected group of his students, Master Robert of Courson (d. 1219), Master Thomas of Chobham (d. 1233–36), and Master Raoul Ardent (c. 1191–1215). As they lectured and disputed in the schools, they wrote biblical commentaries, theological *questiones,* moral treatises, and confession manuals. As moral theologians lecturing and disputing in the schools, they were concerned with administering penance and were particularly sensitive to current issues, such as entertainment by jongleurs, the dangers of tournaments, the practice of ordeals, and sexual behavior. Some, if not all, of their proposals were implemented by their most influential student and colleague, Lotario de Segni, when he was elected Pope Innocent III (1198–1216) and convoked the great Fourth Lateran Council of 1215. Some of their attitudes were likewise adopted by Philip Augustus (1179–1223), the contemporary French king and their neighbor in the royal palace at the opposite end of the Ile de la Cité from Notre-Dame. His reign roughly circumscribes the chronological boundaries of this study, and the royal historiographers Rigord de Saint-Denis and Guillaume le Breton help to contextualize the dialogues between the vernacular writers and the clerical theologians.

Since this study proceeds from a literary base, Chapter 1 addresses literary questions. It introduces the two authors, recounts the plots of their four romances, identifies their designated audiences, and distinguishes the features of their literary craft that set them apart from their predecessors and have tempted me to read them for historical ends. It concludes with a treatment of jongleurs that reveals clues to Jean's and Gerbert's professional identity and offers an example of the interaction between vernacular and Latin texts. Chapter 2 concentrates on the audience—that is, the contemporary aristocrats to whom Jean and Gerbert addressed their romances, along with their entourages. It probes the political context in depth, not only because the romances are thereby situated in history, but also because they are given warranty as historical sources. The next five chapters explore successively the major aristocratic activities of (3) fighting, (4) gift-giving, (5) loving women, (6) celebrating with entertainments, fine food, and elegant dress, and finally (7) worshipping. These are subjects that Jean and Gerbert take evident delight in, but clerics harbored serious misgivings about all but the last. The wealth of vernacular detail is thus both confronted with and corroborated by the criticism of contemporary Latin theologians. On the subject of religion, the obvious speciality of the clergy, the dialogue between the vernacular and the Latin texts is especially intense, but in Chapter 7, I give priority to the romances in initiating the discussion. The concluding Chapter 8 follows the reception of the romances through a series of concentric audiences, which start with Jean's and Gerbert's contemporary public, pass to the later Middle Ages, and conclude with modern critics and historians, among whom I place myself.

In this study I do not concern myself with many issues that have preoccupied modern historians of chivalry. I am not, for example, interested in definitions of knighthood and nobility and their interplay, so important to recent discussion but taken for granted in my texts.[4] Nor are fiefs, vassals, manors, and peasants treated here. In contrast to recent analyses that subject medieval data to modern questions, I have permitted my four romances to set the agenda for this book.[5] In part attempting to reduce the weight of clerical Latin, I have also sought to restrict myself to questions that concerned my vernacular authors. Only in connection with issues they chose to pursue do I seek further help from modern studies. In the last section I seek to evaluate the historicity of the more problematic conclusions offered by the vernacular texts. The contents of this book therefore depart measurably from modern histories.

Neither does a historical knight appear in focus in my pages. Among all the aristocratic individuals who inhabited northern France at the turn of the century, there is a contemporary biography only of William the Marshal, and perhaps of Baudouin de Guines. In fact, much of the modern understanding of twelfth-century chivalry is simply the life of William the Marshal writ large.[6] The main characters of Jean Renart and Gerbert de Montreuil are fictive, except for the patrons to whom their books are dedicated, but I trust that I can convince readers that their distinct features were nonetheless credible to their historical contemporaries. The material that is treated here has not been chosen for its novelty, but for its grounding in the vernacular texts. Although some of it will be familiar to historians, enough, I hope, will be new to justify the effort. Because I believe that many readers will be interested primarily in the individual subjects, the chapters have been written as self-contained units. This presents some repetition to those who read them consecutively, and those who prefer to begin with the historiography and theoretical discussion would do best to start with the last chapter.

Nearly a half-century ago, when I discovered the attraction of northern France around the turn of the twelfth and thirteenth centuries, I affixed myself to that region and to the year 1200 with a tether that stretched little more than two decades in either direction. Within this verdant but circumscribed pasture, I have had the pleasure of ruminating at leisure on varied subjects. The Latin writings of Pierre the Chanter and his theological school at Notre-Dame enabled me to explore the processes of clerical and scholarly thought that culminated in the university of Paris. The registers of King Philip Augustus, also redacted in Latin, later led me to follow the emergence of the Capetian monarchy and plot its ambition to dominate France and to seek hegemony in western Europe. After this sustained diet of Latin documentation, the suspicion emerged that it had prevented me from appreciating other social groups who were beyond the pale because of their illiteracy in Latin. Since my chosen epoch was also rich in vernacular romance, I succumbed to the temptation of trying to understand how this literature both addressed and revealed the appetites of its aristocratic audience. After casting about, my choice finally fell on the two authors whom I trust that this study will vindicate. Chapters on fighting and giving gifts, however, inevitably led to one on making love, and the complexity of that chapter required a book in itself. After the detour of *The Language of Sex: Five Voices from Northern France around 1200* (1994), I have now returned to my original destination.

Like my past writings, this study consists of analyses, paraphrases, and translations of medieval texts, both in French and in Latin, many of which have already been made available in modern languages. While I assume responsibility for all translations and renditions, I cannot conceal my debt to these predecessors. They are grouped with the editions cited in the list of short titles.

Although circumscribed in time and place, this project has led me across a vast terrain of human activity. For help on specific points, I have called upon the expertise of many colleagues, some of whom did not know me personally. Some will no longer recall my question, and I fear I may have forgotten others who responded promptly, but among those who come to mind I wish to thank Rebecca Baltzer, Brigitte Bedos-Rezak, Jacques Berlioz, Thomas H. Bestul, Philippe Buc, Giles Constable, Pierre Desportes, Margot Fassler, John B. Freed, Joseph Goering, Pierre-Marie Gy, Caroline Jewers, William Jordan, Paul Maevert, John Monro, Stephen G. Nichols, Michel Pastoureau, Kathryn Reyerson, Eleanor Roach, Ian Short, Walter Simon, Marc Vaisbroit, Evelyn Vitz, and Michel Zink. As in the past, Margaret Switten has responded to my questions on Jean Renart, and David Hult has helped me with the Old French and interpretative problems. Jean Flori, who has long pioneered in the field, has offered steady encouragement. Finally, this project has yielded the unexpected pleasure of renewing collaboration with Peter Dreyer, my editor for this book just as he was for my study on Philip Augustus in 1986. Since he has long experience with my writing, he knows how to alleviate my faults. I wish to thank him for the distinct improvements he has contributed to the text.

Since 1983, when I first started thinking about it, this project has provided subjects for a number of lectures. I was honored by invitations from the Bertie Wilkinson Lecture at Toronto in 1993, the Quodlibet Lecture at York in 1996, and the Medieval Academy's presidential lecture at Toronto in 1997. In 1995, Pierre Toubert generously invited me to give four lectures at the Collège de France, in which I tried out the present chapters. Other universities and institutes offered opportunities to travel with my ideas: the Haskins Conference in Houston (1988), Princeton University (1988), the University of Pennsylvania (1988), the Institut historique allemand in Paris (1988), the Ecole des hautes études en sciences sociales (1989), Mount Holyoke College (1990), the Midwest Medieval History Conference at St. Johns University in Minnesota (1991), Vassar College (1992), the Kalamazoo Conference (1993), the University of Washington in Seattle (1995), the Medieval Studies Institute at Notre Dame, Indiana (1996), and the Austrian Historical Institute in Vienna (1998). In 1998, too, the universities at Copenhagen, Roskilde, Odense, Aarhus, and Aalborg in Denmark received me in rapid succession. I wish to thank my many hosts for recruiting audiences who provided helpful discussion. At home at the Johns Hopkins University, I have continued to rely on the History Seminar and Medieval Studies Group to provide forums for considering individual chapters.

In 1983–84, the Guggenheim Foundation provided a fellowship and the National Bank of Denmark an apartment overlooking the historic Nyhavn in Copenhagen that gave me the leisure to start thinking about vernacular literature. In 1991–92, the National Endowment for the Humanities made possible free time for writing. Throughout, the Johns Hopkins University was generous in supplementing these opportunities with leaves of absence. I am grateful for this essential support.

The following articles and chapters, previously published, have been adapted in the present book: "Jean Renart et le tournoi de Saint-Trond: Une conjonction de l'histoire et de la littérature," *Annales: Economies, sociétés, civilisations* 45.3 (May–June 1990): 565–88; "The Crisis of the Ordeal: Literature, Law and Religion around 1200," *Journal of Medieval and Renaissance Studies* 24 (1994): 327–53; "'Once there was an emperor . . .': A Political Reading of the Romances of Jean Renart," in *Jean Renart and the Art of Romance: Essays on Guillaume de Dole,* ed. Nancy Vine Durling (Gainesville, Fla., 1997), 45–82; "The Image of the Jongleur in Northern France around 1200," *Speculum* 72 (1997): 636–63; and "From Ordeal to Confession: In Search of Lay Religion in Early Thirteenth-Century France," in *Handling Sin: Confession in the Middle Ages,* ed. Peter Biller and A. J. Minnis (York, 1998), 191–209.

Aristocratic Life in
Medieval France

· ✂ ·

ONE

Literary Craft

Jean Renart,
Gerbert de Montreuil,
and Their Romances

. ∝ .

S INCE this historical inquiry is drawn directly from works of fiction, the literary properties of Jean Renart's and Gerbert de Montreuil's romances are the necessary subject of this opening chapter. I shall quickly identify the two authors and their audiences, recount the plots of their four romances, which are largely unfamiliar to modern readers, and make explicit their literary strategies. Since both Jean and Gerbert considered themselves to be innovators, I shall juxtapose their new techniques with the preceding literature with which their audiences were familiar. In particular, the vernacular romances of Chrétien de Troyes and the Latin treatises of the contemporary theologians at Paris constitute the two "horizons" against which the four romances are read here. Questions normally raised by literary critics are equally essential to the interpretative strategy of employing romance texts as historical sources. Both the identity of the audiences and the hermeneutics of employing literature for historical ends are raised here sufficiently to introduce the reader and are treated at greater length in Chapter 2 and Chapter 8. The chapter concludes with a treatment of jongleurs that serves both to establish the professional identity of the two authors and to provide an initial example of the interaction between vernacular and Latin texts set within a precise historical context, which remains, in effect, the ultimate ambition of this inquiry.

Authors and Audiences

Except for their names, virtually nothing is known about the lives of Jean Renart and Gerbert de Montreuil. Like that of the celebrated Chrétien de Troyes, their identities lie obscured behind their enigmatic nomenclature. Jean, the older of the two, spells his name "Jehan Renart" in the *Lai de l'ombre* (v. 953), but this is patently a nom de plume inspired by the wily fox of the *Roman de Renart* cycle (*Rose* vv. 5420–21).[1] In the *Escoufle* and the *Rose,* he studiously conceals his name in three *engins,* or anagrams, that coyly hint that he is about to pronounce a surname. Jean takes leave of the *Roman de la rose,* for example, by declaring:

> Et cil se veut reposer ore,
> qui le jor perdi son sornon
> qu'il enTRA eN REligion.

> And now he wishes to rest / who lost his surname on the day / that he entered into religion. (vv. 5653–55)

Only by reading the passage backward does his name emerge. The phrase he chose was the stereotypic announcement of entry into the monastic profession,[2] but there is no confirmation that Jean himself, the least monastic of medieval vernacular authors, ever became a monk. Confronted with such obfuscation, there is little wonder that attempts to identify him have remained futile.

In a manuscript that contains Chrétien's *Conte du graal* and five verse continuations (Paris BN fr. 12576), Gerbert identifies himself five times in rapid succession with his baptismal name (*Continuation* vv. 6358, 6998, 7001, 7008, 7016), but only after he has proceeded nearly halfway through the narrative. Saying that death prevented Chrétien from completing his romance (vv. 6984–87), he observes that he himself has taken up the story where other *trouvères* left off (vv. 6998–99). Although he classifies others as clerics, laymen, and monks (v. 6357), he has left no clue to his own status or origin. By comparing similarities in language and style, modern scholars have nonetheless associated this Gerbert with the Gerbert de Montreuil who signed the *Roman de la violette* "Gyrbers de Mosteruel" (v. 6634).[3] Montreuil was the main seaport in the county of Ponthieu on the northeastern coast of France and one of the chief cities under the rule of Marie, countess of Ponthieu, to whom Gerbert sent the romance. Jean and Gerbert are linked by close affinities between the *Rose* and the *Violette.*

If the names of the authors are ciphers, those to whom they addressed their romances are recognizable historical personages.[4] Just as Chrétien had sent romances to Marie, countess of Troyes (d. 1198), and Philippe, count of Flanders (d. 1191), Jean sent his *Escoufle* to Baudouin, sixth count of Hainaut, and ninth count of Flanders (d. c. 1205), his *Lai de l'ombre* to an unnamed bishop-elect (perhaps Hugues de Pierrepont, bishop of Liège, d. 1229), and his *Roman de la rose* to Milon de Nanteuil (d. 1234) while Milon was provost of the cathedral chapter of Reims. Gerbert addressed the *Roman de la violette* to Marie, countess of Ponthieu (d. 1251) while she was lady of the county in the absence of her exiled husband. Since Chrétien's *Graal* already had an addressee, Philippe of Flanders, Gerbert's sequel may have omitted any other as superfluous.[5] All three addressees were francophone, and Jean and Gerbert appropriately composed their romances in Francien, the putative dialect of the region surrounding Paris.

These historical figures help date the romances and contextualize the politics of their audiences, subjects developed in Chapter 2. The audiences consisted both of the known personages and of their entourages. Chrétien coins the phrase "before kings and counts" in his first romance (*Erec et Enide* v. 20). (It is later modified to "told in a royal court" in the *Graal* v. 64.) Adopting the phrase in his three works (*Escoufle* vv. 21, 9076; *Lai* v. 49; *Rose* v. 5646), Jean thereby designates the crowds of knights and ladies who frequented the courts of the high barons and prelates, thus including the lesser nobility in his ultimate audience.[6] Because individuals are identified and the rest socially situated, Jean's and Gerbert's audiences are more accessible to us than the authors themselves.

Narratives

To entertain aristocratic audiences, romanciers adopted the device in the twelfth century of asserting that they had not invented the story they were about to tell but had found it somewhere, usually in written form, and occasionally supplied by the person to whom they addressed their romance.[7] Whether this was true or not in the case of any given story is less important than the ubiquity of the device, which can be illustrated from the prologue of Chrétien's *Cligès* (vv. 8–44). After enumerating his previous compositions, Chrétien announces that he will begin a new story (*an novel conte*) about a young man named Cligès. This history (*estoire*) he claims to have found in a book (*livres*) in an armoire at the church of Saint-Pierre de Beauvais, from which the story (*contes*) has been taken, and he testifies to the truth of this. Opening the *Conte du graal*, Chrétien once again speaks of the romance (*romans*) that he is about to begin (v. 8). By the command of the count (*conte*) [of Flanders], he strives to rhyme the best story (*conte*) ever told (*conte{*) in a royal court. This is the *Contes de graal*, of which the count gave him the book (*livre* vv. 62–67).[8] Chrétien's repetitious conceit of the synonyms *conte* and *estoire* thoroughly permeate Jean's and Gerbert's own prologues and narratives.

In the prologue to his first romance, Jean takes notice of storytellers (*conteors*) who intended to pronounce well and set down stories (*contes*) but with whom he cannot agree (*Escoufle* vv. 10–13). In his own time, he proposes to relate and commit to memory an old story (*conte*) that history (*l'estoire*) tells (*conte*) us—this is the *contes de l'Escoufle* (vv. 35–39). To emphasize its pervasiveness, he plays upon all of the homologies of *conte:*

> K'a cort a roi n'a cort a conte
> Ne doit conteres conter conte, ...
>
> For neither at the court of king nor that of count / should a
> storyteller tell a story. (vv. 21–22)

Like Chrétien, he also emphasizes the link between his story (*conte*) and the aristocratic audience (*conte* = count).[9]

Chrétien's tales have been often rehearsed to both medieval and modern audiences, but since the *contes* of the *Escoufle* and the other three romances are little known to modern readers, I offer brief sketches of their narratives, in the manner in which plots are summarized in opera programs. Like Chrétien's *Cligès,* the *Escoufle* consists of two discrete but related parts. In the preparatory section, Richard, count of Montivilliers (read Normandy) departs on a crusade for the Holy Land, where he defeats the Turks and negotiates a truce for three years. On his return, he passes through Benevento in Italy, where he meets the German emperor, who seeks aid against the depredations of his servile *ministeriales*. Appointed imperial constable, Richard recruits good knights from France and restores the emperor's authority. As a reward, Richard is given a noble wife in marriage, the lady of Genoa, with whom he conceives a son, Guillaume, born on the same day that a daughter, Aelis, is delivered to the empress and emperor.

Guillaume and Aelis, the hero and heroine of the principal story, are raised together from infancy as brother and sister in the imperial nursery, but they soon fall in love. The emperor plans to marry Guillaume to Aelis and make the boy heir to the imperial throne. The empress and high princes of the empire, however, take advantage of Count Richard's death to object to the disparity of the children's birth and their growing intimacy.

They persuade the emperor to separate the lovers, but the youthful couple escape from the court and elope to Normandy to reclaim Guillaume's heritage. During an idyllic *déjeuner sur l'herbe* near Toul in Lorraine, a buzzard, the *escoufle* of the title, succeeds in snatching a purse containing Aelis's ring. When Guillaume finally retrieves this *gage d'amour*, sufficient time has intervened to separate the lovers, and they journey throughout the remainder of the romance in search of each other.

In the company of a servant girl, Ysabel, Aelis finally arrives at Montpellier, where she establishes an atelier to sew belts and purses for a noble clientele. The fame of her work attracts the interest of the countess and count of Saint-Gilles (read Toulouse) who invite her to be their guest at Saint-Gilles. Meanwhile, Guillaume has also been searching fruitlessly for seven years. Employment at an inn at the renowned pilgrimage shrine of Santiago de Compostela enables him to locate Aelis's mule; prayers to Saint Gilles lead him further to the saint's shrine at Saint-Gilles du Gard. Also serving in the *hôtelerie* there, he accompanies a falconer on a hunt, where he catches a buzzard, which he devours raw in a frenzied fit of revenge. His strange behavior is reported to the count, who summons him to court, where the lovers are finally united. Guillaume is knighted and returns to reclaim his Norman inheritance, and the pair are married. Three years after the death of the emperor, they return to Rome, where they are crowned empress and emperor.

The *Lai de l'ombre* is a *conte* of seduction recounted with economy, delicacy, and insight. A young knight from the marches of the Empire between Châlons and Pertois in Champagne attempts to persuade a married lady to become his lover. Her resistance is overcome when he casts his ring to her reflection in a well.

Although Jean is more succinct about narrative technique in his prologue and conclusion to the *Roman de la rose,* the underlying distinctions and terminology remain the same. He opens the romance with the words: "Cil qui mist cest conte en romans . . ." (v. 1). This line can be understood in two ways. It could mean: "He who translated this story [*conte*] into vernacular . . . ," just as Chrétien had translated Ovid's *Ars amatoria* ("en romans mist," *Cligès* v. 3), but following another path, it might also be rendered: "He who turned this story into a romance . . . ," thus creating a distinction between the original *conte* and Jean's present *romans.* At the end of the tale, however,

L'arcevesques par reverence
en fist metre en escrit l'estoire.
Bien le devroient en memoire
avoir et li roi et li conte,
cel prodome dont on lor conte . . .

The archbishop out of reverence / had the story set down in
writing. / Kings and counts should well keep in memory / that
preud'homme of whom one tells . . . (vv. 5643–47)

Although it is not the original tale but Jean's version that is committed to
writing, the salient terms of *conte, estoire, en escrit,* and *en memoire* were retained.

Jean opens the *Rose* by introducing Conrad, the young emperor of the
Germans. Although the flower of chivalry, Conrad gives little thought to
his political obligations of finding a wife and producing an heir to the Empire. Instead, he amuses himself at a spring hunt, where he sings, dances,
and pursues ladies while their husbands are off in the forest. One morning,
to assuage the boredom of this frivolous life, he requests his court jongleur, Juglet, to tell him a pleasant story, and the latter obliges by recounting what is, in fact, Jean's own *Lai de l'ombre.* Asked whether such desirable women still exist, Juglet responds with a description of the beauty of a
maiden, Lïenor, and of the chivalry of her brother Guillaume, a lowly
knight from Dole in Lorraine. Conrad is so enamored with Lïenor's portrait that he wishes to become acquainted with the family. He invites Guillaume to attend a forthcoming tournament at Saint-Trond, where a team
of French knights is recruited against a team of Germans. Guillaume arrives, charms the emperor, and carries away the honors of the tournament
for the Germans. Guillaume's prowess fully persuades Conrad of the family's nobility, and the emperor resolves to propose to the high princes of
the Empire at the forthcoming diet at Mainz that he take Lïenor as his wife,
although he has not yet seen her. The emperor's unnamed seneschal learns
of Conrad's intention and recognizes the threat that the family of Dole
will pose to his own influence at court. He journeys quickly to Dole, where
he is refused an audience with Lïenor but through the indiscretion of her
mother learns of a birthmark in the shape of a rose on the maiden's inner
thigh (hence the title of the romance). Armed with this compromising information, he convinces Conrad that he has seduced the girl, thus causing
the distressed emperor to renounce his marital plans.

Lïenor, however, refuses to accede to this calumny and shows up at Mainz with a counterplot against the seneschal. She sends him a belt and purse as a *gage d'amour* from a lady friend, with instructions that he wear them under his tunic if he wishes to enjoy her favors. Then, in the presence of the imperial diet, she accuses him of rape and theft of her purse, a charge immediately confirmed by the circumstantial evidence under his tunic. Having never seen the girl, the seneschal quickly denies the accusation and offers to prove his innocence by the cold-water ordeal. When he undergoes it, he is straightway cleared, but so is Lïenor. She is the "maiden of the rose" whose virginity the seneschal has falsely claimed to have had, she triumphantly announces. The romance joyously concludes with the seneschal's punishment, Lïenor's marriage to Conrad, and her coronation as empress.

Despite particular points of coincidence with earlier romances, Jean's narratives are essentially his own creations, as far as can be judged. In contrast, since Gerbert's task in the *Continuation* was to complete the *Conte du graal* of Chrétien de Troyes, his underlying story (*conte*) was already provided. Chrétien's original story recounts the initiation of a young boy, Perceval, into knighthood, followed by a complex series of adventures involving his training as a knight, his relations with his mother and family, and his aid to maidens in distress. Among the many episodes, I shall signal only two here. In the first, the knight happens upon the house of the Fisher King, where he witnesses the mysterious ceremony of the Grail, or *graal* (an undefined serving vessel), and a bleeding lance. In the second, he undergoes a penitential experience on Good Friday through the ministrations of a hermit. To these disconnected scenes, Chrétien adds other adventures involving Gauvain, King Arthur's nephew.

Chrétien's story is incomplete in two senses: Perceval fails to ask about the significance of the Grail, and the narrative itself breaks off abruptly during one of Gauvain's adventures. During the following half century, Chrétien's unfinished *conte* spawned a plethora of sequels in both verse and prose. Those in verse were attached directly to Chrétien's original work in manuscripts such as Paris BN fr. 12576, which includes Gerbert's *Continuation*.

The verse continuations, most of which are anonymous, can be sorted into two major families, each containing differing versions. The *First Continuation* is occasionally named the "Gauvain continuation," because it pursues that hero's adventures from the point where Chrétien breaks off.

Gauvain, for example, pays two visits to the Fisher King's castle, but he falls asleep before he can learn of the significance of the Grail. The complex *Second Continuation* consists of a family of versions. It has been attributed to Wachier de Denain and is better known as the "Perceval continuation," because it follows the young hero's adventures after his visit to the hermit, the point where Chrétien's *conte* leaves off. In this series, Perceval revisits Blancheflor and his sister at his mother's house, episodes also found in Chrétien's original story, but he undergoes new adventures as well. In the end, he returns to the Fisher King's castle, where the drama of the Grail ceremony is reenacted for him, but before he learns of its significance, the *Second Continuation* also breaks off. The break is difficult to interpret, however, because it may result from the editor's insertion of a new continuation.

It is at this point that the scribe of the manuscript Paris BN fr. 12576 interpolated Gerbert's version, which takes up the story and subjects Perceval to a further series of adventures, leading him to the Fisher King's castle for a third time, at which point Gerbert breaks off as well. Essentially framed by the Grail ceremony at both ends, Gerbert's *Continuation* focuses on the purification of the young hero through penance. Like his predecessors, Gerbert recapitulates Perceval's visits to his sister, to his chivalric mentor Gornemans, to the ever-patient Blancheflor, whom he finally weds in a spiritual marriage, and to the family of the Red Knight, whom Perceval kills in Chrétien's story, but he also adds new episodes, involving the Dragon Knight, the tournament at Lancien that unites Tristan with the Arthurian knights, and, occasionally, Gauvain. Since Gerbert's *Continuation* ends at the third visit to the Grail Castle without the hero's further enlightenment, the scribe of Paris BN fr. 12756 appended a fourth continuation, that of Manessier, which provides closure to the story. Because Manessier wrote independently of Gerbert and perhaps somewhat later, however, I shall omit him from consideration.

Since Gerbert had received the basic elements of his story from Chrétien and the *Second Continuation,* he punctuates his lengthy narrative with periodic assurances that he is following the original *conte* (vv. 390, 5526, 14074), *histoire* (vv. 10193, 10518, 12220), *romans* (v. 6500), and *livres* (v. 9603), occasionally promising to accelerate the story with greater brevity (vv. 2814–17, 14079). All this terminology is taken directly from the *Conte du graal*.[10] When Gerbert introduces his own name for the first time during the Blancheflor episode, he refers back to Chrétien's original version

(*Graal* vv. 1795–1829) in expostulating on her beauty: "What shall I say of her beauty? You have heard it before another time within the *conte*" (vv. 6353–55). In the most explicit formulation, he affirms:

> But now Gerbert has contributed his part according to the true history [*selonc le vraie estoire*]; may God give him strength and victory . . . that he can attain the end of Perceval, which he has undertaken just as the book [*livres*] teaches him where the matter is written down [*la meterre en est escripte*]. Gerbert who tells it to us from the point where Perceval repaired the good sword with so much pain and toil and has asked the significance of the Grail and the lance that bled. Indeed, it is from that point that Gerbert tells it to us, the one who has drawn from his understanding the rhyming verse [*rime*] that I am reciting. He even completely improved Tristan's battle. I shall not omit a single part of it. (vv. 7001–19)

Gerbert encapsulates his purpose in writing the *Roman de la violette* in two succinct lines of the prologue:

> Por chou me voel jou entremetre
> D'un plaisant conte en rime metre. . . .

> That is why I wish to engage myself / to place a pleasant story in rhyme. . . . (vv. 17–18)

It is, he reiterates a little later, "a fine and delightful story" (*un conte biel et delitable* [v. 33]).

As in the *Continuation*, Gerbert occasionally reminds his listeners/ readers of the *estoire* and *conte*, promising to shorten his story (vv. 1579, 3842–44). At the end, he announces that he does not wish to make it longer because he has reached the other bank of the river with so many rhymes (vv. 6634–36). Gerbert neglects to reveal that he has borrowed narrative elements from the *Roman du comte de Poitiers*,[11] and, more important for my purposes, from the romances of Jean Renart as well. "In the Empire, where the Germans have been for many days and years, as the *contes* says, once there was an emperor . . . Conrad," Jean begins. "Once there was a king in France who was handsome, *preu* and brave . . . Louis" (vv. 65–66, 78), Gerbert echoes. Just as Jean opens with festive singing and dancing on the spring hunt, so Gerbert intones songs and dances in the royal court at Pont de l'Arche. This sets the stage for the hero, Gerart, count of Nevers, to brag about the virtue of his *amie* Eurïaut, and for the villain Lisïart, count of Forez, to wager his county against Gerart's that she cannot withstand his charms. When Gerart accepts, his opponent rides off to Nevers to try his luck, but Eurïaut, true to her lover, resists him. With the connivance of a servant, Gondrée, however, Lisïart spies upon her in her bath and notes a birthmark—not on her thigh, in this case, but a violet on her breast (hence the title of the romance). With this intimate knowledge, he wins the county of Nevers, just as the seneschal blocks Lïenor's marriage.

Gerart drags Eurïaut off to the forest with the intention of killing her, but she warns him of a lurking dragon in time to save his life. He slays the dragon and abandons his *amie* in an unconscious state, where she is discovered by the duke of Metz, who takes her home in hope of marrying her. In the meantime, Gerart disguises himself as a jongleur to spy on Lisïart and Gondrée at their table in Nevers. There he learns of Eurïaut's innocence. Like Guillaume of the *Escoufle*, he takes off in search of his *amie*; like Perceval, he undergoes a series of adventures to relieve besieged damsels and perform other chivalric services; like Gauvain, he is the object of amorous rivalry between two women; and, like Tristan, he succumbs to a love potion, this time administered by the daughter of the duke of Cologne. Meanwhile, at Metz, Eurïaut has lost her ring to a lark and has attracted the unwanted attention of the villainous Melïtir, who, when repulsed, kills the duke of Metz's daughter, who shares a bed with Eurïaut, and plants the incriminating dagger in the sleeping heroine's hand. Caught apparently in flagrante delicto, Eurïaut is condemned to the stake. All the while, Gerart hunts along the banks of the Rhine with his falcon. When his bird captures the lark with Eurïaut's ring, its sight breaks the love potion's spell, just as the buzzard reminds Guillaume of Aelis.

Gerart arrives at Metz in time to save Eurïaut, as Yvain rescued Lunette in Chrétien's *Lion*. To clear the false accusation, an ordeal is proposed, not of cold water as at Mainz, but a judicial duel, in which Gerart proves his *amie*'s innocence. Then it is time to hold a tournament at Montargis, just as Jean Renart organizes one at Saint-Trond. Gerart leads a team of loyal French knights to victory against a team of turbulent barons from the Massif Central headed by Lisïart. In its aftermath, Gerart accuses Lisïart of calumny and proves it with a second trial by battle. The villain is punished with an ignominious death, and the hero marries his *amie* and takes her back to Nevers. In effect, therefore, the *conte* or *estoire* of the *Violette* was cross-fertilized from a variety of literary blossoms. At first glance, these disconnected romantic episodes appear to hold little promise for the historian. I have therefore reduced the plots to their barest essentials, because the fictional *contes* are of less value to me than the peripheries and contexts in which they are set. As had become accepted in romance, all four of these narratives are in octosyllabic verse, with rhymed couplets.

Literary Innovations

Throughout their narratives, Jean and Gerbert make allusions to previous literature, challenging their audiences' literary culture. Comparing a military victory with Roland's exploits at Roncevaux, for example, Jean evokes the name of Charlemagne and recalls the *Chanson de Roland*. He quotes a long passage from *Gerbert de Metz*, another chanson de geste, and Gerbert quotes an equally long stanza from the *Aliscans*. Embroidery on a wedding gown includes scenes from the *Roman de Troie*, and the evocation of Alexander recalls other *romans d'antiquité*. From Breton *lais*, Jean alludes to the anonymous *Graelent Muer* and to Marie de France's *Lai de Lanval*, as well as to the story of Piramus and Thisbe, inspired by Ovid. On one occasion, fabliaux are invoked; on another, the *Roman de Renart*, if only to call attention to Jean's name.[12]

These allusions are brief and fleeting, but Jean and Gerbert draw sustained inspiration from three particular sources, contemporary lyric poetry (discussed later), the Tristan and Iseut legend, and the romances of Chrétien de Troyes. References to the celebrated tragic lovers Tristan and Iseut abound. In the *Escoufle*, for example, Jean draws graphic scenes from the Tristan story on a golden chalice (vv. 579–616), and Gerbert depicts a tournament at Lancien where Tristan, Iseut, and King Marc associate with Arthur's knights of the Round Table (*Continuation* vv. 3610–4869). Chrétien is recalled in Jean's romances by allusions to the Arthurian cast of characters (Perceval, Gauvain, Keu, and Sagremor, as well as the mythic king himself), and Gerbert provides an ending to Chrétien's unfinished *Graal*.[13] As has already been suggested from the narrative strategies, Jean and Gerbert are deeply indebted to the literary craft of their great predecessor.

By evoking this literary panorama, Jean and Gerbert thereby establish what they presumed their listeners/readers to know. In the terminology of Hans Robert Jauss, they create a "horizon of expectation" for their audiences. This "horizon" formed the standard by which the audience "received" or judged the new work, but it is known to the modern reader only through Jean's and Gerbert's texts themselves. Jauss calls the difference between this "horizon" and the work performed before the audience "the aesthetic distance." The shorter the distance, the more conventional the new work is; the greater the distance, the greater the originality.[14]

To position themselves in relation to their predecessors, Jean and Gerbert composed prefaces to their romances. Since the *romans d'antiquité*, writers of romance had employed prologues to offer self-conscious theorizing about literature.[15] Although they might be ironic at times, they were, for the most part, meant to be taken seriously by the audience. Beyond preparing their listeners/readers for their narratives, Jean's and Gerbert's prologues propose novelties that establish "aesthetic distance."

In the preface to the *Escoufle*, Jean attempts to situate himself by distinguishing between truth and fable.[16] To quote just one passage, which may appear repetitive and turgid to modern readers:

> Car ml't voi conteors ki tendent
> A bien dire et a recorder
> Contes ou ne puis acorder
> Mon cuer, car raisons ne me laisse;
> Car ki verté trespasse et laisse
> Et fait venir son conte a fable,
> Ce ne doit estre chose estable
> Ne recetee en nule court;

> Because I see many storytellers who intend / to talk well and to set down stories / to which I cannot accommodate / my heart, because reason does not allow me; / for whenever someone exceeds and takes leave of truth / and transforms his story into a fable, / this should not be an established work / nor recited in any court. (vv. 10–17)

The awkward generalities of this pronouncement are made more concrete in two lines from Gerbert's preface to the *Violette*. His fine story, he says,

> N'est pas de la Reonde Table,
> D'ou roi Artu ne de ses gens;

> is not about the Round Table / nor of King Arthur or his men. (vv. 34–35)

When these two prefaces are joined to the romances that follow, it is clear that Jean and Gerbert have rejected their predecessors' geographic and temporal settings; in particular, they have distanced themselves from Chrétien. As opposed to the fabulous places and times of Arthurian myth, the two propose the here and now as a setting.[17]

The chansons de geste and the romances of antiquity sought to recover the remote geography of ancient France or of classical Greece and Rome. With a few exceptions, notably in *Cligès,* Chrétien's conceives of space as a mythological realm of vast forests mapped with exotic Celtic toponyms and embellished with fictive names like Beaurepaire and Mont-Dolorous. Gerbert naturally adopts Chrétien's universe in his *Continuation,* but his *Violette* follows Jean Renart in constructing a geography directly familiar to their audiences.[18] The itineraries of the fictive characters follow routes that can still be traced on maps. Even Guillaume de Dole's lodgings at Saint-Trond can be precisely located in the city's topography. Although pronounced in Francien to francophone audiences around Paris, Jean's and Gerbert's romances exhibit a predilection for lands beyond the Capetian domain and center on Lotharingia, the middle space between France and the Empire. In the *Escoufle,* the crucial separation of the lovers occurs near Toul in Lorraine. In the *Rose,* Guillaume and Liënor originate from Dole in the same region, and the action takes place in the imperial cities of the Liégeois and the Moselle and Rhine valleys; in the *Violette,* Gerart's and Euriaut's adventures are situated at Cologne and Metz. With little difficulty, Jean's and Gerbert's listeners/readers could immediately orient themselves in the geography of these romances.

The storyteller's formula with which Jean and Gerbert introduce their respective monarchs, Conrad and Louis, "Il ot . . . jadis . . . un empereor [un roi] . . ." ("Once there was an emperor [king] . . .") (*Rose* v. 34; *Violette* v. 65), at first suggests a fictive past. From the crowd of secondary characters, however, the audiences would have distinctly sensed the present. (Here the *Continuation* stands apart.) With the exception of the principal actors, all of the identified personages could have been recognized as well-known contemporaries.[19] In the *Escoufle,* for example, the crusader Count Richard de Montivilliers is a thinly disguised Richard Coeur de Lion, duke of Normandy and king of England; and the count of Saint-Gilles is doubt-less his brother-in-law, Raymond VI, count of Toulouse. The teams of knights participating in the tournaments in the *Rose* and *Violette* are recruited from known adherents of current political factions. Other recognizable names surface in incidental roles. Indeed, Jean and Gerbert's addressees, Count Baudouin, Provost Milon, and Countess Marie would have felt themselves at home with these historical figures of their day—all in contrast to the ancient Charlemagne and Roland of the chansons de geste, the distant Eneas and Alexander of the romances of antiquity, and the legendary Arthur and Gauvain of Chrétien.

Since narrative time was the audience's present, Jean and Gerbert dressed up the decor of their stories with countless details to add verisimilitude to their romances. Meticulous descriptions of clothing, food, entertainments, armor, and techniques of fighting matched contemporary circumstances to provide the tales with realistic effects.[20] The term *l'effet de réel* was coined by the modern critic Roland Barthes to convey Gustave Flaubert's use of small details to create the effect of realism. Thus the barometer that silently records the atmospheric pressure in Flaubert's story "Un coeur simple" plays no role except to provide verisimilitude. By requiring no other significance than its own existence, it stands for the reality of the scene.[21] At times Jean and Gerbert become so enamored of these reality effects that they expand them into entire episodes, such as the falconry scenes. Treating experiences that their contemporaries would have found familiar, they provided their audiences with the "pleasure of recognition." Since the audience immediately recognized the effect or episode, the author had no reason to explain it, but I as a historian can examine it for what it tells me about the life of the aristocracy in northern France around 1200. For that reason I shall seek out the peripheral and notice hundreds of realistic details and episodes that frame these romances. If these details are true *effets de réel*—that is, are divorced from the narrative—they can be considered self-authenticating. When they become implicated with the plot, however—as, for example, in the ordeal episode or the beauty of the heroine—the narrative and rhetorical strategies will also be brought to bear on their interpretation.

Jean's prologue to the *Roman de la rose* announces a second startling innovation that has been often quoted and commented upon:

> Cil qui mist cest conte en romans,
> ou il a fet noter biaus chans
> por ramenbrance des chançons.
>
> . . . .

car aussi con l'en met la graine
es dras por avoir los et pris,
einsi a il chans et sons mis
en cestui *Romans de la rose,*
qui est une novele chose
et s'est des autres si divers
et brodez, par lieus, de biaus vers
que vilains nel porroit savoir.
Ce sachiez de fi et de voir,
bien a cist les autres passez.

He who turned this story into a romance / [*or* translated this story into vernacular] / in which he noted beautiful songs / for the remembrance of these songs / .   .   . / For just as one places red dye / in cloth so that it will be admired and praised / [*or* in order to gain praise and renown], / thus he [Jean] placed songs and melodies / in this *Roman de la rose.* / It is such a novelty / and the interspersed embroidery of beautiful verse / is so different from other works / that a peasant will not be able to understand it. / You may be sure in faith and truth / that this work has surpassed the others. (vv. 1–17)

Jean's metaphor of dyed cloth, it will be seen, was grounded in the technology and economy of the contemporary textile industry. *Graine* (= *granum* [Latin], kermes [English]) was a brilliant scarlet dye that increased the price of fine cloth manyfold.[22] As Jean promised, he inserted forty-eight lyrics into his narrative and thereby became the first to create a new literary genre of lyric anthology.[23] Gerbert was quick to follow in the *Violette*:

Des or commencherai l'ouvraigne
Dou *Roumanch de la Violete.*
Mainte courtoise chançonnete
Orrois, ains que li contes fine, ...

Now I shall begin the work / of the *Roman de la violette.* / You will hear many courtly songs / before the end of the story. (vv. 44–47)

Gerbert's manuscripts include between forty and forty-four lyrics in his narrative, two of which are also found in Jean's.[24]

Jean's and Gerbert's romances were both the earliest and, taken together, the largest of a new genre of lyrical anthologies selected for aristocratic taste. The two collections encompass virtually the entire spectrum of secular music available at the time. Not only does each include a chanson de geste, but both open with *chansons à carole*, rondeaux or refrains suitable for dancing. More important are large selections from the contemporary *grands chants* composed by celebrated southern troubadours such as Bernart de Ventadorn and Jaufré Rudel and northern trouvères such as the Vidame of Chartres, the Châtelain de Coucy, and, most renowned of all, Gace Brulé. Jean identifies a handful of authors, leaving the rest anonymous. All are anonymous in Gerbert. Their repertories also include *chansons de toile*, sung by noble women as they embroidered in the *chambre aux dames*, and *pastourelles*, lyrics celebrating the none too innocent amusements of aristocratic knights and the dangers to peasant shepherdesses in bucolic settings.[25]

Not only does Jean claim that his romance surpasses all others, he further boasts:

> Il conte d'armes et d'amors
> et chante d'ambedeus ensamble,
> s'est avis a chascun et samble
> que cil qui a fet le romans
> qu'il trovast toz les moz des chans
> si afierent a ceuls del conte.
>
> It tells of arms and of love / and sings of both together; / and it will seem to all / that he who made the romance / wrote all of the words of the songs / so well do they agree with those of the story. (vv. 24–29)

Since Jean identifies the composers of certain lyrics, and others were too well-known to be mistaken, he does not ask his audience to take this assertion literally, but merely to appreciate the appropriateness of the insertions into his narrative. The *chansons de toile*, for example, fit well into the scene where Lïenor and her mother are sewing in their chamber at Dole, and the *grands chants* articulate the joys and pains of the emperor Conrad's newly found and lost love for Lïenor, but others accommodate the story only with difficulty, thus generating modern scholarly controversy over Jean's claim.[26]

Equally difficult to interpret is Jean's preceding assertion that his romance is also new because it is to be both read and sung.

> Ja nuls n'iert de l'oïr lassez
> car, s'en vieult, l'en i chant et lit,
> et s'est fez par si grant delit
> que tuit cil s'en esjoïront
> qui chanter et lire l'orront,
> qu'il lor sera nouviaus toz jors.
> Il conte d'armes et d'amors
> et chante d'ambedeus ensamble . . .

> No one will ever be tired of hearing it, / because, he can sing and read it, if he wants; / it is made with such great delight / that all who will hear it sung and read / will take such pleasure, / because it will be new to them forever. / It tells of arms and of love / and sings of both together . . . (vv. 18–25)

This passage, in turn, echoes Jean's opening lines:

> Cil qui mist cest conte en romans,
> Ou il a fet noter biaus chans
> por ramenbrance des chançons . . .

> He who turned this story into a romance / in which he noted beautiful songs / for the remembrance of those songs . . . (vv. 1–3)

Together, these passages raise the question of how Jean's romance was intended to be performed to an audience.[27] If, of course, an individual reader read it privately from a written text, the question did not arise, even if the reader pronounced the words audibly, because he or she was not singing in public. But if the text was performed before an audience, were the songs to be sung as the narrative was recited? In the line "il a fet noter biaus chans," *noter* is ambiguous. It can mean either "take notice of, perform music as on an instrument" (*Rose* vv. 1746, 3402) or, eventually, "to have musical notes transcribed."[28] The unique manuscript of the *Rose* contains no such notation, but each lyric is set off conspicuously with a decorated capital, and occasionally the lyric verses are not transcribed in separate lines (as the narrative of the romance) but are run on like prose, as they are in the later *chansonniers*. By the 1230s and into the fourteenth century, these famous chansonniers were the first collections of secular musical notation and provided music for nearly half of Jean's anthology.[29] When Jean first uses the term *noter*, he closely associates it with memory (*ramembrance*), suggesting that he is taking note of songs sung by fictional characters in imaginary situations. These songs, therefore, resonated only in the memories of the audience. In practice, Jean most often quotes whole stanzas, and on occasion two separate stanzas occur simultaneously in the narrative (*Rose* vv. 306, 528). While the complexity of such techniques might make it difficult to perform the songs vocally to a public audience, Jean nonetheless insists more than once that his romance is to be both read and sung.

In the prologue to the *Violette*, Gerbert, too, reiterates that his romance can be both read and sung, and that the agreement between the songs and the story is a further guarantee of the romance's veracity.

> Et s'est li contes biaus et gens,
> Que je vous voel dire et conter,
> Car on i puet lire et chanter;
> Et si est si bien acordans
> Li cans au dit, les entendans
> En trai a garant que di voir.

> The story is beautiful and noble / which I wish to recite and recount to you, / because one can both read and sing therein. / And the song and recitation / are so much in agreement, / that I take the listeners as testimony / that I speak the truth.
> (vv. 36–41)

Like Jean's, Gerbert's manuscripts contain no musical notation, but one copy follows the *Rose* by highlighting the verse with elaborated capitals, and another transcribes the insertions in red and runs them on, as in the *chansonniers*. In comparison to Jean's, however, Gerbert's practice of inserting lyrics is simplified.[30] He relates them directly, almost crudely, to the plot, so that little ambiguity disrupts their narrative function. When Gerart sets out on the hunt that will result in capturing the lark, for example, he sings Bernart de Ventadorn's popular Poitevin song "Quant voi la loëte moder . . ." ("When I see the lark rise . . .") (vv. 4188–95). Rarely does Gerbert quote an entire stanza; rather, he merely gives the first line as an aide-mémoire to the reader or performer of the intended song. Despite the similarities, Gerbert's text was more accessible to performance than Jean's. While Jean's complexities may have inhibited performers, he nonetheless proposed that his work be read and sung "if one wishes." Gerbert so wished and encouraged the singing of songs. Scribes could have supplied musical notation for both romances according to the format of the chansonniers if their patrons had desired. In effect, therefore, Jean and Gerbert were precocious among medieval romanciers in creating a proto-musical comedy where story and music united to entertain an audience with a romantic fiction.[31]

By anthologizing a corpus of some ninety lyrics, Jean and Gerbert added a new element to the chansons de geste and preceding romances that constituted the literary "horizon of expectation" familiar to their audiences. Unlike the *Chanson de Roland*, which was nearly a century old, or even the works of Chrétien de Troyes, who was only recently dead, these lyrics came from troubadours and trouvères who were near contemporaries. Gace Brulé, for example, was certainly alive when Jean wrote.[32] By inserting songs that were both contemporary and external—that is, originating from other, identifiable authors—Jean and Gerbert reinforced their other outstanding innovation. Like geographic space, contemporary personages, and countless *effets de réel*, these songs connected with contextual referents and corroborated the "here and now" of Jean's and Gerbert's romances.

Hermeneutic Propositions

In their four romances, Jean Renart and Gerbert de Montreuil also adopt other linguistic and literary strategies that have attracted the attention of modern critics, to which I shall return in Chapter 8. But it is the distinct novelty of framing their stories with realistic effects that has encouraged me to use them as historical sources. To this end, I examine their *effets de réel* and "horizon of expectation," alluded to above. The realistic details and episodes framing the peripheries of the narratives provide me with information that is self-authenticating and therefore useful to the historian. Only when these effects become involved in the central narratives do I consider the author's literary strategies. By looking at their "horizon of expectation," I attempt to read these romances from the perspective of contemporary audiences and to understand what literary culture the authors expected of their readers/listeners.

Since Chrétien was the author who loomed largest on their horizon, Jean and Gerbert will be continually compared with their great predecessor to determine what they adopted as conventional and where they distanced themselves as original. In fact, therefore, I devote considerable discussion to the romances of Chrétien de Troyes. While this may have the practical effect of adding a third vernacular author to my discussion, my purpose in evoking Chrétien remains to read Jean and Gerbert through him and thereby to situate their testimony on the horizon of their public's expectations. Finally, to highlight the lay tenor of these vernacular compositions, I shall keep them in dialogue with the Latin writings of contemporary theologians. This will furnish me with a "clerical horizon" and a third technique. The juxtaposing of the vernacular romanciers with the Latin clerics will not only help me to identify the laicity of the former but will also corroborate what is historically significant in the romances. I can be better assured of the social reality of issues raised in vernacular romances when they are also broached by the Latin theologians. The discussion between the vernacular and Latin will enable me to perceive those areas of lay life that the clerics sought to obscure.

Writing at multiple levels of meaning, Jean and Gerbert have attracted the attention of modern literary critics. In their multivocal approach, the two authors were following a widespread practice in the Middle Ages initiated by Latin writers. Inspired by the Church Fathers, the Latin theologians, for example, proposed a figurative as well as a literal meaning to Scripture. By the twelfth century, biblical exegesis was divided among three levels of interpretation: literal (*historice, ad litteram*), allegorical (*mistice*), and moral (*moraliter*). Whereas the last two were useful for doctrine and preaching respectively, Pierre the Chanter concurred with the school of André de Saint-Victor and argued that the figurative meanings could not be constructed without the secure foundation of the literal. In their biblical commentaries, both Pierre and André, for example, place special emphasis upon the historical *superficiem littere*. Analogously, I also propose to concentrate my attention on the literal, surface level of Jean's and Gerbert's romances and leave their more figurative artistry for the appreciation of modern critics. Jean's and Gerbert's linguistic and rhetorical skills certainly created multiple levels of meaning, but like the contemporary theologians, they also intended their romances to be heard or read at the literal, surface level. Doubtless they employed irony as well, but I shall respond to it only when it becomes apparent to me and resist the totalizing hypothesis that all that Jean and Gerbert wrote was ironic and therefore subversive of the literal meaning. My "flat" reading will not satisfy the sensibilities of modern critics, but I trust it will suffice for historical purposes.[33]

Jongleurs

If Jean Renart and Gerbert de Montreuil occlude their identities behind a foxy pen name or laconic toponym, they are less reticent about their profession.[34] Throughout their romances, jongleurs and minstrels abound, suggesting that the authors harbored few equivocal feelings about the *métier* of entertainment.[35] At the imperial coronation in the *Escoufle*, for example, instruments are heard everywhere, songs are sung, and stories are told by jongleurs in robes of silk and ermine (vv. 8276, 8856, 8990–99). In the *Rose*, the spring hunt is accompanied by revelry, song, and dancing. After dinner at an imperial palace

> lors vindrent li menesterel.
> Li uns note un, li autres el,
> cil conte ci de Perceval,
> cil raconte de Rainceval,
> par les rens devant les barons.

> then entered the minstrels. / This one played one piece, that one another, / one recited the story of Perceval, / another that of Roncevaux, / circulating through the rows of barons.
> (vv. 1745–49)

On the eve of the tournament of Saint-Trond, instrumental music drowns out God's thunder (vv. 2348–51); on the morrow, the knights proceed to the field accompanied by flutes and viols (v. 2555). The May Day celebrations at Mainz are an occasion for minstrels to sing songs and lais (vv. 4561–65). A chamberlain named Cupelin plays a new song on his viol for the emperor each morning (vv. 3397–3402); a female jongleur, Doete de Troyes, sings a *pastourelle* at Mainz (vv. 4567–83).[36] The more austere

Capetian court at Pont de l'Arche is likewise a place of singing and danc-ing in Gerbert's *Violette* (vv. 87–238), as is the scene of Gerart and Eurï-aut's wedding (vv. 6584–85). Even Gerbert's pious *Continuation* has min-strels and jongleurs performing music and telling stories at Perceval and Blancheflor's wedding (vv. 6688–89, 6702–8).

Gerbert's favorite device for masking the identity of his heroes is to dis-guise them as minstrels. In the *Violette,* for example, Gerart obtains access to Lisïart's court as a jongleur, where, playing on his viol and reciting four *laisses* of the "Chanson de Guillaume au court nez," he overhears evidence of Eurïaut's innocence. In the *Continuation,* Tristan's insatiable need to visit Iseut prompts the contrivance of disguising the lover and eleven other Arthurian knights as minstrels, with instruments hung from their necks, to obtain access to King Marc's court. When Marc's knights are bested at the tournament of Lancien, the heroes come to the rescue, still clad as musi-cians. Perceval, who happens upon the tournament, is thoroughly discon-certed by their anomalous appearance and concludes that fighting an oppo-nent who slings a fiddle from his neck can only be a joke (vv. 4557–61). Gerbert also assigns the knightly virtue of prowess to entertainers. During a truce in the titanic battle between Perceval and Leander, a minstrel is em-ployed to put the hero to sleep by recounting a story of a strange adven-ture (vv. 11480–89). When three traitors seize the opportunity to attack, the minstrel averts Perceval, helps defend him against overwhelming odds, and dies in combat (vv. 11484–976).

From these crowds of entertainers Jean treats his audience to a portrait of a single jongleur, who bears the eponym Juglet:

> Il ert sages et de grant pris
> et s'avoit oï et apris
> mainte chançon et maint biau conte.
>
> He was intelligent and of great renown, / and had also heard and learned / many songs and many a fine story. (*Rose* vv. 640–42)

Juglet is first identified as a "fiddler" (*vïeleor* v. 635), and his principal tal-ents lie in the realm of music where he performs as singer (vv. 844–52, 1579–84, 1843–51) and fiddler (vv. 1799–1801, 2294). His opening act, however, consists of recounting a lai about a valiant knight from Cham-pagne who loves a lady from the marches of Pertois (vv. 657–74). Later at dinner in the imperial palace, he contributes to the entertainment by narrating a chanson de geste and two or three fabliaux (vv. 1764–76). Although a good friend of the knight Guillaume de Dole, Juglet spends most of his time as the boon companion of the emperor Conrad, who summons him in the morning to alleviate his boredom with a pleasant story and keeps him by his side until long after supper (vv. 4118–40). As exemplified by Juglet, the jongleur exercised multiple talents. Primarily a performer, he both sang and played his viol, but he could be relied on for a good story as well. Terminology identifying these entertainers was equally varied and imprecise. Jean uses *jougleur* and *vïelleors* on occasion, but his preferred term is *menesterel*. Gerbert divides equally between *jougleour* and *menestrel*.[37]

Although Juglet was doubtless maintained in the emperor's household, the jongleur's most visible and lucrative source of income came from the great festive occasions of coronations and marriages, which provided kings and princes opportunities to display their largesse. Chrétien's depiction of Erec and Enide's wedding offered subsequent romanciers an idealized paradigm. The morning after the nuptials, King Arthur rewarded jongleurs to their satisfaction with the most desirable gifts of robes, horses, and money (*Erec* vv. 2055–64). Jean Renart's depiction of the May celebrations at Mainz in his *Rose* follows suit. Minstrels came from many lands to sing for money (vv. 4561–65). To Gerart and Eurïaut's wedding at Nevers, many a musician came on foot but left on horseback (*Violette* vv. 6571–72).

The chief medium of compensation, however, was clothing. At Erec and Enide's wedding, for example, Chrétien details at least a half dozen varieties. At Jean's imperial coronation in Rome, the silk garments bordered with ermine that the jongleurs wear constitute one of the great expenses of the occasion (*Escoufle* vv. 8996–99). At Gerart and Eurïaut's wedding, the minstrels carry off sacks and even chests of furred garments on horseback (*Violette* vv. 6580–81). Not to be outdone, at Perceval and Blancheflor's nuptials at Beaurepaire, knights and *vallets* divest themselves of their coats, surcoats, and furred robes to offer five, six . . . even ten pairs to minstrels (*Continuation* 6709–16). Clothing is equally common as payment to individuals. Juglet's early morning story so pleases the emperor that he gives him a *mantel gris*, saying, "[Y]ou have indeed earned it" (*Rose* vv. 723–24). As in all gift-giving, a reciprocal exchange of services takes place. Festive occasions give princes the opportunity to lavish largesse on jongleurs; jongleurs not only supply the entertainment but also tell stories about these occasions that perpetuate the prince's glory.

In contrast to the vivid accounts in the vernacular romances, the Latin chroniclers take only brief and vague notice of festive occasions at which *joculatores* performed, doubtless because the clerical authors harbored misgivings about the entertainers' activities.[38] This suspicion is elaborated by Pierre the Chanter's school at Paris. The imprecision in terminology and function found in the vernacular romances was shared by theologians who wrote of the profession in Latin. *Joculatores* (jongleurs) were frequently associated with *histriones* (actors), *mimi* (mimes), and *scurri* (buffons), as well as with acrobats, jugglers, and bear trainers. Pierre the Chanter groups them with other dubious *métiers,* such as those of prostitutes, gamblers, magicians, and participants in tournaments.[39] By associating jongleurs with actors and prostitutes, the theologians imposed on them the legal opprobrium and disabilities that the theater and brothel had endured since antiquity.[40] With prostitutes, the actors shared the status of *infamia,* which the medieval canonists translated into specific disabilities. They could not sue in Church courts, enter holy orders, or receive the Eucharist. As virtual excommunicates, entertainers were to be avoided by clerics.[41] This close association between jongleurs, actors, and prostitutes highlighted the use of their bodies. The canonist Rufinus, for example, defines *ystriones* (actors) as *ystoriones* (storytellers) who by transforming their faces and clothing create images that provoke laughter, thus telling an *ystoria* (story) corporally.[42] Jongleurs and actors were equated with prostitutes, confirming that all three put their bodies to shameful and unlawful use. The inherent corporality of the entertainment profession exposed them to the illicit temptations of the flesh. Of equal concern, the entertainment profession generated rivalry with the clerical preacher. The jongleurs were obviously the preachers' most serious competitors for the large crowds on the high holidays. In short, at the turn of the twelfth century, theologians retained the traditional clerical hostility to all entertainers with few distinctions.

Recalling St. Jerome's well-circulated apothegm that to give to actors is to sacrifice to demons, Pierre the Chanter contests the economic foundations of the entertainment profession.[43] Thomas of Chobham dryly opines that actors would abandon their profession if they received no contributions.[44] Discouraging support from audiences therefore became the chief weapon against entertainers in the clerical arsenal. Philip Augustus was the one contemporary ruler who openly enforced the theologians' program, in contrast to the contemporary Angevin, Champenois, and Flemish courts, as well as to Jean Renart's fictional Conrad. Rigord, the royal Capetian historiographer, notes that the courts of kings and princes were crowded with actors, who were able to solicit gold, silver, horses, and garments by jongleuresque words (*verba joculatoria*). A week's work of these entertainers could produce robes worth 20 to 30 silver marks, enough to nourish as many poor souls for an entire year. In contrast, the most Christian king Philip—inspired by the Holy Spirit and remembering the teaching of holy men that to give to actors is to sacrifice to demons—promised his garments to the naked and the poor, thus setting an example to minor princes of the realm.[45] The king apparently kept his word. In the extensive inventories of garments in the royal wardrobe accounts, which first appeared nearly two decades later, no mention is made of gifts to performers.[46]

This royal policy was congruent with Philip's habitual calculation and parsimony in giving to churches and laymen. Applied to entertainers, it concurred with the program of contemporary canonists and theologians. It is likely that this theological-Capetian policy lay behind Gerbert de Montreuil's complaint following Perceval and Blancheflor's wedding. Echoing a common romance sentiment that chivalry is in decline everywhere, Gerbert applies it specifically to gifts of garments. After enumerating robes that knights had once conferred on minstrels, he observes that this custom has now ceased. At many a festival for knighthood or marriage, garments are promised to minstrels but are in fact bestowed upon servants, tailors, plowmen, and even barbers, in the manner in which Philip Augustus rewarded his own agents. The world has become too parsimonious; only the rich are prized (*Continuation* vv. 6720–46). Yet even the Capetians did not fully deserve their tightfisted reputation vis-à-vis the entertainment profession. Between 1205 and 1212, Gace Brulé, the most popular trouvère of his day, enjoyed a *fief-rente*, a regular pension, from Philip Augustus. In 1213, this patronage was continued by Prince Louis, Philip's oldest son, and extended to an actor named Tornebeffe as well.[47]

The Capetians' official policy in this respect was pursued at a steep price, however, because by adopting the ecclesiastical distaste for jongleurs, they deprived themselves of the praise and favorable publicity that other princes enjoyed by reason of their generosity to the highly articulate entertainment profession. The relations between patrons and entertainers were symbiotic. The celebration provided patrons with occasions to lavish their largesse on performers. The jongleurs, in turn, used their narrative talents to publicize the brilliance of the events and the chivalric glory of their patrons. In the end, the investment appears to have been profitable, if the colorful accounts that Count Baudouin, Provost Milon, and Countess Marie received from Jean and Gerbert are compared with what is recorded of Philip Augustus's knighting of Prince Louis at Compiègne in 1209. The Capetian relied on the royal historiographer Guillaume le Breton to publicize the event. Although the chronicler declares that no greater festivity had been seen before that day, he limits himself for the rest to saying that it took place "with such great solemnity, with the assembly of the magnates of the realm, with the multitude of men, the generosity of food and the abundance of gifts" (cum tanta solemnitate, et conventu magnatum regni et hominum multitudine et largiflua victualium et donorum abundantia).[48] Compare this terseness with the nearly three hundred lines that Jean Renart devotes to the crowds of participants during the fortnight of celebrations at Rome for the coronation of Aelis and Guillaume, the solemn processions, the ringing of bells, the festooning of the city, the wardrobe of the empress, the feasting, singing, dancing, and games, and the imperial gifts to those assembled (*Escoufle* vv. 8768–9847). In the mundane world, Latin *veritas* made little effort to compete with vernacular fiction.

The implementation of the clerical program against jongleurs encountered resistance elsewhere too, because patrons could be found even among prelates. According to the Chanter, one entertainer boasted that the contributions of churchmen and towns could be counted on as fixed rents. Enumerating three examples, he expected an annual income of at least 100 livres from the prelates of France.[49] In response, the Chanter demanded the application of the appropriate ecclesiastical sanctions. Like prostitutes, actors should be refused not only the Eucharist but also the hospitality of the table.[50] At the councils of Paris (1213) and Rouen (1214), Robert of Courson prohibited prelates from receiving actors or mimes at their tables or listening to their instruments, and Pope Innocent III invoked the highest ecclesiastical authority of the Lateran Council in 1215 to command all clergy to avoid contact with mimes, jongleurs, and actors.[51]

The question of ecclesiastical patronage was raised in the case of Milon de Nanteuil, the cleric to whom Jean Renart addressed his *Roman de la rose*. At the time, Milon was provost of the chapter of Reims, the second ranking dignitary of the great archbishopric. Although his ambition to become archbishop was not fulfilled, he was elected bishop of Beauvais in 1217. To have received a worldly romance in which jongleurs were esteemed might have caused embarrassment for an ecclesiastic intent upon promotion. Conrad's open and lavish patronage of jongleurs in the *Rose*, moreover, contrasts vividly with Philip Augustus's proclaimed abstention. As provost of Reims, Milon de Nanteuil was forbidden by Church law to associate with entertainers. No evidence has survived of Milon's compliance either at Reims or later at Beauvais, but by chance a rare series of financial accounts from 1203 and 1204 have been uncovered for a contemporary Bavarian prelate, Wolger von Erla, bishop of Passau (1191–1204) and later patriarch of Aquileia (1204–18). Wolger's politics in Germany resembled Milon's in France.[52] Not only was Wolger politically adroit, but the financial accounts reveal that his household supported scores of *joculatores* (including *joculatrices*), *istriones*, *gigarii*, *mimi*, and *cantores*, all forbidden by Church law. Among the latter was Walther, *cantor* from Vogelweide, certainly the most celebrated poet and musician in the German language, who was rewarded with two fur coats.[53] The fortuitous survival of Wolger's financial records illuminates the ubiquity of entertainers in the courts of worldly prelates, and it is not unlikely that Milon's household contained much the same.

Indeed, the prelates' notorious resistance to the prohibition of entertainers may have prompted the theologians to reconsider their unqualified strictures against actors, jongleurs, mimes, and other performers. Pursuing a characteristic theological analysis, Pierre the Chanter and his students sharpened definitions and introduced distinctions. The Chanter and Thomas of Chobham began to distinguish between actors who refrained from bodily wantonness and those who persisted in it. Chobham expands the Chanter's distinctions into his well-known analysis of the acting profession into three groups. In particular, Pierre envisaged a second group of jongleurs whose activities could be tolerated. If they sang of deeds for recreation or information, or, if, as Thomas specifies, they glorified the deeds of princes or the lives of saints for the solace (*solatia*) of humans in sickness or in distress, they might hope for exoneration.[54] Obviously, both theologians were thinking of chansons de geste and saints' lives, genres long established in the jongleurs' repertories, to which the theologians refer elsewhere. On one occasion, for example, Pierre notes without disapproval that jongleurs often selected their chansons to suit the mood of their audiences, switching from Landri to Antioch, to Alexander, to Appolonius, and to Charlemagne.[55]

It is noteworthy that both the Chanter and Chobham introduce music as a factor that might rehabilitate the jongleur's profession. The canonist Huguccio had affirmed that musical instruments could be played without sin for the praise of God, the honorable necessities of the Church, or the health of the body or the soul.[56] Pierre concurred and included licit chansons accompanied by instruments or instrumental music alone. Within the category of actors playing instruments for the delight of humans, Thomas exonerates the jongleur who accompanies his chansons de gestes and saints' lives with instruments for the solace of his audience. To exemplify this exoneration of the newly delineated jongleur, both theologians cite an encounter between a performer and Pope Alexander III. In Pierre's version, when the jongleur, equipped with his instrument, asked the pope whether he could save his soul by pursuing his profession, Alexander hesitated to give him permission to entertain, because he feared that a concession might lead to greater license. According to Thomas, however, when the jongleur averred that he knew no other profession, the pope allowed him to live by his trade as long as he abstained from lechery and turpitude.[57] In effect, Jean Renart's fictional Juglet could now gain his livelihood honorably by reciting edifying stories, singing recreational songs, and playing the fiddle slung from his neck. This rehabilitation may have prepared the way for the last entertainer to appear in Gerbert's *Continuation*.[58] Most likely a musician, this minstrel, as has been seen, helps Perceval to fall asleep by recounting a strange adventure, dies in defense of the hero, and is buried with glory. The epithet engraved on his tomb not only commends his soul to Christ, but concludes

> C'on doit toz menestreus amer
> Por celui. Dieu qui terre et mer
> Estora doint honor a ceus
> Ki onorent les menestreus.
>
> that one should love all minstrels / for the sake of this one. God who created earth and sea / gives honor to those / who honor minstrels. (vv. 11970–76)

The theological concession to chansons de geste and to saints' lives envisaged literary and musical genres that had been sung in France for nearly a century.[59] It is nonetheless noteworthy that at a time when Pierre the Chanter and Thomas of Chobham were proposing that jongleurs redeem their moral status by inserting edifying songs or instrumental music into their performances, Jean Renart, followed by Gerbert de Montreuil, introduced the novelty of inserting lyric verse to be sung into their romance narratives.[60] Whether this would have led the theologians to approve of Jean's and Gerbert's romances depends on their moral evaluation of the lyrics, which we can only surmise. Since the predominant theme of the lyrics is physical love, it is doubtful that the theologians would have recognized their redeeming value. The introduction of music would not have harmed romance, however, and the categories of "for information" and "for the recreation and solace of men" were potent forces in the eventual redemption of literature. Indeed, *solatium* justified storytelling for jongleurs, just as it permitted preachers the use of exempla.[61] Although it may be excessive to infer causality between these two phenomena, their contemporaneity remains important. In the decades surrounding 1200, both the theologians and Jean and Gerbert emphasize music in ways that had not occurred to Chrétien de Troyes or previous romanciers.

Although Juglet is first called a "fiddler," his opening act is to recite a lai about a knight from Champagne who loves a lady on the marches of Perthois (*Rose* vv. 657–74), which, in fact, recalls Jean Renart's own *Lai de l'ombre*. Jean's audience may have known that Jean himself was the author, but in the *Rose*, Conrad constitutes the audience and is presented as believing that the story is Juglet's. In similar circumstances when Tristan, disguised as a minstrel, plays the *Lai de chevrefoil* to Iseut, Gerbert de Montreuil's audience may have recognized Marie de France as the author, but he has Iseut claim that the lai was written by Tristan and herself (*Continuation* vv. 4065–70, 4082–87). Both Jean and Gerbert thereby assert that jongleurs could be authors of literature. Celebrated authors of romance were associated with the entertainment profession. Gerbert is not alone in calling Chrétien de Troyes a trouvère; the latter is likewise grouped with minstrels, along with Gautier d'Arras and Benoît de Saint-Maure, in a poem entitled "Miracle to the Virgin."[62] Chrétien often creates diegetical narrators who tell stories within the story. Juglet exclusively and explicitly performs this function in the *Rose*, until he disappears in the second half, in which Lïenor takes over. Given the abundance of jongleurs throughout the *Rose*, the honor and importance accorded to Juglet, and his talents as a *conteor*, it is not implausible that Jean Renart, who so assiduously conceals his own persona, identified with his creation Juglet.[63] And Gerbert, who takes delight in dressing his heroes as jongleurs, accorded high praise to the minstrel martyred for the sake of Perceval. "One should love all minstrels for the sake of this one," he says. "God honors those who honor minstrels."

TWO

Addressees and
Their Politics

ALTHOUGH they addressed the generic "courts of kings and counts," Jean Renart and Gerbert de Montreuil intended their works for specifically named individuals. Just as Chrétien de Troyes had identified Marie, countess of Champagne (d. 1198), and Philippe, count of Flanders (d. 1191), as recipients of his romances, Jean sent the *Escoufle* to the noble count of Hainaut, the *Lai de l'ombre* to an unnamed bishop-elect, and the *Roman de la rose* to Milon de Nanteuil. Gerbert wrote his *Roman de la violette* for Marie, countess of Ponthieu.[1] These three names not only provide a sample of Jean's and Gerbert's contemporary audiences; of equal significance, they offer a firm basis on which to reconstruct the contemporary context of the romances, since the names can be firmly attached to historical personages.

Even more than Chrétien, Jean and Gerbert took special care to orient their romances to the geographical and political world in which their addressees lived. To enhance their stories with "reality effects," they included places, events, and contemporary personages with whom their addressees and audiences were familiar. (Gerbert's *Continuation* is, however, an exception to this framework. As a direct prolongation of Chrétien's tale, it names no contemporary addressee and remains enclosed in the mythology of Arthurian time and space.) Because of the close interplay between the contemporary world of the addressee and the fictional contents of the romances, a sustained explanation of both the historical context and the "reality effects" will be useful. I shall examine the geography, careers, and politics of the three addressees in detail, along with the space, time, secondary characters, political issues, and other "reality effects" of the romances. Such attention will not only situate the presumed audiences historically; it will also serve as warranty for Jean's and Gerbert's historical consciousness and provide a standard of assessing the reliability of their romances as historical testimony. I shall begin by grouping Jean's addressees together and treat Marie de Ponthieu separately.

Baudouin VI, Count of Hainaut, Milon de Nanteuil, and the Imperial Succession

The undoubted leading candidate for the noble count of Hainaut is Baudouin (born in 1171/72), who became the ninth count of Flanders in 1194 and the sixth count of Hainaut of that name in 1195. He left his lands on 14 April 1202 to take part in the Fourth Crusade, was elected emperor of the Latin kingdom in Constantinople, was captured by the Bulgarians in 1205, and died in prison shortly thereafter.[2] Since Hainaut was his paternal inheritance, he could be appropriately designated "conte en Hainaut."[3] Throughout the *Escoufle*, Jean Renart drops clues that would have been savored by Baudouin. The heroine of the romance, for example, is called Aelis, recalling Alix de Namur, Baudouin's grandmother.[4] The fictional Aelis's fame extended from Montpellier, where she worked, to Mons [-en-] Hainaut (v. 5638), the principal seat of Baudouin's court. The hero, Guillaume, extends his search for Aelis to popular pilgrimage sites. Weeks of waiting at the famous Santiago de Compostela produced only her donkey, but the shrine of Saint-Gilles was decisive in reuniting the lovers. Saint-Gilles du Gard did not enjoy Compostela's celebrity, but it was a favorite of the family of Hainaut.[5]

The story of Guillaume's and Aelis's love and fidelity would, moreover, especially have pleased Count Baudouin. Gislebert de Mons, whose history of Hainaut is dedicated to the same Baudouin, informs us of the count's own marriage to Marie de Champagne, contracted in 1186, when he was fourteen and his bride was twelve. The chronicler expressly states that Baudouin loved his wife chastely and fervently, was content with her alone, and spurned all other women—qualities rarely found among men, Gislebert adds. Baudouin's father's and grandfather's bastards were openly acknowledged, and the well-known opinion that marriage is incompatible with love was attributed to Marie, countess of Champagne, the bride's mother, and Aliénor, duchess of Aquitaine, her grandmother.[6]

Milon de Nanteuil, to whom Jean Renart sent the *Rose*, was precisely located "in the territory of Reims in Champagne." He came from the family of Nanteuil-la-Fosse (Marne, arr. Reims, can. Châtillon-sur-Marne) and first appeared at Reims as a candidate for the archbishopric of Reims in the contested election of 1202–4 following the death of Guillaume de Cham-pagne, uncle of Philip Augustus. His youth and his modest origins in the middle-level nobility made him an unusual applicant for the foremost re-galian see of France, a position that frequently went to members of the royal family. Milon was undoubtedly ambitious, however, and perhaps un-scrupulous. Robert of Courson, who was appointed papal-judge delegate in the affair while he was a theological master at Paris, notes that the young man had offered 3,000 marks from his inheritance to advance his case. In addition to Milon, Philippe de Dreux, bishop of Beauvais, a royal cousin who enjoyed the king's support, and Baudouin, provost of the chapter, likewise sought the post, but all three were obstinately opposed by the archdeacon, Thibaut du Perche, who was a candidate himself. The contro-versy was finally appealed to Innocent III, who imposed his own choice, Cardinal Guy, the former abbot of Cîteaux, in 1204.[7]

Appearing as cathedral canon in 1206, Milon himself became provost of the chapter the following year. For the next decade, he held this position second only to the archbishop.[8] In 1217, he was finally rewarded with elec-tion to Beauvais, vacated by the death of Philippe, the royal cousin, but he was not consecrated until 1222. In the interval, Milon served as guardian of Reims in 1217 during the absence on a crusade of Archbishop Albéric, Guy's successor; he himself left for the East in 1219.[9] Since Beauvais was a regalian see that usually went to men with royal connections, Milon must have enjoyed the king's initial favor, but before his death in 1234, he had antagonized the regency of Blanche de Castile and fallen into a dispute with Louis IX over jurisdiction at Beauvais. In 1225, three years after he arrived at Beauvais, the cathedral was badly damaged by fire. Milon laid plans for rebuilding it as the tallest cathedral in Christendom, and this pro-ject undoubtedly consumed most of his time and energies.[10] Jean includes details in the *Rose* that were likewise meant to catch Milon's attention. For example, seeking to evoke the quantity of cloth used at the emperor's wed-ding, Jean says (v. 5499) that it was sufficient to garb all the monks at Ourscamp and at Igny (a Cistercian house that served as a necropolis for the lords of Nanteuil; along with the nuns at Longueau, Igny was a major beneficiary of the alms of Milon's family).[11]

The identity of the unnamed bishop-elect (*Eslit* v. 41) to whom the *Lai de l'ombre* was sent is less clear. It has usually been assumed that the desig-natee was Milon de Nanteuil during his tenure as bishop-elect of Beauvais between 1217 and 1222, but these dates present difficulties for the chronology of the two romances. Another candidate for the *Eslit* is Hugues de Pierrepont, bishop of Liège (1200–29), whose diocese was of intense interest to Jean Renart, and who was bishop-elect between 1200 and 1202.[12] A bishop-elect might seem an incongruous recipient of verse celebrating courtly love, and even adultery, but like many prelates of his day, Hugues de Pierrepont was not ordained a priest until the eve of his episcopal consecration, and his style of living was indistinguishable from that of lay magnates. A chronicler from Liége notes that Hugues attended the first public session of the Lateran Council dressed as a count, the second as a duke, and only the last wearing his bishop's mitre.[13]

Baudouin de Hainaut and Hugues de Pierrepont were closely involved in one of the great political battles at the turn of the twelfth century. This was the dispute over the succession to the German Empire. Although Milon de Nanteuil's position was not as clear as theirs, he too found himself implicated. Not only does the political stance of Jean's addressees suggest an imperial context, but his audiences would have recognized that his romances were set against the political backdrop of the German Empire and its perennial problem of succession. The *Escoufle* achieves its climax with the coronation of an imperial candidate at Rome who obtains his position by marrying the previous emperor's daughter. Jean limits this emperor's territory to Rome and Italy, but when the candidate is designated a "*parvenu* of the Germans and the Romans," it is evident that Jean considers it the medieval German and not the ancient Roman Empire (*Escoufle* vv. 2792–93). The *Rose* opens with the lines: "In the Empire, where the Germans have been lords for many days and years . . ." (vv. 31–34) and concludes with the emperor Conrad submitting to the demands of matrimony for the sake of producing an heir. A principal question posed in the romances was: who was to succeed to the imperial office? This was precisely the issue that was shaking the foundations of contemporary Germany.

Since the events of the two decades between 1197 and 1218 are familiar to historians, the relevant factors in the succession crisis can be recalled quickly.[14] The sudden death of the emperor Henry VI on 28 September 1197 at the age of thirty-two, leaving an infant son, Frederick, as heir, placed in jeopardy the achievements of the Staufen dynasty, who had successfully ruled the Empire for three generations. Not only had they increased their territory through Henry VI's marriage to the heiress to the throne of Sicily, they had also sought to establish a dynastic claim to the imperial crown. Two conflicting principles governed imperial succession, election by princes and dynastic inheritance. Since their accession, the Staufens had resolved the conflict by persuading the princes to elect members of their family. Now, with an heir less than three years old, they were acutely vulnerable to their enemies both within the Empire and outside it.

The dispute over succession was reduced to two competing parties, one Staufen, the other Welf. The Staufen claims were defended by Frederick's uncle Philip, duke of Swabia, who offered himself as candidate and was crowned king of the Romans (an intermediate step toward the emperorship) at Mainz on 8 September 1198. He probably enjoyed the favor of the majority of the German princes concentrated largely in the south and southwest. Philip was opposed, however, by the princes of the lower Rhine valley, who were encouraged by the kings of England. King Richard lavished subsidies on the archbishop of Cologne, the bishop of Liège, and the duke of Brabant and formed an alliance in 1197 with Baudouin, count of Flanders and Hainaut. The emperor's death in that year provided Richard with a splendid opportunity to promote a rival to the imperial throne. His candidate was Otto of Braunschweig, son of his sister Mathilda, who in 1168 had married Henry the Lion, duke of Saxony, head of the Welf dynasty in northern Germany, and chief competitor to the Staufens. Born in 1175/76, Otto was raised at the English court and was created count of La Marche, of York, and of Poitou by his uncle Richard. Proposed to the citizens of Cologne with financial inducements, he was crowned king of the Romans at Aachen on 12 July 1198 by the archbishop of Cologne.

The rivalry between the two candidates prompted intervention from two outside powers, the papacy and the king of France. Newly elected in 1198, the young and energetic Pope Innocent III inherited traditional hostility to the Staufens because of their harsh treatment of churches and their aggressive designs on Italy, particularly Sicily. Asserting authority to judge the candidates, he pronounced in favor of Otto in 1201.[15] The appearance of a Welf candidate bound by blood and silver to the English king also stirred the fears of a third outsider, Philip Augustus of France. Alarmed by the potential cooperation between a German candidate and the English king, whose immense fiefs in France threatened his own royal domain, King Philip was unfailing in his support of the Staufens.

During the two decades of disputed succession, the balance oscillated wildly between the Staufen and Welf rivals. Philip of Swabia was assassinated in 1208 in an unrelated feud. Innocent finally crowned Otto in Rome on 4 October 1209, thus granting him full recognition as emperor. When the Welf began to follow former Staufen policies in Italy, however, the pope excommunicated him in 1210 and transferred his support to Frederick, who was crowned king of the Romans at Mainz in 1212. In the meantime, Otto's English patron King John (who had succeeded his brother Richard in 1199) suffered losses to Philip Augustus in France, relinquishing Normandy in 1204 and retreating south of the Loire by 1206. To recover his fiefs, he recruited allies from the Lowlands, including the count of Flanders and his nephew Otto. While John attacked from the south, the allies converged on Paris from the north. Both prongs of the invasion were repulsed by the Capetians; most notably to the north at Bouvines, where Philip Augustus defeated the emperor and his English allies in a pitched battle in July 1214. John retired to his island kingdom, and Otto's fortunes never recovered. The following year, the Lateran Council at Rome confirmed Frederick's election. On 19 May 1218, Otto died, with little to bequeath except the remaining imperial insignia, which he instructed be transmitted to the next duly elected emperor.

The importance of marriage and dynasty should be evident from this rapid sketch of imperial history. The marriages of the two Henrys—the Staufen Henry VI to Constance of Sicily and the Welf Henry the Lion to Mathilda of England—shaped the course of imperial politics for decades, but in the case of the German throne, the Staufen family eventually survived inopportune deaths, papal resistance, Welf ambition, and foreign intervention. Not until 1250, when Frederick II died without a legitimate heir, did the dynasty finally come to an end.

Emperor Otto (IV) of Braunschweig, the contemporary Welf candidate for the imperial throne, provides a historical context for reading the *Escoufle* and the *Rose;* in fact, the fictional emperor Conrad can be identified with Otto. This "Welf thesis" was first proposed by Rita Lejeune in 1935, when she argued that Jean Renart fashioned the image of the emperor Conrad to be juxtaposed with that of Philip Augustus, Otto's French antagonist. Otto's role was merely implied, but in an important article in 1974, Lejeune further elaborated the "Welf tonality" of the *Rose* by situating it in the geography of Liège, a bastion of Welf support. Lejeune offered the "Welf thesis" as a hypothesis supported by scattered data. In this chapter I propose to add further evidence and show that Jean Renart can be intelligibly read against the current historical events in the Empire.[16]

Geography and Historical Personages:
The Tournament of Saint-Trond

Since Jean Renart's works were written in Francien, the dialect of the
Capetian lands, it may be presumed that they were composed for an audience—if not living in—at least not distant from the royal domain. Count
Baudouin of Hainaut was ostensibly francophone; his father had sent him
to the imperial court to learn the German tongue and courtesy.[17] The
county of Hainaut was an imperial fief, but Jean Renart clearly hoped that
his *Escoufle* would be known in France. Baudouin's renown was therefore
defined as extending along the French borders from Tournai to Reims (v.
9066). Except for Normandy, however, Jean Renart makes few geographical references to northern France.[18] In contrast, since Milon de Nanteuil
was from Champagne, within the borders of the French kingdom, the references to France are more abundant in the *Rose*. Not only is more attention paid to the French participants at the tournament of Saint-Trond (despite their loss), but France is held up as the ultimate standard of the
chivalrous life. Clothes (vv. 1530–35), wine (v. 1838), and armor (vv.
1661–64) are all judged by French quality. Bishops coveted promotion to
the see of Reims (vv. 797–800) (as did Milon), and only the numerous
daughters of the Capetian royal house were worthy of the emperor's hand
(vv. 3040, 3514, 3515). In one telling slip of the pen, the poet has the emperor ask Guillaume whether he has ever been a familiar of the king of
England, against whom "*our* king of France" ("nos rois de France," v.
1629) has long waged war.

Despite the fact that Baudouin and Milon are addressed in Francien,
both romances are set in lands beyond the French royal domain. In the *Es-*
coufle, Jean Renart takes particular pains to identify numerous places in the
duchy of Normandy, where the story opens with Richard, count of Montivilliers, ready to depart on a crusade.[19] The travels of the young lovers,
Guillaume and Aelis, constitute the major movement in the romance, and
extend north from Italy to Normandy and back south to Montpellier and
Saint-Gilles. The chief dénouement, in which a buzzard causes the separation of the lovers, takes place in Lorraine, near Toul. In other words, the
plot of the *Escoufle* focuses on the middle space between the French royal
domain and the Empire.

Within this setting, the identity of the opening figure, the count of
Montivilliers, would have been apparent to a contemporary audience.

Later in the narrative, he is explicitly entitled "count Richard of Normandy" (*Escoufle* v. 7462). A Norman count called Richard, who confided
his lands to an archbishop and departed on a crusade, where he obtained a
truce from the Saracens, would have been scant disguise for Richard, duke
of Normandy and king of England. Some features of the narrative are, of
course, historically inaccurate (Richard actually embarked from Mar-
seilles) or counterfactual (the German emperor Henry VI imprisoned
Richard rather than welcoming him hospitably). Nontheless, the audience
would have recognized the historical Richard. As the count takes leave of
the duchy, Jean explicitly designates him *cuers de lyon* (v. 298). The em-
blem of the lion was attached to many historical personages, but the epitaph "lion-heart" is particularly associated with Richard.[20] Similarly, the
count of Saint-Gilles (Toulouse), in whose household the lovers reunite,
and who knights the young Guillaume and leads him back to Rouen to be
recognized as count, could only have appeared to contemporaries as Count
Raymond VI of Toulouse, King Richard's brother-in-law. (Jean Renart
recognizes the family ties but mistakenly makes Richard the son of the
count of Saint-Gilles's first [female] cousin [vv. 7748–49].)[21]

A romance addressed to Baudouin, count of Flanders and Hainaut, that
began by evoking Richard the Lion-Heart recalled the origins of the Welf
party by linking the two names. Not only had Richard offered subsidies to
Baudouin in 1194, he had also concluded a treaty of mutual assistance in
1197, to which his brother John and his nephew Otto added their names.[22]
Evocation of a successful crusader who had defeated the Saracens was
likewise pertinent inspiration for Count Baudouin, who had recently
(1200) taken the cross himself. But Jean Renart's account of Count
Richard in the Holy Land recalled another famous pilgrim. When Richard
arrives in Jerusalem, he hastens first to the Church of the Holy Sepulcher
to pray for victory. Offering the guardians a magnificent gold cup that cost
10 marks, profusely decorated with enamels, he places it upon the high altar, above which it is suspended thereafter (vv. 549–639). No report sur-
vives of a comparable gesture by Richard, but when Henry the Lion, duke
of Saxony and Otto's father, came to Jerusalem on a pilgrimage in 1172, he
brought impressive treasures and endowed three lamps to burn perpetually
above the altar of the Church of the Holy Sepulcher. This deed is not only
recorded in an extant charter, it was widely noted by contemporary chroniclers.[23] Once again Jean adds details that could be appreciated by a Welf
audience.

Even more than the *Escoufle*, the *Rose* furnishes Jean with occasions to
map geographical terrain with precision. Dole, from which Guillaume and
his sister Lïenor originate, was located in the Empire, but in the region of
the Franche Comté, that middle space bordering the kingdom of France.
Jean was aware of the traditional imperial cities and castles in the valleys
of the Rhine and Meuse,[24] but he takes particular care to allude to places
situated in the diocese and principality of Liège.[25] With studied precision,
he makes the count of Boulogne break his journey at Mons-en-Hainaut on
the medieval route to Saint-Trond (vv. 2110–11). At Saint-Trond itself,
also not far from Liège, he locates Guillaume de Dole's lodgings at the
crossing of two roads in front of the marketplace so exactly that the site
can still be identified from the city's topography (vv. 2068–71).[26] As the
French and German knights converge on the city for the tournament, the
author distinguishes the Germanic Flemish names Boidin and Wautre (v.
2168) in the German retinues and notes the Germanic greetings *wilecome*
and *godehere* (v. 2595) that were heard in the streets. Francophone himself,
he considered these dialects barbaric and worthy of contempt (v. 2169).
Jean knew well that Saint-Trond had lain for centuries on the linguistic
frontier between the Germanic and French-speaking populations of the
Empire.[27]

Because of the tournament at Saint-Trond, the diocese and principality
of Liège is the central geographical setting for the first half of the *Rose*. As
Lejeune has suggested, this preoccupation with Liège reflects an interest in
Welf politics.[28] Baudouin, count of Hainaut, was a vassal of the emperor,
but his immediate overlord was the imperial bishop of Liège, an early supporter of Otto's bid for the imperial crown.[29] When Otto was elected king
in 1198, his candidacy was favored by the citizens of Liège, the bishop (Albert de Cuyck), and the chapter, of which Hugues de Pierrepont was
provost.[30] In 1200, when Hugues was elected bishop of Liège—the first
French bishop after a long series of imperial incumbents—his candidacy
was contested. Otto threw his support to Hugues by visiting the city and
conferring on him the *regalia*.[31] Until Hugues's consecration in 1202, the
king and the bishop offered close assistance to each other. Thereafter,
Hugues remained favorable to Otto until the latter's excommunication in
1210.[32] When the duke of Brabant, the long-standing enemy of the Liégeois, sided with Otto, the French king came to the defense of Liège,
which obliged the bishop in turn to be loyal to the Capetians. Notwithstanding this, however, Hugues repaired the bridge at Maastricht in 1214,

thus allowing Otto to cross the Meuse en route to Bouvines.[33]

After the tournament at Saint-Trond in the Liégeois, the plot shifts first to Cologne (for two weeks), and finally to Mainz, the scene of the imperial assembly, Lïenor's vindication, and Conrad and Lïenor's wedding. Liège, Cologne, and Mainz were the chief bastions of Otto's supporters in Lotharingia and the Rhine valley.

Jean Renart also populates the *Rose* with scores of secondary characters who are readily recognized as contemporary personages. A number of well-known Welfs play prominent roles in the narrative; for example, among the first of the many who sing lyrics are a valet of the provost of Speyer's (v. 520) and the son of the count of Dagsburg (v. 529). The provost of the cathedral of Speyer, whose name was also Conrad, was entrusted with carrying an important letter for King John after October 1209. He belonged to the entourage of Conrad of Scharfenburg, bishop of Speyer and Metz and imperial chancellor from 1208 to 1212. The count of Dagsburg, it will be seen, was among Otto's earliest supporters.[34] At the opening of the romance, seeking to illustrate Conrad's imperial virtue as a peacemaker, Jean Renart invents a war between the count of Guelde and the duke of Bavaria, in which the emperor intervenes on the side of the count and compels the duke to submit (vv. 621–30). At this time, the count of Gueldre was Otto, who was present at Otto of Brunswick's coronation in 1198 and supported him through 1202,[35] whereas Ludwig I, the contemporary duke of Bavaria, was a partisan of Philip of Swabia.[36]

Most revealing, however, are the secondary figures who fight at the tournament of Saint-Trond. The French knights, who are the flower of chivalry, are the most numerous: [Ansold, or Eudes,] lord of Ronquerolles; [Guillaume] des Barres; [Enguerrand,] lord of Couci; Alain de Roucy; Gaucher de Châtillon; [Guillaume,] lord of Mauléon; Gautier de Joigny; and Count Renaud de Boulogne (vv. 2094–2110). On the tourney field, their champion is Michel de Harnes (v. 2719). All these names can be found in the list of knights in the contemporary registers of Philip Augustus.[37] They are accompanied by unidentified knights from Perche, Poitou, Maine, and Champagne (vv. 2087–88), and from Artois, Alost, Wallincourt, and Balleul in the north (vv. 2674, 2699–2703).[38]

Despite their numbers and the prowess of their champion, these celebrated French knights finally yield to the Germans led by the fictional Guillaume de Dole. Less numerous than the French, the names of the German nobility provide a remarkable muster of Otto's avowed adherents. The duke of Saxony (vv. 2119–20) is none other than Otto's older brother Heinrich, who, as duke and count palatine of the Rhine, provided Otto with sustained help (with one notable lapse).[39] In the final scene of the *Rose*, it is he who urges Conrad to marry Lïenor without delay (vv. 5290–92). The count of Dagsburg (Dabo) (v. 2121) is Albert II, who was the first of the lay princes to write to the pope urging confirmation of Otto's election in 1198.[40] The duke of Limburg and his son Garan (vv. 2122–23) are Heinrich III and Walram III, members of the Welf party from 1198. Heinrich remained true to Otto at Bouvines, but his son sided with Philip Augustus.[41] The count of Bar[-le-Duc] (v. 2125) is Thibaut I, who allied himself with Baudouin of Hainaut against Philip of Swabia and Philip Augustus in 1199, and continued to provide shelter to the king's enemies prior to Bouvines.[42]

These identified champions are followed by companies of knights from Lorraine, the Rhineland, Hainaut, and Burgundy, all imperial territories. In the context of the festivities on the eve of the tournament, two further Welf partisans are mentioned: the duke of Louvain (v. 2315) and the count of Looz (v. 2386). The former, Henri, duke of Louvain and Brabant, was one of Otto's earliest—and most fickle—supporters but was nonetheless a consistent antagonist of the bishop of Liège. Although himself wedded to a daughter of Philip Augustus, he had arranged for his daughter to marry Otto in 1214, and he appeared at Bouvines among the imperial allies.[43] The latter was Louis, count of Looz, close to Saint-Trond, who was caught in the feuds between the duke of Brabant and the bishop of Liège. By 1207, he had become a vassal of John's and pledged support to the Welfs.[44] In the heat of the tournament, another Welf partisan, Dietrich VI, the count of Kleves (v. 2604), is introduced.[45] At the end of the tourney, the author identifies the victorious German knights as those from the Lowlands ("d'Avalterre," v. 2825), thus specifying the center of Otto's support. Since the German champions are, without exception, recognized partisans of Otto's and are victorious against the French, Jean Renart's Welf proclivities can scarcely pass unnoticed.

The final scene of the *Rose* unfolds in the imperial city of Mainz, where Conrad has summoned all the princes of the empire to an assembly on 1 May to hear his matrimonial project. Jean may have selected Mainz in order to recall Frederick Barbarossa's celebrated *Hoftage* in the city in 1184 and 1188,[46] but the archbishopric was equally suitable to the author's Welf politics. When Archbishop Conrad of Mainz died in 1200, at the beginning of the dispute over the imperial succession, one faction in the chapter elected the bishop of Worms, a Staufen partisan. This translation required papal approval, however, and Innocent blocked the move and secured the election of a Welf candidate, Siegfried of Eppstein, who remained archbishop throughout the controversy. Otto took possession of the city at the same time that the bishop was installed.[47] The archbishop of Mainz is, however, inexplicably absent from the *Rose;* in his place, we find the archbishop of Cologne, who joins the imperial entourage after Conrad's brief stay at Cologne, administers the ordeal in the church of St. Peter, officiates at Conrad and Lïenor's wedding, and, finally, commissions the writing down of the story. All of this takes place in Mainz.[48]

It should be noted that, throughout the controversy over the imperial succession, the archbishops of Cologne were the earliest and most influential of Otto of Braunschweig's supporters. Claiming the right to consecrate the king of the Romans, Archbishop Adolf of Altena (1193–1205) promoted Otto's election at Cologne in June 1198 and crowned him at Aachen the same month.[49] When Adolf defected from the Welf party in November 1204, Innocent deposed him and had Bruno of Sayn elected; as provost of Bonn, Bruno had long been Otto's partisan.[50] His death in 1208 led to the election of Dietrich of Hengebach, who likewise remained in the Welf camp.[51]

Otto of Braunschweig

With the fictional emperor consistently portrayed in Welf territories and surrounded by Welf contemporaries, Jean Renart's audience may have been tempted to see a reference to Conrad's historical counterpart, the youthful Otto of Braunschweig. The names of the principal characters also convey family associations. Guillaume, the brother of Lïenor, recalls Otto's younger brother, born in England; Lïenor herself was perhaps named in memory of Otto's mother, Mathilda of England. The troubadour Bertrand de Born, who knew Mathilda at Argentan in Normandy during Henry the Lion's absence on pilgrimage, addresses her variously as Lana, Laina, Leina, and Eleina in his lyrics. Lïenor had therefore become the literary name of Otto's mother.[52] When Jean's audience heard Conrad exclaim to the seneschal that he does not despise Lïenor because she is not the sister of the king of England (he has, after all, sufficient goods and lands for two) (vv. 3574–77), they would have recalled that Otto's mother was in fact the sister of an English king.

In romance and in life, however, the chief device for revealing the identity of knights encased in anonymous armor was heraldry. In the opening scene of the *Rose*, Jean describes the blazon on Conrad's shield: "He carried a shield divided in half between the arms of the noble count of Clermont and a rampant lion of gold on a field of azure" (vv. 68–71). Clermont was a common toponym, and scores existed, but a seigneurie of Clermont-en-Hesbaye can be found near Liège and Huy, the region that preoccupied Jean. This family had adopted the heraldry of the eagle, the famous imperial *Reichsadler*, in use since Henry VI.

In other words, Conrad carries a shield divided between the imperial eagle and the lion of either the kings of England or the house of Welf. ("Welf" means lion whelp.) In the middle of the thirteenth century, the English historian Matthew Paris furnished a colored sketch of Otto's heraldry in the margin of his chronicle, with a half eagle and three half lions, which he describes verbally as half imperial and half the shield of the king of England. Matthew's representation of Otto's shield is confirmed on the reverse of the seal of Marie de Brabant, Otto's second wife, which is divided between three lions and an eagle, as well as on the handle of Otto's ceremonial sword (the "Mauritius sword") and the Quedlinburger casket (made expressly for Otto). Conrad's shield, however, bears an eagle and a single lion. Most of the coins Otto minted while king of the Romans and emperor depicted either the imperial eagle or, more commonly, the crowned lion of the Welf tradition. On occasion, however, coins with both a rampant lion and an eagle were minted, in one case a *Reichsadler*. Despite the discrepancy between one and three lions, those familiar with these coins would have been able to recognize Otto's symbols. This identification was made by another poet who was contemporary to Jean Renart. In a Middle High German *Otteton* addressed to the Welf emperor, the celebrated minnesinger Walther von der Vogelweide declares: "You bear the prowess of two emperors: the eagle's virtue and the lion's strength. These two comrades-in-arms are the emblems on your shield." In effect, therefore, two contemporary writers, French and German, describe the same shield, which Walther attributes to Otto. Whatever the minor discrepancies between the literary descriptions and Otto's actual shield, Jean's audience could scarcely have missed the reference.[53]

Milon de Nanteuil: A Welf?

If Baudouin, count of Hainaut, and Hugues de Pierrepont, bishop of Liège, fit easily into the Welf constituency, Milon, provost of the chapter of Reims, does not. At first glance, his family of Nanteuil-la-Fosse was clearly allied with the Capetians against the Welfs. His father, Gaucher I de Nanteuil, adopted the toponym when he married Helvide, the heiress of Nanteuil, but he was the younger son of Gaucher II de Châtillon-sur-Marne, whose older brother Guy II de Châtillon married Alix de Dreux, a royal cousin. Their oldest son, Gaucher III de Châtillon, accompanied Philip Augustus on crusade and in the Norman campaign, and was rewarded with marriage to Elizabeth, countess and heiress of the county of Saint-Pol; he naturally sided with the French king at Bouvines.[54]

Milon de Nanteuil was therefore the first cousin of Gaucher III de Châtillon, count of Saint-Pol, and an acknowledged supporter of the Capetian cause. In addition to Milon, Gaucher and Helvide de Nanteuil produced four other sons, Gaucher II, Guy, Guillaume, and André. Gaucher, Guillaume, and André are listed among the French knights in Philip Augustus's registers and, most important, Gaucher II de Nantueil and his cousin Gaucher III de Châtillon were recipients of *fief-rentes* from the king, unmistakable evidence of their attachment to the Capetians.[55] Jean Renart recognizes Gaucher de Châtillon's adherence to the Capetians by placing him among the French knights at Saint-Trond (v. 2097).

Although they were securely allied with the Capetians, a family like the Nanteuils might in times of crisis be tempted to hedge allegiances by means of marriage alliances with the opposing side. An extreme form of this behavior was exhibited by the duke of Brabant who, as has been seen, although married to the daughter of the king of France, offered his own daughter to the emperor Otto in 1214. Perhaps the tensions leading up to the battle of Bouvines induced the lords of Nanteuil-la-Fosse to venture such a marriage as well between 1209 and 1214. In July 1209, while Gaucher II, lord of Nanteuil, was absent on a crusade against the Albigensian heretics in the south, his wife, a certain Sophie (perhaps de Chevigny) fell gravely ill and confirmed to the nuns of Longueau donations made by her husband.[56] Apparently, Sophie died soon afterward, because in May 1214, Gaucher, now ill himself, drew up his own testament in favor of the Cistercians of Igny, in which he refers not only to a deceased (first) spouse but also to a second wife, Aleyde de Béthune.[57] (Gaucher did not, however, die from this illness, for he continued to issue charters with Aleyde through 1224.)[58] The daughter of Guillaume II, lord of Béthune, and Mathilde de Dendermonde, Aleyde is named in a charter of 1194, along with her brothers, Daniel, Robert, and Baudouin, and a sister, Mathilde.[59]

At the turn of the century, the family of Béthune held a pivotal position in the conflict between the Capetians and the Welfs. Aleyde's uncle, Robert VI de Béthune, head of the family until he died in 1193/94, had generally been loyal to the French monarchy. Her father, Guillaume II, supported Philip Augustus in the crisis of 1197 with the count of Flanders and accompanied Baudouin to the East in 1202. Her brother Daniel was out of the country on a crusade during the tumultuous years 1213–14. If these members of the family generally acquiesced to Capetian authority, others were prominent on the opposing side. Aleyde's uncle Baudouin accompanied King Richard on his crusade, shared his captivity, and was rewarded with marriage to the countess and heiress of Aumale in Normandy. He was in Richard's original embassy to secure the election of Otto. Aleyde's brother, Robert VII de Béthune, served on two missions between the Welf allies and England, participated in the attack on the French fleet at Dam, and entered the battle of Bouvines on the side of Otto. It was her uncle Jean, however, who was most visible on behalf of the Welfs. He entered his ecclesiastical career as provost of Douai and Seclin, where he was known as a flagrant pluralist and was even suspected of forging papal letters. Despite this reputation, he was elected bishop of Cambrai in 1200 and became Otto's most trusted and active agent in France. As early as 1198, for example, Jean served in Richard's embassy, which promoted Otto's election, and in 1209/10, he was one of the messengers on an imperial mission to seek peace with Philip Augustus.[60] By marrying into a prominent Welf family like the Béthunes sometime between 1209 and 1214, Gaucher de Nanteuil was perhaps protecting himself should the Capetians lose. If Jean Renart was looking for a Welf patron in the form of a recent convert, however, why did he send his romance to Milon, the provost of Reims—a younger brother and a cleric—and not to Gaucher himself?

The answer may lie in the strategic position of Reims on the eastern borders of France. In the fall of 1203, when King John's fortunes were at their lowest, as Philip Augustus's invasion of Normandy proceeded unhindered, success was favoring Otto of Braunschweig's campaign in the Empire. In a burst of generosity, Otto sent his uncle a letter in which he proposed to negotiate a truce with Philip of Swabia for a year or two, enabling him to come to John's aid by attacking France through either Reims or Cambrai.[61] The strategic importance of Reims as an eastern bulwark had long been recognized by the Capetians. In 1124, Louis VI had rallied the French barons there to meet the threatened invasion of the emperor Henry V. Philip Augustus had summoned the armed men of the chapter of Reims in 1197 and 1200 to meet Richard and Baudouin of Flanders. These obligations were renewed in 1207 as the menace from Flanders and the Empire increased. By 1209, the king had loaned money to the archbishop to help strengthen the city's fortifications.[62]

From Otto's standpoint, however, Cambrai was in friendly hands in 1203; Jean de Béthune had been bishop there since 1200, but the archbishop of Reims was not yet known, because the election was still under dispute. It will be remembered that the Nanteuils had attempted to win the position by promoting the candidacy of Milon with a large financial subsidy. In attempting to acquire an episcopal see for their family, they were acting no differently than the Béthunes at Cambrai or the Rethel-Pierreponts at Liège.[63] They were unsuccessful in this, however, and had not yet formed ties with the Welf family of Béthune.

Another family with Welf connections also had designs on the position. The archdeacon Thibaut du Perche had not only opposed the leading contenders in the election of 1202–4 but had also put forward his own candidacy. He was the son of Rotrou IV, count of Le Perche, on the Norman frontier, and Mathilde, daughter of Thibaut IV, count of Blois. In 1189, his older brother Geoffroi IV, count of Perche, had married Mathilda of Saxony, the sister of Otto of Braunschweig. In 1202–4, therefore, the see of Reims was sought by a candidate who was Otto's brother-in-law, although he, too, failed to obtain it.[64]

As has been seen, the contested election was eventually resolved when Innocent III, Otto's leading backer after King Richard, conferred the see on Cardinal Guy, Innocent's agent in promoting Otto's cause in Germany. Guy had formerly been abbot of Cîteaux, and Richard had sent him to Rome to plead for Otto. Innocent elevated him to the position of cardinal-bishop of Preneste and commissioned him papal legate to Germany in 1201 to resolve the dispute over the succession to the Empire. For the next three years, he tirelessly attempted to persuade the German prelates and princes to accept Otto.[65] At the same time, he also supported the candidacy at Liège of Hugues de Pierrepont, whom he finally consecrated in 1202.[66]

So energetic were Guy's Welf politics that the adherents of Philip of Swabia wrote the pope in 1201 protesting the legate's partisanship.[67]

If, in the end, Guy failed to recruit sufficient German princes to secure Otto's cause, his accession to the archbishopric of Reims nonetheless suited Welf interests in France. He was hardly a candidate to please Philip Augustus, since the king undoubtedly remembered that as abbot of Cîteaux he had been part of the papal delegation to investigate the charges of Philip's estranged wife Ingeborg in 1196. Like Jean de Béthune at Cambrai, Guy might have been counted on for continued support, or at least neutrality, if Otto chose to approach France from the northeast. Archbishop Guy was most likely an old man, however, for he died two years later. His successor in 1206 was Master Albéric, archdeacon of Paris, who was recommended for the position by Eudes de Sully, a royal cousin, bishop of Paris and Philip Augustus's chief ecclesiastical advisor. Albéric's career permits little suspicion of disloyalty to the French monarchy, but he was nonetheless absent from the climactic battle at Bouvines, although he and his chapter had long been prepared for the event.[68] Otto's ultimate interests in Reims, therefore, had at least been preserved. A partisan archbishop was succeeded by one who was neutral in the conflict. The role played by Milon de Nanteuil as provost of the chapter remains, however, wholly in the realm of conjecture. During the decade preceding Bouvines, the chapter had apparently contested the king's assessment of its military duties. In October 1207, Milon, as head of the chapter, finally conceded that Reims, like other chapters of France, was obligated to answer a royal summons for the defense of the crown and kingdom; in fact, however, Reims did not appear at Bouvines.[69]

Jean Renart, whose interests in and sympathies for Welf politics I have explored at length, wrote two romances for francophone audiences. The *Escoufle* opens with a crusade reminiscent of King Richard the Lion-Heart's and was appropriately addressed to Baudouin, count of Hainaut and Flanders. Why the *Rose*, which is even more oriented to Welf politics, was sent to Milon, a member of the Nantueil family and provost of Reims, remains open to speculation. If, as I have suggested, it was occasioned by the marriage of Milon's brother to Aleyde de Béthune, whose family had important ties to the Welfs, its purpose may have been to make Milon receptive to Otto of Braunschweig's cause. After the death of Archbishop Guy in 1206, Milon was the head of the chapter of Reims, whereas the new archbishop Albéric was staunchly loyal to the Capetians. During the brief interval between the death of Philip of Swabia in June 1208 and Otto's imperial coronation at Rome in October 1209, the emperor's political fortunes were at their height. Thus encouraged, he explored contradictory policies. He wrote his uncle John, urging him to become reconciled with the English Church and promising him aid against the French. At the same time, he commissioned the bishop of Cambrai to explore the possibilities of peace with Philip Augustus. The French king felt the dual danger most keenly. The chronicler Pierre des Vaux de Cernay reports that Philip excused himself from the expedition against the Albigensians in May 1209 because he had two great and threatening lions at either side of him: the so-called emperor Otto, and King John of England, both seeking to destabilize the French kingdom.[70] In this period of Welf ascendancy, therefore, Jean Renart may likewise have written a romance for an influential dignitary of the strategic see of Reims, whose family was recently allied by marriage with the bishop of Cambrai. A rapprochement with the Welf emperor may explain his choice of the addressee.

The Chronology of the Romances

This political context may also help refine the chronology of Jean Renart's two romances. The dating of the *Escoufle*—1195–1202, as defined by Baudouin's career—may be narrowed to 1200–1202. If it was in order to draw the favor of a prospective crusader that Jean Renart prefaced his romance with a crusade, the work is likely to have been written between 1200, when Baudouin took the cross, and 1202, when he finally departed. Milon's career at Reims ("en Raincïen en Champaigne," v. 5) provides the outside dates of 1202–18 for the *Rose*. The work was probably composed before 1215, however, because the cold-water ordeal performed at Mainz was formally prohibited to the clergy by the Fourth Lateran Council at that date.[71] It was also most likely written before the battle of Bouvines on 27 July 1214. To represent a fictional amicable tournament at Saint-Trond between Capetians and Welfs and to accord victory in a contest between identifiable contemporary figures to the Welfs would have been to undercut the authenticating realism of the tournament after Bouvines. It would also have been provocative, since at least seven of the participants had actually been present at the historic battle, including Gaucher de Châtillon, Milon de Nanteuil's first cousin.[72] Within the framework of Milon's career at Reims (1202–18), the most appropriate time for the composition of the *Rose* may be suggested by the convergence of two factors: the marriage alliance between the families of Nanteuil and Béthune (1209–14), and Otto's political apogee, his coronation in 1209. Without attempting to impose further precision, we may conjecture that the years immediately following 1209 appear to be the most likely time of the work's composition.[73]

Imperial Succession: Consecration, Election, and Heredity

At a time when the German empire was convulsed by struggles over the imperial succession, Jean Renart placed this constitutional problem at the center of his two romances. In the *Escoufle*, the emperor has no son to succeed him; in the *Rose*, Conrad remains a carefree bachelor, untroubled by thoughts of an heir. Beyond its pertinence to contemporary politics, royal succession had also become a topos in the romances that formed the literary horizon of Jean's audiences. It is true that it hardly surfaces in the Arthurian tradition. The legendary monarch never grows old (or older), has no children, makes no effort to designate his nephew Gauvain to succeed him, and takes no thought for the political future of his kingdom. In contrast, the Tristan legend reasserts the dynastic principle of succession. Marc, king of Cornwall and England, adopts his nephew Tristan as successor, but his close barons, fearing that this choice will incite civil war, urge him to take a wife to produce an heir of his body. Accordingly, Marc marries Iseut, but the marriage is compromised by the treasonous love between the queen and the nephew. Chrétien similarly raises the problem in the Greek empire in his *Cligès*, where the uncle Alis contests the nephew Cligès, each desiring the same woman. The objects of their desires, however, are always of royal blood. Iseut la Blonde is a royal princess from Ireland; Fénice is the daughter of the German emperor.

The contemporary crisis over succession in the Empire afforded the papacy opportunity to intervene to its own advantage. Possessing the imperial insignia and asserting the doctrine of *translatio imperii*, Pope Innocent III claimed the right to judge contested elections. In a long speech before the papal consistory at the turn of the century in 1200/1201, he reviewed the qualifications of the three candidates: the infant Staufen Frederick, whom he called a child (*puer*), Philip, duke of Swabia, and Otto of Braunschweig. Judging each by the criteria of what was licit, fitting, and expedient, and citing arguments *pro* and *contra* in scholastic fashion, Innocent analyzed the three fundamental elements governing imperial succession: consecration, election, and heredity. Dynastic succession was the least determinative, because in the case of Frederick, it had produced a child who was unfit to rule, and in the case of Philip, a Staufen who was under excommunication for family policies prejudicial to the Church. Otto had been elected by a minority of the princes, but these were nonetheless the most qualified to choose. Privileging election over heredity, therefore, Innocent decided in favor of Otto, whose election he intended to confirm through his exclusive right of consecration.[74]

Like Innocent III, Jean Renart addressed the three fundamental principles of imperial succession. His two romances show, however, that he differed with the pope on one important issue. He attached little significance to papal consecration. Since Conrad has already been made emperor when the romance begins, the question does not arise in the *Rose;* the *Escoufle,* however, culminates in the coronation of Aelis and Guillaume at Rome, "the master seat of the empire" (v. 8768). In romance fashion, Jean Renart's narrative is preoccupied throughout with the mundane aspects of the festivities. The couple are greeted at the gates by a hundred dukes and counts offering homage. Aelis enters Rome at the right hand of the king of Sicily. The poet lavishly describes the festooning of the city and the clothing of the principals, especially the dress of the future empress. The ecclesiastical element is equally prominent in these celebrations. Church bells peal out on the first day of the couple's entrance into the city. Two weeks later, on the feast of Pentecost, they are led by countless archbishops, bishops, and abbots in procession toward an unspecified destination. Although the pope (*apostoiles*) bestows the scepter, mitre (*cor*), and crown on Guillaume, Jean Renart treats the constitutive ceremony with unaccustomed economy.[75] The consecration, the essential element from the pope's standpoint, is merely alluded to in a simile comparing gold-embroidered garments with ruddy visages.[76] The author then excuses himself from lingering over details and hastens on with evident pleasure to the post-coronation banquet and its attendant entertainments (vv. 8974–76).

If Jean neglects papal rights, the princes' role in electing an emperor figures prominently in both romances, just as it did in the actual German Empire. When the emperor of the *Escoufle* determines to marry his daughter to the young Norman Guillaume and make him his successor, he calls an assembly of high barons of the Empire to secure their consent (vv. 2150–96). Composed of dukes, princes, counts, bishops, abbots, and archbishops, this *parlement* is initially reluctant, but eventually swears to support Guillaume's succession (vv. 2218–2340). After the emperor's death at the end of the romance, these native princes summon Guillaume from Rouen to take his elected place (vv. 8528–91). In the *Rose*, after the emperor Conrad has decided to marry Lïenor, he likewise convokes princes, masters, and dignitaries of the Empire to appear at an assembly at Mainz to obtain their agreement (vv. 3036–95).[77]

Despite the princes' prominent role, Jean nonetheless follows the literary conventions of the Tristan story and of *Cligès*. The princes accept a dynastic solution to the imperial succession. In order to retain the imperial succession within his family, the emperor in the *Escoufle* proposes Guillaume, son of the count of Montivilliers, as his only daughter's husband (vv. 2150–52). In the *Rose*, the imperial succession is threatened by Conrad's insouciance. He has received his name, and therefore presumably his title, from his father, "who was emperor before him" (vv. 35–36). On numerous occasions, the high barons have tried to persuade him to marry and produce an heir (vv. 121–37). They argue that if he dies or goes overseas on a pilgrimage, they will have no king of his lineage, and a king without Conrad's training would treat them cruelly (vv. 3058–71). Indeed, as Conrad himself relates, they are afraid that the kingdom will escheat to another who knows not how to honor and serve them as he does (vv. 5121–27). Both Jean's emperors are, therefore, in search of conventional heirs, the one through a husband for an only daughter, the other through a duly married wife.

Dynastic right was the solution to royal succession utilized by the Capetians and the Staufens. The Capetians had regulated the problem in France by establishing the hereditary right of their dynasty through the "anticipatory association" of son with father before the latter's death. At the birth of Philip Augustus in 1165, who was the seventh of such generations, a monk at Saint-Germain-des-Prés celebrated the Capetian dynastic achievement while rewriting Suger's notes on a biography of Louis VII. To enhance the French success, he notes the difficulties that contemporary English and German kings had had in producing heirs. Henry I's lack of a son in 1135 had brought devastation to the English kingdom, and the problem had been even more acute in the Empire when the Salian emperor Henry V died in 1125 without a direct heir and civil war ensued. In the French view, the kingdom of the Germans had likewise failed to achieve hereditary succession.[78]

After the Salians, the Staufens had likewise sought to establish their dynastic right to the imperial throne, beginning with Conrad III. Although

Conrad had passed over his six-year-old son in favor of his nephew Frederick of Swabia, this Frederick, the renowned Barbarossa, chose his own son Henry as direct successor. When Henry VI died in 1197, leaving an infant son, Frederick, the fate of the Staufens was once again threatened. By baptizing the emperor with the Staufen name Conrad and having him seek an heir of his body, Jean may well have intended to suggest to the Welf Otto that he adopt the Staufen policy of dynastic succession for the Welf family.[79]

Like the fictional Conrad, the historical Anglo-Welfs were singularly uninterested in matrimony, preferring protracted *fiançailles*. Richard the Lion-Heart was affianced to Alix de France (daughter of Louis VII and Constance of Castile) in 1168, when he was eleven and she eight. After more than twenty years, he resolutely refused to marry her, claiming, it was said, that she had been abused by his father. When in 1191 he did marry Berengaria, daughter of King Sancho of Navarre, to protect his fiefs in southern France, their union was without issue, perhaps because of her barrenness or, more likely, because he saw little of her. His unexpected death in 1199 precipitated a disputed succession between his brother John and his nephew Arthur. Whether or not Richard was homosexually inclined, his preoccupations were—to say the least—not matrimonial, for which contemporaries severely blamed him.[80] Like his uncle, Otto of Braunschweig also passed more time as a fiancé than as a husband, and his engagements were equally motivated by politics. Affiancing Marie, daughter of his early supporter Henri, duke of Brabant, in 1198, he broke the engagement in 1206 to become affianced the following year to Beatrix, daughter of his rival Philip, duke of Swabia. He married Beatrix in July 1212, but her death a month later enabled him to return to Marie, whom he wed in 1214, in time to secure her father's loyalty before Bouvines. Childless at his death in 1218, he directed his brother Heinrich in his testament to transmit the imperial insignia to the one whom the princes had unanimously elected within twenty weeks.[81]

Jean Renart saw to it that in contrast to this matrimonial reluctance, his two fictional Anglo-Welfs fulfilled their dynastic duties. When Richard, count of Montivilliers, decides to go overseas to save his soul, the author immediately notes that the count has no children or wife to whom to leave his lands (*Escoufle* vv. 126, 127). His position is effectively that of Richard the Lion-Heart on his departure for the crusade, although technically the latter married Berengaria before he reached the Holy Land. When the fictional Richard does marry and produce a son at Rome, this Guillaume is always considered Normandy's legitimate heir, even though he has never seen the duchy. Shortly before his father's death, ten Norman knights appear at Rome to request his return to take possession of the land (vv. 3488–93); in the end, he claims the duchy as his heritage (v. 8097). The celebrations at Rouen demonstrate that hereditary succession was in full vigor in Jean's Normandy.

At the opening of the *Rose,* Conrad is clearly a *iuvenis,* as yet unmarried, like Otto at his accession in 1198, when the latter was no more than twenty-three. Pleading his youth, Conrad steadfastly resists marriage (v. 136). "If I had a wandering heart, it came from my childhood and youth" (v. 3497), he later explains. By concluding the romance with Conrad's marriage to Lïenor, which the duke of Saxony urges take place without delay, might not Jean have been suggesting to Otto that he initiate a new, Welf imperial dynasty, just as Conrad III had inaugurated the dynasty of the Staufens? In history, however, it was the established dynasty that finally prevailed. Despite the English subsidies and the papal instruments of election and consecration, the Staufens were able to transmit the crown to Frederick II, thus postponing the dynastic crisis for another generation.

Proposed by the Capetians and Staufens and reinforced by romance tradition, dynasty was preeminently a royal-aristocratic solution, but not that of the clergy. Deprived by canon law of legitimate progeny, clerics themselves chose their own prelates through election and recommended the method equally to the laity. In his commentaries on the Old Testament, Pierre the Chanter wrestles with the precedents for dynastic succession among the ancient Jews, but wherever he finds an opportunity, he argues that election was by the people. The popular acclamation of "Vive le roi!" at a royal coronation, for example, implies that the king has been chosen with the people's consent. In the *questiones* in his *Summa,* moreover, he applies the principle of popular election to contemporary institutions. He believes that election was ordained by God for the empire, although hereditary succession was, in fact, employed by kings. Nonetheless, if a candidate for the royal throne was unfit by reason of youth or insufficient qualities, the bishops should refuse to consecrate him. When Innocent III judged the infant Frederick disqualified and confirmed the election of Otto of Braunschweig, he was therefore following the teaching of his former master. The papal policy toward the Empire had been established. What is remarkable is that during the reign of Philip Augustus, and in the capital of the French kingdom, a cleric dared to raise objections to the keystone of the Capetian dynasty.[82] Pierre's proposal threatened the foundations of both the historical aristocracy and its fictional counterpart in the romances of Jean Renart.

In Jean's romances, however, the conflict is not so much over dynastic right as over the choice of the imperial spouse. The princes propose candidates of royal blood, as princes generally do in romances (one thinks of Iseut and Fénice). In the *Escoufle*, they suggest the French king (v. 2166); in the *Rose*, one of his daughters (vv. 3040, 3515). (Since the time of Louis VII, Capetian daughters had been in abundant supply.)[83] Both emperors counter by contracting marriages far below their station. It is true that Guillaume is a count's son, but the values ascribed to him and his father are those of knights (*Escoufle* v. 2799). As Aelis crouches on the windowsill to leap into elopement, her thoughts are torn between *sens* and *amors*, which, in romance fashion, compete for her decision (vv. 3891–3963). Although Guillaume is a count, *sens* upbraids her for disgracing her *lignage* by consenting to this concubinage, but love finally wins her for her *ami*. Since Li̇enor is clearly the sister of a lowly knight, the emperor Conrad must reassure her brother that, as a *prodom*, his *lignage* is worthy of a kingdom (*Rose* vv. 2973–77). The princes and high barons oppose both marriages on the grounds of lineage. Guillaume is condemned as a parvenu of the Germans and Romans (*Escoufle* vv. 2792–93), and Li̇enor observes that the seneschal has always despised her lineage (*Rose* v. 5063). Jean's emperors, therefore, seek to resolve the dynastic crisis by plotting a pair of *mésalliances* with the countal/knightly ranks. To gain the princes' agreement, the emperors ask for a boon, that the princes will swear to follow their request without knowing the oath's contents (*Escoufle* vv. 2186–89, 2280–81; *Rose* vv. 3082–90). Audiences of romance would have recognized these oaths as the conventional *don contraignant* or *don en blanc*, frequently deployed to obtain outrageous goals.[84] With few parallels in contemporary history, this solution must have been a fantasy calculated to please the knights and ladies in the entourages of Baudouin de Hainaut and Milon de Nantueil. In Jean's romances, knightly lineage is conveniently allied with the emperors to resolve the issue of imperial succession; in like manner, the matrimonial successes of Guillaume de Montivilliers and Li̇enor de Dole undoubtedly nourished the wildest dreams of countless knights and ladies at the lower levels of the French aristocracy.

Imperial Ministeriales *and French Knights*

Competition between servile *ministeriales* and freeborn knights for positions in the imperial officialdom is another preoccupation of Jean's romances. Both the *Escoufle* and the *Rose* raise the question of whether the
two emperors should govern their lands with agents of low status. When
Count Richard arrives in Benevento on his return from the crusade, he is
greeted by the emperor in deep distress. Upon his elevation to the throne,
the emperor had dismissed his counts, high barons, and vassals and replaced them with serfs (*Escoufle* vv. 1484–88). Appointed *baillis* (v. 1627),
these serfs so came to dominate forests, castles, and cities that the emperor
could not journey from town to town without an armed escort (vv.
1491–94). Richard agrees to remain for a year or two to deliver his host
from this predicament. Elevated to imperial constable, he recruits a company of French knights and assaults the fortresses of the serfs, who flee
(vv. 1562–88). Toward the end of the tale, the count of Saint-Gilles sums
up the situation in advice to the young Guillaume on the eve of his instal-
lation as count of Normandy: A good prince always loves his subjects according to their merits. He should never forget the emperor's troubles with
his serfs, whom his father had expelled. Elevating the *vilain* (vv. 8396–
8411) is a fatal error.

Jean Renart returns to this theme in his eulogy of the emperor at the
opening of the *Rose*. Conrad distinguishes himself from contemporary
kings and barons who farm out their rents and *prévôtés* to *garçons,* thereby
devastating their lands and shaming themselves. All barons act wrongly
when they hand over their authority to *vilains* (vv. 575–86). Throughout
the episode in the *Escoufle,* Jean contrasts the low rank of the imperial
agents with the highborn men they have replaced: butchers and shoemak-
ers have become castellans, he says (vv. 1603–5). Laying special emphasis
on their servile birth, he designated these newcomers *sers* or *vilains,* which
contrast with *gentix homes* (vv. 1497). How can *vilains* be of good birth and
free (vv. 1630–31)? Despite their arrogance, they have all been in the emperor's service (v. 1489). In the *Rose,* Jean Renart reemphasizes that *vilains*
remain *vilains* even when they are endowed with lordship (vv. 585–86).

Complaints about political agents of low rank were nearly universal
throughout twelfth-century Europe, and they approach the status of a
topos in romance literature as well.[85] Jean's emphasis on the servile hereditary condition of these *parvenus,* however, strongly suggests that he is al-

luding to the ubiquitous German *ministeriales,* a phenomenon characteristic of the Empire and adjacent lands.[86] Unlike France, the Empire retained an influential class of administrative and military personnel who were burdened with hereditary servitude incommensurate with their political and social importance. *Ministeriales* were thus to be found in the lands of Jean Renart's patrons and princes in some form or other. Within the Empire, they had long been employed by both the Staufens in Swabia and the Welfs in Saxony, as well as by the imperial prelates of Cologne and Liège in the Rhineland (a customal regulating their activities at Cologne was drawn up by 1165), and they were deeply entrenched in Brabant. In the French county of Flanders, they were less powerful, although it had been sorely troubled by the ambitions of the *ministerialis* Erembaud clan at the time of the murder of Count Charles the Good in 1127. In the imperial county of Hainaut, under the lordship of Jean's addressee, they mingled with free knights. Even the French city of Reims contained active *ministeriales.*[87]

The term *ministeriales* derived from *minister,* designating an office of service, and since such service was frequently of a domestic and servile nature, the word acquired the connotation of hereditary servitude. Gislebert de Mons offers an example from 1188 of a Hennuyer *ministerialis,* Robert de Beaurain, who despite his social prominence was unable to disavow his servile origins when challenged in a court of law. In 1209, Otto confirmed that if a man of *ministerialis* condition married a free woman, their children nonetheless retained the father's servitude.[88]

Despite the defect of birth, *ministeriales* performed a wide range of duties in the Empire, extending from the household officialdom of the imperial court (seneschal, butler, chamberlain, and marshal) to the seigneurial functions of *prévôt, bailli,* and domanial steward. They supplied leadership and knights for the armies, as well as the garrisons and castellans of fortresses. In each post, they came to enjoy the remuneration and honors appropriate to their position, so that, except for servile status, they could not be distinguished from the freeborn. In Jean's romances, however, these *vilains* by and large perform the local functions of military castellans and of domanial *prévôts* and *baillis.* They recall the Bolandens, a prominent *ministerialis* family who held numerous castles in the principality of Cologne.[89]

Serfs do not, however, fill the high offices of the imperial court in Jean's romances. The emperor of the *Escoufle* appoints Richard, a French count, to the aulic post of constable. The unnamed seneschal of the *Rose* is identified only by the blazon on his shield, which is that of the Arthurian seneschal Kay (vv. 3159–64), the romance prototype of all wicked seneschals.[90] Certainly the villain of the story, this seneschal does not appear to be *vilain* by birth. Holding extensive lands and fiefs around Aachen (vv. 3127–32), he is due to participate in the ceremonies of Lïenor's wedding as one of the aulic officers whose hereditary fiefs require him to serve the emperor when the latter wears his crown (vv. 5406–13).[91]

Neither Count Richard nor the seneschal of the *Rose* resembles the great *Reichsministerialen* who dominated the courts of the competing Staufen and Welf courts during the interregnum. From Henry VI, Philip of Swabia had inherited Heinrich von Kalden-Papenheim as marshal and Markward von Anweiler as seneschal, both *ministeriales* of the Staufen dynasty. On Otto's side, the seneschalcy was held by the Braunschweig *ministerialis* Gunzelin von Wolfenbüttel, who was appointed in 1200 and remained loyal even after 1211, when many deserted the Welf cause.[92] Jean's aulic personages mirror those of his addressees, Baudouin and Milon, more faithfully. Although the court officers of Hainaut are designated *ministeria* in an inventory drafted by Gislebert de Mons in 1212–14, the actual posts were held by the high nobility of the county through hereditary right, as was also true in Flanders. In a similar way, the seneschalcy of the archbishop of Reims, with which Milon was familiar, was the hereditary possession of a noble family from Champagne.[93]

Focusing on servile origins, Jean's criticism of the *ministeriales* coincided with their apogee in the medieval German empire. Encouraged by princes and ecclesiastics for over a century, these administrators profited everywhere from the confusion of the civil war and interregnum.[94] Vaunting his strength to the pope in 1206, for example, Philip of Swabia included among his assets, castles, cities, vast possessions, and also "so many *ministeriales* that it would be difficult to provide an exact figure."[95] The contemporary chronicler Burchard von Ursberg claims that lacking cash to pay his soldiers, Philip alienated so many lands and manors to his barons and *ministeriales* that only nominal lordship and few castles remained. Otto, for his part, feared that Philip's followers would not be easily won over after the duke's death in 1208 and married Philip's daughter Beatrix to secure the loyalty of the *ministeriales*.[96]

Although disregarding the *ministeriales* in the great aulic offices, Jean Renart, like the chronicler Burchard, criticizes their growing local power. To replace the servile castellan and *bailli*, he offers a French solution—the freeborn knight. Refusing the services of the townsmen and other *vilains*, Count Richard recruits his army from among the *bons chevaliers* of France. Finding knights without horses or equipment, he arms them from his own household. To this force he joins the high princes of the land, drawn by his good sense, gifts, and honor to fight for the emperor's cause. Five hundred of this army are worth a thousand *ministeriales* (*Escoufle* vv. 1562–89).[97] Likewise refusing to use *vilains*, the emperor Conrad chooses his *baillis* from *vavassors* who love God, fear shame, and hold honor as the apple of their eye (*Rose* vv. 589–92). This not only follows Philip Augustus's practice of recruiting *baillis* from the freeborn knights of the royal domain,[98] it also points to an underlying distinction between the Empire and France. As a francophone writing for audiences on the border between the Empire and France, Jean Renart may not have been aware of the diversity and complexity of the class of *ministeriales* in the imperial lands, but he did sense the sharp division between unfree and free that distinguished the Empire from France. His simplistic solution was to replace the servile *ministerales* with the free French knights.[99] Addressing the knights who frequented the courts of "kings and counts," Jean therefore not only fed their fantasies by daring to suggest a matrimonial *mésalliance* with the emperor but also proposed that they collaborate in administering the German monarchy as they had in the French.

Marie, Countess of Ponthieu, and the Turbulent Barons of France

The battle of Bouvines not only confirmed the Welfs' defeat in the Empire, it also signaled Capetian domination of the great barons of France. Among the major vassals, John was expelled from Normandy and his Loire fiefs; Ferrand, count of Flanders, and Renaud de Dammartin, count of Boulogne, were imprisoned, and their fiefs were assigned to minor heirs. This extraordinary Capetian victory therefore circumscribed the political context for Marie, countess of Ponthieu (d. 1251), to whom Gerbert de Montreuil addressed the *Roman de la violette*. Two factors shaped Marie's career: her position as a Capetian and her marriage to a turbulent baron, Simon de Dammartin. Marie was the daughter of Guillaume, count of Ponthieu, and Alix de France, who, in turn, was the daughter of King Louis VII and Constance de Castile. For two decades Alix had suffered the humiliation of being affianced to Richard Coeur de Lion, who obstinately refused to marry her, alleging among other excuses that his father had known her sexually. After Richard finally married Berengaria of Navarre, Philip Augustus gave her in marriage in 1195 to Guillaume, count of Ponthieu. Since Alix was the half sister of the king, Marie, her daughter, was Philip Augustus's niece.[100] By blood, therefore, Marie was a Capetian and the cousin of Louis VIII and Louis IX. Jean Renart begins the *Rose* with: "In the Empire . . . once there was an emperor . . ." (vv. 31–35). In conscious mimicry, Gerbert begins the *Violette:* "Once there was a king in France . . ." (vv. 65–66). Gerbert's announcement suggests that he is both following his predecessor and shifting the scene to France.

In 1208, Philip Augustus permitted his niece Marie, the heiress of Ponthieu, to marry Simon de Dammartin, who was brother of the energetic but unstable Renaud de Dammartin, who had abducted and forcibly married the heiress of the county of Boulogne. Wishing to patronize Renaud, the king consented to this aberrant behavior by finally recognizing the marriage. Simon's marriage was doubtless part of Philip's policy to assure Renaud's loyalty, but the Anonymous of Béthune, a well-informed chronicler, remarks that the latter marriage provoked surprise among many people.[101] Shortly thereafter, Renaud began to cooperate with John, and he broke definitively with Philip by 1211, when he refused to render the county of Mortain as security. Because both brothers had sided with John and Otto at Bouvines, the Capetian victory resulted in Renaud's incarceration and Simon's exile. Marie's father, Guillaume, however, had remained loyal to the Capetian on the battlefield and afterward. When Guillaume died in 1221, therefore, Philip prevented the accession of Marie and her exiled husband to Ponthieu and assigned its custody to Robert, count of Dreux, a royal cousin.[102] After the king's death, however, Marie was able to negotiate an agreement with Louis VIII in 1225. Her chief concern was to secure the rights of her sons and daughters to the county. Beseeching royal mercy, she was received as liege-woman for Ponthieu, and her children were restored as heirs. In exchange, she granted that the king could hold her father's lands as long as her husband Simon was alive and promised that her husband would not enter Ponthieu or other fiefs of the king without royal permission.[103] Finally, in 1231, Count Simon also acceded to the terms of 1225. To obtain restoration, he repeated his wife's charter and added that he would not marry his two eldest daughters without royal consent, nor any of his daughters to known enemies of the king.[104]

This brief sketch of the succession of the county of Ponthieu helps to date Gerbert's writing of the *Violette* to the period between 1225 and 1231. Addressing the countess Marie at the conclusion of the romance, Gerbert declares that she was often afflicted before she came into possession of her lands. She had reclaimed them on many occasions but finally recovered her lands and heritage through her faithfulness and loyalty (vv. 6641–48). Employing language remarkably explicit for poetic dedications, Gerbert informs his audience that Marie's persistence had regained her inheritance. He must, therefore, have written after the agreement of 1225 but before that of 1231, because Marie's husband is entirely absent from the romance.

If the appearance of a king named Louis at the beginning of the *Violette* evokes Marie's Capetian blood, her husband, although absent, nonetheless points to the contemporary problem of rebellious barons. Drawn by Renaud, his more famous brother, Simon de Dammartin had likewise revolted against the French king and defied him in battle. Although Philip Augustus had mastered the barons after Bouvines, his death in 1223, which was followed quickly by the unexpected death of Louis VIII in 1226, left the monarchy exposed. When the French crown devolved upon the nine-year-old Louis IX under the regency of a Spanish queen-mother, Blanche de Castille, the great nobility were once again tempted to contest the king's strength. Turbulent barons threatened France until Louis finally diverted their energies by taking them with him on a crusade in 1248. Writing at the end of the second decade of the century, Gerbert introduces the figure of Lisïart, count of Forez, who by treachery is able to calumniate Eurïaut, the *amie* of Gerart, count of Nevers, and thereby dispossess Gerart of his county by means of a wager. Lisïart de Forez is the romance analogue to the historical Renaud de Dammartin, who had captured Boulogne by ruse.

Although Lisïart, Gerart, and Eurïaut are all patent fictions, the county of Nevers, which supplied the political context, had a turbulent history. When the male line of the counts of Nevers died out in 1181, Philip Augustus gave the heiress, Agnès, to his cousin Pierre de Courtenay in marriage, for which he exacted the price of Montargis. Pierre and Agnès produced only a girl, Mathilde (d. 1257), whom the king proposed to give to Philippe, the marquis of Namur, and also brother of Baudouin, count of Hainaut and Flanders (Jean Renart's addressee), but the king's project was defied by Hervé de Donzy, a rebellious vassal of the count of Nevers. Hervé defeated his overlord, seized Agnès, and married her in 1199 against the will of her father and the king (not unlike Renaud de Dammartin).

Faced with this virtual abduction of an heiress, King Philip had to be content with exacting Gien as the price of confirming the fait accompli.[105] In Nivernais fashion, however, the couple produced only a daughter, Agnès, as their heiress.

At the crucial contest of Bouvines between the king and barons, the royal historian Guillaume le Breton believed, Hervé was persuaded to follow Renaud and Simon de Dammartin and to defect to Philip's enemies. Guillaume depicts the allies as planning to divide France among the barons, assigning the Sénonais, Moret, and Montargis to Hervé. It was even believed that Hervé had made a pact with John to marry the heiress Agnès de Nevers. Whatever the truth of these stories, John did intercede with Philip Augustus on Hervé's behalf after the debacle, and the count obtained the king's pardon, unlike Renaud and Simon de Dammartin.[106] To bring Nevers under control, Philip arranged a marriage between Agnès and his grandson Philippe in 1215, but when Philippe died soon after, Agnès was married to Guy de Saint-Pol, a scion of the loyal family of Châtillon-sur-Marne.[107] Death, however, did not spare these matrimonial plans either. Hervé died in 1222, and both Guy de Saint-Pol and Agnès died in 1226, leaving Mathilde once again the sole heiress of Nevers. At this point, however, Mathilde suddenly married Guy IV, count of Forez in July/August of 1226, presumably with the king's approval.[108] On the eve of Gerbert de Montreuil's romantic fantasy of how the count of Forez won Nevers by a wager, therefore, the great barony had undergone a turbulent history for nearly three generations. This history was not identical to Gerbert's fictions, but as Countess Marie reflected on the villainy of Count Lisïart of Forez, she may have been reminded of an equally ambitious and turbulent count of Nevers, Hervé de Donzy, if not of her brother-in-law or her husband. Most important, however, shortly before Gerbert began writing, the county of Nevers was, in fact, united to the county of Forez by marriage and would remain so until Guy's death in 1241.[109] In concluding the *Violette* with a scene at Nevers, Gerbert assigns both counties to his fictional Count Gerart.[110]

Geography and Historical Personages:
The Tournament of Montargis

Abandoning the mythical world of Arthur like Jean Renart, Gerbert de Montreuil set his romance in the actual geography of France and peopled it with contemporary personages. Only twice was he tempted to invent fanciful places as was his custom in the *Continuation* of the Perceval story.[111] When the two lovers are separated, they both head for the eastern borders of France, as in Jean's *Escoufle*.[112] After being abandoned in a forest by Gerart, Eurïaut is discovered by the duke of Metz returning from Compostela and taken to his city. In fact, the two pilgrimages named by Gerbert are to Santiago de Compostela (v. 1119) and Saint-Gilles-du-Gard (v. 307), those of Jean's romance as well. When Gerart learns at Nevers that Eurïaut is innocent, he heads toward Burgundy in search of her (v. 1513). After defending a maiden at the castle of Vergy (Reulle-Vergy in the region of Dijon), he turns north, passing through Châlons-sur-Marne (v. 2268) and the Ardennes (v. 2503) and eventually reaching Cologne, where he defends the city's duke against its enemies (v. 2504). During a drug-induced interlude with the duke's daughter, he indulges in tournaments in Germany and the Hesbaye (v. 3825) and in hunting along the Rhine (v. 4176). The Rhenish Cologne and the Hesbaye in Belgium recall episodes from Jean's *Rose*. (Saint-Trond is in the Hesbaye.) When finally recalled to his senses, he apparently heads south in quest of his *amie*. After lodging at Pont-à-Mousson in the vicinity of Metz, he learns of Eurïaut's imminent danger and arrives at Metz in time to rescue her.

Throughout these journeys, most of the personages encountered are completely fictional. The historical lord of Cologne, for example, was the archbishop, not a duke called Milon (v. 2627). At Metz, however, Gerbert returns to the contemporary world. When Eurïaut is accused of murder, the duke refuses to render a judgment without the counsel of the count of Bar-sur-Duc (vv. 4087–93, 4111–13). At the turn of the century, the dukes of Lorraine (therefore of Metz) were closely related to and dominated by the ambitious counts of Bar-le-Duc. At the time of Gerbert's writing, the duke of Lorraine was Mathieu II (1220–51). His maternal uncle, Henri II, count of Bar (1214–39) had been applying pressure on his nephew, but until 1226, the two remained on good terms.[113] In Gerbert's story, twelve peers are summoned to render judgment, before whom the accusation is brought by the lord of Lansi (who is related to Melïatir, the actual murderer), and Eurïaut is defended by the lord of Asprement (vv. 5379–80). Since Melïatir is doubtless fictional, his relative may be too, but Ancy-sur-Moselle in the vicinity of Metz did possess a lord of knightly rank. The lords of Aprement, however, were an influential family in the region.

Gobert VI d'Apremont (1204–39), Gerbert's contemporary, was the brother of Jean, bishop of Verdun. He was closely allied to the counts of Bar-le-Duc and known for the fairness of his judgments.[114] Although Eurïaut's accusation, trial, and exoneration are figments of Gerbert's imagination, he nonetheless chose historical personages who acted in accordance with their known politics.

Consonant with Gerbert's Capetian orientation, however, the principal events of the romance take place in areas of importance to the French monarchy. The narrative opens with King Louis's Easter court at Pont de l'Arche (v. 86) and then shifts to his court at Melun (v. 698). Except for the Paris region, Pont de l'Arche, downstream on the Seine in Normandy, and Melun, upstream to the south, were the favorite residences of Philip Augustus at the end of his reign.[115] The itineraries within these areas are plotted with precision. When Gerart brings Eurïaut from Nevers to Melun, he stops at Bonny-sur-Loire (vv. 790–98) before crossing the short distance overland to the river Loing, which leads him to Melun. When he returns to Nevers, he seeks lodging at a castle at La Marche on the Loire (vv. 1335–36), a day's journey from the city. Just as Montargis to the south of Melun on the Loing played a role in Pierre de Courtenay's acquisition of Nevers in 1181 (he gave it to Philip Augustus), once again here it becomes the site where the fortunes of the county are to be decided anew. As the knights converge on the city for the tournament, like those at Saint-Trond, they stop at places a day's journey away before entering the city. Arriving from the north, the royal party lodges appropriately at Château-Landon (v. 5735) and the barons from the south with the count of Forez at Châtillon-Coligny on the Loing ("Chastillion-sour-Louain," v. 5959).

As at Saint-Trond, the tournament of Montargis, although fictional, is precisely situated in political geography, and its participants serve to map out Gerbert's political horizons to his audience. Once again, the two opponents, Gerart, count of Nevers, and Lisïart, count of Forez, are fictional, but each leads a team composed of historical personages well known to contemporaries. Although Gerbert offers no first names (with one but mistaken exception), the configuration of nomenclature facilitates their identification when they are placed in the period when Gerbert wrote.[116] Since those on Gerart's side were all faithful to the Capetians, they may be considered a royal party. Four were related to the king by blood. The count of Bologne (v. 5921) was Philippe Hurepel (d. 1234), the son of

Philip Augustus by Agnès de Méranie-Andech, who inherited Boulogne by marrying the daughter of Renaud de Dammartin and acquired the county after the latter's defeat at Bouvines in 1214.[117] The counts of Brittany and Dreux (v. 5914) were brothers of the Dreux (Braine) family who were royal cousins descended through a son of Louis VI. Philippe Augustus gave Pierre de Dreux (d. 1248) the heiress of Britanny in 1212, and he acquired the county the next year. His elder brother was Robert III (d. 1234), who became count in 1218.[118] The count of Saint-Pol (v. 5928) is from the loyal family of royal cousins of Châtillon-sur-Marne, also cousins of Milon de Nanteuil's. He may be Gaucher III de Châtillon (d. 1219), to whom Philip Augustus gave the heiress of Saint-Pol, or Guy II (d. 1226), who married Agnès de Nevers in 1221, or Hugues V (d. 1248).[119]

Including the counts of Dreux and Saint-Pol, five of the party had fought at Bouvines on the Capetian side: the count of Ponthieu (v. 5922) and the lords of Barres and Garlande (v. 5926). The count of Ponthieu is doubtless Marie's father, Guillaume (d. 1221), and not her exiled husband, Simon de Dammartin. The lords of Barres and Garlande, of lower rank, exemplify two families who were devoted "royal knights" in Philip Augustus's household and defended him bravely at Bouvines. Descendants of these families usually bore the name Guillaume in Gerbert's time.[120] To complete the royal party, the count of Roucy (v. 5915) is Jean II (d. 1251), who was allied to the Dreux family through marriage. Before the arrival of Gerart de Nevers, the royal party at Montargis is led by the count of Montfort (v. 5912), who is Amaury IV (d. 1241). As the son of Simon de Montfort, from a barony to the west of Paris, Amaury succeeded to leadership of the northern barons who fought against the Albigensian heretics under Capetian auspices.[121] Shortly after the tournament ends, the king requests information from a counselor, "chelui de Roie" (v. 6132). This person has not participated in the tournament because he is the aged Barthélemy de Roie, a "royal knight" and Philip Augustus's early and trusted lay counselor. He fought for the king at Bouvines along with Barre and Garlande. Created "grand chamberlain of the king in 1208," he held the position until his death in 1237.[122] This royal party cohered and remained loyal to the king until 1229, when the counts of Boulogne and Dreux joined Pierre, count of Brittany, in attacking Champagne.[123]

Those fighting at the tournament of Montargis on the side of Lisïart, count of Forez, were a heteroclite group of turbulent barons who, for the most part, came from the mountainous regions of the Massif Central. The complexity of their marriage alliances (most were interrelated in various ways), combined with their penchant for feuding, make it difficult to group them in a coherent party. Nonetheless, certain patterns help identify five central figures: Archembaud VII (d. 1242), lord of Bourbon (v. 5940); Humbert V (d. 1250), lord of Beaujeu (v. 5942); Guillaume X (d. 1247), count of Auvergne (v. 5948); Robert (d. 1234), dauphin de Montferrand (v. 5950); and the count of Forez (v. 5938).[124] In Gerbert's romance, the last-named is the fictional and villainous Lisïart, but in history the count of Forez was Guy IV (d. 1242), married to Mathilde, countess of Nevers.

Of this cluster, the houses of Beaujeu and Auvergne were long reputed to have been disruptive toward the monarchy. One of Philip Augustus's first actions was to defend the churches of Cluny and Mâcon against the depredations of the lords of Beaujeu and the counts of Chalon, as his father had done before him.[125] In Auvergne, the counts had long asserted their independence of both the king and the duke of Aquitaine, a policy that was continued by the contemporary Guillaume X. In the twelfth century, however, a younger branch split off from the house of Auvergne and established an independent line at Clermont, who styled themselves the dauphins of Montferrand. In contrast to their cousins, they were generally submissive to the Capetians by 1199. To subjugate the major line now established at Riom, Philip Augustus commissioned Guy de Dampierre, lord of Bourbon, to lead an army. Guy's son, Archembaud VII remained the constable of Auvergne and the king's agent to keep the region submissive to royal authority.[126]

As much as they resisted royal authority these barons were prone to feuding among themselves. A marriage treaty in the first decade of the thirteenth century exposes the traditional rivalries. Guy II of Forez and Guy II of Auvergne were to ally themselves by marriages to protect themselves against their respective enemies, identified as Guichard IV of Beaujeu and Guy de Dampierre, lord of Bourbon. Although the terms were never executed, the agreement reveals long-standing cleavages.[127] The disputes between Forez and Beaujeu went back to the reign of Louis VII, and Auvergne and Bourbon remained traditional enemies. By the time Gerbert wrote, however, these enmities had abated. In 1222, Guy IV of Forez made peace with Humbert V of Beaujeu by offering a son in marriage to a daughter of his opponent. Because of problems of potential consanguinity, a waiting period of seventeen years was instituted. A marriage was finally executed in 1247.[128] In 1229, another peace was negotiated between the counts of Auvergne and the dauphins of Montferrand on one side and the lords of Bourbon and the king on the other.[129] These selections are merely a small sample of a myriad of disputes, matrimonial agreements, and other negotiations in which these families engaged. They nonetheless suggest a peaceful, if temporary respite in the traditional feuds among the restless barons of the Massif Central, and would have rendered plausible to contemporary audiences Gerbert's fiction of the families of Forez, Beaujeu, Montferrand, Auvergne, and Bourbon participating amicably on the same side at the imaginary tournament of Montargis. The remaining members of Lisïart de Forez's party are more difficult to group.[130]

At the tournament of Montargis, therefore, a royal party loyal to the Capetians faces off against the turbulent barons of the Massif Central. As romance audiences were entitled to expect, the Capetian forces, led by the hero Gerart de Nevers, win the day, and Lisïart's treachery is unmasked in a subsequent judicial duel. At the court of the good King Louis, royal justice prevailed over baronial turbulence. In the *Roman de la rose,* Jean de Renart had presumed to offer advice to the emperor Otto of Braunschweig and his Welf supporters. Addressing Marie, countess of Ponthieu, who herself was married to a treacherous and exiled baron, Gerbert de Montreuil suggests in the *Roman de la violette* that if Marie remained faithful to the king and her husband Simon submitted to royal justice, they too could be restored to their rightful inheritance and peace.

This lengthy excursion into the historical context of Jean's and Gerbert's romances can be justified by its findings. The close correlation between the political worlds of the three addressees and the contents of the romances cannot be replicated in earlier chansons de geste or romances. Placed against their contemporary worlds, Jean and Gerbert reveal a historical consciousness unprecedented in French vernacular literature. Historians may be able to decipher the vestiges of a distant past in the chansons de geste and the romances of antiquity, but they find it more difficult to relate the romances of Chrétien to the political concerns of a Marie of Champagne or Philippe of Flanders. Whatever may be detected below the surface of these preceding fictions, no previous vernacular author can rival Jean and Gerbert in their acute sense of a "here and now" that would have been immediately familiar to their listeners/readers. The remarkably close

correspondence between the historical context and the fictional "reality effects" of the romances detailed in this chapter encourages me to proceed in
subsequent chapters to read Jean's and Gerbert's vernacular verses as an
opening into the lay environment of the aristocracy of northern France,
which the Latin of the clerical authors obscures.

THREE

Chivalric Prowess

The Solitary Knight,
Single Combat, and Prowess

T H E solitary knight on horseback, clad in helmet and hauberk, and
armed with lance and sword, is the dominating figure of the aristocratic society depicted in romance. Chrétien de Troyes opens his
first romance with the hero Erec and Queen Guenièvre hunting the white
stag in the company of her maidens. Suddenly, they are confronted by "an
armed knight on a warhorse with a shield suspended from his neck and a
lance in his fist" (*Erec* vv. 139–41). Another "splendidly equipped and fully
armed" knight makes his appearance at Arthur's Ascension court in Chrétien's *Charrete* (vv. 43–45). The unexpected arrival of a solitary knight announces a new challenge and prompts the departure of the heroes Erec,
Lancelot, and Gauvain, whose adventures are the *matière* of Chrétien's fictions. Journeying across an immense countryside and through deep
forests, the Arthurian hero punctuates his wanderings with countless single combats to avenge injustices, to relieve castles under siege, to rescue
maidens in distress, to take part in tournaments, and to endure superhuman
trials, all in pursuit of a quest. A creation of Chrétien and his epigones, the
solitary knight-errant provided the ubiquitous "horizon of expectations"
for the contemporary audiences to whom Jean Renart and Gerbert de
Montreuil address their romances.[1]

The specialty of these knights is to fight adversaries in single combat.
So frequent are such combats that their unfolding assumes a stereotypic
taxonomy: first, the initial charge of both knights on horseback, until the
lances are broken or one is unhorsed; then the resort to swords on foot until one cries for mercy, one is killed, or both fall in exhaustion.[2] The engagement may be condensed or expanded, but the audience was conditioned to expect these essential features. This image of the single combat

seems to have originated in the warfare endemic to the society of warriors who inhabit the chansons de geste, but Chrétien's romance world is more at peace, except for occasional sieges of castles. Nonetheless, Chrétien de Troyes and his followers employ countless examples of single combats to emphasize the bravery of their heroes and serve the particular needs of their ingenious plots. Although modern readers may find them tedious, the contemporary listener/reader came to expect scores of such conflicts in a good tale.

Like Chrétien de Troyes, Jean Renart and Gerbert de Montreuil set their stories in times of general peace. Gerbert naturally follows Chrétien's example in the Arthurian *Continuation* and provides Perceval and Gauvain with the opportunity to fight scores of such battles, but in the *Violette*, set in the contemporary world, he reduces such occasions drastically. In contrast, Jean Renart, whose fictional world is equally at peace (except for administrative disruptions in the Empire and the distant warfare of the crusades) omits single combats. In both Jean and Gerbert, the chief exception is the tournament, where the scattered single combats provide the knight with his principal training, amusement, and means of achieving glory. Gerbert adds two cases of the judicial duel, or trial by battle, to decide legal disputes. In both the actual fighting is stereotyped according to romance taxonomy, although the judicial procedures follow contemporary custom. (I discuss them in Chapter 7.) Gerbert's reduction and Jean's omission of the figure of the solitary knight-errant who fights innumerable single combats suggest that he had become a romance fiction that had outlived its use at the turn of the twelfth century in a society now more accustomed to peace. If this figure still possessed any historical reality by that time, it lay not in his particular mode of fighting but in his espousal of an underlying chivalric ethos.

The supreme virtue for the solitary knight was prowess (*proece;* adj. *preus*). From the time of the chansons de geste, this virtue included the qualities of physical strength, endurance, courage, and skill in arms, all requisite for successful warriors. Chrétien's romances, however, extend prowess to connote knightly perfection, embodying the highest values of the chivalric class. The *preudome,* or ideal knight, is defined so broadly that the concept is not restricted to men but includes women, *preudefame,* as well.[3] Jean and Gerbert inherited this broad semantic field and offer few innovations. Accordingly, Jean addresses the count of Hainaut with the flattering epithet of *preudome* (*Escoufle* v. 9101); even the cleric Milon de

Nanteuil is characterized as one of the *preus* of the kingdom (*Rose* v. 7). Both Conrad and Guillaume are consistently identified as *prodomes.* Clearly, the terms were extended to their widest range. The *proece* of Count Richard is equated with all goodness (*Escoufle* vv. 98, 103), and Conrad's people think of him as *preu;* never was there a man better endowed with such good qualities (*Rose* vv. 37–41). Prowess is linked to his good sense, excellence, and largesse (*Rose* vv. 350–51). The heroines Aelis, Isabel (*Escoufle* v. 2055, 4957), Lïenor (*Rose* vv. 3567, 5539), and Eurïaut (*Violette* v. 922) are equally *preus.* Nonetheless, the warrior's bodily attributes are retained throughout. *Preu* is frequently linked with *hardi* (bold) and *valliant* and manifests itself in the context of fighting.[4] As count of Normandy, Guillaume is skilled in arms (*Escoufle* v. 8481); King Louis is *preus et hardis* and bold in arms (*Violette* vv. 66–68), as is the legendary Tristan (*Continuation* vv. 3759–60).

Knights in Groups

Whereas Gerbert remained susceptible to the Arthurian "horizon of expectations," the more innovative Jean replaces the solitary knight with groups of *bons chevaliers.* When the emperor in the *Escoufle* appoints Count Richard to subdue the serfs and *ministeriales* who have usurped imperial authority, the imperial constable looks to France to recruit good knights, making them friends by his generosity. Whenever he sees a knight without arms, horse, or equipment, he supplies these from his household (vv. 1658–89). The emperor Conrad shows a similar preference. Surrounding himself with prized examples of knighthood, he never allows a good knight to wander through his country without an offer of lands and castles to retain him according to his merits (*Rose* vv. 100–103, 856–57).

The earliest and fullest example of knights fighting in groups is when Count Richard leads a force of crusaders to the Holy Land (*Escoufle* vv. 779–1325). The Normans contribute at least 300 knights to the avant-guard of the Christian army, which totals 30,000 men. The principal engagements consist of a surprise attack upon the Turkish camp and a pitched battle between the two armies. Before the latter, however, a Turkish champion breaks ranks and challenges Richard to single combat. In accordance with the convention of such contests in the romances, the Saracen is unhorsed and killed by the Norman's lance. "Quel chevalier et quel preudome!" Jean exclaims (v. 1021).

The temptation to insert such flourishes infected historians as well.

Guillaume le Breton claims that Philip Augustus only with difficulty resisted a challenge to single combat from the count of Flanders at Boves in
1185, and Gislebert de Mons asserts that in 1184, Jacques d'Avesnes offered
to resolve a dispute over homage with the count of Hainaut (the father of
Renart's addressee) by single combat with any knight chosen by the count
(although Jacques eventually backed down).[5] That these are equally romance fantasies and examples of art acting on life is suggested by the observation that although such combats were occasionally proposed, according to the historical record, no evidence has survived of one actually
taking place.

Count Richard succeeded in defeating the Turks, however, chiefly because of his deployment of the Christian troops in battalions (*bataille*),
that is, grouped together in close order (*Escoufle* v. 1238). The Templars
occupied one wing, with two battalions of knights, while the main body
under Richard's command consists of units of footsoldiers and heavily
armed sergeants, interspersed with bands of knights arranged in tight
ranks (vv. 1060–77). As will be seen from tournaments, the last element,
closed ranks, was indeed the key to successful engagement by knights.

When he returns to the Empire, Richard's military skills are applied to
besieging the castles held by the *ministeriales*. No fortress or gate can withstand the companies of "good knights" from France. The first to attack
and the last to disband, five hundred of them are worth a thousand others
(*Escoufle* vv. 1578–85). Comparable expertise is claimed for the knights recruited by Conrad, who drag no siege engines or catapults along with
them but carry only lances and banners. Invariably successful, they take
high towers and burn great castles, devouring with their teeth, as it were,
the wooden pickets outside the walls (*Rose* vv. 103–19). Jean's unconcealed
disdain for modern military equipment is evidently an archaism consonant
with his allegiance to the "good old days of chivalry." It may also reflect
his contempt for the mercenary soldiers who deployed such machines and
made siege operations their specialty. Although Jean assigns the besieging
of castles to knights, he nonetheless recognized that this kind of warfare
had become the specialty of well-coordinated mercenaries.[6]

The Tournaments of Saint-Trond,
Montargis, and Lancien

The field of honor on which prowess was most visible was undoubtedly
the tournament.[7] Its importance is signaled by the attention that Jean Re-

nart and Gerbert de Montreuil devote to the tournaments of Saint-Trond, Montargis, and Lancien in their romances. The enjoyment of the sport had probably attained its pinnacle a generation earlier. Gislebert de Mons reports, for example, that from 1168 to 1184, Count Baudouin V of Hainaut, the father of Jean's addressee, participated in at least thirteen tournaments in the Rhine valley and northeastern France.[8] At precisely the same time, the English-born William the Marshal attended eighteen different contests in the same area. It is not surprising, then, that Gerbert has his hero Gerart de Nevers on the road tourneying in Germany and the Hesbaye (not far from Saint-Trond) (*Violette* vv. 3824–25). Since the sport had been outlawed by Church councils as early as 1130, clerics like Gislebert were reluctant to divulge many details in their Latin writings, but vernacular writers were not as inhibited vis-à-vis their aristocratic audiences. The *Histoire de Guillaume le Maréchal,* a biography of William the Marshal commissioned by his family in 1225, devotes at least 2,500 verses to William's tournaments and undoubtedly constitutes the richest source on the subject available to historians from the twelfth century.[9]

Four romances by Chrétien de Troyes tell at length the stories of four fictive tournaments that coincide in time and place with those attended by Count Baudouin and William the Marshal. In *Erec et Enide,* at a contest between Evroïc and Tenebroc shortly after his wedding, Erec sets out to demonstrate that marriage has not affected his knightly prowess (vv. 2072–2222). In the *Cligès* (vv. 4583–4969), King Arthur sponsors a four-day tournament between Oxford and Wallingford that affords the protagonist opportunity to fight incognito in four different sets of armor. In the *Charrete* (vv. 5369–6056), the ladies take charge of this male sport when Queen Guenièvre presides over the celebrated tournament of Noauz (the renowned Lancelot is obliged, for example, to fight well or poorly according to the queen's pleasure). And in the *Graal* (vv. 6211–7033), Gauvain becomes involved in a dispute between two damsels that obliges him to exercise his prowess on the tourney field.

The behavior of Chrétien's fictional knights differs, however, from that of the historical knights who participated in the contemporary events recorded in the *Histoire de Guillaume le Maréchal.* The question is not whether Chrétien or the author of the *Histoire* is more faithful to historical reality. Rather, they present competing perspectives. Chrétien privileges chivalric ideals over practical tactics, and the *Histoire* tactics over ideals. Both perspectives are present in each author, however, and, in fact, chivalry and tactics interacted as well on the historical tournament field.

As noted, however, Chrétien provided the literary "horizon of expectations" of Jean's and Gerbert's audiences. Since the latter's *Continuation* is a direct sequel to the Perceval story, it comes closest to Chrétien's ideals (vv. 3752–4779). Gerbert situates his tournament at Lancien, the fictional residence of King Marc.[10] The tournament is initially introduced to permit Tristan to pay a visit to his *amie,* Iseut. He persuades Arthur to allow his best knights (Gauvain, Lancelot, Yvain, etc.) to accompany him to Lancien disguised as minstrels. While there, they join the tournament (still in disguise) to help Marc's forces, who are faring poorly on the field. This allows Tristan to demonstrate his prowess in the company of the knights of the Round Table. Perceval appears belatedly on the scene, however, and proceeds to defeat Tristan and the Arthurian knights, until King Marc finally brings the contest to a close. It is clear that literary preoccupations are uppermost here. In this parodic tournament of knights fighting apparent minstrels on the field of Lancien, Gerbert has succeeded in reintegrating the romance world. Tristan joins Arthur's knights, and Perceval, who is usually absent, joins in for the pleasure of the sport and to demonstrate his superiority to the Arthurian universe.

The underlying tension between literary chivalric ideals and practical tactics is nonetheless best embodied in Jean's *Rose* and Gerbert's *Violette.* It will be recalled that the narrative function of the tournament in the *Rose* is to enable Guillaume de Dole to demonstrate his prowess and thereby prove that his sister is from a family worthy of marriage to the emperor. In the *Violette,* the tournament allows Gerart to show himself superior to Lisïart. Since neither is essential to the central story of the romance, Jean and Gerbert are free to expand upon the event for their audiences' pleasure of recognition. Occupying a quarter of the *Rose* (vv. 1644–2967), Jean's tournament takes place at Saint-Trond, a well-known town in the Liégeois, as has been seen, and is staffed with historical figures. Gerbert's tournament at Montargis is also geographically situated and historically peopled. Modeled on the Saint-Trond tournament, it is reduced in length and accorded fewer details. Espousing Chrétien's chivalric ideals, the two nonetheless seek to create an effect of realistic versimilitude like that of the *Histoire de Guillaume le Maréchal.* Rather than setting literature and history at odds, they manifest a reciprocal relationship between the two genres of texts. When read together with Chrétien and the *Histoire,* they show both how the practices of the tournament were given literary expression and how the chivalric ideals of romance shaped actual knightly performance.

To explore the tensions in the fictional tournaments at Saint-Trond, Montargis, and Lancien, I shall pose four questions: (1) How do the participants fight: singly or in groups; and what weapons do they emphasize: lances or swords? (2) Do knights enter the lists for glory alone, as recommended by the romances, or for material gain, as suggested by the histories? (3) Are women present at tournaments as spectators? And (4) since these combats had long been proscribed by ecclesiastical councils, how do churchmen attempt to exercise their influence over the practice. More specifically, do knights attend Mass before fighting?

In all accounts, both literary and historical, knights invariably enter the tournament on horseback, protected by helmet, hauberk, and shield and armed with lance and sword. During times of peace, the tournament offered aristocratic warriors the fullest opportunity to train themselves in the use of this equipment. Upon arrival, they divide into two sides, such as those organized by two noble ladies at Noauz, by the French and the Germans at Saint-Trond, by the Capetian partisans and the turbulent Auvergnese barons at Montargis, and by the knights of King Marc (those inside) and those of the King of One Hundred Knights (those outside) at Lancien. In the *Histoire de Guillaume le Maréchal*, numerous regional groups appear at the contests, but they polarize into two teams on the field, such as knights from Anjou, Maine, Poitou, and Brittany against the French, Normans, and English at Valennes in Maine. Scores to hundreds of men normally take part.

In one out of three contests recorded in the *Histoire*, the tournament opened with a preliminary exercise called *jostes de plaideïces* (v. 1310) or *commençailles* (v. 3214).[11] These jousts paired less experienced knights in single combat before the main event began. Between Maintenon and Nogent, for example, young men tried their skills on the eve of the tournament, but the experienced barons restricted their knights to observing. When the young William the Marshal entered his first tournament with forty knights of the Chamberlain de Tancarville's, his biographer exclaims that this was not a joust of *plaideïces* but a well-ordered squadron of closed ranks, which had not come to "plea" but to win or lose all (vv. 1307–12). As in the *Histoire*, preliminary exercises are also announced on the eve of Saint-Trond, but like the highborn men of the *Histoire*, Guillaume de Dole declines to participate, invoking an earlier oath never to bear arms on Sunday (*Rose* vv. 2218–22, 2296). Gerbert likewise opens the tournaments at Montargis and Lancien with *commençailles* (*Violette* vv. 5969–70; *Continuation* vv. 4002–3).

When Chrétien's romances turn to the main event, attention focuses on the single combat. In the case of the tournament at Oxford, for example, the romancier proclaims that ancient custom decrees that the contest be opened by a knight from Arthur's household taking on an opponent (*Cligès* vv. 4592–97). Accordingly, the hero Cligès must fight four knights of the Round Table, Sagremor, Lancelot, Perceval, and Gauvain, on successive days. Not until the initial combat is decided does the general mêlée begin. Even at the later stage, Cligès brings the action on the field to a standstill because all the opposing knights prefer to queue up to challenge him, so as to have the honor of being captured by the hero (vv. 4648–54). The tournament at Tenebroc opens with a general mêlée between the opposing sides, but Erec soon enters on a white horse at the head of his line in search of an opponent; singly, he unhorses three successive challengers. Lancelot and Gauvain in their respective romances make solitary appearances and defeat all opponents singlehandedly.[12] Throughout the engagements, the couched lance, tucked tightly under the armpit, is the chief weapon with which to strike and unhorse the adversary. Only when Cligès and Gauvain both lose their mounts do they fight on foot with swords until King Arthur calls a halt to the battle (vv. 4884–89).[13] Chrétien is preoccupied with the single exercise for the simple reason that it best enables him to display his protagonist's prowess. At the end of each contest, the hero is judged the best knight of the day.[14]

Although it will be seen that the author of the *Histoire* concentrates on the maneuvering of squadrons and the confusion generated by fighting in groups, like Chrétien, he also must not lose sight of his hero. Throughout the action, William is pictured busily defending the youthful King Henry, known as the Young King, son of King Henry II of England, taking prizes, and keeping himself from capture, but his opponents are only rarely identified, and then only in unusual and often humorous circumstances. At Anet, for example, he captures Simon de Neaufle, but through inadvertence retains only the latter's horse (vv. 2827–74). Mathieu de Walincourt is named at Eu because he has twice lost his horse to the Marshal in the same tourney (vv. 3255–73). Throughout the eighteen tournaments, the only adversary defeated in single combat and identified is Philippe de Valognes, whom William took at Valennes. In romance tradition, the Marshal singles out Philippe from among his opponents, rides out in front of his ranks, spurs forward his horse, strikes Philippe squarely with his lance, and leads him away by the reins (vv. 1324–41). The author obviously pays special attention to this incident because Philippe was William's first prisoner. Despite the humor of some incidents and the confusion of mêlées, the *Histoire* never records a defeat for the Marshal. At the end of each tournament, the author carefully notes that William, like a romance hero, was accorded the prize of the day.[15] At the conclusion of the tourney of Pleurs, for example, a noble lady granted a magnificent pike to her friend the duke of Burgundy. In courtly fashion the prize was passed down the ranks, from the duke to the count of Flanders, to the count of Clermont, and to the count of Troyes. Finally, the count of Flanders suggested that it be conferred on William the Marshal, who had proved himself the most worthy knight of the day. The knights delegated to make the presentation finally found William in a blacksmith's shop with his head on the anvil as the smith tried to extract his head from a battered helmet (vv. 3041–3164).

Like Chrétien, Gerbert de Montreuil and Jean Renart must display the chivalric virtue of their heroes in single combats scattered throughout the tournament. At Lancien, Gerbert's focus is on Tristan disguised as minstrel, who wins all the single jousts until Perceval arrives on the scene and begins to defeat the Arthurian heroes. Similarly, the tournament at Montargis opens with a single combat when the villain Lisïart gallops between the lines and challenges anyone to a joust. The count of Montfort responds, but it is the hero Gerart, disguised in white, who finally unhorses Lisïart (*Violette* vv. 5971–6005). At Saint-Trond, Jean is obliged to exhibit the prowess of his hero Gillaume de Dole to demonstrate the worth of Guillaume's sister. As the French and German lines converge, heralds call out: "Let him pass in front. It's Guillaume de Dole." Guillaume singles out a Fleming ready for battle and charges. He is met with a blow that, but for God's help, would have felled him, but he responds with a well-aimed lance at the Fleming's chest, thus unhorsing his first adversary (vv. 2638–65). In the following action, Guillaume jousts with eight knights from Artois, discomfiting seven. The tournament's high point, however, is a duel between the leaders of the two sides, Guillaume for the Germans and Michel de Harnes for the French. The combat follows the preceding pattern. Michel delivers the first blow and would have succeeded if his lance had not broken, but Guillaume responds with two strikes that break the straps of Michel's saddle and cause him to slide to the rear of his horse.

This permits Guillaume to seize the reins and lead him off as prisoner (vv. 2717–51). A final combat pitting Guillaume against Eudes de Ronquerolles ends inconclusively with them charging and implanting their lances in each other's shields. Only the courtesy of approaching dusk finally separates the combatants (vv. 2792–2803). Although Guillaume de Dole has taken the honors of the day, as required by romance, his victories are not as conclusive as those of Chrétien's heroes, owing to the renown of the French opponents. The literary objective behind these single combats is nonetheless offered without ambiguity. The hero—whether Cligès, William the Marshal, Perceval, Gerart de Nevers, or Guillaume de Dole—has won the prize and is worthy of the title of "the best knight" of the day.[16] Throughout, the sole weapon is the long lance, "more rigid than a club" (*Rose* v. 3738).

Despite the need to glorify the hero, the emphasis in the *Histoire de Guillaume le Maréchal* is nonetheless on groups. The combat units are called *conrei* ("squadrons," v. 1307), *bataille* ("battalions," v. 1420), and *rote* ("troops," v. 3627), and they are led by bannerets like the Chamberlain, who carried his pennant to Valennes. At the magnificent event of Lagny-sur-Marne, the author fills successive columns of text by reciting the names of bannerets who followed the Young King, the French, the Flemish, and the Normans, along with hundreds of their most distinguished knights (vv. 4457–4776). Victory went to those squadrons that could keep their ranks tightly closed and in good order ("li conrei seréement et sanz desrei," v. 1308). At Saint-Brice and at Gournay, for example, William noticed which units kept their ranks and which came onto the field in disarray (vv. 1417–20, 2497–2501). Although the French had a good reputation (vv. 2577–2606), they rode carelessly in loose formation onto the field at Anet. William and the Young King let them advance, but then attacked, pierced their lines, and put them to flight (vv. 2801–14). Since those who broke ranks were the first to be captured, it was deemed foolish to succumb to the temptation (vv. 2732–35).[17] Throughout the action, squadrons were kept together by the deployment of banners and the shouting of battle cries (vv. 2947, 3824, 4806).

Never was there a better tournament, exalts the author of the *Histoire*, reviewing the last contest at Gournay. The field was so strewn with broken lances and swords that horses lacked paths to charge. Helmets resounded with the blows of swords. So many knights fell and banners lay in the mud that it was customarily said that one found the truly valiant beneath the horses' feet. A coward would not have risked his life in such a press (vv. 6069–97). So confused were these tournaments that they could scarcely be distinguished from actual warfare, except for the constraint against killing one's opponent. In the mêlées of the *Histoire,* moreover, no one set of weapons is privileged. Lances break like glass (vv. 4856–60, 4952–55, 4981), and maces and swords batter heads and arms (vv. 2509–13, 2966), but most often blows are delivered and returned without identifying the weapons.[18]

The general mêlée also lurks in the background behind the brilliant exploits of Chrétien's heroes. The tournament at Tenebroc, for example, begins with fighting between groups before Erec appears (*Erec* vv. 2081–2116). Gerbert de Montreuil also acknowledges the participation of groups at Montargis and Lancien by the use of the terms *conroi, batailles, compaignies,* and *mellee,* but these maneuvers are not at the center of attention.[19] Recognizing the importance of group action, however, Jean Renart intersperses it among the single combats. As soon as Guillaume hears the tournament announced, he writes three companions at Dole to join him at Saint-Trond (vv. 1943–49). They accompany him throughout the tourney (vv. 2432–33) and help him to extract an oath of submission from his first prisoner (vv. 2670–73).[20] The participants arrive on the field in *batailles* (v. 2450) led by bannerets, the count of Kleves with 100 knights, Guillaume with 60 (vv. 2606, 2632). Knights from Lorraine enter shouting their battle cry "Au Bar!" (deriving from the name of their patron saint, Nicholas de Bari), followed by 140 men of the count of Boulogne on the other side crying, "After their reins!" ("as frains") (vv. 2780–87). Although Guillaume's single combats uphold the Germans' honor, the French fight better in groups. The German count of Kleves, impatient to be the first, rides at full gallop with lines in disarray, while the French in full armor close ranks tightly ("tuit armé, serré et rengié") (vv. 2604–11). After the first victory, Guillaume is assaulted, as if by one man, by the knights of Walincourt and Artois, who shower on him eight blows to his one (vv. 2674–75). His singular prowess withstands them, but he is never able to breech the closely knit (*seré et clos*) ranks of the men of Walincourt, Bailleul, and Alost (vv. 2700–2703). In the end, as at the last tournament of Gournay, it looks as if carpenters have amused themselves with lumber on the field at Saint-Trond (vv. 2804–11).[21] Never since the Maccabees have such blows been delivered. The pride of the Empire and the kingdom have assembled on the field. Despite individual gains and losses, they separate that night amicably and without bitterness, the Germans honoring their emperor and the French and Lowlanders a credit to the lordship of France (vv. 2814–35).

Jean Renart shared the task of glorifying individual prowess within the confusion of the late twelfth-century tournament with all those who wrote for aristocratic audiences. A writer of fiction like Chrétien, he was free to emphasize his hero's individual exploits as he levels his lance in single combat, but like the author of the *Histoire de Guillaume le Maréchal,* he did not ignore the fundamental group dynamics of the twelfth-century mêlée. Knights were trained to fight in closed ranks in squadrons, where they employed swords and maces as well as lances. The *Histoire* confirms the tactical claim of the *Rose* that optimum effectiveness is attained in groups. Within this framework, however, the romance ethos privileges the knight's individual prowess. Not only did it tempt the author of the *Histoire* to situate his hero in occasional single combats, but it undoubtedly inspired historical knights like William the Marshal to try their hand at individual exploits. How often twelfth-century knights fought singly like Cligès or Lancelot or in groups like William cannot be measured, but Jean's *Rose* reveals the tension between the two modes. Undoubtedly, historical knights fought both ways.

A parallel tension arose between romance and practice as to the motives for participating in tournaments, my second question. Were knights content to fight for glory alone, as proposed in literature, or were they also induced by material rewards, as suggested in the historical accounts? In other words, what importance was attached to booty and prisoners?

The romances and histories agree on the deepest motivation: the perfect knight entered the lists to seek glory. At the end of each day, Chrétien's Erec, Cligès, Lancelot, and Gauvain are adjudged the best on the field. In identical language, Gerbert de Montreuil proclaims that Gerart and Tristan had all of the prizes at Montargis and Lancien; Lisïart had none (*Violette* vv. 6062–66; *Continuation* v. 4290). The *Histoire* seeks throughout to demonstrate, in conventional romance hyperbole, that William was without doubt "le meillor chevalier del monde," winning the prize at the end of each tournament. Jean's Guillaume de Dole must likewise win at Saint-Trond to convince the emperor that he is a *preudom* of lineage worthy of imperial marriage (vv. 2968–77). In a well-known diatribe against tournaments, the contemporary preacher Jacques de Vitry confirms the priority of glory. Among the seven capital sins committed in these contests, pride is foremost, because in their circuits, knights strive for the praise of men and vain glory. The fifth sin is avarice, or plunder—taking a prisoner for ransom and despoiling him of his horse and arms.[22]

Gerbert and Jean Renart attribute importance to the number of opponents their heroes unhorse and capture. Tristan, for example, takes twenty at Lancien (*Continuation* v. 4289), Gerart seven at Montargis (*Violette* vv. 6063–64), and Guillaume de Dole fifteen at Saint-Trond (*Rose* v. 2913). Chrétien's heroes, however, display a singular disdain for prisoners and horses. Erec refuses to join the others who are busy rounding up captives. Concerned only with prowess, he allows Gauvain to collect the more material rewards (vv. 2113–72). At Oxford, Cligès has made heavy investments in three additional sets of armor, but at the end of each day his defeated opponents cannot find him to pay their due ransoms (vv. 4660–72). Lancelot gives away his captured horses to whoever wants them (*Charrete* vv. 5982–83). Although many engage in taking booty on the first day at Tintagel, on the last, Gauvain unhorses four knights and gallantly presents their mounts to lady admirers.[23] The taking of horses and ransoming of prisoners form a backdrop to Chrétien's tournaments, but his protagonists are too absorbed with the chivalric virtue of largesse to take part.

Life was less simple, however, for a landless knight without resources like William the Marshal. At Lagny, for example, knights of the Young King were paid 20 shillings a day by their bannerets (vv. 4762–67). The chronicler Gislebert notes for each tournament whether Count Baudouin reimbursed his knights or whether they entered at their own expense.[24] Throughout his tourneying career, however, the Marshal devoted close attention to horses, prisoners, and ransoms. Some were windfalls, such as at Saint-Pierre-sur-Dives, where an injured knight collapsed in front of William while he was lunching with companions (vv. 7203–23), but in most cases the prize was won fairly. The trick was to take one's opponent *al frein*, that is, by the horse's reins, and lead him off the field. The Marshal's first capture was acquired this way (vv. 1324–41). In one day at Eu, he took twelve horses (v. 3372); on another, fifteen knights at Anet (vv. 4020–21). Becoming more proficient, he formed a partnership with a Flemish knight, Roger de Gaugi. Their earnings were so great that a scribe was engaged to keep accounts; he reckoned that between Pentecost and Lent, at least 103 knights had been taken, not counting horses and equipment (vv. 3403–24). On his deathbed, the Marshal estimated that he had captured more than 500 knights over a lifetime (v. 18483). William learned one particularly effective technique from Count Philippe of Flanders. The count waited on the sidelines until the battle was under way. When parties showed fatigue and lines were weakened, he swept across the field and carried off the exhausted prey (vv. 2723–35).[25] The appetite for horses and prisoners was, of course, whetted by economic necessity. Whenever William tourneyed apart from his patrons' company, it was assumed that he met his own expenses. The windfall of the hapless knight at Saint-Pierre-sur-Dives, for example, could not be resisted because William thereby found the means to pay the innkeeper (vv. 7220–32). As in the rodeos of the American Far West, such prizes kept the itinerant knight alive.

Such success might suggest that William was well on his way to making a fortune, but the contrary ideal of largesse was also at work, urged on by romance literature. Among Count Baudouin's expenses, Gislebert de Mons occasionally records the names of prisoners who were set at liberty.[26] The *Histoire* frequently narrates the activities of the evening following the tournament, when the participants circulated from hostel to hostel to eat, drink, talk of the day's events, and settle accounts.[27] To these lodgings, the winners sent their prizes, and the losers offered pledges and swore to pay ransoms (vv. 3292–3300). William is occasionally depicted as giving away his earnings in the negotiations. At Pleurs, where the Marshal was awarded the prize pike, the author remarks that he had not come for gain but to do well and win honor (vv. 3007–12).[28] Those captured at Joigny had not really lost, because the Marshal acquitted their pledges and made gifts to defeated knights and crusaders (vv. 3553–62).[29] At Anet, fifteen French knights were released in one stroke (vv. 4063–67). At Joigny, however, William made his most conspicuous display of largesse. While the knights were waiting for the ranks to form, the Marshal and his companions amused themselves by dancing with ladies to the tune of William's singing. A herald took over William's place as singer but changed the song by ending each stanza with the refrain: "Now, Marshal, give me a good horse."[30] In response, William immediately mounted, rode out to capture the first approaching knight, and presented the herald with the steed without breaking the cadence of the dance (vv. 3455–3520). Openhandedness undoubtedly reduced the profits of tourneying. It was not booty that made the Marshal's fortune, however, but the chivalric reputation that qualified him to marry Isabel de Clare, a rich heiress. This marriage elevated a poor knight to the richest baron in England.[31]

Jean's fictive Guillaume finds himself at Saint-Trond in a position comparable to that of the historical Marshal. Guillaume enters the contest with financial liabilities. He is missing a helmet, which he lost the previous week at a tournament in Rougemont, and must accept a replacement from the emperor (vv. 1650–63). Later, the emperor bestows on him 500 livres of Cologne, two warhorses, and two silver cups (vv. 1894–1903). Undoubtedly, this munificence enables Guillaume to send money and jewels to his mother and sister to cover expenses at home. Like Cligès, however, he must also procure new equipment. He writes a bourgeois whom he knows at Liège to order 120 lances and three shields (vv. 1927–64). Lacking cash, he asks for credit. These expenses, along with food and lodging at Saint-Trond, have put him deeply into debt at the outset. The contest, opening with a Flemish knight and ending with Eudes de Ronquerolles, nets him fifteen captures. His first victory provides a horse, which he immediately dispatches to the bourgeois of Liège to pay his debt to him (vv. 2670–73). His second victory procures a knight, who is sent to his landlord in Saint-Trond (to settle his account?), and a horse for the jongleur Juglet (to reward him for the introduction to the emperor?) (vv. 2688–93).

With debts settled, Guillaume can finally afford the luxury of largesse. In an exemplary gesture, he releases the French champion, Michel de Harnes, on the field (vv. 2760–63). As in the *Histoire,* the participants return to their hostels to eat, drink, bathe, and circulate through the town, looking for companions, paying ransoms, or offering pledges (vv. 2894–2921). Guillaume returns to his own hostel empty-handed because he has given his arms and horse to the heralds (vv. 2875–79). After washing, he sits down to supper with his companions and his fifteen prisoners, whom he then acquits of their ransoms. Unable to turn down a request, he prefers honor to money (vv. 2908–28). For all his pains, he retains only his shredded padding and leaves Saint-Trond poorer than he had arrived (vv. 2957–59), but like Chrétien's Erec, neither an Alexander nor a Perceval had won as much glory in a single day (vv. 2880–81, 2960–61).[32] Like the Marshal, moreover, his reputation as a brave and generous knight remains his greatest asset, because it will enhance his lineage with an imperial marriage.

On the field of Saint-Trond, however, unhorsed knights are at the mercy of the charging men of Lorraine (vv. 2776–82). Like the count of Flanders in the *Histoire,* the count of Boulogne, the renowned Renaud de Dammartin, waits in the wings while Guillaume engages the men of Artois, Walincourt, and Bailleul. Not until Guillaume has been wearied by the contest with Michel de Harnes does Renaud appear on the field with 140 knights shouting: "As frains, as frains!" (vv. 2784–89). By sundown, riderless horses wander aimlessly, reins dangling at their feet. "God, there's a fortune to be gained there!" the author observes (vv. 2804–23).[33]

That night Saint-Trond is ablaze with the light of torches, and God's thunder cannot be heard above the revels (vv. 2336–57).[34] Come the sobering dawn, Guillaume has saved enough to give presents to his host (vv. 2950–56), but many of the high barons are not so provident. Jean notes that with resources depleted, they resort to perjury to escape their debts and even pillage their lodgings to meet bills due to the bourgeoisie. This is apparently not implausible. When King Richard licensed tournaments in England in 1194, he made all participants swear to abide by the terms of his peace, which stipulated that no knight traveling to or from tournaments should take food or necessities without payment according to reasonable market rates.[35] The emperor Conrad's solution at Saint-Trond befits a romance hero—he generously pays all outstanding ransoms. What he loses in money, he gains in friends in both the Empire and France (vv. 2929–47).

Although writing in the romance tradition, which prized chivalric honor, Jean Renart nonetheless stresses the economic exigencies described in the *Histoire*. Both authors must acknowledge largesse, but both concur that the taking of booty is the business of the tournament. Horses and prisoners are the medium of exchange. Despite these necessities, the romance ideal nevertheless prevails. Horses and prisoners offer the opportunity and satisfy the imperative to exercise the generosity requisite to glory. Both the *Histoire* and Jean, therefore, incorporate the tension between the romantic ideal and the economic practice. We need not doubt that this tension was deeply felt by the twelfth-century participants. How each historical knight personally resolved the tension cannot be determined. Whether he was as generous as the fictional Erec or as ruthless as the historical count of Flanders, however, the tension itself was real.

In the *Histoire de Guillaume le Maréchal*, the tournament is scarcely a spectator sport. Ranging over fields and vineyards, across the countryside, and through village streets, it offered few vantages from which the exploits of knights in squadrons could be observed and admired. It is little wonder that with one important exception, the eighteen contests contain no word of women looking on (my third question), not to speak of their taking part.

The romance tradition established by Chrétien de Troyes, however, offers a stark contrast; in the *Graal* and the *Charrete*, women are not only present but play commanding roles.[36] In the former, the tournament enacts the rivalry between the two daughters of the lord of Tintagel, who take seats in a tower to watch the event. The younger is championed by Gauvain, who wears her sleeve as a token. When he unhorses his opponent, he bestows the captured mount on her and departs from the scene promising fidelity whenever she should require his service. In the *Charrete*, the tournament of Noauz is convoked exclusively at the bidding of the ladies, who are in search of husbands from among the attending knights. Queen Guenièvre is elected to preside, and messengers are dispatched to announce the event. Lancelot, who is incapable of forgoing a good tournament, manages to attend incognito and fights well or badly on alternate days at the queen's secret command. The spectacle is carefully observed by the ladies from a wooden tribune built for the occasion. No reversal of roles could be greater than between the eighteen (save one) tournaments in the *Histoire* and that of Noauz in Chrétien. William the Marshal's masculine sport has been so subverted by women that Chrétien's tournaments are best read as parody for the delight of the aristocratic ladies in his audience.

Women appear only twice at tournaments in the *Histoire*, and on both occasions they are limited to the final and beginning phases. At Pleurs in Champagne, in romance fashion, an unnamed lady presented the prize pike to the most worthy knight. Since she appears after the event, the author gives no indication of whether she had observed the contest (v. 3042). Whatever the ambiguity at Pleurs, women are clearly evident at the opening of the tournament at Joigny in the Auxerrois on the borders of Champagne. As William's company wait for the tournament to begin, they pass the time dancing with the ladies, while William sings, dances, and honors a herald's request for a horse (vv. 3455–63). Not only does he thereby win the admiration of the audience (they say they have never seen a finer deed [vv. 3511–20]), but the ladies' spell is borne by the knights into the fray. The tournament begins auspiciously. The least courageous heart vows to win that day for the ladies present. Although each wishes to increase his own glory, the company prudently close ranks so that no one precedes the others. From the other side, one knight moves up quickly and charges the middle, but he is immediately taken by the reins. The knights who have danced with the ladies are so set in their bodies, hearts, and souls to do well, however, that they surprise those on the other side. As lightning clears a path, so those who come from the side of the ladies excel in every way (vv. 3524–52).

The unfolding events at Joigny are noteworthy. Not only are ladies un-mistakably evident, but their very presence induces the knights to greater prowess. Courage is stirred, and discipline is reinforced, closing the ranks tightly. It is no coincidence that William both performs his dancing and jousting act and displays his most exemplary largesse at this time (vv. 3553–62). All of these are romance topoi whereby the lady's love valorizes the knight's prowess. Of further note, the tournament at Joigny contrasts starkly with all other examples, which are totally devoid of the female presence. Even as William visits the baronial hostels during the evenings to balance accounts and talk of the day's events, women remain absent, unlike in Jean de Joinville's *Histoire de Saint Louis* a half century later, when the count of Soissons cannot wait to return to the ladies' chambers to recount his exploits.[37] The parallel between Joigny and Tintagel/Noauz suggests, therefore, that art is here acting upon life.

Although Jean Renart sings "of arms and of love" in romance tradition (*Rose* v. 24), the two are not connected at Saint-Trond.[38] Guillaume excels at arms, but Conrad is the lover of the story and does not participate.[39] As the knights exit the town, the noble ladies are eager to know Guillaume's name. When they hear it, they exclaim, "His *amie* must return his love most willingly. Happy is the lady who holds the heart of such a *preudom*" (vv. 2542–45). In fact, however, Jean has already revealed that Guillaume is without an *amie* (vv. 2035–36). At Montargis, the connection resurfaces. Gerart enters the fray in disguise, but wearing Eurïaut's wimple, as Gau-vain carries the sleeve of the younger daughter at Tintagel (*Violette* vv. 5890–5901). Every time he scores a hit, he cries, "Chevalier, m'amie Eu-rïaut!" (vv. 6006–10, 6019–30). Tristan, however, takes advantage of King Marc's absence in the lists at Lancien to return to Yseut's chamber and re-join his *amie*.

As at Joigny and Pleurs, women are present at Saint-Trond as observers and witnesses before and after the tournament. As Guillaume leaves his hostel to attend the evening exercises, noble damsels remark on his cloth-ing and countenance and wish him good luck (vv. 2308–11).[40] On the mor-row the procession of knights from the town to the field is witnessed from balconies, upper floors, windows, and doors by crowds of ladies of high nobility. Admiring Guillaume's clothes and envying his supposed *amie*, they affirm that he surpasses the Arthurian hero Graelent Muer (vv. 2528–67). That evening there is not a townsman, maiden, or lady at Saint-Trond who does not come to the door to see what each knight has brought back. Guillaume has nothing to show, because he had already given away his horse and arms to the heralds. His handsome face nonetheless wins the love of many a lady (vv. 2868–88). It is clear, therefore, that in Jean's and Gerbert's scenarios, women do not observe the actual battle but wish the combatants well at the outset and witness the results at the end. Unlike Chrétien's romances and Gerbert's *Violette*, Jean's *Rose* portrays neither the hero nor any other as fighting because of a lady's love.

Jean's fictive Saint-Trond may help resolve the tension between the masculine sport and the inclination to introduce women. The *Rose* confirms the impression arising from the *Histoire* that by the twelfth century, feminine participation was limited to observation before and after the battle. Although authors like Jean and Gerbert might have placed ladies on grandstands, towers, walls, or even the field, their concern for versimilitude apparently inhibited them from depicting women as leaving town or attending the contest. On the other hand, the *Rose* and the *Violette* also attest to a romance impulse to enlarge feminine participation. Finding strongest expression in Chrétien's fantasies at Tintagel and Nouaz, this tendency also surfaces in the *Histoire* at Joigny, where the ladies inspire the resulting prowess and generosity. They do not demand individual combats as yet, but continue to reinforce the traditional tactics of closed ranks. The brief appearance of ladies in Jean Renart, therefore, suggests that their presence had not been institutionalized by the turn of the century. The romance ideals have not yet succeeded in reorienting masculine habits, although the mounting pressure is signaled by the ladies at Joigny and at Saint-Trond. By the end of the thirteenth century, however, ladies did undoubtedly insert their presence into tournaments as spectators.

Tournaments and the Clergy

Since churchmen were predictably hostile toward this life-threatening sport, my fourth question explores how the clergy sought to exercise their influence. At the council of Clermont in 1130, Pope Innocent II had formulated the Church's position, which was repeated at all the major French councils and at universal councils held in Rome prior to the great Lateran Council of 1215. The language of the Third Lateran Council of 1179 is most explicit: "Following the footsteps of our predecessors, Popes Innocent and Eugenius, we forbid these detestable fairs or holidays, which are called *torneamenta* in the vernacular, in which knights are accustomed to fix a date and to gather to demonstrate their strength and rash bravery with frequent loss of life and danger to the soul. If any one of the participants dies there, he shall be refused ecclesiastical burial, although he may receive penance and the host if he requests it while yet alive."[41]

These injunctions not only inhibited clerics from narrating the details of tournaments in Latin, they also prompted the theologians of Pierre the Chanter's school to approach the task of implementing the decrees in actual practice, which was particularly difficult, because the sport was immensely popular in aristocratic circles. The Chanter admitted that tournaments were customary, pleasurable, and naturally pertained to human nature. Two preliminary questions emerged: Since the tourneyers frequented the courts of princes and prelates, how could contact be avoided with people who were thereby under automatic excommunication? And were knights required to make restitution for the ill-gotten gains of horses and ransoms acquired in tournaments?[42] At William the Marshal's deathbed, for example, certain clerics had insisted that William restore all the profits gained from the some five hundred knights he had taken during his life. The Marshal refused, protesting that the clerics were shaving him too close; if this standard were applied, no knight could be saved (*Histoire* vv. 18476–96). This question echoed the debates in the Paris schools, with Pierre the Chanter arguing for full restitution, such as was demanded of usurers, whereas Robert of Courson began to permit knights to keep their earnings from tournaments, which, he argued, although immorally acquired, were retained legally, like wages from prostitution.[43]

A particularly perplexing question arose from an apparent discrepancy in the conciliar decree: How could a dead knight be refused burial in a consecrated cemetery when he had been received as a penitent while still alive? The Chanter's response followed the precedent for champions in judicial duels, examined in Chapter 7. The prohibition of burial should remain as a public and powerful deterrent to the sport.[44] Yet the problem persisted and was highlighted by the celebrated case of Geoffrey, count of Brittany, son of King Henry II of England, who was killed in 1186 in the prime of life and buried at Notre-Dame in Paris. The Capetian historian Guillaume le Breton states enigmatically that he died on the field of Champeaux, but the Englishman Benedict of Peterborough less discreetly asserts that he was killed in a tournament. Philip Augustus, who loved Geoffrey dearly, summoned his doctors to Paris to minister to his wounds. When their remedies failed, the king's grief was so great the he had to be restrained from leaping into the grave. Not only was Geoffrey buried with great honor in the choir of Notre-Dame, where two polyphonic *conductus* were composed for the occasion, but the king established two chaplains to sing perpetual masses for his soul.⁴⁵ If the count had been killed in a tournament, how could he be buried at Notre-Dame? The debates in the Chanter's school suggest that the theologians were under pressure to mitigate the severity of the decree. Pierre began to highlight certain gestures, such as beating one's breast, which might indicate that the knight had truly repented of his crime before he died. Thomas of Chobham tells of a knight killed in a tournament and buried in unconsecrated ground. When his friends found that his right hand covered his face in the form of a cross, the pope accepted this as a sign of repentance, however, and authorized transferal of the body to a church cemetery.⁴⁶ Such reasoning may have facilitated Count Geoffrey's burial.

A final point raised by the theologians queried whether knights could attend Mass before a tournament. No mention is made of church attendance, or even of clergy, in connection with any of the eighteen tournaments of the *Histoire de Guillaume le Maréchal*. Chrétien likewise consistently ignores the issue of the Mass; the sole exception is Gauvain (*Graal* vv. 6854–65), who attends mass on the second day of the contest, but he is alone, and no connection is drawn between his devotion and the tournament.⁴⁷ A generation later, however, in the romances of Jean and Gerbert, church attendance is represented as a regular preliminary to the sport. On the Sunday evening before the tournament at Saint-Trond, Guillaume de Dole merely attends the opening jousts (*vespres*), refusing to participate out of respect for the holy day (*Rose* vv. 2218–22). On the morrow, however, he and his three companions, accompanied by sixty other knights, form a solemn procession, two by two, to church. After rendering offerings, they hear Mass in honor of the Holy Spirit sung by the chaplain of an abbess (vv. 2432–45). After breakfast, Guillaume joins the brilliant defile of knights leaving town for the tournament, followed by musicians and crowds. Three barons carry the knight of Dole's shields on their chests as if they were relics or holy treasures (vv. 2481–89). Mounting his horse, and commending himself to God that he be spared from dishonor, Guillaume joins the slow cortege, which proceeds step by step, two by two, like monks in a procession (vv. 2506–11). Following Jean's lead, Gerbert depicts knights hearing a Mass of the Holy Spirit before the tournament at Montargis (*Violette* vv. 5869–70), and the Arthurian heroes do likewise at Lancien (*Continuation* vv. 4034, 4103–10). By depicting public church at-

tendance and parades that incorporate ecclesiastical rituals, Jean and Gerbert appear to be sanctifying an activity that churchmen vigorously opposed.

The theologians' discussions suggest that they were not unaware of
these practices. The Chanter notes that those who frequent tournaments
should be barred from communion, but that because of priestly cupidity—
apparently an allusion to the offerings—the Church is accustomed to
overlooking the offense.[48] In another version, he asks why the Eucharist is
given to knights en route to tournaments and thereby under excommunication. Some argued that this was allowed by toleration or dissimulation.[49]
Apparently, one accommodation was drawn from the parallel with hired
champions, who were permitted to hear Mass before they fought but not to
receive communion. It is difficult to know precisely what the romance
knights actually did in church. Both Jean and Gerbert say explicitly that
they heard Mass, perhaps implying acceptance of the Chanter's distinction, which prohibited receiving the host. The Chanter and Thomas of
Chobham had also raised the possibility of knights who defend themselves
in battle receiving the Eucharist if they are able to suppress fraternal hatred, a sin against the Holy Spirit.[50] Theologians doubted whether this was
humanly possible, but Gerbert specifies that the knights hear the Mass of
the Holy Spirit at Montargis so that God will grant them the power to
abandon all ill-will (vv. 5869–72). (Indeed the votive Mass of the Holy
Spirit may have been expressly sung to aid participants in suppressing this
very sin.)

At the turn of the century, however, churchmen were perplexingly ambivalent about enforcing the prohibition. Not only did the Paris theologians discuss possible attenuations of the conciliar decrees, but the papacy
itself was willing to make accommodations, particularly when churchmen
sought to recruit knights to go on crusade. As the tournament at Ecry in
Flanders demonstrated in 1199, Innocent III learned that these contests
assembled audiences of aristocrats ready to hear the preaching of the crusade.[51] In the diocese of Soissons and the province of Tours, the pope relaxed the sentence of excommunication against participants in tournaments to encourage the taking of the cross. At the Lateran Council of 1215,
he frankly admitted that since the interdiction of tournaments had im-
peded the launching of a major crusade, he suspended these prohibitions
for three years.[52]

Philip Augustus was likewise ambivalent about tournaments, but perhaps for different reasons. Unlike the Angevins and Staufens, the Capetian is never openly associated with these pastimes in the contemporary chroniclers, and no mention is made of tournaments at Paris.[53] The only recognition of the activity in royal documentation appears when Philip demands that his son forswear the sport, presumably to protect the royal succession. Philip was doubtless mindful of Geoffrey of Brittany's fate. When Prince Louis was made a knight at Compiègne in May 1209, he swore to his father that he would attend tournaments only as a spectator. To reduce temptation, he further promised not to bear arms but only to wear a hauberk and an iron cap. His half-brother Philippe Hurepel, next in line in royal succession, also promised his father not to bear arms in tournaments without express permission as long as the king was alive.[54]

The history of the tournament in the thirteenth century deserves a chapter to itself. Suffice it to say that what the romances proposed at the opening of the century became historical reality by the end of it. The brutal mêlée of knights fighting in groups gave way to single combats that were increasingly regulated, ritualized, and transformed into games in which personal danger was reduced. As tournaments increasingly became spectator sports, the women who are absent in the *Histoire de Guillaume le Maréchal* became the prerequisite onlookers for all tournaments, as the romances had originally proposed. Although churchmen continued to protest against the dangers to body and soul, they finally capitulated to the sport's popularity. In 1316, Pope John XXII withdrew the penalty of excommunication, citing among other reasons the argument from the crusades. And knights routinely attended Mass before the spectacle. In the interaction between text and history, the evolution of the tournament demonstrates the potent influence of literary norms on social practice.[55]

The Order of Chivalry

Just as a person is not born a Christian but is created one through the new birth of baptism, so in the twelfth century a young man was not born a knight but was made one at his dubbing. This is well illustrated by the young Perceval at his first encounter with a knight. Having never seen one before, he asks:

> "Fustes vos ensi nez?"
> "Naie, vallet, ce ne puet estre
> Qu'ensi peüst ja nus hom nestre."

"Qui vos atorna dont ensi?"
"Vallet, je te dirai bien qui . . . ."
"N'a pas encore cinc ans entiers
Que tot cest harnois me dona
Li rois Artus qui m'adouba."

"Were you born like this?" / "Certainly not [the knight
responds]. No one can be born like this." / "Who then equipped
you like this?" / "I shall tell you, young man . . . / five years[56]
have not yet passed / since all of the equipment was given me /
by King Arthur who dubbed me." (*Graal* vv. 282–90)

And yet birth did count in the romance world, because no one was dubbed
a knight who was not *gent*, that is, from a family of knights or higher. The
Arthurian heroes Erec, Cligès, Yvain, Gauvain, and even Tristan, claim
royal lineage; only Lancelot and Perceval are introduced as stemming
from lesser families.[57] Shortly after the above experience, Perceval's
mother reveals to her son that he is descended from a *lignage* of illustrious
knights on each of his parents' sides (*Graal* vv. 416–31). Only later does he
learn of his royal blood through the matrilineal line (*Graal* vv. 6415–19).
In the world of the chansons de geste, the knightly virtues mentioned most
frequently are those related to birth: the ideal knight should be *franc* (free),
gentiʒ (noble), and *noble*. This emphasis upon lineage is continued in Chrétien's romances.[58]

Jean Renart is acutely sensitive to the issue of lineage in both of his romances, because his hero and heroine contemplate *mésalliance* with the imperial family. Although the son of a count, Guillaume de Montivilliers is
opposed by the high princes on account of his lesser birth, and Aelis ago-
nizes over the question as she prepares to elope.[59] The situation in the *Rose*
is comparable. Speaking for the imperial princes, the seneschal lists the
requisite conditions for Conrad's wife: *bone* (goodness), *sage* (prudence),
bele (beauty), *pucele* (virginity), and *bon lineage* (proper birth) (vv.
3020–22). Lïenor admits that the seneschal has always despised her *lignage*
(v. 5063), but Jean frequently describes Lïenor and her brother as *gentil*,
the term that he applies to the emperor.[60] Jean keeps returning to the theme
of *lignage* throughout the romance (vv. 1644, 2975, 3025, 3448). As *gentils
chevaliers*, Guillaume's family is sufficient to recommend Lïenor as a
spouse worthy of an emperor.

Although lineage was assumed, dubbing nonetheless remained essential for creating new knights. Since descriptions of dubbing are rare in Latin around 1200, Jean's and Gerbert's audiences formed their "horizons of expectations" both from actual practice and vernacular literature.[61] Before Chrétien de Troyes, the chansons de geste commonly use the verb *adouber*, "to dub," to mean simply "to arm," that is, to give arms or equip a knight militarily for combat. Starting with Chrétien, however, the meaning of the word changes significantly: henceforth *adouber* almost always signifies "to make a new knight." Although this included supplying the knight's first set of arms, the word also conveys the notion of promotion to the rank of knight, even of conferring the status of knighthood itself. Since knighthood was both a profession and an honor, its institution was almost always ceremonial and public. The dubbed or new knight in the romances is invariably a young man; the dubber is most often King Arthur, or more rarely a relative of the dubbed. Almost never is there a vassalic connection between the two men.

Dubbing could take place at any time, but the religious feasts of Pentecost and Nativity, when Arthur's court holds festive sessions, are the preferred occasions in the romances. None of the elements of dubbing are depicted as profoundly ritualized, however, or endowed with exclusively religious significance. The making of new knights is accompanied by the offering of gifts, usually of garments, but never of cash or lands. The ceremony itself consists of a number of gestures, none of which is required without exception. Most often, the new knight is belted with a sword; occasionally he is given spurs. Often he takes a preparatory bath; at times, he receives a *colée*, or blow from a sword.[62]

The chief male characters are already experienced knights when Jean's and Gerbert's narratives open. The sole but noteworthy exception is the young hero Guillaume de Montivilliers in the *Escoufle* (vv. 7885–7929). After Guillaume and Aelis are reunited at the court of the count of Saint-Gilles, the next morning the count announces: "My dear cousin, my first task will be to make you a knight as soon as possible." He summons to his court all the young men in his land who desire arms and to be dubbed in honor of the count of Normandy.[63] Jean Renart protests that he will not waste words on describing the ceremonies that took place in a fortnight. He does not specify the constituent gestures but employs the generic term *armes*, doubtless the sword. As in Chrétien, the honored knight is accompanied by others, in this case, thirty young men. On this occasion, which

Jean hyperbolically claims rivals the burning of Troy, Aelis and Guillaume distribute gifts to the attending maidens, ladies, and knights. Unlike
Chrétien's normal regime, however, family ties unite the dubber with the
honored candidate; the others are the young sons of his vassals.

Jean's audiences could draw on personal experience for their familiarity
with the practice. The family of Baudouin, the count of Hainaut, to whom
the *Escoufle* was sent, had all undergone the ceremony. According to the
Hainaut chronicler, Count Baudouin IV, the addressee's grandfather, had
fervently desired to see his sons knighted and his daughters married within
his lifetime, because misfortune had denied these achievements to his fore-
bears. Baudouin V was therefore "ordained" a knight on Easter 1168 at Va-
lenciennes, and subsequently he himself saw his sons follow in his footsteps: Baudouin VI (Jean's addressee) at the age of eighteen by Henry,
king of the Romans, at Spire in 1189; Henri by Renaud, count of
Boulogne, in 1194; and Philippe, aged twenty-one, by Philip Augustus on
Pentecost in 1195.[64] In respect to ties of family and vassalage, therefore,
Jean's single example follows contemporary practice rather than Chrétien's inspiration.

Although Philip Augustus consented to knight young boys (such as
Arthur of Brittany, Geoffrey's son, at fourteen),[65] he was less generous
with his own son, Prince Louis. It was not until Pentecost of 1209, when
Louis was twenty-two, that the king conferred the belt of knighthood on
his firstborn, along with a hundred other new knights, with his own hand.
If the father was fearful for his son's safety, he was nonetheless uncharac-
teristically generous on this special occasion, as will be seen.[66] The creation
of new knights was, however, a regular duty for the king of France.
Philip's sole surviving financial account, from May 1203, for example,
records robes given to three new knights at Pentecost.[67]

Jean's narrative of Guillaume's knighthood in the *Escoufle,* therefore,
substantially fitted the literary horizons and the contemporary customs of
his audience. These sources concur on an absence of religious ceremonial,
although the date usually followed the high feasts of the Church calendar.[68] Chrétien's *Graal,* however, raises an important exception to this pervasive secularism (vv. 1622–95). Not only is Perceval, the young naïf, a
humorous parody as he stumbles into knighthood despite his mother's opposition, but his attainment of knighthood is accompanied by strong religious motivation. When the *preudom* Gornemans de Gorhaut accedes to
the young man's request to make him a knight, he confers a spur, belts a

sword on him, kisses him, and offers practical advice, which accords with
that furnished by the boy's mother: never kill a knight in battle who pleads
for mercy, do not speak too much, and offer help to men, women, or or-
phans in distress. What is new, however, is Gornemans's solemn declaration that the sword is remitted with

> le plus haut ordene . . .
> que Diex ait faite et commandee:
> C'est l'ordre de chevalerie,
> qui doit estre sanz vilonnie.

> the highest order . . . / that God has instituted: / This is the
> order of chivalry / which should be free of wickedness.
> (vv. 1635–38)

Further obligations were added to attend church frequently, to pray for
one's soul, and to request protection as a Christian in this worldly age.[69]
Appropriately, then, the *preudom* makes the sign of the cross and blesses
the boy with hand raised high.

As Gerbert recapitulates Perceval's adventures, the religious implications of the order of chivalry are increasingly emphasized. After Perceval
passes through the woods where he has previously first met the five knights
and arrives at the hermitage where his mother is buried, the hermit reminds him that a knight who desires to love God and to be *preus* and *vaillans* carries a sword with two cutting edges. One edge defends Holy
Church, and the other defends earthly justice to safeguard Christian people (vv. 2762–72). When the young knight reencounters the *preudom*
Gornemans, who once again confers on him the order of chivalry by belting a sword on him, this order is now identified as that which God has established in the world to do justice and preserve Holy Church (vv.
4992–97, 5018–21). Toward the end of his journey, when Perceval seeks
pardon for his sins, a hermit admonishes him with a brief sermon: God
does not create knights to kill people or make war, but to do justice and defend Holy Church (vv. 15819–23).

This simple formula, which defines the order of chivalry by means of
the image of the double-edged sword, "por tenir droite justise" and "por
desfendre Sainte Eglise," originated in the royal ideology of the early
Middle Ages and was perpetuated in the coronation ceremonies of kings.[70]
At his consecration in 1179, Philip Augustus promised to abide by *tria pre-*

cepta: to preserve the peace of Christian people and the Church, to prevent rapine and iniquities, and to enforce equity and mercy in all judgments.[71] It appears therefore that the two duties emblematized by the sword and formulated by Gerbert were those that kings had traditionally assumed for centuries. Whereas the royal duties were defined by clerics and imposed in ceremonies that from the outset took place in churches, the order of chivalry for knights arose from a lay milieu. Despite the religious orientation, Chrétien's order of chivalry is first enunciated by a *preudom,* and the initial belting does not take place in a church. The *Conte du graal,* in which the order of chivalry is first mentioned, is dedicated to Philippe d'Alsace, count of Flanders, whom Chrétien fittingly praises as one who loves *droite justice* and the *sainte eglise* (vv. 25–26).

In the early thirteenth century, however, Jean and Gerbert in the *Violette* are silent about the order of chivalry and its twofold duties. For Jean, the term *chevalerie* often means simply an assemblage of knights (vv. 857, 2172, 2424), as it does in the chansons de geste, but it could connote a mode of behavior or system of values appropriate to knights as well. For example, hospitality at Dole includes fine words of chivalry and love along with the meal (*Rose* vv. 1255–57). The precepts of this *chevalerie* remain unexpressed, however, and it is not attached to any religious order. Moreover, in an apothegm that became a traditional complaint, Jean laments:

> Por ce s'enledsit et efface
> chevalerie hui est li jors.

> For this reason chivalry today / is debased and dying out.
> (*Rose* vv. 555–56)[72]

Resuming the Perceval story in his *Continuation,* Gerbert resurrects the order of chivalry, but now assigns its promulgation to hermits. Chrétien's and Gerbert's formulations of the order, written in the vernacular for lay audiences, represent the internalization of ecclesiastical principles by aristocratic society. Rearticulation of the code of *chevalerie* in the Latin liturgy of the Church was yet to come.

The appearance of the order of chivalry in Chrétien's *Graal* is accompanied by elaboration on the concepts of prowess and the *preudom* not found in Jean or in Gerbert's *Violette.* Surfacing as bravery, but expanded to include the highest values of knightly perfection, the term *chevalerie* already had a broad scope. In the *Graal,* it appears more frequently and acquires a religious dimension. Perceval's mother advises her son to keep company with *preudomes,* because they will never give bad counsel (vv. 563–66). All who offer the neophyte good advice are thereafter designated by the term: Gornemans, the Fisher King, and, most important, the holy hermit (v. 6303). Gerbert's *Continuation* regularizes the practice of calling hermits *preudomes.*[73] "If knights wish to be *preus* and *vaillans,* they should love God" (vv. 2762–63), counsels the hermit who tends the grave of Perceval's mother.

In effect, therefore, the chivalric ideal of prowess approximates the religious connotations of the virtue of fortitude, the second of the four cardinal virtues of the Patristic schema. St. Augustine defines the first, prudence, as choosing what should be chosen, and fortitude as resisting all vexations. "Fortitude should be attached to prudence," Pierre the Chanter continues, "so that we may strongly resist rising vexations to hold to that which we have prudently chosen. . . . This kind of bravery is the virtue by which we conquer the world, the devil, and ourselves, if we fight well."[74] Parallel to the romance attribution of prowess to hermits, the Chanter extends fortitude to magnanimity, which was appropriate for prelates. "Magnanimity pertains to resisting the enemies of the Church, just as fortitude patiently tolerates diverse troubles. . . . Magnanimity is the mother of fortitude, fortitude of patience, and patience is the nurse of all virtue. . . . Magnanimity is therefore the virtue that cultivates . . . the roses of martyrs and the victorious crowns of confessors."[75]

The most memorable expression of the evolution of the term *preudom* around 1200 was left to Philip Augustus himself, as recalled by his grandson, Louis IX, and reported to Louis's seneschal, Jean de Joinville:

> There is a great difference between a *preu home* and a *preudome.* There are many *preus* (brave) knights, not only in the lands of the Christians but also [in those] of the Saracens, who do not believe in God or his mother. God bestows a great gift and grace on the Christian knight that he endure bodily bravery and service to God but is kept from mortal sin. One who so governs himself should be called a *preudome,* because this prowess comes as a gift from God. But the first-mentioned should be called *preuʒ homes,* because they are brave in body but do not fear God or sin.[76]

Jean and Gerbert could produce examples of heathens or wicked people who were known for physical courage. The Turkish champion, for example, is "prex et frans et hardis" (*Escoufle* v. 1165), the villain Lisïart is *preus* in arms (*Violette* v. 6355), and the treacherous Leander is "preu et hardi et dur et fort" (*Continuation* v. 10857), but only the exemplary Christian knights of Chrétien's *Conte* and Gerbert's *Continuation* are truly *preudomes*.

FOUR

The Economy of Romance

Largesse and Hospitality

THE economy of the early Middle Ages was doubtless complex and is obscured by the lack of documentation, but modern historians have identified the military leader as one of its driving forces. By waging endemic warfare, these leaders amassed great wealth from pillage and booty. They secured authority for themselves through distribution of these riches to their military supporters and churchmen. Germanic kings had pursued these objectives as early as the great migrations accompanying the disintegration of the Roman Empire, but the most spectacular success was achieved by Charlemagne in the ninth century, and Scandinavian chieftains played a similar military-economic role during the Viking invasions that followed. In the eleventh and twelfth centuries, this power was extended to local lords, who from their castles dominated the surrounding regions through their military and legal authority. Lords channeled wealth to their retainers through gifts, and the latter were expected to respond with counter-gifts, thus creating a vast network of gift exchange.[1] Wealth was distributed ostentatiously, without restraint. The supreme virtue in this economy was largesse, or generosity.

The earliest and most visible mechanism for displaying largesse was the great ceremonial feast, during which food, entertainment, and gifts of clothing flowed in spectacular abundance. Following ancient Germanic traditions, such feasts were offered both by Carolingian kings on the Continent and by Scandinavian chieftains in the north.[2] During the eleventh century, the obligation of largesse devolved to territorial princes, and by the twelfth it had become the duty of castellans and local lords as well.[3]

The Largesse of the King:
The Royal Ideal

In the twelfth century, the economic technique of gift exchange, by which wealth flowed from the top down through society, was fast becoming archaic, but its image nonetheless persisted in imaginative literature and eventually devolved to romance. In depicting the largesse of the mythical King Arthur, Chrétien de Troyes provided a "horizon of expectations" for the audiences of Jean Renart and Gerbert de Montreuil.[4] Chrétien is mute as to where Arthur found his riches, but the king is credited with maintaining the best knights in his kingdom. Arthur's immense wealth is fully displayed at his great feasts. To honor Erec's marriage to Enide in Chrétien's first romance, for example, Arthur organizes an extraordinary celebration at Pentecost, summoning his tenant kings, dukes, and barons to a feast that lasts a fortnight. Arthur is not stingy: doors are closed neither to rich or poor, and royal pantlers, cooks, and butlers distribute bread, wine, and venison with abandon (vv. 1870–2021). Similar abundance is lavished on the participants in the festivities of Erec's Christmas coronation at Nantes in Brittany (vv. 6488–6878). Becoming weary of describing the crowds of illustrious guests in attendance, Chrétien concludes that Arthur's liberalities exceeded even those of the kings of the chansons de geste and the Roman Caesar. The great Alexander, who conquered so much and was so *larges* and *riches*, had been poor and stingy by comparison (vv. 6611–23). Beyond food, entertainment, and money, clothing is particularly noteworthy among the gifts. Before his coronation, for example, Erec clothes 169 misfortunates and provides copes and *pelices* for poor clerics and priests (vv. 6470–81). For his part, Arthur opens his chests and spreads out mantels throughout his rooms so that his guests can take as much as they wish (vv. 6624–27).

Like the feasts of Scandinavian chieftains or the potlatches of the Indians in northwest America publicized by anthropologists, these Arthurian celebrations appear on the surface to be entirely gratuitous and disinterested, but as in Germanic gift exchanges, each gift requires acceptance and a counter-gift from the receiver, so that society becomes enmeshed in complex webs of mutual obligations.[5] Although both festivities are ostensibly to honor Erec, the Breton Arthur profits from them to create new knights. At Pentecost, he orders a hundred young men to take the ritual bath before knighting, and he rewards each with fur-lined robes of silk, arms, and horses—the meanest worth more than 100 livres (*Erec* vv. 1963–72). At Christmas, he dubs more than four hundred new knights, all sons of counts and kings, and on each he bestows three horses and three sets of costly clothing, not of rabbit and linen but of ermine and silk embroidered with gold (vv. 6596–6610). In *Cligès*, Arthur knights the young prince Alexander and his twelve Greek companions, giving arms, horses, and equipment to each (vv. 1112–26). Although these gifts are offered with seeming disinterest, they nonetheless serve to recruit new knights, who circulate throughout the Arthurian world performing exploits that enhance the glory of the mythical king. Arthurian largesse thus generates and perpetuates chivalric society. The loyalty of his knights is controlled through acts of creation and gift-giving. Largesse reinforces the equality of the Round Table, thus preserving peace within the Arthurian realm, since no knight could raise an economic or preferential excuse for picking a quarrel with another. As Chrétien apostrophizes in his *Cligès:*

> Que largesce est dame et reine
> Qui totes vertus anlumine
> Ne n'est mie grief a prove
>
> .   .   .   .
>
> Par soi fet prodome largesce,
> Ce que ne peut feir hautesce,
> Ne corteisie, ne savoir,
> Ne gentillesce, ne avoir,
> Ne force, ne chevalerie,
> Ne proesce, ne seignorie,
> Ne biautez, ne nule autre chose;
> Mes tot ausi come la rose
> Est plus que nule autre flors bele,
> Quant ele neist fresche et novele,
> Einsi la ou largesce avient,
> Desor totes vertuz se tient,
>
> .   .   .   .
>
> Tant a en largesce a conter
> Que n'an diroie la mitié.

> For largesse is the lady and queen / who illuminates all other virtues, / and it is not difficult to demonstrate. / .   .   . /

> Largesse alone makes one a *prodome;* / high birth cannot do it, /
> not courtesy, wisdom, / nobility, wealth, / strength, chivalry, /
> prowess, lordship, / beauty, or anything else. / Just as the rose is
> more beautiful / than any other flower, / when it buds fresh and
> new, / thus largesse holds itself /above all other virtues when it
> appears, / . . . / There is so much to say about largesse /
> that I could not even tell you the half. (vv. 189–91, 197–208,
> 212–13)

Largesse thus supplants the prowess of the *prodome.*

Just as jongleurs competed for largesse at the great feasts, romance authors rivaled each other in describing festivities for the pleasure of their
patrons. Jean's emperors maintain Arthur's tradition of largesse at their
solemn festivals. When Count Richard returns victorious from the crusade, for example, he is met at Benevento by the emperor, who insists that
the count stay at the imperial palace, which is decked out with many-col-
ored silks in honor of the occasion. Like Chrétien, Jean excuses himself
from describing the abundance of the food and wine, but never has such
bounty been seen since the death of Merlin. During the festivities, which
last for two weeks, the emperor showers the count with gifts of gold, jewels, satins, silks, and warhorses (vv. 1370–1455). When Richard's son, in
turn, succeeds as emperor, the imperial coronation held in Rome at Pentecost is a lavish occasion for entertainment and gift exchange. After the ceremony, the barons give presents to the empress, and both Guillaume and
Aelis honor their knights and ladies reciprocally to retain their friendship
(vv. 8974–9047). In the *Rose,* Conrad celebrates his marriage to Lïenor
with comparable festivities. A resplendent banquet follows the church services at which the imperial baronage perform their honorific table-service
according to the dignity of their offices, accompanied by music and
singing (vv. 5389–5421). After the tables are cleared and the jousts and
other amusements have begun, an elaborate gift exchange takes place before the royal couple retire. So much clothing and equipment are distributed that no one who arrives in hope of profit leaves disappointed. For
their part, the barons are so eager to gain the emperor's good graces
through capes, surcoats, tunics, and mantles that if these garments were
converted into white serge, they would clothe all the Cistercian monks of
Igny and Ourscamp for three years (vv. 5489–99). The success of the nup-

tial night is further evident in the profusion of the *morgengabe* the next morning. No request for rich presents is refused, and the high barons depart enriched with jewels according to their dignity and service (vv. 5516–24).

The emperor's example devolves upon lesser princes. Jean opens the *Escoufle* with Count Richard de Montivilliers honoring his men with fair gifts (vv. 66–68). Many a good knight is saved from poverty through these gifts and profitable marriages (vv. 80–82). He wins the love of his vavasors and their wives with gifts of clothing (vv. 91–93). Because of his open-handedness with gold and jewels, he attracts many foreign knights to his service, like the historical King Richard (vv. 734–51). After accepting the task of expelling the oppressive serf *ministeriales* from the Empire, he seeks the favor of the high princes through gifts and recruits good knights from France with comparable enticements (vv. 1562–76). We have seen that the count of Saint-Gilles matches the generosity of his cousin Richard and celebrates Guillaume and Aelis's reunion with festivities and the conferring of arms (vv. 7889–7903).

The chief beneficiaries of this royal and princely largesse were the knights at the bottom of aristocratic society, but they incurred comparable obligations themselves. Just as the chivalric ethos of maintaining peace, according justice, and protecting the helpless may be seen as the devolution of royal duties of early medieval kings down the social scale to the knights, by the twelfth century the royal duty of largesse had also reached this level in the prescriptive literature written in Latin.[6] Chrétien extends the scope of the virtue in principle but finds few occasions to apply it in practice. His panegyric to largesse asserts that, unlike other virtues, largesse alone is sufficient to create a *prodome*, regardless of rank (vv. 197–203), but since the heroes of his romances are poor knights-errant, they rarely find the means to comply. Erec, for example, is likened to Alexander for his liberalities at the tournament of Evroïc (vv. 2213–14), but the listener/reader has to wait until he becomes king before his gifts can be enumerated. Similarly, when the young Guillaume of the *Escoufle* is at the imperial court, his father's resources enable him to win friends through generosity (vv. 2046–53), but in exile the gesture cannot be repeated, and he can only do so again after he becomes emperor.

The knight Guillaume de Dole is expressly said to be poor in land—his holdings can scarcely support six squires (*Rose* vv. 761–65)—yet the habit of exchanging gifts is deeply ingrained in his family. His mother recognizes the importance of appearances and gift exchange for advancement at the imperial court. Before Guillaume departs, she articulates family policy: don't let anyone in Germany say that you are poor or destitute (vv. 1084–88). At the imperial court, Guillaume accordingly presents the chamberlain Baudouin, the jongleur Juglet, and his hostess and her daughter with such resplendent robes and jewels (vv. 1815–45) that the emperor takes notice of their value (vv. 1871–90). Lïenor likewise offers jewels to her hostess at Mainz (vv. 4503–8).

We have seen that the tournament offers a stage on which Guillaume displays his largesse, and Chrétien's knights likewise exhibit both their prowess and their generosity at tournaments. At Saint-Trond, Guillaume engages the most prominent quarters, where he entertains lavishly; moreover, since he releases numerous prisoners and gives away his horse and armor, he leaves the city poorer than he had entered it, but resplendent in chivalric glory.

The ancient Alexander the Great set the highest standard of largesse, but by the end of the twelfth century, his renown was shared not only with the mythical Arthur and his knight Erec but with the lowly knight Guillaume de Dole. In concluding that Alexander had not won as much honor in a single day as Guillaume does (vv. 2880–81), Jean Renart expresses the final devolution of the royal ethos to the chivalric class.

Although Jean Renart's Guillaume de Dole is only a lowly knight, his exercise of largesse competed with the reputation of the historical young King Henry, son of the English king Henry II. The *Histoire de Guillaume le Maréchal* portrays the Young King as reviving chivalry in the 1180s through a phenomenal display of prowess and generosity, in contrast to the miserly times in which the author is writing (vv. 2637–41, 7175–84). By pouring out largesse, Henry attracted hundreds of knights to his retinue (vv. 2656–62, 3197–3210). Throughout his life, neither Arthur nor Alexander could rival him in bravery and expenditures (vv. 3573–82). During his journeys, whenever he arrived at a castle or city, he spent with an open hand. When he departed, he did not know how to leave without lavishing horses, robes, and foodstuff on his hosts, often amounting to 600 livres a visit (vv. 5073–83). Generous above all Christians, he wedded largesse in a good marriage, loving her, and she him, as loyal *amis*, unlike the concubinage with which largesse is now dishonored (vv. 3645, 3661–68).

The romance vocabulary of largesse is lucidly simple, centered on the word *don* (gift) in all its noun and verb permutations. These semantics had been established by the time of Chrétien. Arthur, for example, offers Erec the festivities of both marriage and coronation as a *don* (vv. 1873, 6498), characteristically expressing a redundancy in the latter case: "cest don et cest enor vos doing." Although synonyms, such as *livrer* (*Erec* vv. 2009, 2012), *despandre* (*Erec* vv. 2213, 6621), and *baillier* (*Cligès* v. 1125), are also employed, *doner* is the word of choice for largesse: "The king was very powerful and generous; he did not give coats of serge" (*Erec* vv. 6605–6). Jean follows Chrétien's vocabulary closely, even to the point of redundancy. At the wedding in Rome, for example, the barons give gifts to the empress ("des dons que la baron donerent," *Escoufle* v. 8986), and at Conrad's wedding, the emperor gives clothes and equipment to his barons (*Rose* vv. 5489–90), which the barons give in return to gain his love (v. 5495). The terminology remained constant throughout the aristocratic ranks. Not only is Count Richard forever distributing fine gifts (*Escoufle* vv. 68, 82, 1569), but Conrad explicitly transfers the royal ideal to Guillaume at the bottom of the scale. When the knight gives a very expensive surcoat to the chamberlain Baudouin, the emperor warns that such extravagance will soon exhaust his funds, but then revises his opinion, concluding that the coat was well bestowed, because he who knows how to give is truly a king ("si oi bien, / si est rois qui puet doner rien," *Rose* vv. 1889–90).

Almsgiving: The Ecclesiastical Ideal

The largesse that the aristocratic ethos prescribed was mutually beneficial to kings, lords, and knights. As Christians, however, they were also bound to give alms to God's Church and the poor. In principle, alms were distinguished from largesse in that they were ultimately destined for the poor, whereas largesse was not so restricted. In practice, however, there was an overlap and confusion between the two regimes. Upon learning of his father's death, Erec orders vigils and masses sung for the repose of his soul. He exceeds his promises to hospitals and churches by providing new clothing for some 169 poor men, as well as black capes and fur-lined coats for impoverished clerics and priests. And to the needy, he distributes a bushel of coins (vv. 6470–84). Ritualistic gifts made during the *offrande* of the liturgy are particularly noted by Jean and Gerbert. These occur at the morning masses preparatory to the tournaments at Saint-Trond (*Rose* v. 2440) and Lancien (*Continuation* v. 3354), as well as at the nuptial mass for Perceval and Blancheflor at Beaurepaire (v. 6637), but not during daily services. Although Perceval acquires the habit of attending mass each morning before setting off on a new venture, he is never depicted as making offerings. Gifts to God were not entirely disinterested, however, but were understood to be an exchange of services. Not only is Count Richard's gold mark to the nuns of Montivilliers given in exchange for their prayers (*Escoufle* vv. 231–56), but his sensational offering of a gold cup worth 10 marks to the Church of the Holy Sepulcher in Jerusalem is likewise payment for victory over the enemies of the faith (vv. 564–79, 615–23). The connection between his son Guillaume's prayers and the *offrande* to St. Gilles is even more explicit. Jean notes that the saint hears the boy's supplication, sends him employment immediately, and brings about the lovers' reunion in the near future (*Escoufle* vv. 6484–6501). Perceval, however, discovers that there are limits to these gift exchanges with the Divine. One hermit instructing the young knight declares that a single mortal sin that remains unconfessed will drag a soul to Hell, from which even alms cannot deliver him (*Continuation* vv. 14221–27).

These reports on almsgiving in the romances are unexceptional and accord with the universal Christian obligation to give to the Church and the poor. In the second part of the *Verbum abbreviatum*, on virtue, Pierre the Chanter devotes five chapters to this religious duty. "Almsgiving is a daughter of mercy," he begins, "concerning which it should be noted, what is its effect, what should be given, how, in what order, how much, in what way and from whom, to whom, how many, and of what sort."[7] To answer this schedule of casuistic questions, the Chanter as usual resorts to a mosaic of biblical quotations. Within the comprehensive discussion, he is particularly interested in the limitations applied to the universal imperative. In effect, almsgiving should be disciplined by necessity. In answering "how much," for example, one should retain what is necessary for oneself and one's family before distributing what is left over to the poor, which should be further governed by the recipient's necessities according to time and place. Alms should be offered, furthermore, only with regard to God, not for material profit, thereby eliminating the reciprocity inherent in aristocratic gift exchange.[8] The rigor of such disinterestedness is relaxed, however, when alms are given to benefit one's soul. Thibaut II, count of Champagne (d. 1152), was one of the great French barons whose benefactions caught the Chanter's attention. When distributing shoes to the poor near Pontigny, for example, the count insisted on making the donations with his own hands, because, as he explained, this would excite greater gratitude from his recipients and more prayers for his soul.[9]

Pierre the Chanter offers no sustained discussion of *largitas*, the worldly analogue to the spiritual duty of almsgiving, but he does touch upon the subject in related chapters in the first part of the *Verbum abbreviatum*, on vice. The closest he comes to unbounded largesse is the concept of *prodigalitas*, which emphasizes extravagance. Although spiritual prodigality, by which the soul is given unreservedly to Christ, is unquestionably praiseworthy, the temporal form is associated with cupidity, avarice, and rapine. Such prodigality is expressed in material goods, such as buildings, clothing, food, and any unnecessary superfluous expense motivated by curiosity or vanity. Like unrestrained almsgiving, superfluous expenditures are unnecessary by nature and grace.[10] Two other chapters inveigh against giving to the non-needy, defined as the rich, family relatives, and malefactors.

As in vernacular romance, Alexander the Great furnishes Pierre with an ancient example of unbounded largesse. When a retired legionnaire requests his back wages, Alexander offers him the revenues of an entire city. The soldier demurs that he is unworthy of this preposterous reward, and Alexander agrees, explaining that he merely wished to demonstrate that such munificence is more appropriate for a king to give than a subject to receive. The Roman philosopher Seneca, from whom the anecdote is excerpted, castigates Alexander as a bloated beast who gives only to enhance his own glory.[11] Raoul Ardent also takes Alexander to task for his largesse, claiming that he bestowed it only to win the Macedonians' favor. Raoul quotes a letter from Alexander's father Philip: "What error has induced you to hope that these will be your *fideles* whom you have corrupted with money? Will not the Macedonians judge you to be not their king but their servant or guardian?"[12]

After this ancient example, Pierre offers a more recent case, clothed in the conventions of romance. In 1112, two nephews of the chancellor of the cathedral, Master Anselm, had been unjustly implicated in the insurrection at Laon that resulted in the assassination of Bishop Gaudri. Anselm, who was celebrated for his theological learning, pleaded for the release of the two boys, and out of respect for him, the royal chancellor Etienne de Garlande not only granted the request but proposed in addition to endow them with his own goods, dub them knights, and provide them with noble brides. Anselm refused this extravagant offer, however, arguing that his nephews should not be raised above their poor origins.[13] This example is cited to discourage striving for family advancement, but Etienne de Garlande's largesse nonetheless also extends to unrestrained prodigality.

Raoul Ardent seeks to carry the Chanter's discussion forward by proposing *parsimonia* as the remedy for the excesses of largesse. Parsimony is the virtue of modestly dispensing the goods entrusted to us. We use for ourself as much as is necessary and bestow gifts on others according to their faculty to receive. Retaining for ourselves only what is necessary, we give the surplus to others. Largesse without parsimony is prodigality; parsimony without largesse is avarice, but frugal largesse and generous parsimony are virtues. It is for the religious to be frugal with themselves and generous to the needy. By adopting the moderating effects of Christian almsgiving inherent in parsimony, the extremes of worldly largesse can be restrained.[14]

Limiting both almsgiving and largesse, the discipline prescribed by the theologians, is also acknowledged by the writers of romance. In dedicating his *Conte de graal* to Philippe of Flanders, Chrétien is explicit about the theological influence (vv. 1–59). Philippe is lauded as one who exceeds the great Alexander in largesse, for which the latter is justly celebrated, while avoiding Alexander's vices. Obeying the Gospel commandment (Matt. 6:3), when the count gives, he does not allow his left hand to know the good the right hand is doing. In the biblical interpretation (*selonc l'estoire*), the left hand signifies vainglory and hypocrisy; the right, charity, which does not boast of good works but conceals them. God is charity, St. Paul says, and he who abides in charity, lives in God, and God in him (1 Cor. 13:4). Philippe's gifts are given in charity, because he consults no one but his good heart. Despite its patently clerical inspiration, Chrétien's panegyric to largesse is neither precisely that of the theologians nor without ambiguities. In one passage (vv. 45–46), only God knows of the charity performed by the count's right hand, but in the preceding lines (vv. 33–36), this knowledge is shared by the recipient as well, as might be expected.[15] Moreover, notwithstanding that Chrétien prefaces his last romance with an encomium to Count Philippe's generosity, the ensuing story contains fewer examples of largesse than his previous writings. The largesse of Arthur's court is only implicit, and Perceval's and Gauvain's wanderings offer few occasions for festive celebrations. Unreciprocated largesse did not in any case apply to the author himself, who gave his romance to Philippe according to the biblical aphorism, "He who sows little, reaps little, but he who casts good seed on fertile ground harvests a hundredfold" (vv. 1–12).[16]

Although Jean Renart celebrates the lavish gift-giving of emperors, lords, and knights, his successor is more reticent on the subject. Like Chrétien, Gerbert does not neglect, however, to include largesse (v. 55) among the virtues of his patroness, Marie, countess of Ponthieu. Known participants at the tournaments of Montargis, such as the counts of Boulogne (v. 5919) and of Ponthieu (v. 5924), are similarly praised. Also like Chrétien (*Lion* vv. 5–6), Gerbert cannot resist the temptation to pun on Pentecost, a festival that he says is so named because it costs so much (v. 6285). King Louis's Easter court at Pont de l'Arche (vv. 79–95), although well attended, is nonetheless devoid of conspicuous acts of royal generosity. Only at Gerart and Eurïaut's wedding, which Gerbert declares outstripped even Arthur's Pentecost and Christmas feasts (vv. 6588–90), are the great sums of money that the barons of Nevers and Forez expend on their lord and lady specified (vv. 6606–9). Gerbert's *Continuation* offers few opportunities to describe great festivities. The exception is the wedding at Beaurepaire (vv. 6687–6747), where an abundance of food and entertainment is lavished on the guests. Performers are rewarded with as many as ten garments each, but, as will be seen, Gerbert complains that this customary extravagance is no longer practiced in his own day.

If Chrétien in his *Graal* and Gerbert in his two romances appear to have been susceptible to the theological program of limiting the largesse of the aristocracy, their restraint coincided with a comparable attitude on the part of Philip Augustus. Although he bore the epithet *dieu-donné*—given by God to his parents—he himself was not remarkable for his own gifts. Two generations later, his grandson, Louis IX, vividly remembered the old king's advice that one should reward one's household more or less according to the service provided, because no one could be a successful ruler unless he knew how to withhold as well as to give.[17] Neither exemplary almsgiving nor largesse is celebrated in the official accounts of his reign. Rigord notes that the king did not neglect the patron saint of the kingdom at Saint-Denis, making periodic visits to lay costly silks on the altar and bestow relics and other benefactions, but his regular alms to churches were not abundant and his new foundations were limited to the abbey de la Victoire, established to commemorate Bouvines.[18] When famine threatened the royal domain in 1195, Philip, like Count Thibaut, contributed generous alms to the poor and encouraged his bishops and abbots to participate in the program of relief.[19] Unlike the chroniclers who record the contemporary generosity of Henry II and Richard of England, however, Rigord and Guillaume le Breton are equally restrained about Philip's secular benefactions. Rigord details the king's gifts to crusaders at Messina in 1190—in undoubted competition with Richard's—and notes that when King John was entertained at the royal palace in Paris in 1201, gold, silver, clothing, horses, and other precious gifts were lavished on him.[20] The one ceremonial occasion on which Philip Augustus could not avoid the expectation of a near-Arthurian display of largesse, however, was his son's inaugural feast of knighthood. Concerning the gathered assembly at Compiègne on Pentecost 1209, the royal chronicler remarks in quasi-romance fashion that the solemnities were accompanied with such generous abundance of food and gifts ("largiflua victualium et donarum abundantia") never recorded before.[21] Gifts to new knights at Pentecost were apparently the custom at the Capetian court. The surviving financial accounts record 23 livres for three pairs of robes to new knights on the feast day,[22] but neither the number of knights nor the sum of money could be mistaken for Arthurian largesse.

Romance Hospitality

If the liturgical feasts of Christmas, Easter, and Pentecost, and celebration of life-events such as knighting and marriage, provided spectacular occasions for royal and princely generosity, the obligation of largesse was equally involved in the daily and practical routine of hospitality. Like largesse in general, the duty of hospitality emerged from the archaic economy of the early Middle Ages. When kings, princes, and great landholders circulated through their domains each year, they were owed prescribed amounts of free board and lodging, or *gîte*, by their subjects. By the twelfth century, this right had devolved from kings to princes and finally to local lords and castellans.[23] Of equal importance, warlords were reciprocally obliged to maintain their warriors in their households, which involved expenditures on food and lodging, as well as clothing and arms. Hospitality both to lords and to knights had become a chivalric virtue subsumed under largesse, meeting the regular practical needs of knighthood.

The Arthurian myth of the knight-errant, however, virtually ignored the economic requisites of knighthood. Clad in a steel helmet and a coat of chain mail, armed with a lance, sword, and shield, and mounted on a powerful warhorse, this central figure of romance was vested with enormously expensive equipment. Although the romance knight typically traveled alone on his mount, historical knights were often accompanied by a squire and two other horses, a traveling horse (*palfrey*) and a packhorse (*sumpter*) loaded with supplies and gear.[24] Such outlays in equipment and horses required substantial resources of land, which, in turn, demanded a seigniorial economy in which peasants supplied the labor. Concerning these underlying economic foundations, the Arthurian romances are totally mute. Most Arthurian knights make their appearance mounted and fully equipped; new knights, like Perceval, seek their horse and armor from the king or acquire them by conquest. Only the more realistic Jean Renart notes in passing that notwithstanding his lavish habits of dress and hospitality, the lowly Guillaume de Dole's land was barely sufficient to support six squires (*Rose* vv. 763–65).

Oblivious of the economics of initial investment, the romances nonetheless acknowledge the necessities of the knight-errant's day-to-day support through the literary convention of hospitality.[25] The lone knight wanders interminably through the *gaste forest*, with no fixed itinerary, no accompanying provisions, and no money with which to procure them. The accommodations provided each night through the generosity of a local personage are therefore an indispensable condition for the journey. Expanding upon suggestions in Chrétien's *Graal*, Gerbert introduces some twenty-two episodes of hospitality into Perceval's and Gauvain's prolonged quests for the Grail, which serve to punctuate the narrative. As night approaches on one occasion, for example, St. Julien, the patron saint of travelers, enables Perceval to find a *chastelet* belonging to an old man (*Continuation* vv. 16056–57).

Although the obligation of hospitality may have stemmed from the ancient royal right of *gîte*, by the second half of the twelfth century, romance writers had assigned it to all lords of castles and extended it to lesser vavasors of manor houses (witness Chrétien's *Erec*) for the benefit of aristocratic travelers. By 1200, the literary convention of aristocratic hospitality followed an established protocol, which, although incorporating a variety of motifs, nonetheless distributed them into four distinct stages. Canonized in the twelfth century in both Arthurian and non-Arthurian romances, the motifs can be illustrated from Perceval's journeys in Gerbert's *Continuation*. The first occurrence at the castle of Cothoatre may serve as an example. The opening stage (vv. 344–85) is a cheerful welcome. When Perceval approaches the castle, he is greeted by the inhabitants with joy. They help him disarm and dress him in fine robes. (Although omitted in this particular episode, Gerbert is normally careful to report that they attended to stabling and feeding the horse.) The second stage is supper, which, although briefly described here, is usually understood to be sumptuous in dishes and plentiful in wine (vv. 600–606). Then follow the preparations of the bed, which at Cothoatre is fitted with sheets from Constantinople and adorned with golden bells hanging from the bedposts. If there is to be an amorous interlude—in this episode his hostess, Escolasse, does not neglect to pay Perceval a visit—it is inserted at this point (vv. 609–72). The fourth and final stage is the taking of leave early next morning, which in Perceval's case is nearly always accompanied by attendance at Mass, occasionally followed by breakfast (vv. 673–97).

Because of Gerbert's religious preoccupations, monks and nuns are Perceval's hosts in nearly half of the episodes in which he receives hospitality (9 cases). A few are communities of nuns (such as the Chastel as Puceles [v. 3008], the abbey of Saint-Domin [v. 9070]), and a group of thirteen hermits (vv. 8430–31), but most are hermitages consisting of a small chapel and a single hermit isolated in the recesses of the forest. Again, the reception unfolds according to the four stages of aristocratic hospitality, but the quality is markedly inferior. To take as an example the first hermitage at which Perceval lodges, his arrival is cheerfully welcomed and he is relieved of his arms, but his horse is fed straw rather than wheat or oats. His own supper consists of barley bread and cress (occasionally expanded to roots and wild fruits), and his drink is limited to water from the fountain. His bed, sometimes just leaves and grass, is narrow and hard. After an uncomfortable night, the next morning the knight has access to the religious services of the adjoining chapel and the spiritual counsel of the holy man (vv. 7070–7139).

Whereas numerous castellans, vavasors, and hermits in romance unbegrudgingly dispense the hospitality essential to an itinerant knight, Gerbert underscores chivalric obligation by including the negative example of the castellan Parsamans, who forces wandering knights to pay the toll of doing battle with four of his men and then with himself before opening his household to them. When travel-weary strangers cannot pass this test, they forfeit their equipment. Perceval, of course, refuses to accede to this robbery and successfully defends his own armor against the five adversaries. He denounces such villainy as a breach of *l'ordre de chevalerie*, which prescribes courteous and pleasant reception of knights (vv. 7769–81). Before the hero departs, Parsamans swears on the relics of St. Amand that he will hereafter abandon this abuse of hospitality (vv. 8145–52).

The peregrinations of Perceval and Gauvain in the *Continuation* require full use of the conventions of hospitality to move the two heroes toward the goal of their quest. Although the journeys in the *Violette* are mainly those of a hero in search of a heroine, the custom of aristocratic hospitality is retained. Lisïart de Forez's opportunity to spy on Eurïaut is supplied by the latter's offer of hospitality for the night (v. 414). As Gerart de Nevers seeks Eurïaut, he receives free lodgings at the castles of Monglai (v. 4590) and Bien Asis (v. 4967). Even the inhabitants of the castle of Vergy, suffering under siege, cannot refuse him, something that happens frequently in the Perceval legend (vv. 1548–50). When Duke Milon serves dinner to Gerart at Cologne, Gerbert interjects that he has never seen *hostel* so plentiful, except at the court of his patroness, Marie, the lady of Ponthieu (vv. 3205–12).

As a corollary of largesse, the romance obligation of hospitality shared the same semantic field as gift-giving. The operative word is *doner*, either explicitly pronounced or implied by the context. Throughout Gerbert's *Continuation* and the *Violette*, the mechanism remains constant, whether the host be lay or religious. Most often it occurs at the request of the traveler, invariably granted by the host. When, for example, Perceval and a maiden ask for lodgings out of charity, the vavasor Gaudins au Blanc Escu grants their request and makes them a gift ("et li preudom / lor otra et lor fist don," *Continuation* vv. 1094–96). The lady in the castle by the sea affirms that compliance with such requests is the custom of her castle (*Continuation* vv. 10674–76). Even the dire straits of a castle under siege do not excuse noncompliance. "You shall have whatever we are able to give you," is the response of the defenders of Vergy. "We don't seek any such excuse not to lodge you" (*Violette* vv. 1540–41, 1548–49).[26] It will be seen, however, that the bourgeois hospitality portrayed by Jean Renart employs an entirely different semantic field.

This picture of the solitary knight by pure chance finding a convenient hostel where all of his material needs are supplied virtually every night is, of course, a fantasy. Yet, when Gerbert links the fictional duke of Cologne with the historical countess of Ponthieu, he suggests that the romance convention of hospitality played a prescriptive role valid in the contemporary context. Although it may be difficult, if not impossible, to determine how far the convention was practiced by historical castellans, vavasors, and hermits, it was nonetheless recommended to the aristocratic world as a social ideal. In reiterating the stereotypical stages of courtly reception within a long tradition, Gerbert is articulating a code of behavior that united the aristocracy in a shared communion. The gratuitous nature of the host's hospitality is only apparent, however; services are, in fact, exchanged. The knight-errant punishes robbers, relieves besieged castles, and rescues maidens in distress (at times serving them in bed too), always helping to restore peace and good order. Churchmen also stood to benefit from the pious zeal behind the quest for the Grail. The reciprocity implicit in hospitality, however, was strictly limited to hosts and guests of the aristocratic classes. At Vergy, for example, the defenders' impoverishment does not prevent them from receiving the noble Gerart, because, as they are quick to observe, he does not appear to be a herdsman (*Violette* v. 1550). Reciprocally, peasants are never required to provide lodging for knights in the romances. There is little doubt that the conditions of a peasant home would have been too primitive and demeaning. The bourgeoisie are likewise absent in Gerbert's *Continuation*, although in the *Violette* they share these tasks with the aristocracy. In Jean's romances, however, which opened up new vistas for Gerbert's *Violette*, the bourgeoisie take over the *hôtellerie*. In contrast to the apparently gratuitous aristocratic hospitality, they accept cash.

The Emergence of Bourgeois Commerce and Hospitality

The principal features of the archaic economy of the early Middle Ages were still intact at the beginning of the twelfth century. Unfree peasants remained the major workforce. Kings, princes, castellans, and knights continued to command the land and its people with military force, to appropriate its products for their consumption, and to distribute the surplus to their warrior retainers. The success of these lords, however, stimulated competition among them to accentuate the flamboyant style of their courts. Bread remained the staple of life on their tables, but more and more the white flour of wheat replaced dark barley, and it was served with *companagium* (literally, that which accompanies bread): legumes, cheeses, and meats. At the same time, the quality of the wine that filled their cups improved. The clothing on their backs conformed to new fashions, which prized silks, furs, and luxury woolens. Their weapons, armor, and the harnesses of their horses were crafted with greater artistry and refinement. Wealth still flowed in gifts from high princes to lowly knights, as in the past, and as competition increased, great lords were tempted to live beyond their means and resorted to borrowing.

Moreover, the appetite of the lords for delicate food, premium wine, elegant clothing, and burnished arms transformed the sources of supply. No longer could such luxuries be produced on the lord's estates; they had to be manufactured in specialized centers, which were increasingly situated in conglomerations of population called *bourgs,* or towns. The manufacture of fine cloth and armor was thus taken over by towns, many of which were also surrounded by belts of vineyards where quality wines were produced. The inhabitants of these centers, now called the bourgeoisie, or townsmen, not only manufactured these goods demanded by the seigniorial courts but facilitated their distribution and exchange as middlemen or merchants.

To promote commerce, the mints of the lords increased the quantity of coinage in circulation, and to satisfy the voracious consumption of the aristocracy, merchants began to extend credit. Although the older mechanisms of peasant agriculture and lordly domination persisted, the new elements had become irreversibly established by 1180, on the eve of the epoch when Jean Renart and Gerbert de Montreuil composed their romances. The mentality of selling and credit, which postulated the profit motive, overtook the aristocratic preference for gift exchange and largesse, yet a nostalgia for the old habits of conspicuous consumption and extravagant generosity remained strong in aristocratic circles.[27]

In the romances, written for the distraction of the aristocracy, the peasants of the countryside, although comprising perhaps as much as 90 percent of the total population, are exceptional figures. The gross features of the *vileins* who appears in the opening section of Chrétien's *Lion* are obviously caricatured to shock or amuse the audience (vv. 286–325). In Chrétien's *Conte du graal,* the narrative function of the harvesters who harrow oats for Perceval's mother is to provide directions for a company of knights (vv. 300–325). In like manner, Gerbert employs a lone *païsant* sowing wheat to inform Perceval about the lord of the nearby castle (*Continuation* vv. 348–55). Towns and their inhabitants likewise rarely make an appearance in Chrétien's romances. The evocation of Escavalon in the *Graal,* with its bustling money changers, arms manufacturers, weavers, goldsmiths, and merchants, who are becoming rich because of the shortages caused by the siege, remains the major exception (vv. 5758–82). When Gauvain declines to participate in the tournament at Tintagel in the same romance, the elder sister questions his honor by calling him a merchant disguised as a knight to escape paying tolls (vv. 6438–63). The bourgeoisie are completely absent in Gerbert's *Continuation* and marginal in his *Violette*, but in the romances of Jean Renart they move to the center of the stage.

Like the chorus in a nineteenth-century opera, the crowds at all festive occasions contain representatives of the *borgois*. They are identified when Count Richard departs from Montivilliers (*Escoufle* vv. 149, 183), when the lovers are reunited at Saint-Gilles (v. 7778), and when Guillaume is invested with his father's duchy (v. 8204). The delegation that conveys the keys of Rouen is composed of bourgeois (vv. 8234–37), and they display their riches on balconies at Rome during the couple's imperial coronation (vv. 8852–53). On Lïenor's triumphal entry into Mainz in the *Rose*, her beauty so entrances the bourgeois at the money exchange that one could easily have cut their purses as they strained to watch her pass (vv. 4539–46). And at Saint-Trond, they join the crowds of ladies who from their doors watch Guillaume's return from the tournament, battered and depleted, but covered with honor (v. 2872).

The principle functions of the bourgeoisie in Jean's romances are the production and exchange of goods and the service of *hôtellerie*. After the separation of the lovers in the *Escoufle*, the princess Aelis enlists the impoverished Ysabel to accompany her in search of Guillaume. When, after two years, their money runs out, she decides that despite her exalted lineage, she must gain a living with her two hands. Her early training at court has taught her to embroider portraits of lovers on *chainture* and to make rings, purses, ribbons, and *attaches* (vv. 2060–69). Aelis and Ysabel set up an atelier at Montpellier, where, to Ysabel's experience in making towels and wimples, Aelis adds her aristocratic skills in gold and silk work to produce gold embroidery, belts, and ribbons (vv. 5434–61). Their artistry transforms the enterprise into a huge success, attracting the attention of knights and bourgeois from afar. They soon become rich from selling their luxury items, since their work commands whatever price they choose to name (vv. 5478–5501).

The highborn Aelis dislikes buying on credit, and when she closes her shop at Montpellier, she is quick to pay her neighbors what she owes them (*Escoufle* vv. 6048–53). Credit plays an essential role, however, in the affairs of the lowly knight Guillaume de Dole. When he assembles his armor at Saint-Trond for the tournament, Guillaume has to buy 120 lances with pennants and three shields with silk and embroidered straps on credit (*créances*) from a bourgeois in Liège, although the emperor has bestowed on him a helmet manufactured at Senlis (*Rose* vv. 1952–61, 1650–68). Not only does Guillaume order these arms from the bourgeois supplier by letter, unaccompanied by money, he takes lodgings at Saint-Trond without payment and runs up debts at Dole, which he covers by sending money to his sister and mother (*Rose* vv. 1930–40). The bills for arms and lodging are not paid until he captures opponents and collects ransoms (vv. 2670–73, 2690–91).[28] The bourgeois are happy to lend to him, however, because he can be trusted to pay on time (vv. 1884–87).[29]

Although the emperor Conrad numbers his fortune in good knights (*Rose* vv. 92–93), he too must take account of bourgeois commerce (vv. 593-620). Like the young Philip Augustus and the count of Champagne, he takes merchants under royal protection even during times of war. So severely are brigands punished that a merchant traveling anywhere in his lands is safer than if he were in church. Unlike the French king and other contemporary princes, however, Conrad declines to exact *tailles* from his *vilains* and bourgeois. An important tax upon the royal domain and towns, the *taille* was considered particularly oppressive because of its arbitrary character and its annual collection in lump sums. In 1202/3, for example, *tailles* from the towns produced 7 percent of Philip's total income. In one sense, Conrad looks on the townsmen's property in the manner the Capetians viewed that of the Jews.[30] Since both capital and earnings ("le chatel et le conquest," v. 601) are at the king's disposal, the bourgeois are only custodians of their wealth. In contrast to Philip's practice, however, Conrad feels it more honorable to maintain the aristocratic fiction: townsmen are allowed to keep their earnings and encouraged to offer gifts to the emperor in exchange for protection and reciprocal liberality.

Throughout Jean's romances, the preeminent service that the bourgeois render is the very same provided by the romance convention of hospitality—the lodging of aristocratic travelers. Although there was precedent in romance, it is rarely acknowledged in Chrétien.[31] Bourgeois hospitality is distinguished from the courtly variety by the fact that the guest normally pays for the services he receives. Since Jean is little concerned with the knight-errant, however, aristocratic hospitality is largely absent, and the bourgeois mode dominates his romances from the start. The first voyager to appear in the *Escoufle* is the crusader Richard, whose itinerary to the Holy Land takes him through Lombardy, Brindisi, Acre, Jerusalem, back to Brindisi, and finally to Benevento, where he meets the emperor. Since Jean specifies the cash, silver, gold, silk, and clothing that Richard has amassed before departure, he merely asked rhetorically when the count is crossing Lombardy, "[W]hy speak of lodging [*ostex*] and food [*viande*]? They had all they wanted" (vv. 365–69). Approaching Brindisi, the count dispatches a messenger to seek the best available lodging for a high lord. Thereafter, the terminology and procedure for finding lodging are identical on each occasion. The procuring of provisions, ships, horses, and supplies amply corroborates the bourgeois and cash character of the phrase "por prendre ostel" (to take lodging). Richard has already engaged the best accommodations at Benevento when the emperor imposes his own aristocratic hospitality, which, although gratuitous, is nonetheless valued at 500 marks (vv. 1372–80).

Guillaume and Aelis's elopement provides a second series of journeys in the *Escoufle*. Like Richard, the couple collect clothing, mules, jewels, and money before departure (vv. 3728–34, 3792–95, 3866–69). Although only children, they employ good sense to *prendre ostel* off the main road. While Guillaume obtains wheat and oats for the mules, Aelis procures wine and provisions to make patés for the next day. While dining with the host, they settle their accounts, always paying more rather than less (vv. 4238–93). After their separation, Aelis implores St. Julien to find her lodging at Toul. The saint leads her to a poor woman and girl (Ysabel) who are caretakers of a grange and press. The accommodations are mean, but the princess rewards them handsomely, neglecting to count out the money (vv. 4868–5046). Thereafter the two girls wander through many towns, among them Châlons, where Aelis's money furnishes lodging and food for two years (vv. 5326–39).

As for Guillaume, he loses his money to a robber in a woods and is likewise forced to earn his living. Although the son of a count, he chooses the *hôtellerie* trade, working for wages for nine months in a hostel for pilgrims owned by a bourgeois and situated in front of the money exchange at Santiago de Compostela (vv. 6186–6205, 6308–23). His second employment is at a similar establishment in Saint-Gilles du Gard. His duties consist of making bread, serving at table, preparing beds, attending to the harnesses of horses, and conducting hunting excursions with dogs and falcons, for which he contracts with the bourgeois owner for an annual wage of 50

sous, which, Jean explains, was the market price. His skill, industry, and af-
fability, combined with the hostel's popularity, earn him more in tips (vv.
6510–6607). When, after three months, he finally quits his job to rejoin his
amie, the count of Saint-Gilles provides warranty for what remains of the
contracted service to his master (vv. 7838–34). Although Guillaume will be
the emperor of Germany and is endowed with courtly skills, Jean engages
him to a bourgeois master in the *hôtellerie* trade without derogation of his
birth or future promotion (vv. 7252–55).

Jean's *Rose* is likewise populated with messengers, knights, and ladies
seeking lodging from bourgeois hosts in towns. The imperial messenger
Nicole, for example, engages lodgings at Dole before visiting Guillaume's
family and reciprocates the service for the knight when they return to the
emperor (vv. 943–45, 1368–74). So many knights arrive at Saint-Trond for
the tournament that three such towns could not house a quarter of them
(vv. 2156–59). Guillaume is fortunate to find the best house in town, without regard to price, situated overlooking the marketplace (vv. 1996–2005,
2068–73). When the scene shifts to the imperial city of Mainz, the emperor
naturally does not need St. Julien to find him a residence (vv. 3632–39), but
Lïenor is obliged to invoke God's help; she encounters two bourgeois
women returning from Mass whose house, located on a side street, suits
her needs perfectly (vv. 4197–4226).

The distinguishing feature of these bourgeois accommodations is the
cost. The crusading count and the highborn elopers begin their journeys
well funded for the ensuing expenses. The less affluent Guillaume de Dole
has to rely on his prizes at the tournament to cover expenses. He dispatches
his second prisoner to his landlord as payment on his account there (*Rose*
vv. 2690–92). The entertainment and hospitality dispensed by knights during the evenings both before and after the tournament are unusually lavish
(vv. 2336–51). It has been seen that the modest Guillaume apparently had
enough left to offer presents to his hosts the next morning (vv. 2950–56),
but many high barons were not as fortunate and resorted to perjury to escape their bills with the innkeepers. Unlike the historical King Richard,
who provided a legislative remedy, Conrad's solution befits his image as a
romance hero.[32] With extraordinary generosity, he opens his purse and
pays off the ransoms (vv. 2929–47). It need not be added that the chief
beneficiaries are the bourgeois proprietors of the urban hostels.

In the *Violette*, Gerbert adds bourgeois elements to the traditional aristocratic hospitality already noted, but the romance ethos nonetheless prevails. Since the tournament at Montargis is merely a replay of that at Saint-Trond, the town is likewise crowded with converging knights. Gerbert's hero Gerart, like Guillaume, sends his squires ahead to take lodging on bourgeois terms. Likewise in imitation of Guillaume, he offers everyone brilliant hospitality both before and after the fighting (vv. 5856–64, 6074–80). Since the terminology and procedures are identical, we may presume that Gerart paid for his accommodations. In an episode at Cologne, which is under siege according to the romance scenario, Gerart takes lodgings (*ostel prist*) near the marketplace with a bourgeois named Adam the Greek, and the joyful welcome, the stabling of the horse, and the sumptuous dinner that follow are standard features of romance. When Gerart offers his services in defense of the city, his host accepts with alacrity and lends him weapons and a full set of armor (vv. 2505–32, 2577–94). Whereas the knight may initially have intended to pay the bourgeois for his accommodation, this understanding appears to have been supplanted by an exchange of hospitality for defense, as envisaged in Arthurian romance. No remuneration is mentioned. Whatever the ambiguity here, aristocratic hospitality supersedes the bourgeois variety at Châlons. Sick at heart and in body over the loss of Eurïaut, Gerart finds lodgings with a bourgeois called Guyon the Gray, whose daughter Marote nurses the knight back to health. When Gerart takes leave and asks what he owes in accordance with bourgeois procedure, the girl perceives that he has little money and refuses cash payment, asking rather that he accept a hawk as a courteous token of their friendship. The bird is followed by gifts of clothing for the journey. In Gerbert's treatment, therefore, the cash terms of bourgeois accommodations are commuted to the exchange of love services congruent with aristocratic hospitality in romance.

Pierre the Chanter is also nostalgic about free hospitality without the commercial conditions of the bourgeois variety. Although ignoring the aristocratic hospitality depicted in the romances, he nonetheless promotes the ecclesiastical virtue of *hospitalitas*, which, like almsgiving, clothing the naked, visiting the sick, and burying the dead, is one of the daughters of mercy. In a short chapter, he collects Gospel injunctions and Old Testament examples to note the frequency of the word, particularly in the Pauline epistles. Titus 1:8, for example, commands bishops to be hospitable, but Pierre sadly concludes that this kindness has since disappeared from episcopal and clerical practice, which now resembles that of the laity: no-body will offer lodging without a price.[33] Aristocratic and episcopal hospi-tality had yielded to bourgeois *hôtellerie*.

By the end of the twelfth century, the growing presence of townsmen in northern France left its imprint on the lexicon of romance. Although the economics of largesse and gift exchange continue to dominate Chrétien's semantics, he begins to introduce words like *despans* and *créance* (*Lion* v. 1582), although as yet not in a commercial context. At Erec and Enide's wedding, for example, although Arthur offers to pay the jongleurs to their satisfaction (v. 2052), he withholds payment until the next morning, so that credit has in fact been advanced (v. 2057), but the transaction is none-theless entirely overshadowed by the king's largesse of fine robes (vv. 2058–59).[34]

It is Jean Renart, however, who employs the vocabulary of commercial exchange and credit in appropriately commercial contexts. At Brindisi, Count Richard sends his men to lease ships and vessels (*Escoufle* v. 387), and at Acre his marshal goes into town to buy horses (vv. 430–31). At each stop on their route, Aelis and Guillaume buy wine and fish in great quan-tity (vv. 4260–63) and settle with their hosts for their expenses (vv. 4288–89). Aelis and Ysabel's customers at Montpellier pay no heed to cost (vv. 5492–93), because the girls' skill can command any price. Credit (*créances*) rules the market at Saint-Trond for both equipment and lodging. Aelis may have avoided it at Montpellier, but Guillaume de Dole cannot abstain from its advantages. It is also at Saint-Trond that Jean Renart most vividly contrasts the bourgeois commercial mentality with the aristocratic largesse displayed from the emperor down to the knight Guillaume. As has been seen, Guillaume bestows upon the imperial chamberlain a surcoat so mag-nificent that even the emperor takes notice. When Conrad asks who gave it (*dona*), the chamberlain replies that the giver is noble and generous (*larges*), not one who prefers to lend at interest (" . . . qui n'a / talent de prester a usure," *Rose* vv. 1872–73), or, in other words, is not a merchant. In reply to the emperor's warning that Guillaume will thereby impoverish himself, the chamberlain goes on to say that Guillaume is well received by the bourgeois when he comes to borrow (*emprunter*), because he gives gifts (*done*) freely and pays his bills on time ("bien à point paié," v. 1887).[35] Conrad likewise prefers gifts from his bourgeois to *tailles*. As has been seen, the emperor concludes that Guillaume has made good use of the robe, because he who knows how to give is truly a king (v. 1890). And to implement this royal truism, Conrad sends 500 livres in Cologne currency to Guillaume the next morning and two warhorses and two silver cups to his companions (vv. 1894–1903). Summing up aristocratic largesse, Jean comments that a fine gift is worth more when it has not been promised ("mout vaut uns biaus dons sanz promesse," v. 1907). The gratuity of aristocratic largesse is thereby contrasted with the obligation of a bourgeois contract.

The romance economy of largesse prominently displayed in periodic feasts and quotidian hospitality to itinerant knights derived from an archaic past. The romances of Jean and Gerbert say almost nothing about the agricultural economy that underlay their own society. The peasants who worked the fields are thoroughly marginalized. The fiefs that support knights, that impose military service, and that enmesh the knights in complex webs of obligations with their lords are all but absent from their narratives. And moreover, the landed economy itself had been undergoing fundamental change for nearly half a century. Goods were increasingly exchanged in markets, commercial practices were being perfected, money circulated rapidly, and towns emerged with burgeoning bourgeois populations.

Among the romanciers, Jean Renart is virtually alone in taking notice of this evolving economy, but his attention is largely limited to *prendre ostel*, the hiring of lodgings for his principal characters. For Gerbert, as for Chrétien, however, the motor of the economy remains the archaic exchange of gifts, still a potent force in his own day. The rhythm of great feasts continued, gifts were still lavished, and hospitality was offered. The prescriptions of the romances remained relevant to contemporary society. Lordly patrons might need the services of jongleurs to entertain their guests and publicize their glory, but the jongleurs themselves were likewise dependent on aristocratic largesse. Gerbert thus felt free to urge that his patroness, the historical Countess Marie of Ponthieu, to be as hospitable as his fictional Duke Milon of Cologne.

FIVE

Women and Love

. ⚬ .

MEN and warfare stand out in the pages of the chansons de geste when they emerge in France early in the twelfth century. In the romances that follow by mid-century, the men continue to fight, but they share the stage with women and love. This traditional formulation of the relation between the two literary genres is one of those generalizations that invites objections and nuance the more it is studied, but on the surface, where it was first perceived, it retains a certain validity. By the end of the century, however, the chansons de geste and romances had doubtless begun to interact and efface the generic distinctions.[1] It is equally true that vernacular romances were far more involved in portraying women and love than the Latin texts of the clerics, whether imaginative or didactic.

The consideration of women opens the broader issue of gender—that is, the constructed relationships between women and men. The feminine condition can never be assessed in isolation, but must always be kept in comparison with the masculine. Since this process involves the vast totality of society, it is impractical to implement it systematically in the scope of a chapter. For this reason, comparisons between men and women will be limited to a few examples and the rest left understood. It may be hoped that sufficient examples are given to highlight the role of women and love in the romances.

Although Jean Renart and Gerbert de Montreuil do their best to conceal their own identities, there is little doubt that they, like almost all French vernacular authors, were men. Whatever the possibility of women disguising themselves behind masculine noms de plume, only two, Marie de France and Christine de Pizan, dared to write under a female name during the first three centuries of French literature. Male writers, however, did address their works to highborn women on occasion. Out of hundreds of French romances, nearly two dozen were sent to female recipients.[2] In addressing his *Roman de la violette* to Marie, countess of Ponthieu, Gerbert follows the example of Chrétien de Troyes, who wrote his *Charrete* at the prompting of Marie, countess of Champagne.

We may be confident, therefore, that the "courts of kings and counts," Chrétien's and Jean's phrase to identify their audiences, contained not a negligible number of women. How this female public influenced the male authors remains conjectural. What is clear, however, is that during the second half of the twelfth century, the proportion of female characters in romance texts increased dramatically, and their portraits became distinct, enabling audiences to recognize the characters of Queen Iseut, Marie de France's unnamed but individualized ladies, and Chrétien's dynamic but unsettling heroines—Enide, Fenice, Laudine, Lunette, and Guenièvre—with greater assurance than any woman found in contemporary Latin imaginative or historical texts. These forceful but fictive women prepared Jean's and Gerbert's audiences for the female characters they placed at the center of their narratives. Again, to what extent these fictive heroines responded to the demands of the women in the audience can only be surmised. How historical women accepted or resisted identification with these fictional characters can be approached only indirectly. Little testimony has survived of historical women actually hearing and reading this burgeoning genre of romance replete with vivid females. Even in the romances themselves, there are few images of women reading. Chrétien's often-commented-on scene of the girl in the garden reading a romance to her parents is a rare instance of this (*Lion* vv. 5336–64). The presumption cannot be avoided, therefore, that the male authors were prone to follow their own interests and to create female characters that responded to the men in their audiences.

Misogyny

In medieval society, gender relations were asymmetrical; patriarchy was ingrained and misogyny was prevalent. (The term *misogyny* is used here restrictively to denote any speech act that attributes a generalization to women with the effect of devaluing them, comparing them unfavorably or subordinating them to men.) Jean's and Gerbert's four romances, however, contain few utterances of overt misogyny. When they do occur, they are closely linked to moments of crisis and stress in the narrative. When

the empress, for example, blandishes her husband in bed to persuade him
to separate Aelis and Guillaume, Jean interjects:

> Ahi! ahi! feme que fame
> > Com le set ore bien atraire!
>
> Oh! a woman is a woman / who knows well how to win!
> (*Escoufle* vv. 2880–81)

And when Guillaume de Dole's nephew discovers Lïenor's alleged seduction, he shouts:

> Femes getent adés dou mains
> por fere honte a lor amis.
>
> Women will always play fast and loose / in order to bring shame
> to their *amis*. (*Rose* vv. 3836–37)

Bloiesine's seduction of Gauvain in the *Continuation* evokes a *vallet*'s opinion:

> Mais biauté de feme a maint home
> Trahi et dechut, c'est la some . . . .
>
> Women's beauty has betrayed and deceived many men, /
> that sums it up. (*Continuation* vv. 12767–68)[3]

These scattered flashes of misogynistic lightning are given a sustained
rationale in Gerbert's *Violette*. As Gerart reflects on the losses he has suffered through Eurïaut's supposed betrayal, he identifies himself with the
heroic figures of Scripture whom women brought low:

> Mais or me sui bien aperchus
> Que par femme est mains hom dechus.
> Salemons, ki molt par fu sages,
> Rechut par femme mains damages,
> Car par sa femme fu il pris.
> Sanses, qui refu de grant pris,
> Qui tant fu fors et resoigniés,
> Refu par sa femme engigniés;
> A ses anemies le vendi,

En dormant ses crins li tondi,
Apriés li fist crever les iex.
Absolon li biaus, l'amoureux,
Rechut par une femme mort.

Now I clearly perceive / that man is often deceived by woman. / Solomon, who was exceedingly wise, / received great loss from a woman, / because he was overcome by his wife. / Samson, who, in turn, was of great worth, / strong and feared, / was tricked by his wife. / He was sold to his enemies; / while asleep she cut his hair; / she had his eyes put out. / Absolom, the handsome lover, / received death from a woman. (*Violette* vv. 1292–1304)

St. Jerome's *Adversus Jovianum* may be an obvious source of inspiration for this, but Abelard and Heloise drew up a catalogue of Old Testament men, including Adam, Job, Samson, David, and Solomon, who had been betrayed by women, from among whom Gerbert selected two noteworthy examples.[4]

Misogyny is not limited to a few overt expressions, but pervades all medieval literature in more subtle and indirect ways, which feminist critics have sought to expose. Nor is misogyny limited merely to negative evaluations of women. The praise of female attributes or the introduction of forceful female characters may also have served to manipulate, co-opt, marginalize, or otherwise entice women to conform to asymmetrical gender positions within a male-dominated society. Since these covert and subversive techniques are difficult to uncover, I shall simply take it for granted that both my authors and their society were patriarchal and misogynistic.[5]

Social Rank

Following their romance predecessors, Jean and Gerbert introduce remarkably vivid portraits of female characters into their narratives. When these women are set in realistic contexts, as in the *Escoufle, Rose*, and *Violette*, historians may be tempted to look to them for evidence of the lives of contemporary women. I shall not resist this temptation, but shall attempt to control my inquiry by two conditions. First, unlike recent literary analysis of women in medieval fiction, I shall not limit myself to a few select examples to be examined in depth but shall survey comprehensively the entire range of female creations of my two authors.[6] What I lose in this search is an appreciation of the authors' literary craft, as well as the subtleties and nuances of their creations. What I hope to gain is to minimize the bias of those modern critics who select a small sample to justify a predetermined conclusion. Second, to approach the subject from the perspective of the contemporary audience, I shall keep in view the "horizons of expectations," or familiarity with precedents, that the authors expected of their audiences. Since Gerbert's precedent for the *Continuation* was, of course, Chrétien's Perceval story, his characters are less distant from the Arthurian world than those of the *Escoufle*, *Rose*, and *Violette*, set in contemporary contexts. I shall therefore attempt to keep the Arthurian characters separate from those situated in contemporary settings. In this way, I may be able to distinguish novelties from conventions and conventions from realities.

Like their men, virtually all of Jean's and Gerbert's women are identified with the free and aristocratic ranks of society. The chief exceptions are Ysabel and her mother Erme, two working women in the *Escoufle*. Aelis makes their acquaintance at Dole, where she seeks lodging. She meets Ysabel as the latter exits her dwelling burdened with two water pots, her face wet with perspiration. Ysabel and her mother inhabit a grange and presshouse, where they serve the bourgeois owner as guardians and eke out a livelihood by sewing wimples. Their abode is sparsely furnished with a single bench, a table, and rude beds (vv. 4879–5044, 5212–35). Euriaut's personal servant Gondrée is of equally low station; her father was a robber and her mother a renegade beguine (*Violette* vv. 502–8). Occasionally, bourgeois women make their appearance, as in the hotel trade at Brindisi (*Escoufle* vv. 375–78) and Saint-Trond (vv. 4217–21). In the *Violette*, Gerart finds similar lodgings at Châlons-sur-Marne with Marote, the daughter of a bourgeois, Guyon le Gris, but her behavior and skills are equally appropriate to noble culture (vv. 2266–2310). Gerbert's *Continuation* is virtually devoid of women of non-noble rank.

At the pinnacle of birth was the imperial family of Germany, and since both of Jean's romances deal with imperial succession, this level is fully represented in them. Aelis, daughter of the emperor and future heiress, shares the center of the *Escoufle* with her *ami* Guillaume. (Her scheming mother, the empress, is also included.) Preoccupied with the Empire, Jean ignores other royalty with the exception of the daughter of the king of

Persia, a non-westerner, who is the *amie* of the Turkish champion in the Holy Land (*Escoufle* vv. 1155). King Louis in Gerbert's *Violette* is not accompanied by a spouse at Pont de l'Arche or at Montargis, and in the *Continuation,* Queen Guenièvre is barely visible at the incident of the "Perilous Seat" at Carlion (vv. 1341, 1410). Only Iseut, wife of King Marc of Cornwall and England, makes a cameo appearance at the tournament of Lancien (*Continuation* vv. 3862–4233). The Arthurian Pucele au Cercle d'Or, who is besieged at Montesclaire, is revealed to be a king's daughter (*Continuation* vv. 1915–18).

Although royalty is sparse, the high aristocracy is most fully represented in all four romances. In the *Escoufle,* the emperor gives Richard, count of Montivilliers (Normandy), a wife of comparable rank in the lady of Genoa, who becomes the hero Guillaume's mother (vv. 1696–1753), and the lady of Montpellier rivals the countess of Saint-Gilles for the affection of the count of Saint-Gilles (vv. 5828–92). In the *Violette,* Aigline, the first maiden in distress to be rescued, is the châtelaine de Vergy, to whom all in the county of Beaune submit (vv. 2168–72). Aiglente, who competes with her *chamberiere* Flourentine for the attention of Gerart, is the daughter of Milon, duke of Cologne (vv. 2678–82), while Ysmaine, the unfortunate victim of Melïatir's assassination, is the daughter of the duke of Metz (vv. 3989–4031). Blancheflor, the maiden whom Perceval rescues and promises to marry in Chrétien's *Graal* (vv. 2417), is the lady of Beaurepaire, surrounded by numerous knights holding fiefs (*Continuation* vv. 6464–65), as well as fourteen bishops, whose regalian lands she holds. "Outside of Arthur, there was no queen or king who held such power in Brittany," Gerbert comments (vv. 6773–94). Female religious are also present from the ecclesiastical hierarchy. The abbess of the historic Benedictine nunnery of Montivilliers in Normandy provides chants and prayers at Count Richard's departure on his crusade (*Escoufle* vv. 225–63), and the holy Ysabiaus, Perceval's kinswoman, presides over the Chastel as Puceles, an Arthurian nunnery, to whom the hero confides his sister for protection (vv. 3009–3247).

In numerical terms, however, a clear majority of women in the romances are identified simply as *pucele, damoiselle,* or *dame.* Except for the *Escoufle,* they comprise over half of the women; in the *Continuation,* over three-quarters. Although these terms were customary for designating aristocratic females, without further qualification, they indicate the lower levels of aristocratic society. These women perform services for the itinerant knight heroes, especially in Gerbert's stories, but they also furnish the leading heroines. The belle Lïenor of the *Rose*, along with her brother and mother, are from a modest fief that takes its name from the nearby town of Dole in the Lorraine (vv. 784–86). Eurïaut of the *Violette*, although identified as a niece of the queen of Hungary and the count of Montfort (vv. 5738–45), appears only as the *amie* of the hero, without prestige or the protection of family.

The feminine world of Jean's and Gerbert's romances replicates the hierarchy of the contemporary masculine aristocracy from royalty through high nobility down to the lower reaches of knighthood. It approximates the divisions constructed by the clerics of Philip Augustus's chancery, who roughly divided the aristocracy into counts and dukes, barons, castellans, and vavasors.[7] Also like the masculine world, it is a world to which one belongs by birth. Among the scores of noblewomen, no one questions this assumption. Only when a disparity emerges is lineage raised. The princes of the Empire object to the marriage between the imperial-born Aelis and Guillaume, the son of a French count (*Escoufle* vv. 3910–13). As the young couple travel, however, strangers cannot detect the difference in their birth. Everyone who sees them remarks, "He is certainly the son of a high baron and she the daughter of a high lady" (vv. 4278–82). The imperial princes raise the same objections to Lïenor's marriage to Conrad in the *Rose* (vv. 5062–65). *Mésalliance* became a problem at the imperial level; apparently, all other noblewomen felt secure in their birthrights.[8] Gondrée, the quintessential traitress, is provided with depraved parentage to underscore the depths of her villainy.

Conventional Female Beauty

If virtually all romance women are noble, their beauty conforms to a universal convention that tolerated few exceptions. Inspired by Ovid, the Latin rhetoricians Mathieu de Vendôme and Geoffroi de Vinsauf made this convention canonical in handbooks of Latin poetics.[9] The technique was to start with the head and move to the feet, dissecting the female body into its components, and assigning to each part a natural attribute. For example, hair is golden, forehead milky, eyes sparkling like stars, visage rosy, lips flaming, teeth ivory, neck white, and so on. Breasts are always small and firm, and when the poet reaches the abdomen, he averts his eyes. "What particulars should I relate?" Ovid exclaims. "Who doesn't know the rest?" ("*cetera quis nescit?*").[10] Marie de France's portrait of the fabulous lady in

Lanval (vv. 564–70) and Chrétien's account of Soredamor (*Cligès* vv. 761–849) show the extent to which romance poets of the twelfth century adopted these canons.

So ubiquitous was the stereotype that Jean felt free to parody it. Aelis's beauty is not sufficiently mature to provide a canvas for his talents (the emperor notices that her breasts are very small [*Escoufle* vv. 2320–21]), but Jean assures his audience at pertinent stages of her budding beauty. At age three, the rose of her cheeks matched that of her dress (vv. 1934–27). At her wedding, no one had seen such beauty, so richly had nature endowed her (vv. 8938–41). The belle Lïenor, however, offers Jean his first extended opportunity when the jongleur Juglet paints a verbal portrait of the heroine for Conrad:[11]

> sa bloie crigne recercle
> en ondoiant aval le vis;
> a flor de rose, a flor de lis
> samble la face de color,
> car la rougeur o la blanchor
> i fu mout soutilment assise . . .
> Les oils ot beaus por esgarder,
> vairs et clers plus que n'est rubis,
> sorcils bien fez, lons et tretiz,
> non pas joignanz, c'est veritez;
> les denz de la bouche et le nez
> avoit toz fez par maiestire. . . .
> Mout par avoit simple la chiere,
> blanche potrine, blanc le col. . . .
> cors ot gent, biaus braz, beles mains.

> Her blond curls encircle her face; / the red and the white of her cheeks / subtly contrasted like roses and lilies . . . / her hazel eyes sparkled beautifully / and clearly like rubies, / her long arched eyebrows were delineated / and not joined; / the teeth in her mouth and nose / were masterful creations. . . . / her visage simple, / her neck and chest white. . . . / her body noble, her arms lovely, and her hands fine. (*Rose* vv. 694–722)

Halfway through this patently potted exercise, Juglet mocks himself:

N'aprist pas hui si a descrire
qui l'embeli en tel meniere.

. . . . .

Ce sachiez vos de verité
qu'ele ert tel com ge la devis.

The one who embellished her in such manner / hasn't learned to
depict only yesterday / . . . / Know it for the truth / that
she is exactly what I am describing. (vv. 711–12, 721–22)

And Jean expects his audience to accept Conrad's hopeless descent into
love with a cardboard doll whom he has never seen.

Since heroines are invariably clothed in twelfth-century romances,
dress is closely melded to the body. Geoffroi de Vinsauf again provided a
model, this time of attire, emphasizing gold, gems, and jewelry. At Aelis's
coronation in Rome, Jean devotes more lines to her garments than to her
beauty (*Escoufle* vv. 8914–37). To prepare her imposing entry at the imperial court at Mainz, Lïenor carefully selects wardrobes for her knights and
herself (*Rose* vv. 4341–62) so as to produce the same *éclat* as the fabulous
lady in Marie de France's *Lanval*.[12] Like Aelis at Rome, she pays particular
attention to her décolleté. Her firm breasts fill out her silk gown. To call attention to her chest, she pins a gold clasp at the opening of her chemise,
which reveals a landscape whiter than snow (vv. 4359–80). Grasping her
horse's reins in one hand, she holds the clasp with the other, manipulating
the aperture as she rides through the streets. For Jean, décolleté marks the
liminal boundary between clothes and the feminine body.[13] At her coronation, Lïenor wears robes embroidered with the legend of the fall of Troy
that rival Erec's mantle at his coronation (*Erec* vv. 6671–6747).

Eurïaut's entry to the royal court at Melun competes with Lïenor's at
Mainz. Beginning with the clothes, Gerbert embellishes their richness by
offering comparisons with historical and mythological figures. The clasp
on the collar of her *blïaut* contains precious stones worth the entire city of
Piacenza. It belonged to Florence when she was empress at Rome and was
presented to Eurïaut by her aunt, the queen of Hungary. Her belt is
adorned with rubies and emeralds equal to the fortune of the count of
Toulouse. Roland sent it to his fiancée, Aude, before departing for Roncevaux. Lined with ermine, her mantel is embroidered with tiny flowers,

each containing a silver bell (vv. 812–54). Although her garments are
greatly admired, they are nothing in comparison to her beauty. Ten literary heroines are evoked as demonstration: Helen, Dido, and Antigone
from the *romans d'antiquité*, Iseut from the Tristan legend, and Galiene
from more recent romance. In the process of segmenting the physical,
Gerbert increases the precision and the natural resemblances:

> Cief ot crespé, luisant et sor,
> De couleur resambloient d'or:
> Front ot blanc come voirre poli . . .
> Qu'ele avoit les sorcius brunés;
> Les iex avoit et clers et nes;
> Le nes avoit droit et traitiç . . . .
> La rose qui naist en esté,
> Quant s'aoevre la matinee,
> N'est pas si bien enluminee
> Com el ot la bouche et la fache; . . .
> Plus blanc que argent ne yvoire
> Ot la fache entre le vermel;
> Mais d'une chose m'esmervel,
> Qu'ele ot plus blanc col et poitrine
> Que flour de lis ne flour d'espine.
> Blanches mains ot et bien fais bras . . . .
> Si n'avoit pas plus de quinse ans; . . .
> Mameletes ot haut levees,
> Ki nouvielement li poignoient.

> Her head of curls / was a resplendent gold, / her forehead as
> white as polished glass, . . . / her eyebrows brown, / her eyes
> clear and pure, / her nose straight and delicate. . . . / The sum-
> mer rose / that opens in the mornings / was not as radiant /
> as her mouth and complexion. . . . / Her cheeks were whiter than
> silver or ivory / enhanced against the red. / But of one thing I
> marvel / that she had a neck and chest more white / than the lily
> or the pine in flower. / She had white hands and well-formed
> arms. . . . / Although not more than fifteen years of age, . . . /
> her small breasts were raised high / and newly pointed. (vv.
> 868–900)

After this performance, Gerbert offers an encore on the beauty of the demoiselle des Illes Pertes, in which he abbreviates Eurïaut's features (vv.
5005–25).

In the *Continuation*, Gerbert turns his talents to Escolasse, the first demoiselle whom Perceval encounters after he leaves the Fisher King's castle. Whether Escolasse's portrait expands Eurïaut's or is simply common
convention, this time the author is more self-conscious (vv. 386–453):
"The story tells us," he begins, "that she had a noble body and an affable
face. If I describe her beauty to you, don't become bored by listening because I wish to tell it right." Later he interjects: "Please do not become ir-
ritated, if I tell you the truth, because I want to relate all her qualities as
best as I can." "I was foolish to try to describe her," he concludes, "If I had
learned to do it a hundred times, I could not tell the half, as much as I
tried." He enumerates Escolasse's attributes at a slower pace from head to
breast, assigns them the same properties as Eurïaut's, and finishes summarily with her clothes. Unlike in Eurïaut's case, however, he begins with
her torso, declaring that her hips are broad for pleasure, the better to enjoy
the games of bed. This unusual acknowledgment of sexual attributes is
doubtless to establish Escolasse's role as a good-natured seductress, offering herself to Perceval and constituting his first temptation in the quest for
the Grail.

Gerbert's powers of describing feminine beauty were evidently exhausted by Escolasse, because nowhere else in Perceval's interminable
journeys is another demoiselle so treated. Even Blancheflor, the sole heroine of the story, is slighted. More than once, Gerbert assures his audience of her beauty (vv. 6248–49). "You have heard it before [in Chré-
tien], but I can tell you with certainty that as Gerbert testifies in his story,
never has cleric, layman, or monk seen one so beautiful" (vv. 6353–60).
On the eve of the wedding, he takes the unusual step of expatiating on
Perceval's handsomeness from head to foot (vv. 6588–6603)—romance
authors were reluctant to treat the male body in detail—but not on Blancheflor's. All comment is limited to her wedding garments (vv. 6612–27).[14]
Gerbert's greater attention to her clothes than to her body accentuates her
chastity to prepare the audience for her spiritual marriage. Jean's and Gerbert's public would have had difficulty in distinguishing Aelis, Lïenor, Eurïaut, and Escolasse from their physical descriptions. So stereotypically is
the female body treated that the writers are hard pressed to vary their metaphors and versified expressions. The difficulties are signaled by Gerbert's

two portraits in the *Violette* and confirmed when he tries to repeat them in the *Continuation*.

The longevity of the stereotypical image of the flaxen-haired beauty, constructed by male desire, suggests that it was well received by Jean's and Gerbert's audiences. Since the audiences were mixed, the women may have concurred with the men; if they did not, they were not influential enough to bring about change. The only alternative offered by the romance authors is a complete reversal, the portrayal of female ugliness. Chrétien introduces it in the *Graal* in the appearance of the demoiselle on the mule at Carlion. No creature could be uglier, not even in hell, he avers, and proceeds to compare her features with those of animals. Her eyes, for example, are smaller than a rat's, like two holes (vv. 4610–37). Gerbert reintroduces the figure in the old woman with the casks of ointment. "Never has such an ugly creature been described," he reiterates, but he then goes on to compete with Chrétien in finding more revolting comparisons. "Her eyes were uglier than any beast's; one, red and small was buried in her head, the other, large and black, was thrust forward" (*Continuation* vv. 5515–17). It would be fastidious to pursue such comparisons, because both portraits are simply meant to shock. Preceding romances may have found occasion for male ugliness as well, but Jean and Gerbert create no grotesque men. In the male construction of the female body, therefore, little intermediate space separates beauty and ugliness, where most humans assuredly reside. The modern reader looking for historical women at the turn of the twelfth century in both the Arthurian and contemporary romances of Jean and Gerbert may, therefore, be permitted to read these literary portraits of female beauty as male fantasies and nightmares.

Female Education

With one exception, all women make their appearance in Jean's and Gerbert's narratives after puberty, thus obscuring their upbringing in childhood. The exception is the imperial princess Aelis, whose exalted position may reduce her pertinence to our understanding of medieval aristocratic women. The skills she was taught as a child were, however, common among her aristocratic *consœurs* in adulthood. Jean details the training of the two children after Guillaume is taken to the imperial court at the age of three to be educated. While the boy is occupied with horses, shields, lances, and swordplay (*escrime*) (*Escoufle* vv. 2018–45), Aelis and her accompanying maidens acquire the two basic skills of singing and embroidery. "And bele Aelis," Jean continues, "was she not the most *prex* and courteous? Her favorite companions were happy that she excelled them in singing songs, telling tales of adventure and in embroidering belts with images of *amis* and *amies*. . . . There was no distraction or skill a girl should know to which she did not apply herself better than any other woman" (vv. 2054–71).[15]

Aelis's needlework will be considered first. As a child at the imperial court, she becomes proficient in sewing belts, purses, ribbons, and straps for helmets. These skills later serve her well. "What does my lineage matter to me," she says to Ysabel, "when it is necessary to gain my livelihood with my two hands" (vv. 5434–36). They rent a shop at Montpellier, where to Ysabel's experience in making towels and wimples, Aelis adds talents in sewing with jewels, gold thread, and silk to make gold-embroidered work, belts, and ribbons (vv. 5451–61). Their atelier is a great success. So great is their customers' satisfaction that the women are able to charge any price they please. Ambitious to acquire the lady of Montpellier as a client, Aelis creates a belt and purse in gold work on which she embroidered the arms of the lady's husband (vv. 5560–69). This chef d'oeuvre, accompanied by Ysabel's best wimple, wins the lady's admiration and friendship.

At the bottom of the aristocratic scale, Aelis's skill with the needle is shared by the demoiselle of Dole and her mother. Guillaume introduces the imperial messenger into the "chambre à dame . . . à pucele" where Liënor and her mother are seated on a cushion at work with their needles. Just then the mother is embroidering a stole, but they also produce ecclesiastical trappings and vestments, such as pennants, ornaments, chasubles, and aubes. They sew both for their own amusement and for charity, donating their work to poor churches (*Rose* vv. 1116–39), and as they work, they customarily sing *chansons de toile* that echo the tasks they are performing: "A daughter and a mother are seated at gold making; with gold thread they sew crosses" (vv. 1159–60). In another song, "bele Aye" has *paile d'Engleterre*, an English cloth (vv. 1183–84), in her lap, which may allude to the famous English embroidery known as the *opus anglicanum*.[16]

Gerbert similarly depicts the bourgeoise but courtly Marote seated in her father's chamber embroidering an ecclesiastical stole in gold and amict with small crosses and stars and amusing herself with a *chanson de toile* (*Violette* vv. 2296–2302) and Flourentine, the *chamberiere* of Aiglente, the daughter of the duke of Cologne, seated alone on a cushion embroidering a coat of arms (vv. 3596–3600). Euriaut also teaches Ysmaine, the daughter of the duke of Metz, this skill, appropriate to the tranquility of the *chambre aux dames* (vv. 3991–92).

No scene could be more unremarkable than an aristocratic lady alone in her chamber sewing and singing. Thus, when Lïenor fabricates the charge of rape against the seneschal, she can plausibly claim that she was sewing alone when he entered (*Rose*, vv. 4778–84). The image, however, is limited to Jean's and Gerbert's contemporary romances.[17] Like Chrétien before him, Gerbert depicts no woman at her needlework anywhere in the *Continuation*.[18]

Maternity

The *Escoufle*, *Rose*, and *Violette* share the theme of political succession transmitted through inheritance, which obviously requires the birth of legitimate heirs. Only the *Escoufle*, however, deals overtly with the subject of maternity. Count Richard de Montivilliers marries the lady of Genoa whom the emperor has given to him as wife; their nuptial chamber is blessed by bishops; that night, on beautiful white sheets, they conceive a son, Guillaume, who is born in a castle near Venice. After baptism the boy is confided to three nurses, one who nurses him, another who attends to his crib, and a third who carries, bathes, and puts him to bed. The same day as Guillaume, a daughter, Aelis, is born to the empress (vv. 1718–97).

Childbirth is explicitly mentioned only in the *Escoufle*, but the romances give fuller expression to maternal love, of which Perceval's mother in Chrétien's *Graal* is the prototypical example. Bereft of her husband and two sons by the violence of knighthood, she struggles fiercely to protect her last son from its seduction and accedes to his wishes only with anguish (vv. 407–88). When he neglects to return home, she dies of heartbreak. In the *Escoufle*, Guillaume's mother sheds tears at each departure of her son, because she loves him more than anything else, but she recognizes the advantages of being raised at the imperial court; later she furnishes him with supplies for his elopement in the hope that he may regain his fortune (vv. 1846–1919, 3728–79). Ysabel's mother Erme similarly relinquishes her daughter to Aelis in a flood of tears (vv. 5308–19). Like the lady of Genoa, Guillaume and Lïenor's mother is ambitious for her children and recognizes the advantages of the imperial court. "You should go immediately," she says. "The emperor offers you a great honor when he summons you so courteously" (*Rose* vv. 1023–25). Her indiscretions to the seneschal are doubtless prompted by overweening ambition for her daughter. On the other hand, the empress's machinations against Guillaume may be attributed to a desire to protect her highborn daughter from the pretensions of a parvenu family (*Escoufle* vv. 2832–37, 2900–2904). In the *Violette*, the parents of Gerart and Euriaut are absent, and daughters like Ysmaine and Aiglente are directly under their father's supervision. Perceval's mother is dead by the opening of Gerbert's *Continuation*, and few women play maternal roles in the following adventures.

The principal exception occurs during the mayhem at the castle of Urpin de la Montaigne Irouse. Gauvain and Bloiesine have conspired to pretend that he will kill her if her father, Urpin, threatens him. At this point, Bloiesine's mother, believing her daughter in danger, rushes in, pleads for mercy, and threatens to take her own life. She has already lost three sons; if Urpin proceeds with his attack, he will further lose a wife and daughter, thus wiping out his heirs. This maternal intercession succeeds in saving Gauvain and Bloiesine, but it is only an interlude in the continuing mayhem (vv. 13548–611).

Demoiselles in the Service of Knights

When Count Richard arrives at Brindisi, the daughter of the innkeeper, a maiden *bele et sage*, leads him to his rooms (*Escoufle* vv. 375–78). While convalescing at Châlons, Gerart is nursed back to health through the ministrations of the courteous Marote, daughter of Guyon le Gris (*Violette* vv. 2415–35). After leaving the Grail Castle, Perceval's first stop is at Cothoatre where, after he has shed his arms, a girl brings him a set of fine clothes (*Continuation* vv. 372–81). Personal and domestic services to knights on their incessant journeys are also provided by many other demoiselles, inspired by examples in Chrétien,[19] and aristocratic women avail themselves of female servant-companions as well. Ysabel is confident that she can be of profit to Aelis (*Escoufle* vv. 5022–25); Gondrée is Euriaut's personal *maitresse*, although she is false and treacherous (*Violette* vv. 368–69); and Flourentine is the competitive *chamberiere* of Aiglente, the daughter of the duke of Cologne (*Violette* vv. 2678–82). In characterizing the disloyal Gondrée, Gerbert de Montreuil says that she knew more tricks than Iseut's Brangien or Fénice's Tessala (vv. 518–19). Jean and Gerbert draw portraits of these named women and allow them important roles, just as Béroul and Thomas had depicted Brangien and Chrétien had created Tessala or Lunette. The social origins of the servant women are either low, as in the cases of Ysabel (a tradesperson), Gondrée (daughter of a robber), and

Marote (a bourgeoise), or unclear, as in the case of Flourentine, but their services to the hero and heroines are in great demand both in the contemporary and Arthurian romances.

Unnamed demoiselles—invariably described as beautiful, and therefore presumably noble—also appear in the Arthurian romances, however, where they perform more than routine or personal service. Gerbert, for example, introduces a girl who carries a shield with a red cross and reliquary. Inscribed on the shield is the message that no knight except the bravest and one who has confessed his sins will be able to carry the shield and be worthy of finding the Grail and the lance that pierced Jesus' side. Any undeserving knight who tries to take the shield will be destroyed. Perceval naturally has no difficulty in removing the shield from the girl's neck (vv. 8466–8517). When he forgets to ask where the shield came from, however, the girl deprives him of further use of it (vv. 9836–51).

The most spectacular task of unnamed maidens is to perform the awesome Grail ceremony at the Castle of the Fisher King. In Chrétien's first episode, the sword, lance, and two candlesticks are carried by boys (*vallés*), but the resplendent Grail is born by a beautiful, noble, and finely clad demoiselle, followed by another who holds the silver trencher (*Graal* vv. 3165–3231). These participants reappear in the ceremony as Gauvain observes it in the *First Continuation* (vv. 1327–70).[20] Their ceremony is slightly modified in the *Second Continuation*, however, which is the version to which Gerbert attaches his continuation. Although the sword appropriately remains with the boys, the girls are now entrusted with both the holy objects. "They had not been seated long . . . when a noble demoiselle, whiter than the flower on the bough, came out of the chamber with the holy Grail in her hands. . . . Shortly afterward, another girl arrived, more beautiful than anyone had seen, dressed in white silk and carrying the lance, which dropped blood from its tip" (vv. 32396–407). In the inner sanctum of the Grail Castle, with its exalted but inscrutable significance, young, beautiful, but unnamed maidens are entrusted with the near sacerdotal service of bearing the sacred objects before the most worthy of knights. Whereas the demoiselles who perform personal and domestic services may plausibly fit the historical context, the mysterious Grail maidens doubtless belong to the realm of male fantasy.

On a less elevated plane, but equally objects of male desire, are the numerous seductresses of Arthurian legend who offer sexual service to knights. Memorable archetypes are Chrétien's demoiselle who seeks to undermine Lancelot's fidelity to Queen Guenièvre by exacting company in bed in exchange for hospitality (*Charrete* vv. 931–1280) and even Blancheflor, who joins Perceval between the sheets. It is not clear whether her embraces and kisses are intended to seduce him or simply to persuade him to defend Beaurepaire against her enemies (*Graal* vv. 1935–2079). Following this tradition closely in the *Continuation,* Gerbert presents Perceval as the privileged "victim" of these advances. Escolasse, the first person he encounters at Cothoatre, feeds him well, leads him to his chamber, and whispers that she will join him in bed for his delight. The hero trembles but, remembering the Grail, politely declines (vv. 621–57). The next assault is by a devil in the guise of a beautiful daughter of the Fisher King, who promises the secrets of the Grail in exchange for submitting to her desires (vv. 2517–62). Even the noble shield maiden desires the hero to join her so that she may have the pleasure of bearing a son to the best knight who ever lived (vv. 8809–21). When Perceval rejoins Blancheflor at Beaurepaire, the demoiselle, whose motivations remain unclear, repeats the performance of their first night. Perceval welcomes her, and they pass the night with kisses and embraces, but without the *sorplus* that would have deprive them of their virginity (vv. 6521–66).

Gerbert doubtless subjects his hero to this barrage of attempted seduction the better to test his chaste aspirations, but Gauvain enjoys a reputation in Arthurian literature for submitting more readily to female charms,[21] and his extended encounter with Bloiesine in the tent adds a new dimension to the topos of the seductive maiden. Only an abbreviated version of this lengthy episode can be offered here. Although Gauvain makes the first advance, the girl is not interested until she discovers that he has killed her brother. Then she plots to take revenge by enticing him into her bed and stabbing him there. Gauvain discovers the dagger, however, but forces her to resume the game she has initiated. Apparently, this is not entirely disagreeable to her, because Bloiesine warns him of an impending attack by her cousins, and after they are repelled, the couple gladly return to their sport. Thereafter, Bloiesine continues to aid Gauvain against her brothers and her father in exchange for further evenings together (vv. 12381–13927).

The topos of the seductive maiden appears to have been a creation of the Arthurian legend, because it is absent from the contemporary romances of Jean Renart. In Gerbert's *Violette,* the convention is similarly altered. Faithful to the memory of Eurïaut, Gerart is able to resist the blan-

dishments of Aiglente, daughter of the duke of Cologne, until he succumbs to a love potion, a standard device since the Tristan legend (vv.
3566–75). Aside from this unfair taking of advantage by Aiglente, however, no other maiden in the romances attempts to disturb the hero's devotion to his *amie*.

Maidens render further service to wandering knights in the romance
convention of the damsel in distress ("la demoisele deconseilliée") which
enables men to combine women with prowess and achieve the twin objects
of their desires. The topos is fully developed in Chrétien's first romance,
when Enide, the original cause of Erec's loss of prowess, is sent ahead to
attract the assaults of predatory knights so that Erec can regain his prowess in defending her. So many examples occur throughout Chrétien's oeuvre that he finally has it formulated as one of the tenets of chivalry in the
last romance. "If you find near or far a lady in need or a maiden in distress,
offer them your help if they ask for it, because that is true honor" (*Graal*
vv. 1656–62, alluded to in Gerbert's *Continuation* vv. 5017– 21), is Perceval's mother's advice, seconded later by Gornemans (vv. 1656– 62). Following their admonition, Perceval applies himself to rescuing maidens
wherever they appear (e.g., *Graal* vv. 3428–93, 3691–3949), and he continues to do so unabated in Gerbert. His beneficiaries include two girls suspended by their hair in a tree (vv. 910–54); his cousin Ysmaine, jilted by
her fiancé (vv. 1622–1788); his sister attacked by Mordres (vv. 2862–2959);
Rohais about to be raped by Dragoniaus li Cruels (vv. 7140–7377); and the
Pucel au Cercle d'Or besieged by the Dragon Knight at Montesclaire (vv.
9012–49).

Although such victims are absent in Jean's two romances, the convention was sufficiently strong to induce Gerbert to include examples in his
Violette, set in a historical context. Thus Gerart defends Aigline against
her besiegers (vv. 1538–2038), prevents a new bride from being raped by
Durlus, the justiciar of Ardennes (vv. 4423–4559), and saves the demoiselle of Illes Pertes from the giant Brudaligaus (vv. 4728–4963). The climax is, of course, his rescue of his *amie* Euriaut from being burned at the
stake. In a scene inspired by Yvain's rescue of Lunette (*Lion* vv.
3557–3725), Gerart arrives on the scene just before the fire is lit and offers
to defend the damsel in a judicial duel (vv. 5332–48). To this procession of
maidens awaiting deliverance, Gerbert adds a modification at the end of
his *Continuation.* After Perceval rescues Dyonise de Galoee from the fountain where she has been humiliated by Brandon Dur, she repays his gal-

lantry by attempting to assassinate him (vv. 15003–268). Her treachery is replayed by Felisse de la Blanclose, whose calls for help lure passing knights into a trap prepared by robbers (vv. 15300–473).

The frequency of the knight rescuing maidens in Gerbert suggests that it was a theme demanded by romance audiences. The prevalence of rape in successive episodes reinforces the impression that it fed male fantasy. The vulnerability of women—especially to rape—was not, of course, limited to fantasy, but its remedy in romance depends on the plausibility of knights being available to come to the rescue. This may not have been an unlimited source, as suggested by the absence of the topos of the victim damsel in Jean. Gerbert does, however, offer an alternative solution that may have struck audiences as more realistic. After defending his sister, Perceval accompanies her to the Chastel as Pucelles, where they receive hospitality and medical treatment. The castle is inhabited by a company of ladies and maidens seeking to preserve their chastity and virginity. They are presided over by *la sainte* Ysabiaus, who is identified as Perceval's kinswoman. When an orphaned sister is left there for protection, it becomes clear that the Chastel functions as a contemporary nunnery. Resembling Montivilliers, a historical Norman nunnery mentioned in the *Escoufle*, this legendary house both promotes sexual purity among noblewomen and constitutes a refuge created by noble families to shelter their women against masculine depredations in a patriarchal society. Like contemporary nunneries, the Chastel as Pucelles welcomes kinswomen.[22]

A final service rendered by demoiselles and ladies is the reconciliation of warring parties. Not only do mothers intercede for their children, but Bloiesine, fully enamored with Gauvain, attempts to negotiate between him and her infuriated family. Ysmaine, wife of Leander, similarly serves as intermediary between her family and Perceval. The hostilities begin when it is discovered that Perceval has slain Leander's father, the Red Knight, back in Chrétien's version, for refusing to hand over armor that Perceval believes King Arthur gave to him (*Graal* vv. 1076–1196). Rejecting Perceval's explanation, Leander challenges him to battle, and when Leander is bested by the hero, Ysmaine pleads for mercy for her spouse. It is granted, and she tends to Perceval's wounds in hopes that Leander will pardon him. Four traitors, however, pursue revenge by attacking Perceval while he is asleep. The wife summons her husband to save Perceval from the traitors, and once again she cares for the hero's wounds. Despite her pleas that he pardon Perceval, Leander proposes still another battle to set-

tle accounts. When Perceval prevails for a second time, Leander and his
kinsmen finally accept reconciliation (vv. 10614–12202). What has been
enacted in this lengthy episode is a classic blood feud or vendetta over the
death of a warrior, killed in a society where fighting is endemic. In the end,
the persistent search for revenge is finally resolved by the hero's prowess,
combined with the equally persistent desire of a woman to achieve peace.

Not all ladies, however, play pacifying roles. After leaving the hermit
king, Perceval meets Claire, a demoiselle furiously driving a cart bearing
the charred remains of her *ami*, killed by the Dragon Knight. She has
taken a vow to wear her clothes backward and to abstain from meat and
wine until her *ami* is avenged. Since no kinsman dares take up her cause,
she is heartened to see that Perceval carries the red cross shield, which is a
match for the Dragon Knight's powers (*Continuation* vv. 8906–9037). After Perceval releases the girl from her vow by killing the Dragon Knight,
she buries her *ami* at the abbey of Saint-Sorplis and founds a hermitage,
where she lives out her days praying for his soul, herself, and Perceval (vv.
10103–131).

Love

> Il conte d'armes et d'amors
> et chante d'ambedeus ensamble . . .
>
> It tells of arms and of love / and sings of both together.
> *Rose* (vv. 24–25)

Although Jean unites arms with love in the prologue to the *Rose*, the two
qualities are not combined in one hero, as in most romances. Women,
however, are assigned the function of love in all of Jean's and Gerbert's
romances.[23] To desire men and become the reciprocal objects of men's desire is their principal role. Both authors explore the entire spectrum of amatory relations between women and men. (Gerbert dismisses love between
men with passing but unqualified disapproval, and neither author makes
mention of love between women.)[24]

Since the transfer of property and power informs the political contexts
of three of the romances, the institution of marriage is featured prominently, resulting in the unions of the principal characters. This royal and
aristocratic pursuit of matrimony concurs with contemporary ecclesiastical teaching. By the mid twelfth century, the Paris theologian Pierre the

Lombard had included marriage among the seven sacraments in his *Libri sententiarum,* and the Bolognese canonist Gratian had discussed it at great length in his *Decretum.* Debating the essence of marriage, Gratian had argued that it has two stages: first, an exchange of words that conveys the consent of the two parties, and, second, sexual consummation, which completes and perfects the marriage bond. Pierre the Lombard contends on the contrary that consent alone constitutes marriage. It is expressed through future words (*verba de futuro*) in the engagement, but most fully in the present words (*verba de presenti*) of the marriage agreement itself.[25] Despite this controversy, canonists and theologians agreed on four chief "causes" or goals of marriage by the turn of the century, defined by the canonist Huguccio and the theologian Robert of Courson as: (1) progeny; (2) "rendering the marital debt" (or performing coitus in marriage, as discussed by St. Paul in 1 Cor. 7:3–5); (3) restraining incontinence, or avoiding sin; and (4) the fulfilling of lust. The first two can be performed without sin, and the third with venial sin, but the last only with mortal sin.[26]

Of the two romance authors, only Gerbert acknowledges the ecclesiastical doctrine explicitly, citing three of the four "causes." The morning after Perceval and Blancheflor's nuptials, the hero sees a bright light and hears a voice say: "Perceval, dear brother, think truly on God. You have wedded your wife, who is full of goodness. Now know truly what I have come to announce to you from God: No man should touch his wife except for holiness alone and two things. The one is to propagate, the other, to avoid sin. . . . But it often happens that when young people are together they think that whatever they do in carnal delight is done well. But know truly that they are committing a misdeed and do not live rightly" (*Continuation* vv. 6882–99).

The clerical axiom that thoroughly informs all four romances is the mutual consent of both parties. It undergirds the emerging love of Aelis and Guillaume, who refer to each other as brother and sister to avoid the compromising word *amis.* The passion between Conrad and Lïenor is likewise mutual, although for different reasons, and Gerart's search for his *amie* is matched by Eurïaut's patience. The rapturous reunions of all three couples undoubtedly confirm their reciprocal desire. At least two marriages in the four romances, however, are arranged by politics. As overlord of the lady of Genoa, the emperor in the *Escoufle* commands her to be the wife of his constable Richard and fixes the date of the wedding (vv. 1696–1707). In answering objections to the proposed match between the two children, he later explains that as father and emperor, his daughter is his to dispose of (vv. 2168–79). Such political marriages were common in contemporary royal and aristocratic society. As overlords, kings and emperors claimed the right to monitor the matrimonial alliances of their immediate vassals, and child marriages were frequently arranged. Louis VII, for example, had given two daughters from his wife Aliènor to the counts of Troyes and Blois, and those from his second wife, Constance, to the Angevin family of England. All of the children were engaged at an age below the minimum set by canon law (twelve for girls and fourteen for boys). Even contemporary theologians acquiesced in such arrangements. Robert of Courson sums up generations of clerical discussion when he lists reconciliation of enemies and confirmations of peace and treaties as additional but legitimate "causes" for wedlock.[27] Female characters in the romances are, however, depicted as assenting to such unions: the lady of Genoa, for example, received the emperor's command with joy because she has heard good reports about the count (*Escoufle* vv. 1702–3), and the emperor's matrimonial plans merely legitimate the children's own desires.

How fully the romance authors concur with the ecclesiastical program of consent can be best seen in Gerbert's *Continuation*. For example, having killed the demoiselle Rohais's *ami*, Dragoniaus li Cruels tries to force her to marry him by beating her severely. When he demands that a hermit marry them, the latter responds that he will comply only if she grants it (v. 7192). Never, by St. Paul, she protests; she would prefer to die than to spend the night with Dragoniaus, and Perceval defends her right to free choice by battle, finally forcing Dragoniaus to swear on a Psalter that he will stop ravishing demoiselles (vv. 7141–7377). In another incident, a knight, Faradien, seduces Ysmaine, Perceval's cousin, by promising to marry her, but then abandons her the next morning to seek the hand of another. As the bans are being read—"If any knows why this marriage should not take place, let him speak now"—Ysmaine appears and declares that Faradien has already pledged his faith to her in loyal marriage (vv. 1776–91, 2072–73, 2188–96). Faradien denies this, but Perceval proves his kinswoman's case in battle and finally forces the reluctant fiancé to marry Ysmaine. Throughout this prolonged episode, the promise of faith ("fïanchast sa foi," v. 1779, v. 2038) enacts an engagement (*verba de futuro*) that embodies consent. The subsequent consummation confirms that this consent constitutes a valid marriage, which cannot be abrogated (vv. 1749–2389).

Gerbert's most noteworthy case of consent constituting matrimony is doubtless the spiritual marriage of Perceval and Blancheflor. After rescuing Blancheflor from her tormentors in Chrétien's version of the *Graal*, Perceval promises his *amie* to return after he finishes searching for his mother (vv. 2933–37). Gerbert transforms this promise into a formal engagement: "I have made a covenant with her that I would be her *ami* and wed her as my wife" (*Continuation* vv. 5143–46), he tells Gornemans. His failure to fulfill this promise is one of the sins that prevents him from achieving knowledge of the Grail. Unlike Faradien, therefore, Perceval intends to honor his word as a fiancé. Before arriving at Beaurepaire, however, Perceval has already announced his intention that it not be an ordinary marriage. "I wish to wed her as my wife. If I live chastely as a man who leads a holy life and keeps his purity, chastity, and virginity, it shall be to my advantage" (vv. 6044–52). For a third time during the series of continuations, the couple spend a chaste premarital evening in bed before the official ceremonies. After the blessing of the nuptial chamber by Blancheflor's bishops, they enter the marriage bed and once again lie arm in arm, skin to skin under the sheets. Although trembling with desire, Blancheflor expresses the thought that is on her husband's mind: "Chastity is a holy thing, but just as the rose exceeds the beauty of all other flowers, virginity surpasses chastity" (vv. 6830–35). They rise from bed, kneel facing east and beseech Jesus to preserve their virginity. Then, returning to bed, they fall asleep without touching each other. Unlike Chrétien's Enide, who is transformed from a maiden into a lady (*Erec* vv. 2052–54), Gerbert's Blancheflor goes to bed a maiden and arises a maiden the next morning (vv. 6954–55).

Despite the absence of consummation, Perceval and Blancheflor's marriage remains fully valid, because it is founded on mutual consent. Before the church ceremonies, Perceval addresses Blancheflor's vassals, saying: "Lords I have come to ask for your lady as my wife in good faith, as I ought to do. I wish to do it with your agreement and with hers. . . . It is better that we unite in the sacrament of marriage than to put our bodies to foolish use" (vv. 6466–75). The girl heard this, Gerbert comments, and sighed with joy, for she would not have exchanged the empires of Greece and Rome for her Perceval. Just as the chaste marriage of the Virgin Mary and Joseph provided the defining example for the Paris theologians, so Blancheflor and Perceval epitomize the foundations of matrimony, because their union rests solely on mutual consent. Perhaps for that reason,

Gerbert omits the second "cause" of the canonical-theological scheme, which is the rendering of the marital debt. Although all four causes implicate sexuality, the marital debt most closely links consummation with consent, because if a couple agree to marry, that consent entails a further obligation to respond to each other's sexual demands.[28] The phenomenon of "spiritual marriage" was not without precedent in western European history. Some thirty historical examples of these unions have been uncovered before Gerbert's time. Among the most renowned were those of Edward the Confessor, king of England, and Edith, and the emperor Henry II and Cunegunde—both couples who had thereby avoided the royal duty of procreation.[29]

Although Gerbert unequivocally endorses consent, his two romances nonetheless portray a society where the principle was under constant assault. Abandoned by her lover in a forest, Eurïaut is discovered by the duke of Metz, who is so taken by her beauty that he wishes to marry her immediately. Only Eurïaut's fabrication of an unsavory past and the objections of his knights deter the duke's resolve (*Violette* vv. 1167–1253). Episodes later, the duke would succeed in pressing his suit were it not for his barons' resistance (vv. 3851–55). As is traditional in romance, many suitors resort to more violent means to woo unwilling maidens into matrimony. Aigline has lost her father and two brothers and is without an *ami* to defend her castle against a determined suitor (*Violette* vv. 1621–33).[30] Like Blancheflor besieged by Clamadeu in Chrétien's *Graal*, Gerbert's *Continuation* also contains other maidens who are able to resist displeasing aggressors solely by appeal to wandering knights who come to their defense. A prime example is Perceval's rescue of the Pucele au Cercle d'Or, besieged by the Dragon Knight (vv. 9012–21); or, in another case, when he defends his own sister against the rapacious Mordrés (vv. 2872–2993) and confides her to the safety of the Chastel as Pucelles.

It is not entirely clear whether the ravishers of Blancheflor and Perceval's sister, as well as other maidens in distress, are intent on matrimony, but the threat of rape is endemic. Throughout the entire romance world of Jean Renart and Gerbert de Montreuil, rape—the ultimate violation of consent—is an ever-present danger. Even Jean, who eschews the conventional figure of *demoiselles deconseilliées*, includes a case of criminal rape, albeit a fabricated one. The verisimilitude of Lïenor's charges against the seneschal lend credence to her claim. She was at work sewing and, most important, alone when her alleged ravisher came upon her, she says. After violating her, he flaunted his contempt by stealing her jewelry (*Rose* vv. 4777–90). Such incidents are commonplaces in preceding romances and pastourelles.[31] Melïtir's attempted rape of Eurïaut is more graphically violent. Once again, the villain finds his victim alone and attempts to entice her with gifts. When she tries to dissuade him by reminding him of her dissolute past, he forces her on to the bed. His physical brutality is matched by her kicking out his teeth and pummeling him with her fists before she escapes (*Violette* vv. 3950–84). The wife who is abducted, stripped down to her chemise, and beaten by the lord of Durlus while held by three knights is an apparent victim of gang rape (*Violette* vv. 4482–95). The procession of *demoiselles deconseilliées* through Gerbert's *Continuation* furnishes plentiful examples of brutal rape—for example, the rape of Lugarel's *amie*, who loses her life in the process (vv. 14895–906).

If Jean's and Gerbert's principal heroines respect the sanctity of marriage for either dynastic or pious reasons, their lesser female characters are not as scrupulous. The *Escoufle* contains a prominent episode of adultery among two couples of the high aristocracy, brought to light by Aelis's gift of a purse to the lady of Montpellier embroidered with the arms of her husband. The lady has been openly receiving visits from her lover, the count of Saint-Gilles, and takes mischievous pleasure in his jealousy when he is shown the fine purse. When the count succeeds in obtaining the purse for himself and quickly returns home to conceal his absence, his countess is not as indulgent when she sees the purse and perceives the *gage d'amour* (vv. 5826–5914). Despite Gerbert's overarching interest in penance, he also introduces a case of adultery into the *Continuation* in the cameo appearance of Iseut and Tristan. Eager to revisit his old *amie* at the tournament of Lancien, Tristan disguises himself and his Arthurian companions as minstrels. When Tristan sings the lai de Chievrefueil, Iseut recognizes him. Taking advantage of Marc's absence in the lists, she leads her lover to her chamber where they resume their old habits. "There," Gerbert comments, "they enjoyed the pleasure that *amis* are wont to have with *amies*, certainly of kisses, but of the *sorplus* I cannot tell you, because I was not present" (vv. 4203–7). Gerbert includes this adulterous episode in his pious story without apology. Although he adopts the equivocations of the original legend, there is no love potion here to exonerate the lovers.

Adultery normally required the complicity of both partners, but fornication permitted greater scope to the initiative of the parties. Jean introduces Conrad as a young man indulging his freedom by preying upon the females of his entourage. Sending the older men off on a spring hunt, he and two companions return to the tents to sport with the ladies. "Chevaliers aux dames" is their battle cry. As the bachelors extend their arms, the ladies, whatever their marital status, come willingly to their embraces (vv. 121–227). Conrad is the only principal hero of the four romances whose amatory energies are not limited to his future spouse—a circumstance doubtless excused by his youth (*genvrece*). All the other initiators of consensual fornication in the romances are female. The most shameless is the châtelaine of Dijon, Lïenor's fictive seductress, who succeeds in ensnaring the seneschal. Although the châtelaine admits to having rebuffed the seneschal's courtship, she now repents and sends tokens of her love. If he will wear them, she will consent to see him and accede to his desires (*Rose* vv. 4289–4332). Although a ruse, the ploy must have been sufficiently plausible to shield the seneschal in the eyes of the audience from the ignominy of having been completely duped. Gerbert creates competition at Cologne between Aiglente and Flourentine as to who is to win the love of Gerart, whose resistance endures until he is finally drugged into submission (*Violette* vv. 2674–3575). A parade of seductive maidens is introduced into the *Continuation*. As has been seen, they exercise their ingenuity to overcome Perceval's devotion to his quest. Bloiesine's seduction of Gauvain is less apparent, however, because of the latter's habitual receptivity.

One variety of extramarital behavior nearly absent in the romance tradition is prostitution. Jean omits it entirely, and Gerbert includes it only in hyperbolic form. To dissuade the duke of Metz from marrying her, Eurïaut pretends to practice the trade, saying she is the daughter of a wagoner who became a whore (*femme legiere*) three years before and took up with a notorious highway brigand, who kept her in fine clothes (the robe she is wearing was recently stolen at Coucy). Although her boyfriend has been captured, she says, she escaped and intends to resume her profession (*Violette* vv. 1192–1216). This caricature is introduced to outrage both the fictive duke of Metz and the sensibilities of Gerbert's audience, who were unaccustomed to such women in courtly entertainment. (Prostitutes appear in the less refined fabliaux and bawdy clerical verse.)[32] Lisïart's insult to Gerart during their final battle is thus understandable: "You would do better to wander across the countryside and to pimp her [Eurïaut] from town to town, because she could make you a wealthy man" (vv. 6430–38).

Fin'amours

If Jean and Gerbert were reluctant to include common women in their stories, they were equally convinced that their audiences expected the romance conventions of *fin'amours*. Chrétien had explored the interaction between love and prowess as a dominant theme. For him, one of the principal functions of *fin'amours* was to inspire prowess. Since Erec's love for Enide debilitates his prowess, he undertakes a series of hazardous adventures in the company of his wife to regain his lost virtue. At crucial moments, his love for Enide enables him to survive the ensuing tribulations. In parallel fashion that became paradigmatic, Lancelot's love for Gueniévre likewise enables him to endure extraordinary hardships and to achieve remarkable feats of prowess. Jean and Gerbert do not neglect to include examples of *fin'amours* that encourage chivalric bravery. Except for the initial crusade, individual combats are largely absent in the *Escoufle*, but we remember that the battle between the Franks and Turks is preceded by a duel between Count Richard and the Turkish champion. Since Richard has no *amie*, Jean attributes the courtly convention to the infidel Turk, who bears on his right arm a silk sleeve on which the daughter of the king of Persia has embroidered a declaration of love. "The love of his *amie* incites him to be *preu*, noble, and brave" (vv. 1138–65). In the *Rose*, chivalric prowess is limited to the tournament at Saint-Trond. Once again, the hero Guillaume enters the lists without an *amie* (vv. 2035–36), despite female adulation (vv. 2542–45), but Gauthier de Joigny, a minor participant, who is dying for his love, is now ready to fight again (vv. 2101–6).

The convention of prowess inspired by love is used sparingly by Jean, but Gerbert makes it the mainspring of Gerart's search for Eurïaut. In the titanic combat with Galerant, the two knights collapse from exhaustion, but the memory of Eurïaut revives the hero to deal the final blow (vv. 1996–2004). Devastated by his wounds and dispirited by the loss of his friend, Gerart takes to bed at Châlons in a state of severe emaciation and abject depression. When Marote entertains him with a *chanson de toile* containing a heroine called Eurïaut, the very name reinfuses him with strength. "Whoever forgets his true love, saps his sense and vigor. It is no wonder that I am so weak when I have forgotten her whose love imputes value to my life" (vv. 2273–2326). At the climactic tournament of Montargis, Gerart gallops into the fray with Eurïaut's wimple around his head

(vv. 5894–95). As Lisïart crashes to the ground, Gerart lets loose a cry of victory, "Chevalier, m'amie Eurïaut!" (vv. 6601–10).[33]

Gerbert appears to have reduced the convention in the *Continuation*, however. The unfortunate Lugarel, for example, defends a statue of his dead *amie* against all strangers. Although he regains strength from viewing the likeness, it is not sufficient to win against Perceval (vv. 14768–809). Before the tournament of Lancien, the lovers Tristan and Iseut are both prompted by memories of love (vv. 3763–85, 3864–73), but Tristan joins Iseut in the less perilous combat in bed, while Marc fights in the tournament. Afterward the queen arms her lover and his companions to rescue her husband, but love's inspiration is not sufficient to give Tristan victory over Perceval (vv. 4549–91), Gerbert's central chivalric figure, who is resolutely uninterested in fighting for the love of women. After deflecting Escolasse's advances in the opening narrative, Perceval turns to deep thought over the Grail (vv. 658–72). All prowess is directed toward this single goal, which effectively displaces love as the motivation of his quest.

The memory of love is crystallized in romance convention in the ring, both the key symbol of marriage and the prime *gage d'amour* (see Iseut's gift to Tristan), which is central to Jean's and Gerbert's narratives. Among the jewels that Aelis amasses to finance her elopement is a ring with a stone greener than ivy, given her by her mother as a token of affection (*Escoufle* vv. 3806–13). During the lovers' idyll in the meadow, this is the ring that Aelis bestows on Guillaume, "with her body and her love" (vv. 4870–93). Rather than placing it on his finger, however, Guillaume returns it to the purse, and after the buzzard steals the purse, Guillaume recovers the ring but loses Aelis. At their reunion at Saint-Gilles, the ring becomes the talisman of their rediscovered identities and love. "Don't you recognize me? I am Aelis, your *amie*, who gave you my mother's ring, from which we have received so many troubles," she says. Aelis then demands that Guillaume produce the ring. Despite poverty and misfortune, he has nonetheless kept it sewn in his belt. The assembled company admire the ring while the couple are engrossed in embraces and kisses (vv. 7698–7745). "This ring, for which the buzzard was destroyed, is worth more than a thousand marks." Given its singular significance, the audience may not have expected Guillaume finally to bestow the ring on the count of Saint-Gilles, his cousin and Aelis's former admirer. The count accepts it as a token of generosity, which binds their hearts together (vv. 8430–45). The ring's final destination may be meant to be equivocal, if not ironic, but Jean employs a ring in like manner in the *Rose*. To loosen the tongue of Lïenor's mother, the seneschal gives her a ring *par drüerie*. Weighing more than five *besants* of gold and with a bright red ruby, it supplies him with the information with which the heroine's reputation is destroyed (vv. 3342–61). In the preceding *Lai de l'ombre*, Jean Renart also assigns a ring to the service of *drüerie* when the knight bestows it upon the lady's reflection in the well and thereby overcomes her resistance.

In the *Violette*, however, Gerbert returns to Jean's *Escoufle* and reemploys the ring unequivocally as a love token. In despair at Metz over the loss of her *amie*, Eurïaut is feeding a lark in her lap when the ring that Gerart has given her slips off her finger. In a repetition of the buzzard episode, the bird seizes the ring in its beak, but it slides over its head and down its neck, and the lark flies off (vv. 3892–3946). Not long afterward, as Gerart is hunting with his hawk along the banks of the Rhine, he hears the lark's song, which reminds him of *fin'amours* and of Bernart de Ventadorn's celebrated lyric about the lark (also sung in Jean's *Rose*, vv. 5212–27). He is still under the potion's spell, however, and his love is Aiglente. When Gerart's hawk captures the lark and the knight recognizes the red stone in the ring, the magic is broken and the memory of Eurïaut floods over the hero (vv. 4174–4279). At the final scene of reunion at Metz (recalling Saint-Gilles), Eurïaut confesses that she has lost Gerart's ring, but her *ami* reassures her that it has been found and recounts his adventures (vv. 5703–14). The retrieval of the ring marks the lovers' reunion, and Eurïaut never parts with it again. Rings and *fin'amours* are absent in Gerbert's *Continuation*, however, doubtless obscured by the penitential Grail.

Ja fine amors ne sera sanz torment,

Fin'amours will never be without suffering, (*Rose* v. 3188)

sings the emperor Conrad, in a *grand chant* allegedly of his own composition. If love's highest aspiration in the romances is *fin'amours*, it is often accompanied by *mal d'amour*.[34] (Lovesickness, or *amor heroicus*, was epidemic even in classical antiquity, if one believes literary accounts and ancient medical treatises.) Afflicting mainly the aristocracy, its symptoms were many and diffuse, but paleness, nausea, insomnia, and mental distress were among the most common. From the beginnings of romance, *fin'amours* is depicted as accompanied by both joy (*joie*) and grief (*dolor*), but aggravation of the latter leads to the general morbidity of lovesickness. Romance literature equates *mal d'amour* with seasickness, as when Thomas de Bretagne depicts Tristan and Iseut on shipboard with his celebrated threefold pun on *la mer* (sea), *l'amer* (bitter), and *l'amour* (love).[35] Chrétien transmitted the analogy to succeeding writers in Soredamor and Alexandre's comparable episode at sea (*Cligès* vv. 541–44). Following this tradition, Jean and Gerbert cause their heroes and heroines to slip from love pangs into the pathological depths of lovesickness. Jean's young couple in the *Escoufle* precociously exhibit the symptoms of sighs, sobs, and *angoisse* in the nursery (vv. 1992–2001), but their mutual love never achieves acute morbidity. In the Provençal tradition of distant love (*amor de lonh*), the emperor Conrad, however, has fallen in love with a woman whom he has never seen but only heard about. When his dreams have been shattered by the seneschal's accusation, he cannot check the onslaught of lovesickness:

> Amours a non ciz maus qui me torment;
> mes n'est pas teuls com les autre genz l'ont.
>
> . . . . . .
>
> Et ge di: "Las! mi mal, quant fineront?"
>
> Love is the name of the disease that torments me, / but it is not like love that other men suffer / . . . / I exclaim, "When will my illness cease?" (*Rose* vv. 4587–88, 4591)

Gerbert's first report of an outbreak of *mal d'amour* is in an early episode in the *Violette*, when Lisïart attempts to seduce Eurïaut. "Lady have pity on me! Ever since I have heard so much of your appearance, beauty and qualities, my heart has forced me to come here. Whatever happens to me, I shall never be able to tell you of the ills that love has made me endure. I cannot describe the suffering I bear for you; my complexion pales and my heart constricts in my chest. Since I have heard speak of you, *mal'amor* has infected me . . . . Love has shot his arrow into my heart" (vv. 376–98). Because Lisïart's symptoms are stereotypical, Eurïaut has good cause to reject them outright: "Have mercy sir! If I can endure your talk and do not respond with obscenities, it is only by courtesy. . . . If you have nothing better to do, know that you are wasting your time here" (vv. 401–10). The illness that afflicts the hero, Gerart, is genuine, however, and his hostess, the courteous Marote, diagnoses it as *mal d'amer* when she hears him singing deliriously in bed (vv. 2346–80). Advising him never to test the love of an *amie*, she serves him hot bouillon, covers his head against drafts, and soothes his face and temples with rose water (vv. 2387–2450). Gerart pronounces himself healed, but bouts of illness return when he is at Cologne. As others play at games, he retires to the window lost in thought. The poignant memory of Eurïaut so seizes his weakened body that he can scarcely remain standing. Once again he articulates his symptoms:

> Destrois, pensis, en esmai. . . .
> Ma douche dame ou j'ai pris
> Les maus dont ja ne garrai,
> Ains en trai
> Les painnes come fins amis.

> Distraught, thoughtful, deeply disturbed. . . . / from my sweet lady I have caught / the sickness from which I shall not be healed, / but from which I suffer / the pains of a *fin'amant*.
> (*Violette* vv. 3236–43)

The coquette Aiglente takes pleasure in his lament, because she imagines herself to be its object. When disabused, she too takes to her bed. The ailments of love touch her heart, rendering her weak, sad, and dispirited. Tossing back and forth, complaining, sighing, and trembling, she endures ten to twenty attacks within an hour (vv. 3362–97).

The *Rose* and *Violette*, therefore, present lovesickness as an epidemic to which aristocrats of both sexes could succumb. Inhibited by his high position, the emperor Conrad can only watch helplessly as the seneschal destroys his dream. Although believing Eurïaut to be innocent, Gerart occasionally lapsed into despair of ever recovering his love. Not all heroes and heroines, however, are thus infected. Perhaps too young, Aelis and Guillaume are certainly preoccupied with their mutual search. Lïenor is resolutely determined to recover the position that was so close to her grasp. Although Eurïaut pauses to remember her lover (*Violette* vv. 3856–59), she is too busy defending herself against the duke or avoiding the stake. But lovesickness appears entirely absent from Gerbert's *Continuation*. None of the numerous knights, ladies, or demoiselles are afflicted, not even the long-suffering Blancheflor. Perceval, whose adventures are both martial and amatory, is securely innoculated against *mal d'amour* by his resolve to attain the Grail.

To the romance topoi of the exchange of tokens, prowess inspired by love, and *mal d'amour*, modern scholars have added still another, the prominence of adultery, implied by Andreas Capellanus's well-circulated contention that love and marriage are incompatible.[36] The contemporary popularity of the Tristan and Iseut legend would seem to give support to this view. In Chrétien de Troyes, however, the relation between *fin'amours* and marriage is more complex. The love between Lancelot and Queen Guenièvre in the *Charrete* is, to be sure, adulterous, but *fin'amours* likewise governs the love between the married Erec and Enide. Jean Renart, for his part, includes adulterous couples in his narrative, and both he and Gerbert attribute *fin'amours* pursued within the bonds of matrimony to their princi- pal heroes and heroines. Marriage and *fin'amours* are thus proposed as in- dependent strategies, but *pace* Andreas and his modern interpreters, they are not mutually exclusive.

In addition to the essential features of *fin'amours*, modern scholars have also debated whether courtly love, as it is often called, was actually prac- ticed by the historical French aristocracy, or whether *fin'amours* is merely an ironic convention of romance, perhaps derived from Andreas Capella- nus's scholastic manual, or even a fabrication on the part of the nine- teenth-century scholar Gaston Paris. The historian John F. Benton has as- serted that no trace of courtly love has been found in the charters and other archival records.[37] Yet the theologian Pierre the Chanter, reputed for his rigorous moralism, devised a *questio* in direct response to Andreas ar- guing that the art of love (*ars amatoria*) could be legitimately taught as a remedy against the misuse of love.[38] His student Thomas of Chobham further recognizes the symptoms of lovesickness and proposes therapy for a cleric and his mistress.[39] And the archives have yielded a charter from King Richard of England addressed to his constable in Normandy on which the ribbon attaching the seal bears a message to the constable's wife: "Jo sui drüerie / ne me dunez mie / ki nostre amur deseivre / la mort pui si ja receivre" ("I am *drüerie* [romantic love]. Do not give me to one who might separate our love. May he then instantly incur death").[40] This *gage d'amour* powerfully suggests a *fin'amant*. Although one may suspect that historical archives are not the best place to look for courtly love, even these repositories are not devoid of traces of it.

Women in Love

One of the foremost achievements of romance in the second half of the twelfth century was to create heroines with distinctive and forceful characters. We may assume that aristocratic audiences could appreciate and distinguish the qualities of Iseut, Guildeluec, Enide, Fénice, Laudine, Lunette, and Guenièvre, just as these women continue to attract the attention of modern readers and critics. Striking female figures were of no professional concern to Paris theologians, however, and they are strangely absent from the clerical chronicles and underplayed even by Latin poets. It should be unnecessary to remind ourselves that these vernacular figures were the fictive creations of their authors' imaginations. No historical model has so far been proposed for any of them, and recent critics have preferred to remove them from their historical context and to treat them as exercises and metaphors for modern theoretical concerns.[41] As fictions, however, their only historical significance may lie in the plausibility of their traits and actions to contemporary audiences.[42] Undoubtedly, the chief function of the heroine in romance is to love the chivalric hero and thereby to become the object of his desire. Thus interacting with men, these female figures are best understood in terms of gender. Since Gerbert is less concerned with female fictions than Jean is, I shall treat the principal heroines beginning with Blancheflor of the *Continuation,* continuing to Eurïaut of the *Violette* and Aelis of the *Escoufle,* and concluding with Lïenor of the *Rose.* Many of their traits have already been noted, but they will be recalled here to construct composite images.

Blancheflor, the damsel in distress under siege from Clamadeus and his seneschal, was originally Chrétien's creation. Introduced in stereotypical fashion, her beauty is the mirror-image of Perceval's. Observers remark: "He is so handsome and she so beautiful that never did a knight or maiden go together so well" (*Graal* vv. 1869–71). Since Blancheflor is in grave peril, it is she who must take the initiative. When Perceval remains silent, inhibited by Gornemans's advice, she opens the conversation. She comes to his bed at night dressed only in her chemise and silken mantel and awakens him with her tears. Despite her déshabillé, she protests that she is innocent of base intentions, but nonetheless threatens to kill herself in despair (vv. 1985–98). Later she opposes his arguments to defend her against the seneschal so skillfully that she is able to strengthen his resolve (vv. 2128–37). But it is Perceval who invites her between the sheets in the celebrated scene where they lie arm in arm, mouth to mouth, with no further comment from Chrétien except that the maiden was not displeased (vv. 2049–69). These dalliances are repeated at Blancheflor's behest (vv. 2354–62, 2574–77), but they are not sufficient to dissuade Perceval from fighting Clamadeus, if that is her ultimate intent (vv. 2630–41). Nor can they retain the hero after his victory. Although he now commands Blancheflor's land and heart, his own heart is fixed on his mother. The most his *amie* can obtain is a promise to return with or without his mother. Perceval leaves and Blancheflor resumes her tears.

In the *Second* (Wachier de Denain or Perceval) *Continuation*, which mediates between Chrétien and Gerbert, the lovers' second reunion is fortuitous, despite Perceval's earlier resolve to return, and they do not recognize each other until their names are pronounced. During the replay of the bed scene, Blancheflor comes to Perceval's chamber, and the knight draws her into his arms. The author will not mention the rest (*seurplus*), "but if Perceval did not fail to do more, Blancheflor did not object" (vv. 22834–837). The heroine proposes that Perceval marry her the next morning and become the lord of her lands (refusing other suitors, she has been busy restoring her domain in his absence). Once again the hero demurs, citing an undisclosed journey, but promises this time by Saint Gilles of Provence that he will return as soon as possible (vv. 22893–99, 23065–70). For a second time the knight takes leave of his *amie* in deep sorrow.

Whereas Chrétien and the Second Continuator granted Blancheflor certain initiatives—to dramatize her distress, to slip into his chamber for love trysts, and to propose marriage, albeit to no avail—Gerbert reduces the heroine's role to enhance the hero's. Now it is Perceval who resolves to return to Beaurepaire to wed his *amie*, reminded by Gornemans, his chivalric mentor, that his failure to keep his promise has hindered him from learning the Grail secrets (vv. 5116–77, 6040–46). Messengers are sent ahead to announce his arrival. Although Blancheflor joyously receives the news and dons her finest attire, she is subdued when she meets him (vv. 6378–87). In the now almost obligatory bed scene, Blancheflor arrives undressed in her chemise and mantel, and the boy takes her into his arms and kisses her, but Gerbert explicitly says that he does not take the "rest" ("du sorplus n'i ot il point," vv. 6551–61). After the wedding ceremonies and the blessing of the nuptial chamber, the young couple once again find themselves together in bed (vv. 6809–13). Although the two are not unaffected by desire, Perceval has previously announced that his union will be chaste

(vv. 6040–52), and Blancheflor yields to the requirement of virginity (vv. 6822–35). They pray to Jesus to keep them pure.

Perceval's marriage vows, *hélas,* no more prevent him from abandoning his bride the following morning than his other promises did. Assigning Gornemans as *bailli* of Blancheflor and her lands, Perceval asks for his arms and horse. Because she had hoped to live with him in peace "as a *preudom* does with his wife," the heroine nearly dies of grief when she hears the familiar words (vv. 6970–79). This is, in fact, her narrative death; at this point, Gerbert evokes the death of Chrétien and never mentions Blancheflor's name again.

Gerbert's penchant for passive heroines is reinforced in the *Violette.* Throughout the romance, Eurïaut's actions are subordinated to those of her lover, Gerart. It is he who vaunts Eurïaut's beauty, suffers disinheritance through Lisïart's treachery, learns of her innocence by investigation, searches for her near and far (while at the same time enjoying chivalric and amorous adventures), rescues her from the stake, excels at the tournament, exacts justice from the villain, and finally arranges for the marriage. Although often inspired by her memory as a *fin'amant,* Gerart, not Eurïaut, is the dominant figure in Gerbert's *Violette.* In contrast, Eurïaut's chief role was to defend her fidelity to her lover. She resists Lisïart's advances, the duke of Metz's proposal of marriage, and Melïatir's brutal rape. At moments of crisis, religion is her principal succor. At Lisïart's calumny, she calls upon Saint Mary and God's body (vv. 972–77); a chapel at Metz offers her the solace of prayer (vv. 3845–47); at the stake she pronounces her long confession of faith, concluding with a Pater Noster (vv. 5182–5332). On occasion, her passive resistance rises to more direct deeds. When Gerart leads her into the forest to kill her, she alerts him to a menacing dragon, saving his life (vv. 1041–84). Melïatir is repulsed with the loss of teeth (vv. 3977–84). She offers to undergo the ordeal to clear herself of the charges of murder (vv. 5477–78). At the reunion of the lovers at Metz, it is she who, with inner torment, takes the first step, falls on her knees, and begs forgiveness (vv. 5661–72). Yet despite these bursts of action, as well as her beauty and her talents as a singer, Eurïaut remains the nearly abject pawn of men, just as Blancheflor suffers Perceval's comings and goings.

Jean Renart's principal heroines are markedly more enterprising. Aelis exercises virtual parity with Guillaume throughout the *Escoufle,* emblematized by their common birthday.[43] When Guillaume is moved into the imperial nursery at age three, they are raised as brother and sister. Each is taught comparable skills for the court. Guillaume's coaching in conversation, games, swordplay, and horsemanship is matched by Aelis's lessons in singing, recounting stories, and embroidery (vv. 2018–75). When opposition to their eventual marriage emerges at age twelve, they both come to the decision to elope (vv. 3548–57). From the children's nursery to the end of the romance, Jean's audiences would have found it difficult to detect differences in the quality and intensity of their youthful ardor. Guillaume's confession of the kisses and caresses he has lavished on Aelis is paralleled by the girl's own reveries of her lover's hands on her stomach and thighs. By switching scenes from one to the other, Jean allots equal time to the pair in their search for each other during the succeeding seven years.

The chief asymmetry is the vast superiority of Aelis's imperial lineage to Guillaume's comital family, but the girl resolves the conflict within her heart in a rhetorical debate between *sens* and *amors* (vv. 3906–63). After their separation by the buzzard, Guillaume supports himself in the hotel trade, and Aelis employs her ingenuity to keep searching with Ysabel, her companion. When her money runs out, she moves to Montpellier, where she combines her embroidery skills with Ysabel's expertise to set up an atelier. The success of their enterprise permits the girls to enlist the lady of the town among their customers. This wins them access to the highest circles of the nobility and transfers them to Saint-Gilles, where Aelis shares the amenities of the *chambre aux dames* with the philandering count. This familiarity apparently does not diminish her love for Guillaume, because at their reunion it is she who first recognizes him. Struggling again between *sens* and *amors,* she finally breaks loose at the sound of her name and throws her arms around his neck (vv. 7548–64, 7680–93). Thereafter Aelis's personality recedes. Countess of Normandy through her marriage to Guillaume, she becomes the empress of Rome when her father dies three years later and reciprocally bestows the emperorship on her husband. At the end of the coronation services, Guillaume and Aelis are pictured bestowing gifts on their knights and maidens respectively. Jean concludes: "These two, who possessed every goodness, held the imperial honor all their lives" (vv. 9046–47). Both Gerbert and Jean tell stories about separated lovers in mutual search for each other. Whereas Gerart's efforts largely surpass those of Eurïaut, Aelis's actions are accorded virtual equality with Guillaume's.

Jean's bele Lïenor is the most independent of the heroines under consideration and one of the striking female personages of the romance genre
up to that date. Without doubt, the maiden outshines the male protagonists
of the romance itself. Her brother Guillaume de Dole takes advantage of
the tournament at Saint-Trond to display his prowess and thereby demonstrate that his lowly family is worthy of a marriage to the emperor, but
at no time does he fall in love. When his family ambitions are frustrated by
Lïenor's alleged scandal, his reactions are withdrawal and tears. The male
lover in this "story of arms and love" is the emperor Conrad, but Jean reduces him to a literary convention. Conrad is introduced to the audience at
the spring hunt as a young man whose wandering heart inhibits commit-
ment to any one woman. When he is smitten by Juglet's conventional portrait of Lïenor's beauty, he follows the troubadour tradition of *amor de
lonh*, exemplified by Jaufré Rudel's classic lyric "Lors que li jor sont lonc
en mai," which Jean includes in his repertory (*Rose* vv. 1301–7). His passion for a woman whom he has never seen is nourished merely by hearsay.
When he is deprived of his love by the seneschal, he too becomes a helpless troubadour lover, further isolated by his high estate. His love symptoms alternate between joy and grief, stereotypically those of the trouvère
grands chants, which the emperor sings throughout the romance.[44]

In contrast, Lïenor's resolve and effectiveness raise her above the surrounding males. From the outset, Jean endows her with ambition. When
Guillaume detaches the imperial gold seal from the letter summoning him
to court and bestows it upon his sister as a broach, she scrutinizes the image
of the armed king on horseback and exclaims to her mother, "I should be
certainly happy now that I have a king in my household" (*Rose* vv.
1002–8). Although she cannot know why her brother has been summoned,
she has already intuited consequences for herself. This family ambition is
shared by her mother, who urges her son to depart quickly (vv. 1023–25)
and to take care of his appearance, so that no one can accuse him of poverty (vv. 1084–88). When she falls victim to the seneschal's ruse and reveals the rose on Lïenor's thigh, her indiscretion is as attributable to family
ambition as to greed (vv. 3340–61).

Lïenor's refusal to submit to the disaster of the calumny contrasts markedly with the response of her brother and emperor. "Before the end of April, which approaches, dear mother, I shall have completely uncovered his
villainy and deception" (vv. 4026–29). Calling upon the Holy Spirit, she
coolly calculates how to counter the seneschal's trick. She enlists the aid of

two vavasors, carefully selects her wardrobe, and engages lodgings at Mainz. Her entrapment of the seneschal has elicited admiration from modern critics.[45] Through forged letters, she induces the seneschal to wear compromising evidence. His verbal deceit and games are now matched by hers; his body violated as was hers; the belt around his naked waist responds to the *ensaigne* of the rose on her thigh. Lïenor's procession through Mainz and arrival at the imperial palace is pure theater, rivaling Marie de France's *Lai de Lanval*. She chooses her gown to accentuate her décolleté, which she manipulates as she rides through the crowds. Her luxuriant hair cascades to her shoulders as she removes her mantel. Her astounding beauty and sincere plea before the emperor elicit the sympathy of the onlookers. When the seneschal is cleared by the ordeal, she snatches the victory with the avowal: "Je suis la pucele a la rose," by which she both identifies and exonerates herself (v. 5040).

Throughout this high drama, Jean has dropped no hint of Lïenor's love for Conrad. She expresses feelings toward her mother and brother but not the emperor. Only on the nuptial evening, after the coronation has been completed and she has assured her imperial status, does Jean turn to her love and this indirectly:

> Je ne vos ai mie conté
> quel siecle li rois ot la nuit.
> Se nus hom puet avoir deduit
> a tenir s'amie embraciee
> en biau lit, la nuit anuitiee,
> donc pot on bien savoir qu'il l'eut.
> Quant Tristans ama plus Yseut
> et il s'en pot miex aaisier
> et d'acoler et de baisier
> et dou sorplus qu'il i convint,
> et Lanvax, et autretex .xx.
> amant com cil orent esté,
> ce sachiez vos de verité,
> ne peüst on aparellier
> lor siecle a cestui de legier.

> I have not told you / what pleasure the king had that night. / If any man can have delight / to hold his *amie* in his embrace / in a fine bed the whole night, / then one can be sure that he had

it. / When Tristan loved Iseut the most / and he could best take
his ease / to embrace and kiss her / and the *sorplus* that was
appropriate, / and Lanval, and twenty other / lovers could do
the same, / then you truly know / that one cannot compare /
their happiness to this one very easily. (vv. 5501–15)

By evoking the legendary loves of Tristan and Lanval and assuming that
their *amies*, Iseut and the fabulous lady, reciprocated, Jean only suggests
Lïenor's response to Conrad. The next morning, Lïenor remains fully in
command. The seneschal's friends negotiate the villain's fate with her; he
is forced to thank her personally in tears for sparing his life and banishing
him from the realm. So forceful is the heroine's character that a modern
critic has proposed renaming Jean's work the "Roman de Lïenor."[46]

How Jean's and Gerbert's historical audiences heard or read these four
romance heroines is open to speculation. Baudouin de Hainaut, Milon de
Nanteuil, and their retinues were provided with an abundance of objects
for male desire, but of differing character. How would they have distinguished among the teasing of a Blancheflor, the passive fidelity of an Euriaut, the equality of an Aelis, or the taking charge of a Lïenor? No chronological progression can be perceived among the possibilities; nor are the
traces of influence between Jean and Gerbert or between the latter and
their predecessors clear. Chrétien's invention of Blancheflor's equivocal
entry into Perceval's bed may have been a popular motif, because his con-
tinuators—even Gerbert, for whom its inclusion might have subverted
spiritual marriage and the hero's devotion to the Grail—did not omit the
scene. With the possible exception of Perceval's peculiar solution, all the
male heroes are apparently satisfied both with their brides and with the institution of matrimony. We have seen that resolution must have especially
pleased Baudouin de Hainaut, whose court chronicler informs us that his
marriage to Marie de Champagne took place at the ages of fourteen and
twelve respectively, making it comparable to the youthful expectations of
Guillaume and Aelis. Moreover, the chronicler continues, unlike the philandering of his father and grandfather, Baudouin loved his wife chastely
and spurned all other women.[47]

The response to the four heroines by the females in the audience is
equally problematic. Blancheflor's repeated weeping suggests that she is
less than satisfied with Perceval's habitual elusiveness, but she does not re-
bel. The remaining heroines indicate little discontent with their lovers or

marriages. As modern critics warn, however, the idealization of female figures can pose more insidious traps for a feminine audience than vilification, because the heroines are thereby controlled and manipulated.[48] If the response of historical women in the Middle Ages to these figures escapes us, we do possess a single clue to the expectation of one author toward a designated woman in his audience. Gerbert de Montreuil makes it clear that Eurïaut's faith in and loyalty to ("vo fois et vo loiautés," *Violette* v. 6625) Gerart exemplifies Countess Marie de Ponthieu's identical virtues ("sa fois et sa loiautés," v. 6647) when she endured similar disinheritance by the king.[49] Eurïaut's fidelity could thus provide moral instruction for a female audience.

SIX

Embellishments

*Festivities, Entertainment,
Food, and Clothing*

Des armes a parler vos les,
qu'il fet mellor a la vïande.

I shall let you talk about arms,
for I would rather speak of food.
(*Rose* vv. 2142–43)

WITH this couplet Jean Renart switches from the tournament at
Saint-Trond to the subsequent festivities. "Now it would be
good to hear about the dishes for dinner," he observes a few
lines earlier (vv. 2138–39). Turning from the grave matters of prowess and
fighting, he takes evident delight in expatiating upon food and banqueting.
While the latter may appear frivolous to the modern reader, they were of
great importance to writers of romance as embellishments that valorized
aristocratic life and distinguished it from the rest of society.

car aussi com l'en met la graine
es draps por avoir los et pris,
einsi a il chans et son mis
en cestui *Romans de la rose,*
qui est une novele chose
et s'est des autres si divers
et brodez, par lieus, de biaus vers
que vilains nel porroit savoir.

For just as one places red dye / in cloth to increase its value, /
thus he [Jean] has added poems and melodies / to this *Roman de
la rose.* / It is such a novelty / and the interspersed embroidery

of beautiful verse / is so different from other works / that villeins will not be able to understand it. (vv. 8–15)

This opening passage in the *Rose* announces that Jean is indeed proud of the embellishments that make his romance fit for aristocratic ears. To introduce the novelty of inserting lyric verse, as we have seen, he evokes still another embellishment, that of dyeing fine cloth crimson red. Vernacular authors had long furnished their romances with lavish descriptions of the particular luxuries separating the refined lifestyle of their audiences from that of peasants. These amenities included not only dress—as suggested by the brilliant cloth—but festive occasions, entertainment, and food as well. I shall begin with the general and proceed to the particular.

Festivities

Previous romances had fully accustomed Jean's and Gerbert's audiences to elaborate depictions of high festivities. These consisted mainly of coronations, weddings, the making of new knights, tournaments, and the arrivals and receptions of important personages. Often these occasions coincided with the annual round of ecclesiastical high holidays, Christmas, Easter, and Pentecost; at times, the holy days themselves were sufficient excuse to hold court and celebrate. We have had ample opportunity to notice that in his first romance, Chrétien de Troyes, for example, features Erec's wedding at Pentecost and later his coronation at Christmas, held at Nantes in Brittany. Both occasions are sponsored by King Arthur and accompanied with spectacular gifts to participants. Lasting two weeks, the first is preceded by the knighting of a hundred new knights, followed by sumptuous entertainment, feasting, and a tournament (*Erec* vv. 1870–2078). The second repeats the dubbing of new knights—this time four hundred—and concludes with a regal banquet (vv. 6490–6878). Apparently, Chrétien exhausted his descriptive energies on these two festivities, because thereafter he explicitly declines to provide details of similar occasions. Of Alexandre and Soredamor's wedding at Windsor, for example, he asserts that no one could express the riches and food, the joys and pleasures without falling short of the truth. In any event, he will not waste words trying to do so (*Cligès* vv. 2316–22). Alis's wedding feast at Constantinople (vv. 3203–5) and Arthur's banquet following the tournament at Wallingford (vv. 4982–84) are treated with the same brevity, and so are

Yvain's wedding to Laudine in the *Lion* (vv. 2161–65) and the reception of Perceval by Gornemans in the *Graal* (vv. 1566–69). At Laudine's reception of Arthur, however, Chrétien does pause to evoke the festooning of the city and the popular entertainment. Silken cloths decorate the façades of the houses, and tapestries are spread across the pavements. Trumpets resound, girls dance, and acrobats perform (*Lion* vv. 2342–58).

The contemporary Latin writers who chronicled highborn careers could not ignore these occasions, which punctuated the lives of their patrons, but in stark contrast to the vernacular and fictive accounts, they studiously avoid the illuminating details. Among the royal French historiographers, for example, Rigord's attention to Philip Augustus's coronation is limited to the crowning itself and the acclamation by those assembled, both rituals performed inside the cathedral of Reims. A subsequent banquet can only be inferred from other chroniclers.[1] At the coronation and the nuptial blessing of Queen Isabelle of Hainaut on Ascension Day a year later, Rigord again notices only the events that unfolded inside the abbey of Saint-Denis.[2] When King John of England conceded a treaty favorable to the Capetians in 1200, he paid a visit to Paris the next year, where, according to Rigord, he was received with *mirabili reverentia et honore*. The royal chronicler dilates on this reception by noting solemn processions at Saint-Denis, an abundance of all kinds of wine at the royal palace, and a profusion of gifts. Aside from the implied drinking of wine, no mention is made of the kind of festivities that have since made French hospitality renowned.[3]

We have seen that the festive highpoint of Philip's reign occurred at Compiègne on Pentecost in 1209, when Prince Louis, the royal heir, was knighted. The royal historiographer Guillaume le Breton reports "that Louis, the firstborn son of King Philip, put on the belt of knighthood from the hand of his father with such solemnity and in the presence of the assembly of the magnates of the realm and of the multitude of men and accompanied with such a generous abundance of food and gifts as was never seen or read of before that day." Roger of Wendover adds that a hundred other nobles were knighted with him, as at Erec's wedding. The Anonymous of Béthune, writing in the vernacular, identifies the high barons who served at the subsequent banquet. Despite Guillaume's superlative language, echoing romance rhetoric, neither he nor other contemporary chroniclers divulge details of the festivities, which were doubtless splendid.[4]

Compare now Jean's account in the *Escoufle* when the hero, Guillaume, is made a new knight by his cousin, the count of Saint-Gilles. The count begins to amass the requisite wealth and goods for the event and summons all vassals who hold land from him and desire to be dubbed in honor of the count (vv. 7885–99). Then Jean interposes his own voice:

> Why should I prolong the matter? In two weeks Guillaume was made a knight. The count gladly created him and thirty others for the love of him. Why should I recount the joy, the festivities, and the honor? Since the great city of Troy was burned down, never were there so many high ladies and worthy maidens assembled for the making of a knight. The belle Aelis offered riches of value. There was not a lady or maiden, I believe, to whom she did not give jewels, belts, rings, and clasps before they took leave. Guillaume enriched his friends even more. . . . By gifts of furs, he enlisted into his household around him those who became knights because of his honor and nobility. (vv. 7900–7923)

The Latin chroniclers share a penchant for superlatives with the vernacular romances and allude to written precedent, but in practice they exercise the brevity that Jean only professes, following Chrétien's example. Despite these protestations, the romancier could not resist the temptation to embellish the whole event, culminating in Guillaume and Aelis's largesse. In contrast, Guillaume le Breton characterizes Philip Augustus's gifts in three words: "largiflua . . . donorum abundantia."

In the Capetian record, Philip's festive occasions consist of the coronation, Isabelle's wedding, King John's reception, and Louis's knighting. Composing for audiences conditioned by Chrétien and others, however, Jean and Gerbert delight in signaling any occasion calling for "la joie, la feste et l'onnor" (*Escoufle* v. 7906).[5] Unlike knightings, coronations and weddings were political and familial events that normally occurred only once in a lifetime. (Philip's second legitimate marriage to the Danish princess Ingeborg was so disastrous that it effaced all excuse for celebration.) Among the romances, the *Escoufle* achieves its dramatic climax at the imperial coronation of Aelis and Guillaume in Rome on Pentecost, accompanied by a fortnight of festivities (vv. 8768–9045); their marriage has been performed previously at Rouen, accompanied by an equally *grant feste* (vv. 8234–8351). In the *Rose*, however, the emperor Conrad is too impatient to await the approaching feast day of Ascension to marry his beloved. Their hastily arranged nuptials at Mainz fulfill the dual service of the empress's marriage and coronation, like Philip's wedding to Isabelle at Saint-Denis, but Jean does not omit the appropriate banquet (*Rose* vv. 5301–5634). In addition to the monarchs, the two romanciers celebrate the weddings of Count Richard de Montivilliers to the lady of Genoa (*Escoufle* vv. 1704–52), of Count Gerart de Nevers to Euriaut at Montargis on Pentecost (*Violette* vv. 6572–96), and of the knight Perceval to the lady Blancheflor at Beaurepaire (*Continuation* vv. 6633–6808), all accompanied by a plethora of entertainment.

No record has survived of Philip Augustus's attendance at tournaments, but those in Jean's and Gerbert's romances at Saint-Trond, Montargis, and Lancien provide occasions for extended celebrations in the towns, as well as knightly exercises on the field. The Capetian is never portrayed on the hunt by his historiographers. Philip almost lost his life in a hunting mishap in the forest of Compiègne shortly before his coronation.[6] Doubtless this trauma removed all taste for the sport. Jean's opening scene in the *Rose* shows Conrad chasing ladies rather than deer, followed by lunching, singing, and dancing (*Rose* vv. 136–572).

Count Richard's entry into Jerusalem (*Escoufle* vv. 532–778) and Benevento (vv. 1366–1473) prompts joyous receptions by the people, as does his son Guillaume's into Arques (vv. 8081–8227) and finally Rome (vv. 8768–9047). Count Gerart is similarly greeted when he brings his bride back to Nevers (*Violette* vv. 6597–6633), and on his return to Beaurepaire to marry Blancheflor, Perceval receives no less of a reception (*Continuation* vv. 6308–6808).

Each year the citizens of Mainz leave the city at midnight on the first of May to bring in the May tree, flowers, boughs, and greenery in the morning, accompanied by singing, dancing and minstrels (*Rose* vv. 4147–63, 4559–60). King Louis summons his barons to his court at Pont de l'Arche at Easter, where they amuse themselves with eating, dancing, and singing the lyrics that Gerbert anthologizes (*Violette* vv. 78–103). On these occasions, the cities are appropriately festooned, as when Laudine's subjects decorate their streets to welcome Arthur. Among the five or more examples included in the romances, Aelis and Guillaume's reception at Rome is perhaps the most spectacular: "All of the city was strewn with gladioli, rushes, and mint. It is needless to ask how kings could pay such a price. Under the cortege and their horses, the streets were lined and carpeted with all kinds of silks, satins, and taffetas. From the churches the carillons rang forth the feast day of the lady" (*Escoufle* vv. 8836–44).

The modest knight Perceval is similarly welcomed at Beaurepaire: "[Blancheflor's] people did not wait, but adorned their streets and curtained them with silk and satin. So much wealth was displayed at the window that it seemed like an earthly paradise. Carpets were spread on the ground without regard to their harm. . . . The noise of drums and bells was so loud that the city shook" (*Continuation* vv. 6308–40). At Jerusalem, the humble people greet the crusader Richard by spreading greenery before their doorways. "The wealthy paved the chief streets with satin, cloth of silk, woven with chains and embroidered with gold, rich and costly. . . . Never since the time of Pierre the hermit was a French knight so honored in the city of Jerusalem" (*Escoufle* vv. 540–53).

It is possible that the festivities welcoming King John at Paris were, in fact, not comparable, but whatever the actuality, Rigord's phrase "cum mirabili reverentia et honore a civibus receptum" does not measure up to the specificity of the vernacular accounts. Of course, much was formulaic, but it appears that aristocratic audiences never tired of the repetition. Most strikingly, the romanciers attend to the details of entertainment, food, and clothing, which are totally missing from the Latin accounts.

Entertainments

As we have seen in connection with jongleurs, these public festivities provided the stage for professional entertainers. In the paradigmatic account of Erec's wedding, Chrétien observes: "When the court was fully assembled, there was not a minstrel in the land who knew any kind of entertainment who was not present. There was joy in the hall, with each performing that which he knew: some leaped, others tumbled, others performed magic, some whistled, others sang, some played the flute, others the reed pipe, some fiddled and others played the *vïele*. Maidens circled and danced" (*Erec* vv. 1983–93).

Of the many descriptions of entertainment in Jean's and Gerbert's romances, that of the imperial coronation is given the fullest treatment: "Great noise was made by the instruments and merrymaking in the palace. In more than seven or eight places, one played at chess and *tables*. Some sang songs, some told stories, others played at dice. . . . Girls put their efforts into dancing their rounds; wherever one went, one found a hundred kinds of pleasures. Across the courts greyhounds pursued boars, bears, and wolves. These festivities lasted for a full two weeks" (*Escoufle* vv. 8990–9007). And to leave little doubt about the role of professionals, Jean interpolates: "Jongleurs paraded about with their robes of silk fringed with ermine. No expense was spared to honor the lord of this day" (vv. 8996–99). In Jean's and Gerbert's pages, the variety of entertainments is expanded. Bear- and boar-baiting occur at Count Richard's wedding (vv. 1710–11). At the tournaments of Saint-Trond and Montargis, minstrels keep up such a din with their *vïeles,* flutes, and other instruments that Jean protests that God's thunder could not be heard above them (*Rose* vv. 2348–51).[7] Perceval's wedding at Beaurepaire affords Gerbert comparable opportunity to expand on the variety of entertainers: "After [dinner] they went to dance; jongleurs sang, fiddled, and played their harps and pipes; each according to his turn came forward to show his skill. Raconteurs told beautiful tales before ladies and noblemen; when they had performed enough, the minstrels were well rewarded" (*Continuation* vv. 6702–10).

Throughout the *Rose,* the eponymous Juglet earns his keep by telling stories, singing songs, and playing the *vïele.*[8] In the *Violette* and the *Continuation,* Gerbert introduces unnamed jongleurs who play "sons et notes et conduis" on their *vïeles* at dinners (*Violette* vv. 3089–90) and weddings (*Violette* v. 6584; *Continuation* vv. 6687–88). The *vïele* is their principal instrument, but others are noted as well.[9] The guests at Erec's wedding (*Erec* vv. 1988–2000) hear the ubiquitous bowed instruments (fiddle [*vïele*] and gigue [*gigue*]) and a variety of wind instruments: the flute (*freteles*), the trumpet (*busines*), the reed pipe (*chalemeles*), the panpipe (*estives*), and the bagpipe (*muses*), as well as percussion instruments, the drum (*tabor*) and the tambourine (*timbre*). At Laudine's wedding, bells (*sain*), horns (*cor*), and trumpets (*busines*) resound so loudly through the castle that they too drown out God's thunder (*Lion* vv. 2350–52).[10] At Count Richard's wedding, the procession to church is accompanied by hurdy-gurdies (*symphonies*), rotes (*rotes*), psalteries (*sautier*), harps (*harpes*), flutes (*fleuhutes*), and fiddles (*Escoufle* vv. 1732–33). Describing King Marc's tournament at Lancien, which Tristan and a company of Arthur's knights attend disguised as minstrels, Gerbert provides an inventory comparable to Chrétien's at Erec's wedding. Tristan carries a *vïele,* slung from his neck (*Continuation* vv. 3828, 3881) and others have *estrument divers,* including other string instruments, such as the harp, psaltery, and hurdy-gurdy, wind instruments, such as the horn, flute, reed pipe (*calemel*), Cornish pipe (*estive de Cornuaille*), and bagpipe (*pipe a forrel*), and a drum (vv. 3823–28).[11] Marc hires them on the spot (vv. 3912–17). For his part, Tristan gains access to Iseut by sweetly playing the *lai de chievrefueil* on a flute (vv. 4066–70).

That Arthur's knights were able to pass themselves off as professional musicians raises the question of whether the aristocracy possessed the skills and inclination to play instruments in public. Gerbert appears to be asserting that the knights are accomplished players, because they are able to persuade Marc that they are minstrels. Those among the audience who remembered the Tristan legend would have known that the hero's courtly training had rendered him proficient with musical instruments. In the *Violette*, Gerbert likewise has Count Gerart disguised as a jongleur, and he accompanies himself on the *vïele* as he sings a chanson de geste at Lisïart's table (vv. 1379–1429). Jean Renart never depicts a nobleman with a fiddle or any other instrument in his hand,[12] however, and Gerbert limits his examples to knights in disguise. Unlike the aristocracy of southern France, therefore, those of the north did not permit themselves to be seen in public with musical instruments.

Singing, however, was different. Although none of Chrétien's knights or ladies break forth in song, Jean and Gerbert represent singing as a talent cultivated and exercised in public by the entire aristocracy. Both Aelis and Guillaume are instructed in this courtly skill in the imperial nursery (*Escoufle* vv. 2030, 2058). Of the eighty *chants* anthologized in the *Rose* and the *Violette*, a few are performed by jongleurs, but most are sung by the principal characters, including the emperor, counts, demoiselles, knights, and *vallets*. Many of the performers are young, as suggested by the terms *bachelers*, *damoiseau*, and *pucele*, and women figure prominently among them.[13] In the *Rose*, as we have seen, Lïenor and her mother are observed singing *chansons de toile* as they go about their needlework. Jean assigns singing parts to other women too, particularly at the spring hunt that opens his romance, but as it progresses, Conrad, Juglet, and other men take over the singing. In the *Violette*, however, Gerbert divides the music more evenly between the sexes. When the romance opens at the royal court at Pont de l'Arche, the company are entertained by seven noble ladies, including the duchess of Burgundy and the countess of Besançon, as well as sisters of the counts of Blois and Saint-Pol. Eurïaut is given opportunity to sing three songs. Featured maidens, such as Aigline, Marote, Aiglente, Flourentine, and the demoiselle des Illes Pertes, perform as well.

Telling of stories accompanied singing at public festivities. Chrétien opens his *Lion* with a scene from Arthur's Pentecost court at Carduel, where knights, ladies, and maidens amuse themselves with tales of love (vv. 8–17). Aelis knows how to tell stories of adventure (*Escoufle* vv.

2058–59); her shop at Montpellier is renowned for both the recitation of romances and the singing of songs (vv. 5525, 5818). The revelers on the spring hunt likewise recite love songs and fine stories (*Rose* v. 229). As a jongleur, Gerart de Nevers offers a musical performance of the chanson de geste "Guillaume au court nes" (*Violette* v. 1405). After the adventure of the perilous seat at Arthur's court at Carlion, the assembled company tell stories and other frivolities, while Perceval withdraws to reflect upon his solemn quest (*Continuation* vv. 1615–18).

The profusion of vocal and instrumental music naturally encourages dancing. Erec's wedding finds the maidens dancing and performing *caroles*, "each competing with the other to show their joy" (vv. 1993–94).[14] In the *Escoufle*, girls perform *caroles* in the imperial nursery (v. 2829), at the emperor's court (v. 3798), at the reunion of the lovers (v. 7767), and finally at the celebrations in Rome (vv. 9000–9001). Tournaments (*Rose* v. 2364), receptions (*Continuation* vv. 6091, 6412–17), and especially weddings (*Violette* v. 6587; *Continuation* vv. 1959, 6702) provide other occasions. At Perceval and Blancheflor's nuptials, ladies and maidens dance in more than thirty or forty places (*Continuation* vv. 6412–17). The normal phrase to indicate this entertainment is "a danser et a caroler" (*Escoufle* v. 9001), without a clear distinction being made between the terms. Most often the performers are girls and women, but occasionally they are joined by boys and knights (*Rose* v. 509; *Violette* v. 97). The music is usually limited to singing, although instruments accompany the dancers at wedding festivities (*Erec* vv. 1988–2000; *Continuation* vv. 6702–4). At Ysmaine's wedding, "some go singing, while others dance . . . *rotruengues* and *chansonetes*" (vv. 1958–63). At Gornemans's castle, they rejoice, sing and dance (*Continuation* v. 6090).

Jean's and Gerbert's scenes of the aristocratic *carole* illuminate the dancing procedures and introduce the musical repertory. After dinner is finished on the spring hunt, the ladies and emperor's companions exit the tent to a meadow, where the maidens and *vallets* remove their coats and begin to *carole* hand in hand. The music is sung by a lady dressed in crimson, the *vallet* of the provost of Spire, the son of the count of Dabo, and the duchess of Austria, and lasts until time for bed (*Rose* vv. 505–50). At the Capetian court at Pont de l'Arche, the king invites all those assembled to dance after dinner. The ladies return from dressing to select a knight and begin the festivities. Once again, the music is supplied by seven singers, all of the high nobility and, on this occasion, all women. Each partner takes the other by the hand, and they proceed as couples. The king arises and begins to sing as he takes the first steps (vv. 92–159).

Evidently, the dancers always held hands, at times arranging themselves in a circle, as suggested by the *Rose,* and at other times, marching two by two in procession, as in the *Violette.*[15] Jean's lyrics further suggest that the steps were accompanied by arm movements (*Rose* vv. 326, 517). Named "de Robin . . . d'Aaliz" (v. 548), the four songs recorded in the *Rose* constituted the earliest repertory of the *chanson de carole;* later they were associated with the rondeau. Since Gerbert's seven examples include only the opening lines, they are more difficult to identify (his term for them is *cancho* or *chançon*). In all likelihood, aristocrats also danced to songs other than the dance rondeaus.

Among the distractions offered to the Roman populace at the coronation are games. In seven or eight places, people play chess and *tables,* while others play games of chance (*Escoufle* vv. 8992–95). In the romances, however, these amusements are limited to the aristocratic maidens and knights; Chrétien's scene in a pleasant meadow offers a paradigm. Some play at *tables,* chess, and games of chance (*dez, mine*); others indulge in childhood rounds (*baules*), reels (*quaroles*), and dancing, singing, tumbling, and leaping; still others wrestle (*Charrete* vv. 1634–38). The trilogy of chess (*eches*), *tables* (a form of backgammon or *trictrac*), and dice (*dez* and similar games of chance, *san, la mine*) becomes canonical in Jean's and Gerbert's romances. Jean's knights and ladies imitate Chrétien's on the spring hunt (*Rose* vv. 498–503); the same amusements are provided at Jerusalem (*Escoufle* v. 762) and in Cologne (*Violette* vv. 3223–24). Contrary to their custom, the army of the Franks refrain from the pleasures of chess and *tables* on the eve of the battle with the Turks (*Escoufle* vv. 870–73 f.). As the paragon of all courtiers, Tristan is well instructed in chess, *tables,* and dice (*Continuation* vv. 3705–6).[16] Competing with this legendary figure, Jean has Guillaume de Montivilliers attain these skills by the age of ten: "He had a master who taught him the martial arts . . . and knew well how to hold an agreeable conversation and also play at dice, chess, and games [*de gius partis*], in which he was most expert" (*Escoufle* vv. 2027–29). Aelis offers the same diversions to knights, ladies, and clerics at her shop in Montpellier (vv. 5526–27), but they could be enjoyed in privacy as well. When Lïenor's mother summons her knights to receive the emperor's seneschal, she finds them playing chess with the priest at Dole (*Rose* vv. 3300–3303). Among the many scenes, Jean offers the closest

glimpse of these amusements after dinner on the spring hunt. While minstrels play their instruments and the young people dance, "some went to
play at *tables;* three knights return to dice to test their luck [*as des au ha-
ʒart*]—which extended to 6 deniers a throw—while still others sat down
either to chess or other games of chance" (*Rose* vv. 498–503).

Jean and Gerbert do not need to explain the rules of these games, because their audiences were familiar with them. Chess was played on a lined
board (*eschiquier*) with pieces and rules comparable to the modern version.
Tables covered a series of games likewise played on a diagrammed board
with pieces and perhaps dice; eventually it evolved into the English backgammon and the French *trictrac*. Dice was apparently played with more
than one cube because the plural *deʒ* is employed; the rules may not have
differed greatly from the modern ones. Related games of chance—*la
mine*, for example—lie hidden behind their names.[17]

One diversion, however, led the aristocrats away from the gaming tables, court, and meadow and into the forest. The romanciers take for
granted that hunting wild game is of high priority in noble society. The
pleasures of the woods and streams ("deduit de bois et de riviere," *Lion* v.
2470) entertain the wedding guests of Chrétien's Yvain and Laudine, as
also of Jean's Count Richard (*Escoufle* v. 96). *Bois* stands for the prey of
the forests, *riviere* for that of the streams, the habitat of fowl that could be
hunted with birds of prey.[18] Conrad knows the delights of the birds and
woods (*Rose* vv. 54–55) better than anyone, as does the young Guillaume,
accompanied by Aelis (*Escoufle* v. 2080). Tristan's chivalric upbringing has
taught him the skills of the woods and streams better than any *vilains* or
man of the court (*Continuation* vv. 3707–8). When Tristan is exiled from
the court or Yvain roams the forests as a demented wild man, these skills
furnish food (Béroul vv. 1279–98; *Lion* vv. 2816–28), but for the most part,
Chrétien introduces the aristocratic hunt to launch his knights on a new
adventure. Arthur's renewal of the tradition of hunting the White Stag,
for example, starts Erec on his quest (vv. 35–38), and Jean employs the
spring hunt to get Conrad's entourage into the forest so that the emperor
can prey upon the ladies.

As with games, Jean and Gerbert feel no need to elucidate the hunt, but
because birds play important roles in their romances, they devote more
time to episodes of falconry. Chrétien had already supplied the basic vocabulary of which Jean and Gerbert avail themselves.[19] When Guillaume
applies to the innkeeper at Saint-Gilles for employment, he brags that he

knows dogs and birds better than anyone in France (*Escoufle* vv. 6524–30). This expertise qualifies him to offer his services to the master falconer of the count, who wants to hunt birds by the river but lacks a *vallet* to help with a second hawk (vv. 6682–6847). The falconer is obliged to carry his falcon (*faucons*) on one wrist and a goshawk (*ostoirs*) on the other, the first moulting (*muiers*), the other red (*sors*). Mounting his horse, Guillaume knows immediately on which wrist to take the tamer of the two. Although the youth professes willingness to learn more, his expertise with both the bird and the horse becomes evident. As they approach the river, the well-fed falcons beat their wings in anticipation, but after a full league of hunting, they find neither bird nor duck, although the river had formerly teemed with mallards and herons. With nightfall approaching, the hunters decide to make one last turn through the marshes and fields. Guillaume's falcon stirs, stretches its head, and struggles to see something beyond, but Guillaume calms the bird and keeps it low by his thigh. Not seeing what is agitating the bird, the boy asks the falconer whether he should release him. "If you do not follow quickly after he has downed his prey, you will lose him, because he is eager to fly far," the master replies. Adroitly Guillaume shifts the falcon from one wrist to the other to throw it ahead, releases the jess (*loinge*), opens his fist, and the bird takes off, with Guillaume in close pursuit. The falcon alights upon an *escoufle* (buzzard) devouring a chicken in a field strewn with manure. Although the buzzard takes flight, the falcon brings it down. After Guillaume separates the falcon from its prey, he proceeds to take revenge on the buzzard, which has separated him from Aelis. Furiously tearing the buzzard apart, he devours the heart raw.

Like the buzzard in the *Escoufle,* Gerbert has a lark escape with Euriaut's ring in the *Violette* in conscious replay (vv. 4145–4375). Drugged by Aiglente's love potion, Gerart indulges himself one day in the pleasure of pursuing game and of training his sparrow hawk (*esprevier*) to hunt larks (*aloe*), quail (*quaille*), magpies (*pie*), teals (*cerciele*), and lapwings (*vaniel*). Exiting the main gate of Cologne on his horse with his hawk on his wrist, he rides downstream along the Rhine, where he hears the song of a lark in flight. When the lark folds its wings and comes to rest, Gerart spurs his mount and releases the hawk's jess, which he passes to his companion. Espying the lark afar, the hawk crouches on Gerart's wrist and takes off in a beautiful flight. As the lark arises to flee, the hawk accelerates and catches its prey, holding it in its claws. Gerart gallops up to the pair and quickly dismounts. Allowing the hawk to deplume the lark for a moment and taste its blood, Gerart seizes the two birds, feeds the hawk the lark's head, but then quickly removes the prey. At this point, the hero spies Eurïaut's ring, which breaks the magic spell. His gesticulations are so violent that the sparrow hawk escapes to a bush on the riverbank. Because the bird is well trained, Gerart is nonetheless able to retrieve it and return it to Aiglente as a token that his love remains without baseness, but the hapless girl would have killed the bird on the spot had not her father reproached her for taking revenge on an innocent creature.

The buzzard and the lark play comparable roles in the denouements of the *Escoufle* and the *Violette*. In developing the two climaxes, however, Jean and Gerbert exceed the demands of their narratives to exploit their knowledge of the art of falconry. Setting the scene, assessing the falcons' qualities, following the maneuvers of the masters, and celebrating the captures, the two romanciers surely afforded their audiences the pleasure of recognition of a sport for which they shared a common enthusiasm.[20]

Food

Guillaume le Breton characterizes the banquet at Prince Louis's knighting on Pentecost in two words: *largiflua victualium,* "the generosity of the victuals."[21] This phrase is expanded on in detail by the vernacular romanciers, because eating was one of the distinguishing occupations of the aristocratic court. It has long been recognized that these lengthy descriptions are infused with formulas such as "they had every dish they could want," "they were served to their satisfaction," and "the food was delicious."[22] Following the lead of anthropologists, critics have interpreted such conventions as *codes alimentaires,* or symbolic systems, which were not inscripted to describe food habits but offered as schemes of representation to express the underlying mentalities of contemporary society.[23] But these two readings need not be mutually exclusive. Within different levels of fictional meaning, food can be mentioned both for its own sake and as a metaphor for semiotic, anthropological, or cultural structure.[24] Read within the formulaic framework, these long passages can also reveal much about aristocratic eating that clerical unwillingness in the Latin chronicles to pay undue attention to a bodily function leaves obscure.

Chrétien codifies the conventional framework when he characterizes the Arthurian feasts in terms of their impressive abundance, the care of their preparation, and the astounding variety of their dishes. At Erec's Pentecost feast, for example, the romancier declares that the king was not stingy, but ordered his bakers, cooks, and butlers to provide bread, wine, and venison in such abundance that all could satisfy their desires (*Erec* vv. 2006–14). Before being allowed to observe the Grail at the Fisher King's house, Perceval is served, as first course, a haunch of venison cooked in its fat with hot pepper, along with an abundance of clear wine. It was a repast, Chrétien avers, fit for a count, king, or even an emperor (*Graal* vv. 3280–83, 3315–17). In addition to the generic trinity of "pain et vin et veneison" (bread, wine, and venison) at Arthur's Pentecost feast, fowl such as plover, pheasant, and partridge are offered at Chrétien's meals (*Erec* v. 489; *Graal* v. 7482). Arthur feeds Erec fish, including pike, perch, salmon, and trout on Saturday night, presumably to observe the ecclesiastical regime of fasting (*Erec* vv. 4237–39). At Erec's coronation, thousands of knights serve bread, wine, and other dishes in great abundance. Chrétien assures us that he could tell what those dishes consisted of, but he will not talk about food, because he has other things to say (vv. 6872–78). Obviously, this is an excuse to end the story quickly, because the romance terminates at this point, and Chrétien repeats the excuse to move the narrative along in other romances (*Cligès* vv. 2316–21, 3204; *Graal* vv. 1566–69).[25]

Jean Renart, we have seen, prefers to talk about the food at Saint-Trond. Working within Chrétien's framework, he and Gerbert adopt their predecessor's formulae to convey quantity, quality, and variety, but unlike Chrétien's feigned reluctance, they are eager to give details. Abundance is succinctly conveyed by the frequent use of the terms *plenté* and *assez* (*Escoufle* vv. 1432, 5746; *Rose* vv. 1036–37, 1242; *Violette* v. 494; *Continuation* v. 16658). At Jerusalem, wines and meats circulate in a vast whirlwind ("blowing like straw in the wind"), but Jean is careful to describe each item with a quality. The larded venison, sweetmeats, and bacon (*lardés*) are not rancid; the fresh- and saltwater fish are neither spoiled or sharp. The fish is roasted or steamed like beef (*Escoufle* vv. 706–21). At Saint-Trond, the meats, fowl, and game are those in season; the wine is dry and clear (*Rose* vv. 2336–39). To emphasize the superiority of these meals, Jean has the imperial messenger ironize on a counterfactual meal. The emperor feeds his servants venison that is rotten, boar and deer meat out of season, and patés that are old and moldy, ones that even mice would refuse (vv. 1044–49). Where Chrétien declines to enumerate the variety of courses, both Jean and Gerbert delight in supplying the particulars. Like Chrétien, they tacitly acknowledged the season of fasting, when only fish is offered.

The lady of Montpellier, for example, serves a large fish for supper (*Escoufle* vv. 5746–47), and Gerbert enumerates rockfish (*roches*), pike (*lus*), brochets (*beches*), and *barbiau* in season, which probably coincided with a Church fast, because they are found on a priest's table (*Continuation* vv. 2452–56). Jean's and Gerbert's hosts do not, however, hesitate to include fish along with a variety of meat, venison, and fowl. The river Seine provides Count Richard with fish, and his forests provide venison (*Escoufle* vv. 54–57). Unlike Chrétien, Jean and Gerbert apparently fail to respect the churchmen's distinction between feasting and fasting (the separation of eating meat and fish). A succession of dinners that mix the culinary regimes follow.[26]

Jean, in particular, expands the romance categories of food in his *Rose*. Although Dole is a modest seigneury, Guillaume's family impresses the imperial messenger with a menu that includes milk pudding, suckling pig, good rabbits, larded chicken, pears, and ripe cheeses (vv. 1242–46), to which the messenger reciprocates with good wines and stuffed cakes (*gastelez fourrez*) at Saint-Trond (vv. 1513–15). At Maastricht the emperor's dinner consists of meats, venison, waterfowl, and all kinds of fish, along with good wine (vv. 1976–80). The gastronomic climax is naturally achieved at Lïenor's banquet at Mainz. Jean confesses that it is not easy to render an account of the dishes served, so great was their diversity: boar, bear, and deer, cranes, geese, roast peacock, lamb ragout (it being May), fat beef, and fattened gosling, served up with white and red wine as desired (vv. 5449–58). As Jean approaches the parallel banquet in the *Escoufle*, he adopts Chrétien's excuse about continuing, doubtless for the same reason, to bring the romance to a close (vv. 8980–85). Gerbert is more heavily indebted to Chrétien, however, and the topos appears twice in connection with Perceval's wedding at Beaurepaire (*Continuation* vv. 6449–52, 6696–6701). Gerbert also adopts another device for suggesting the variety of dishes without troubling with the details. To celebrate victory over the Saxons, Duke Milon of Cologne has a meal prepared in the great hall at which more than six courses are served (*Violette* v. 3076). Throughout the *Continuation*, Gerbert repeats the formula, "five or six courses, I do not know" (vv. 1126, 6096, 13143, 15649).

Great feasts on high holidays naturally called for culinary exertion, but similar results, if on a reduced scale, are produced by lesser lords on ordinary occasions. When Erec happens upon a modest vavasor, the latter, at a moment's notice, is able with the aid of only one servant to come up with a supper of meat and fowl, of which the former is both braised and roasted (*Erec* vv. 488–92). The remarkable variety of the kitchen of Dole has already been noticed. Similarly, Euriaut's cook is able to serve roast fowl, venison, and fresh fish in plentiful courses to Lisiart, even though the count of Forez is unwelcome (*Violette* vv. 491–95). And Perceval's first request for hospitality at Cothoatre is satisfied with a roast salted capon (*Continuation* vv. 688–89).

The aristocratic banquet table invariably consisted of boards laid across tressels, quickly assembled and covered with white table cloths. Before eating, guests were always offered water in basins to wash their hands, because, except for knives, fingers served as the utensils. Chrétien evokes this etiquette at the banquet after the tournament of Wallingford (*Cligès* vv. 4970–77) and goes into detail at the great hall of the Fisher King. The water is warm, the boards are ivory, the trestles are ebony, and the table cloth is white enough to satisfy any cardinal or pope (*Graal* vv. 3254–79). These rituals become obligatory throughout Jean's and Gerbert's feasts.[27] At Saint-Trond, knights who have just returned from the field particularly need to wash (*Rose* vv. 1260–63), as do most diners after the meal while the tables were being removed. The emperor, empress, and archbishop wash before the others at Liénor's wedding (*Rose* vv. 5481–84).

On high occasions, banquet service was assigned to the aristocracy according to rank. At Louis's knighting in 1209, the one aspect that caught the attention of the anonymous vernacular chronicler of Béthune was the identity of those who served the dishes. The first were brought in by royal cousins, the counts of Brittany and Dreux; the last by the count of Boulogne. The highest honor was accorded to the count of Auxerre, another royal cousin, who carved the meat before the newly knighted Louis.[28]

Chrétien focuses on the hyperbolic scale and gradation at the banquet following Erec's coronation. Five hundred tables are crowded into five halls; each table is presided over by a king, duke, or count and seats a hundred knights; and a thousand knights in fur-lined livery serve them dishes of food, bread, and wine (*Erec* vv. 6857–74). To rival this display, Jean has a hundred men serve Count Richard with venison and fish each day at Rouen (*Escoufle* vv. 51–59). As at the contemporary Capetian court, certain nobles are designated to perform particular tasks. As nephew of the emperor, Cligès, for example, serves his uncle at the wedding feast in Constantinople (*Cligès* vv. 3225–27), and a *vallet* carves on a silver platter before the guests at the Fisher King's supper (*Graal* vv. 3285–87). Jean's coronation feast at Mainz comes closest to the Capetian ceremony. The emperor and empress are joined by the archbishops, bishops, dukes, and other barons on the dais, and vassals serve them courses according to the rank of their fiefs. To accentuate his disgrace, the seneschal is deprived of the traditional service assigned to his ancestral fiefs; he celebrates the occasion manacled in the donjon (*Rose* vv. 5386–5413).

After the tables are dismantled in the great hall, lordly hospitality continues to provide food and drink before bedtime. The *vallets* of the Fisher King who prepare the beds bring Perceval a great variety of expensive foods—dates, figs, nutmegs, cloves, pomegranates, and confections for desert, Alexandrian gingerbread, pliris, *arcoticum, resontif et stomaticum,* accompanied with sweet wine without honey or pepper, mulberry wine, and clear syrup (*Graal* vv. 3322–32).[29] Although without the exoticism, Jean follows the custom of providing fruit and wine before retiring. When the empress wishes to ingratiate herself with her husband, she has chamberlains serve them in bed with wine and fruit, both raw and cooked (*Escoufle* vv. 2862–64). The count of Saint-Gilles customarily joins the ladies in the *chambre aux dames* to relax by the fire, while his pears and apples are stewing (vv. 7020–97). When the objective is seduction, the quality of wine receives more attention. The insistent demoiselle plies Lancelot with two jars, one of red and the other of strong white (*Charrete* vv. 990–91); Lunette serves Yvain a full jug of wine of good grapes (*Lion* vv. 1048–50); Leander's wife includes a strong wine along with the perch and salmon she serves Perceval; and Gauvain's love tryst is supplied with wine as well as with paté (*Continuation* vv. 11456–57, 13383–84).

Even away from court, the aristocracy's dining is no less sumptuous. When Perceval comes upon the tent of the demoiselle in the forest, he finds ready for his ravenous appetite a keg full of wine, a silver goblet, and three tempting venison patés, laid out on a bed of rushes under a fresh white towel (*Graal* vv. 738–44). Patés or pastries of all sorts are frequent fare for knights and ladies away from court. Jean pays particular attention to Guillaume and Aelis's provisions during their elopement. Each evening they buy meat and fish to make patés. Bottles are filled with cold, light wine, and salt and cakes are folded in a towel. The patés are wrapped and placed in a wallet, along with galettes, cold meat, and roast *geline* (pullet) (*Escoufle* vv. 4260–67, 4296–4305). For their *dejeuner sur l'herbe* near Toul, they cool the wine in a fountain where they wash their hands, spread a coat for a cloth, open the patés, and adroitly carve the *gelines*, separating the meat from the bones. They intersperse morsels with kisses, and neither salt nor pepper could have made the lunch more tasty (*Escoufle* vv. 4428–61). Neither could the dinners and suppers in the forest on the spring hunt have been more sumptuous. The victuals are excellent and wholesome, the Moselle wine clear and cold, the plate all new. Patés of goat meat, lard, and venison of roe, red, and fallow deer are plentiful, and the cheeses from the valley of Clermont are good and rich. There is no summer dish in season that they do not enjoy in abundance. *Vallets* attend to the tables, cloths, and water basins before and after the dinner (*Rose* vv. 343–98). At supper this service is repeated, and the hunters are offered a first course of beef marinated in garlic and verjuice, followed by young geese, gruel, and the best wine (not the kind in which you soak bread) (*Rose* vv. 461–96). Except for a roof, little could distinguish these picnics from court festivities.

Voyage by sea is one form of travel that diminishes aristocratic opulence. On Alexandre's journey from Constantinople to Britain, Chrétien substitutes biscuits for bread but retains the staples of meat and wine (*Cligès* vv. 229–30). When Count Richard sets sail from Brindisi, Jean provisions his ship with sea biscuit and other unspecified food, but substitutes fresh water and *vins cuits* (strong wine, or wine cooked with spices?) for ordinary wine (*Escoufle* vv. 390–92).

By repeatedly inscripting these meals of unsurpassed abundance, quality, and variety, the romance authors construct an alimentary code distinguishing the aristocracy from the rest of society. The nobility eat for pleasure, not merely for survival. They wish to be remembered for their incessant feasts, not for fear of famine. Although bread was a staple of the age, it seldom figures in the romance accounts because of its quotidian banality. Nor are the aristocracy in the romances overly concerned with the dietary regime of fasting imposed by churchmen. The lean days of Wednesday, Friday, Saturday, the vigils of feast days, and the three Lenten seasons are signaled only by an occasional notice of fish eaten alone. More frequently, pike and salmon are interspersed with meat dishes, indicating that the occasion was not a fast day. Without doubt, highest priority is accorded to meat, and especially to venison and game fowl, the goal of the aristocratic hunt. This abundance of meat distinguished the nobility from the peasants, whose diet, beyond the staple of bread, was weighted more heavily toward vegetables. Although not absent, spices receive little notice. Not a necessity, because of the freshness of the meats, these costly items were appreciated more for their taste than for their preservative or corrective powers.[30]

To underscore the abundance of the aristocratic feast, Chrétien introduces a counterexample of famine at the siege of Beaurepaire. The devastation of the countryside by Blancheflor's enemies has brought the mills and ovens to a halt. There are neither bread nor paté, neither wine, cider, nor beer (*Graal* vv. 1772–73). When merchants finally replenish the city's stores from the sea, they bring bread, wine, salted bacon, beef, and pigs for slaughter (*Graal* vv. 2539–41, 2568–73).[31] The crusade apart, Jean's romances by and large take place in peacetime, thus excluding periods of turmoil, except for an occasional siege, but Gerbert elaborates on Chrétien's situations. The inhabitants of the territory of Montesclaire, ravaged by the Dragon Knight, for example, are reduced to eating roots and crab apples (*Continuation* vv. 9082–85). After defeating the enemy, Perceval has the city provisioned with barrels and casks of wine, cattle, sheep, and pigs, thus signaling the restoration of the aristocratic diet.

The starkest contrast to aristocratic abundance is provided by the forest. Following the example of Tristan, who lives by hunting while in exile, Chrétien has the demented and naked (and therefore uncourtly) Yvain feed on the raw flesh of animals he hunts in the wilderness. A hermit takes pity on him and exchanges bread and water, his own fare, for the savage's game. Close to starvation, Yvain devours the bread, although it is made of barley mixed with straw, moldy, and dry as bark (*Lion*, ed. Hult, vv. 2848–51). Thereafter in the romances, the diet of the hermits who dispense hospitality in the forest is the archetypical antithesis to that of the court.[32] In contrast to the aristocratic triad of bread, meat, and wine, the sylvan hermit's food consists of bread, vegetables, and water. In contrast to the nobles' presumably white bread, the hermit's bread is always dark, either of barley or oat flour. Although Chrétien's repast for Perceval is specifically penitential, Gerbert adopts it for all the hermits who receive Perceval throughout the *Continuation*. The first whom the young knight meets provides a supper of spring water, cress, and barley bread, a regime as severe as the bed on which he has slept (vv. 7118–24). At the last hermitage, it is the same: barley bread kneaded with sedge grass, herbs, lettuce, and cress, no claret or other wine, only water from a basin. To this regime is added wild fruit gathered from the woods (vv. 15775–81). Variations consist of roots, wild apples, and acorns gathered in the woods (vv. 10157–82) and juniper berries offered to Gauvain (vv. 13969–71). The one exception to this vegetarian regime is when a hermit catches a young goat. After boiling and roasting it, he and Perceval have plenty of meat, but little bread. Nor do they enjoy pepper or garlic. As usual, they drink from a fountain because there is no beer or wine (vv. 14146–60). Gerbert reinforces the contrast between the alimentary codes in an incident at the hermitage of Elyas Anais, the hermit king. When Perceval arrives, thirteen hermits are attempting to divide a single loaf of bread. They offer the knight a portion, for which he has little appetite. When the maiden who carries the red cross shield arrives, however, she brings two barrels of wine and two rabbit patés wrapped in a cloth, which are refused by the monks, because they never eat flesh or drink wine (vv. 8430–8535).

Aside from assessing the jongleurs' profession, as we have seen, Pierre the Chanter and his fellow theologians take scant notice of aristocratic festivities and entertainments, but they could not ignore the basic human needs of food and clothing. As to the former, the Chanter sets the pattern by proposing a fourfold analysis of food consumption: "Nebuzardan [King Nebuchadnezzar's captain at 2 Kings 25:8], that is, the stomach, has four guards, which consist of what, how much, what sort, and when. Respectively they concern the categories of substance, quantity, quality, and time."[33] Pierre's follower Raoul Ardent dilates this casuistic schema into fourteen extensive chapters on the virtue of *abstinentia*, covering the whole range of human alimentation.

Most clerical discussion sought to prescribe the general principle of moderation to unspecified social groups, but Pierre and Raoul touch upon the aristocratic diet's characteristic variety, abundance, and care of preparation. For the Chanter, "what," or "substance," is a question of kinds of edibles, in particular their taste. Raoul notes the propensity of the great and powerful of the world to reject common foodstuffs in favor of delicious, costly, and rare ones. They choose taste not to satisfy their hunger but their gullets; price, not for the food's cost, but for its costliness and their vainglory; and rarity, not for possession, but for the pride that they alone possess it.[34] To provide a variety of dishes to satisfy just one stomach, hunters scour the land, fowlers the air, and fishermen the sea.[35] Savory foods require more work and take more care to acquire than they furnish in pleasure to those who consume them, unlike the bread and water that nourish numerous monks, recluses, and hermits, who survive even on bitter roots, herbs, and fruits.[36]

The Chanter defines quantity as gorging oneself, converting the stomach into a great sack. Since excessive eating pertained to all levels of society, Raoul does not single out the aristocracy. This vice is attributed to the Sodomites in Scripture, whom the prophet Ezekiel accuses of having had an overabundance of bread (Ezek. 16:49). Food should be consumed like medicine, sufficient to succor life but not too much to harm. Necessity, not fashion, should impose the limits of eating.[37]

When the Chanter turns to quality, he is especially concerned with the care of preparation that pertained above all to the aristocracy. Quality is a question of how food is cooked. By boiling, roasting, or frying? What are the varieties of salt and spices? How is it sliced? Is it served cold, warm, or hot? In elaborating, Raoul distinguishes between foodstuffs that are naturally delicious and those that are unworthy but rendered pleasing to the taste of the gluttonous by the cook's adulteration. With art, great care, and ingenuity, master cooks transform foods by means of a diversity of stuffings, flavors, condiments, mixtures, frying, and roasting.[38] To accommodate the whims of the gluttonous, for example, eggs are prepared in different ways—boiled, fried, or baked in ashes, some soft, others hard.[39]

The temporal category of "when" prohibited eating immediately before or after other meals, at inappropriate hours (during the morning), and too frequently. Raoul specifies that although eating three or four times a day is permissible, an honorable man might restrict himself to once or twice. Once a day was the limit for the Church's fast days, when one should not eat before noon; on all other days, one should not eat before terce (9 A.M.).[40] Such temporal regulations envisaged all levels of society, but Raoul's attention to the time spent at table pertains particularly to aristocratic festivities. Some spend the better part of the day at banquets, thinking that they were born to eat, he complains. They live to eat, whereas they should eat to live. Their god is their belly, the kitchen their temple, the table their altar, the various courses their sacrifices, and the different wines their libations.[41] The category of time, however, could serve to exonerate aristocratic feasting.

The rules of abstinence could be relaxed not only for sickness and old age, however, but also on solemn festive occasions and at the arrival of guests. Since the solemn feasts of the Church are figures of the eternal heavenly solemnities, we are permitted to enjoy their abundance, and the arrival of guests permits not only the relaxation of normal abstinence but even the breaking of mandatory fasts.[42] Although not fully exploited in

Raoul's treatise, these two conditions offered potential accommodation for holding great feasts. If lordly patrons held their celebrations on ecclesiastical feast days, churchmen could not object to the abundance, quality, and variety of food on their tables. Moreover, since participants could be considered guests (*hospites*) of the lordly patron, he could lavish his largesse on them without the deprivations of fast days. Fish and meat could be abundantly served together, as they are in Jean's and Gerbert's romances.

Clothing

Like their food, their clothing distinguished aristocrats from the rest of society. Alongside the alimentary code, an equally distinctive code governed their dress as a social class. Beginning with *Erec et Enide*, Chrétien models aristocratic clothing drawing on the social world he perceived,[43] and his descriptions correspond to the evidence from archaeological and iconographic sources. Textiles and clothing likewise serve Jean as metaphors. The opening verses of the *Rose*, for example, compare the lyric insertions that embellish the text to dyes that increase the value of fine cloth.[44] Jean's appreciation of textiles increases his sensitivity to clothing, but like Chrétien's, his representations of sartorial practice are grounded in the world of fashion of which his audience was aware, and Gerbert de Montreuil follows his lead in both the *Violette* and the *Continuation*.

The wealth of vestimentary detail in the romances can be juxtaposed with the equally revealing fiscal accounts of the Capetian household that survive for the year 1202–3, around the time Jean began to write. Three times that year, at All Souls (1 November), Candlemas (2 February), and Ascension Day (April–May), the royal chamberlain, Jean de Betefort, acknowledged receipt of funds from which he deducted for the purchase of wardrobes for Philip Augustus, for his queen, Ingeborg, for his son, Louis, and for his daughter-in-law, Blanche, as well as for the infant children of his mistress Agnès de Méranie, Marie and Philippe, in the nursery at Poissy.[45] The items in these Latin inventories correspond remarkably to the vernacular fictions of the romanciers' imaginations.

Unlike the clothing of peasant men, who wore short robes over pants to facilitate manual labor, the aristocratic wardrobe for both men and women was modeled on a long, loose-fitting tunic dating from the early Middle Ages. While peasant garb changed little, the long aristocratic robes began to be fitted with laces and buttons to hug the body more closely and were embroidered and decorated more richly during the course of the twelfth century. Around 1200, however, the basic garments of both men and women still retained their characteristic patterns and names.[46] The romance writers normally identify clothing according to cut (shifts, robes, coats) and by materials (silk and wool), but they pay special attention to embellishment with color, furs, linings, borders, and the application of precious metals and stones. Their objective is to accentuate newness and expense.

Closest to the body were the undergarments, consisting of trousers, stockings, and the chemise, or shift. Trousers were worn only by men. Chrétien has Gornemans supply the young Perceval with linen pants and hosiery dyed red with brazilwood (*Graal* vv. 1600–1602), along with a chemise.[47] Since these articles were rarely seen beneath the long robes, Jean omits them and concentrates on the chemise, which was worn by both sexes. Made of light material, loose and flowing, the chemise figures prominently in Chrétien's descriptions. Enide is first introduced in a flowing chemise of fine cloth, white and pleated, which enhances her beauty, despite her ragged outer garments (*Erec* vv. 402–4). Soredamor sews a chemise for Alexandre out of white silk, delicate and smooth, to which she adds her own golden hair in the stitches on the sleeves and neck (*Cligès* vv. 1146–54). Jean also exhibits this undergarment on his major characters. As Aelis dresses to meet her lover, she puts on a white chemise arranged in folds. With panels broader than a fathom (*toise*), it is very supple (*Escoufle* vv. 3293–97). As the knights and ladies perform their ablutions on the spring hunt, the absorbent shifts serve admirably as towels (*Rose* vv. 278–79). Under Lïenor's magnificent dress at Mainz is a white, flowered chemise, which does not conceal her firm, small breasts (*Rose* vv. 4355–62). When Guillaume de Dole returns to his lodgings at Saint-Trond, he undresses except for a fine chemise under his *surcot* (vv. 2194–96). At the court of Duke Milon, Gerbert notices Gerart de Nevers's pleated chemise embroidered with gold thread; he is doubtless dressed lightly because of the heat (*Violette* vv. 3465–67). In the royal wardrobe accounts, chemises (*camisie*) and cloth to make them are recorded only for the nursery of Poissy, most likely because these garments were not costly enough to be listed among adult clothing.[48]

Closely related to the chemise was the *chainse*, an outer garment, usually white and of lightweight material. At her initial appearance, Enide wears a white *chainse*, ragged at the elbows, over her shift (*Erec* vv. 405–10). The tightly laced pleated *chainses* of the ladies on the spring hunt do little to hide their bodies (*Rose* vv. 196–97). In the *Violette*, Aigline's white *chainse* is old and coming apart, recalling Enide's (v. 1580). Preparing for the summer, the nursery at Poissy required cloth for making *unum cheinse* as well as shifts.[49]

The garment that aristocratic women and men wore for public dress was the long tunic, variously termed a *robe*, *bliaut*, or *cote*. Enide's *bliaut*, which she exchanges for her old *chainse* at her wedding, becomes a model of elegance in subsequent romances. A gift of Queen Guenièvre, tailored expressly for the daughter of the lowly vavasor, it is lined with ermine, and its wrists and neck are adorned with beaten gold and precious gems (*Erec* vv. 1575–83). Jean's and Gerbert's heroines follow her example. As she dresses to meet her lover, Aelis likewise dons a *bliaut*, this one made in Syria, lined with fur, and trimmed with ermine (*Escoufle* vv. 3290–92). The terminology of Lïenor's attire at Mainz is somewhat confusing. Over her chemise, she wears a tunic (*cote*) of green silk, whose body and sleeves are lined with fur. It is cut to fit closely around her waist and hips and not to hide her chest. But Jean also says she wears a *robe* of dark-blue samite lined with white ermine. This must certainly be her *mantel*, an outer garment, which she adjusts for her ride to court (*Rose* vv. 4349–60).[50] Recalling Lïenor, Gerbert has Eurïaut enter Melun in a wondrously tailored purple *bliaut* embroidered with gold crosses. In competition with Enide's, the materials and precious stones display extraordinary wealth (*Violette* vv. 812–39). And Gerbert naturally does not neglect Blancheflor's wedding gown (*roube*) of blood-red silk, covered with stars and trimmed with dazzling stones (*Continuation* vv. 6612–25).

If described in less detail, the men's tunics are equally sumptuous. Chrétien's Gornemans gives Perceval a *cote* of purple silk, woven in India, to replace his mother's rustic garb (*Graal* vv. 1603–4). Jean robes the youthful Guillaume in a red samite *cote* bordered with ermine (*Escoufle* vv. 2574–75). To meet the emperor for the first time, Guillaume de Dole puts on a *robe* of *escarlate* lined with ermine, which the jongleur Juglet recognizes immediately as the latest French style (*Rose* vv. 1530–35). For his wedding, Gerbert's Perceval also wears a well-tailored robe of *escarlate* (*Continuation* vv. 6584–87). *Roba* and *tunica*, taken together, outnumber by far all other items inventoried in the royal accounts. Numerous commissions are recorded for the royal family; in particular, robes are specified for the high holidays of All Saints, Christmas, Easter, and Pentecost. *Roba* were apparently more costly than *tunica*, occasionally requiring the expensive material *scarlata,* and were commissioned expressly for the holiday.

On festive occasions, the tunic was combined with an outer garment called a *mantel,* or cloak. Along with the *blïaut,* Guenièvre's wedding gifts to Enide include a *mantel* of equal worth. Its collar has sables and jewels on each side. Lined with white ermine, the outer fabric is stitched with multi-colored crosses (*Erec* vv. 1567–1601). Although Aelis's tunic (*cote*) at her coronation is neglected, Jean notes that her *mantel* has a double-faced train, with gold brocade and links. The lining of black sable in diamond patterns is bordered with ermine whiter than snow. The entire cloak is hemmed in gold and studded with gems (*Escoufle* vv. 8914–25). When Lïe-nor rides to court at Mainz, her outer garment, already described as of dark-blue samite lined with white ermine, is now termed a *mantel.* She pulls back both sides to expose her throat and bodice (*Rose* vv. 4529–32). Eurïaut decks herself in a green *mantel* lined with ermine and embroidered with gold flowers, each containing a tiny bell (*Violette* vv. 842–49). Sim-ilarly, Blancheflor's wedding attire includes a cloak lined with ermine up to the border (*Continuation* vv. 6626–27).

An innovation that surfaced toward the end of the twelfth century was the *sorcot,* apparently a sleeveless "overcoat" worn over the *cote.* It makes its first appearance in Chrétien's last romance, and Jean notices it briefly in this early *Escoufle.*[51] When Aelis moves from Montpellier to Saint-Gilles, for example, her trunk is packed with *chainses,* cloaks, pelisses, and *sorcos* (vv. 6046–47). As she relaxes before the fire in the *chambre aux dames,* she familiarly embraces the count by inserting her arm through a side aperture of his *surcot.* She too is informally attired in a chemise and a pelisse without sleeves (vv. 7048–57). In all likelihood, the *sorcot* was preferred at home for occasions of déshabillé. In his lodgings at Saint-Trond, Guillaume de Dole removes his clothes except for a *chemise* and a *surcot* lined with red silk, edged with fur, and decorated with gold English brocade across the back (*Rose* vv. 2194–2201).[52]

Mantels were dress overcoats for festive occasions, but more practical against cold weather were the long, furred overcoats, or pelisses. Count Richard's gifts to his vassals' wives include these garments, along with cloaks (*Escoufle* vv. 92–93),[53] but the lovers' elopement demands out-erwear more serviceable against inclement weather. Their baggage in-cludes rain capes (*chapes a aige*), homespun tunics (*cotes bures*), and *cotes* of dark Flemish cloth (*Escoufle* vv. 3583–85). At the moment of departure, Aelis dons a *cote* of Flemish cloth and a fine cape (*Escoufle* vv. 3996–4001).

Perhaps the cool, moist climate of northern France necessitated as many outer garments as festive tunics in Philip Augustus's wardrobe. With the absence of references to *mantels*, the frequent use of *supertunicalis*, a direct translation of *sorcot*, must imply that it served as the generic term for both *mantels* and *surcots*. Like the vernacular *mantel*, it was most often lined with fur.[54] Also prominent in the accounts are the *pelicio* and *capa*, equivalent to the French *plichons* and *chape*. Rain capes (*capae pluviales, ad aquam*) are also noted, one expressly designated for the king's use during Lent.[55]

Surpassing their attention to tailoring, the romanciers take note of the luxurious materials expended in the confection of aristocratic clothing.[56] King Arthur, Chrétien boasts, offered *mantels* not of serge (*sarges*) or brown cloth (*brunetes*) but of samite as Christmas gifts (*Erec* vv. 6606–8). Among the silks, the heavy samite figures prominently; among the woolens, *escarlate* and *porpre* are singled out for special notice. The last two terms chiefly designate a fine grade of wool cloth, and only secondarily the colors to which their names were eventually attached.[57] Jean and Gerbert are particularly sensitive to the quality of materials in clothing. Upon arising, the courtiers on the spring hunt don tunics and cloaks of samite and cloth from overseas (*Rose* vv. 234–36). Never before were so many luxurious baldachins (*baudeguin*, or gold-embroidered silks), other exotic silks (*ciglaton*), and good satins (*bon diaspre*) and samites seen in tunics of so many styles as at the wedding in Mainz (vv. 5364–67). After the tournament, Gauvain gives Tristan two *bliauts*, one of silk from Aleppo (*de halepin*), the other of baldachin (*Continuation* vv. 3665–66). Only Gerbert, echoing Chrétien, takes notice of the fine cloth called *porpre*, but both are fascinated by costly *escarlate* in all hues.[58] Jean, for example, notes that Liënor's saddle cloth is of *escarlate* from England, so hemstitched that the yellow silk lining can be seen beneath it (*Rose* vv. 4488–92).[59] In the Capetian royal wardrobe, silk was frequently used for tunics, cloaks, capes, and headgear. Camel hair (*camelinum*), not mentioned in the romances, was also employed to make outer garments, as well as robes, but not tunics. *Escarlate* (*scarlata*) was occasionally chosen for capes, but most frequently for expensive robes for the king and his children on the holidays of Christmas, Easter, and Pentecost.[60]

Aristocratic tastes were not satisfied merely with expensive materials, but demanded further embellishment with colorful dyes, fur linings, and trimmings, and the application of gold and precious stones. Much of the cost in manufacturing fine cloth consisted of the process of dyeing. *Escarlate* was an expensive cloth because of the dye, whatever the final color might be.[61] One of the most costly dyes was kermes (*granum* in Latin, and *graine* in medieval French), which produced a brilliant red color.[62] When Jean therefore proclaims:

> ... com l'en met la graine
> es dras por avoir los et pris
>
> ... that one placed kermes / in cloth to increase its worth
> (*Rose* vv. 8–9)

he is grounding this much-discussed analogy on a widely known current textile-making practice. Similarly, when Erec wishes to exchange Enide's impoverished garb for an expensive dress from the queen, he asks for one not only in silk but also dyed red with kermes ("qui est de soie tainte en grainne," *Erec* v. 1336). Jean himself refers to a *surcot* made so recently of *escarlate* that it was still redolent with the red dye ("qui fleroit la graine," *Rose* vv. 1816–18).

The most striking reference to the dyeing process is found in the Anonymous of Béthune. Describing Prince Louis's attack on Steenvoorde in Flanders in 1214, he quotes Brother Guérin, the king's chief agent, as saying, as he put the city to the torch: "'My lords ... have you ever seen an *estanfort* more beautifully dyed with red kermes than this one [nul estanfort miels taint en graine de cestui]'? He said this while the red flames poured forth, but many a *preudome* took it badly because it was said by a man of religion."[63] Guérin was punning in bad taste on Estanfort, the French name of Steenvoorde, and the cloth, doubtless red in color, of which Philip Augustus's accounts record one robe and five tunics.[64]

If *estanfort* was reputed to be flaming red, *escarlate* was not always that shade. It could be blood red (*sanguine*) (*Escoufle* v. 5766), vermilion (*vermeille*) (*Escoufle* v. 7997; *Continuation* v. 6586), purple (*violette*) (*Rose* v. 4343), or as dark as blackberry ("d'escarlate noir come meurs," *Rose* v. 1530). *Porpre*, on the other hand, could also be blood red (*sanguine*) (*Continuation* v. 6618).

In addition to these differing shades of red, green was another color of choice. Lïenor's tunic is of green silk (*Rose* v. 4357), and, always in competition, Eurïaut's *mantel* is greener than cabbage leaves (*Violette* v. 843). The seductive Escolasse is clad in two layers of samite, one green, the other vermilion (*Continuation* vv. 447–48). Along with red *estanfort*, the other favorite color in the Capetian wardrobe was green. Capes, *sorcots*, and silk robes were so designated. Blanche, wife of Prince Louis, had a green robe for Christmas; her husband's robe was black.[65]

As in Chrétien, most of the festive tunics and cloaks of Jean's and Gerbert's heroes and heroines are lined and trimmed with fur, with highest preference being given to white ermine and sable. Occasionally, the less valuable fur of the squirrel (*vair*) and rabbit (*conins*) is included in gifts of clothing (*Erec* v. 2060; *Rose* vv. 1538, 1818) or interlaced in linings with ermine ("de gris chevronees," *Rose* v. 238). Jean vaunts that Lïenor's wedding robe is not lined with *grise* or *vair* but with alternating black sables and ermines (Rose vv. 5352–56). These fine furs are always new (*fres*), that is, fresh. Chrétien has Yvain dress in a robe of *escarlate* lined with *vair*, sewn so recently that it still bore the chalk marks (*Lion* vv. 1885–87). Odor is the best indication of newness for Jean. On three occasions, he notes that ermines are fine and sweet smelling (*soëf flerans*) (*Rose* vv. 239, 1532, 1539). In addition to furred pelisses, at times identified as squirrel (*gris, ver, escurellorum*) and hare (*leporem*), the royal wardrobe accounts point to the abundant activity of pelletiers. It is specified of many of the inventoried robes, *surcots*, and capes that they are *furura*, or *foderatura*, indicating that fur linings and edges were added. No expensive pelts are recorded, but only the less costly *ver* and *gris*.

Enide's wedding *blïaut*, which so influences Jean's and Gerbert's rhetoric of clothing, is edged at the neck and wrists with gold braid, on which are set gems of various colors. The *mantel* has a jacinth and ruby, more brilliant than carbuncles, on either side (*Erec* vv. 1575–94). Aelis's coronation cloak is likewise edged with gold and adorned with numerous stones and gems (*Escoufle* vv. 8920–23). The culmination is Blancheflor's wedding gown, which is trimmed with gems so dazzling that it appears to be consumed with tongues of fire (*Continuation* vv. 6614–25). Enide's *mantel* is tied at the neck with silk laces worked with gold (*Erec* vv. 1602–3). Jean notes that young Guillaume's laces are not of string but of silk and gold laminate (*Escoufle* vv. 2976–78). As Lïenor rides to court at Mainz, she manipulates the laces of her cloak to display her bodice better (*Rose* vv. 1535–36). Ribbons (*fresellae*) appear in the royal wardrobe accounts as well.[66]

At her throat, Enide wears two golden clasps (*fermaillez*), each sealed with a topaz (*Erec* vv. 1245–47). Jean focuses his attention upon this jewelry because of his preoccupation with décolleté. The gleaming clasp points to the breasts as the boundary between the clothed body and what can be seen.[67] Aelis's *afice* is skillfully fashioned with stones that reflect all the colors of summer flowers and shown against the whiteness of her chest (*Escoufle* vv. 8926–37). Lïenor's *fermail* is positioned a full finger below the opening of her chemise to enhance her chest, which is whiter than snow (*Rose* vv. 4373–80). Mindful of Jean, Gerbert describes Eurïaut's *afice* as formerly having belonged to the empress Florence of Rome, a gift from Queen Margaret of Hungary, her aunt. Below the clasp, she wears a silk belt embellished with hyacinths, rubies, and emeralds (*Violette* vv. 818–36). Chaste Blancheflor's wedding gown is not so adorned, but Gerbert provides men with this article of jewelry as well (*Violette* v. 5659).

Enide wears a gold chaplet (*cercle*) on her head, designed with flowers of many colors (*Erec* vv. 1639–41). In place of a wimple, Aelis likewise dons a gold wreath (*cerlet*) (*Escoufle* vv. 8288–90); the wreath of rubies she wears at Rouen was made by an Arab (vv. 3300–3301). At her moment of triumph, Lïenor wears a wimple as she rides to court (*Rose* v. 4383), but when she removes her *mantel*, the wimple falls off, entangled with her hair, and reveals a gold *chaplet* beneath, such as girls of her country are accustomed to wear (vv. 4716–43). Eurïaut's *chapiel* is set with precious stones (*Violette* vv. 840–41). Relaxing in his chemise and *surcot*, Guillaume de Dole also wears a fine wreath (*Rose* v. 2203).

For all the attention they devote to cloth and furs, the royal accounts virtually ignore precious metals and jewelry, except for the sole mention of a small sum paid to the goldsmiths.[68] An occasional *capella* (chaplet?) is recorded in silk, but none in gold.[69] The jewel accounts transcribed into the royal registers inventory gold broaches (*firmacula*), some set with sapphires, scattered among the diamonds, rubies, sapphires, emeralds, and other precious stones.[70]

All this attention to fine cloth, dyes, furs, gold work, and precious stones merely reminded the audience that the ultimate standard for romance clothing was its expense. Chrétien's perception of aristocratic sartorial value is summed up in the lines:

> Molt estoit riches li blïauz,
> mes por voir ne valoit noauz
> li mantiax de rien que je sache.

The *bliaut* was very expensive, / but to my knowledge / the
mantel was not worth any less. (*Erec* vv. 1583–85)

Enide's robe is bordered with 200 marks' worth of beaten gold, Chrétien
marvels, and the *bliaut* itself costs 100 silver marks (*Erec* vv. 1579, 1616).
Doubtless these figures are hyperbole to suggest extravagance. Jean omits
the figures, but after detailing the cloth, furs, gold, and jewels of Aelis's
coronation robes, he concludes in romance style that never was a lady
garbed so richly ("si riche," *Escoufle* vv. 8924–25). Gerbert resorts to contemporary literary hyperbole to evaluate Euriaut's *bliaut*. The gems on
her clasp are equal in worth to the city of Piacenza, and the silk of her belt
to the fortune of the count of Toulouse, whereas the jewels rival those that
Roland gave to Aude before leaving for Roncevaux (*Violette* vv. 818–39).
Blancheflor's gold and gems are worth more than the possessions of the
king of Frisia (*Continuation* vv. 6345–47).

Jean de Betefort's accounts provide data useful for comparison with
these imaginative flights. Jean received 500 livres *parisis,* or 10,000 sous,
from the Temple to clothe the Capetian family for the fiscal year 1202–3.
Since he actually spent 11,160 sous, he was obliged to borrow another
2,000 to cover the difference. The king's wardrobe accounted for 40 percent of the expenses, those of Prince Louis and Princess Blanche for 33
percent, and that of Queen Ingeborg, living in stringent disgrace, for less
than 10 percent. The greatest expenditure was 2,331 sous (or 1,165 sous
apiece) for two robes for Louis and Blanche at Pentecost. Below that, the
most costly item was the habitual expenditure of 320 sous apiece for the
king's robes of *escarlate* for the feasts of Christmas, Easter, and Pentecost.
Capes of *escarlate* for Philip were procured for the same price. Blanche
paid 275 sous for her green robe at Christmas but Louis only 97 sous for
his black robe on the same occasion. The most Queen Ingeborg spent was
557 sous for a robe and fur-lined cape.[71] It is difficult to measure what fur
linings or trimmings added to the price. Furred *surcots* ranged between 57
and 70 sous; a furred green silk robe cost from between 27 and 40 sous.
Pelisses in various kinds of squirrel fur could average between 30 and 50
sous apiece. On the other hand, a camel-hair robe lined with *vair* was
priced at 160 sous; single squirrel pelts brought around 5 sous. The cheap-
est cloth appears to have been red *estanfort,* which regularly cost 15 sous
for tunics and 36 sous for robes. All told, the customary price of 320 sous

for a new robe for the king on each high holiday was not a great extravagance. It would have paid for only a half a horse (normally selling for 720
sous) or the military services of a mercenary knight for a month at the
highest rate of 10 sous per day. It would have paid the salary of Philip's
best *bailli* for only a fortnight. Since the women of the royal family did not
normally outspend the king, the Capetians' sartorial sobriety would seem
to contrast markedly with the opulence conveyed by the romance authors.[72] Louis's and Blanche's robes are the one real extravagance, added at
the end of the accounts, after the nursery expenses at Poissy. No further
evidence of prodigality surfaces in a surviving fragment of Louis's own
household accounts from ten years later. Louis paid his chamberlain Richard only 24 sous for his robes at Christmas.[73]

Pierre the Chanter, who takes scant notice of aristocratic celebrations
and amusements, deals with the eating habits of the medieval ruling class
only obliquely, but examines their garb more directly. As a cleric formed in
the schools, he is quick to quote Ovid's complaint: "We are carried away
by clothing. Everything is hidden under gems and gold; the girl is the least
part of herself." Geoffroi de Vinsauf had dilated in his rhetorical manual
upon the gold, gems, and jewelry that enhance the image of feminine
beauty.[74] Pierre's chapter "Against the Superfluity and Expense of Clothing" in his *Verbum abbreviatum* identifies current excesses in materials,
dyes, form, composition, diversification, and mutation of materials. Beginning with the first two, he notes that the Lord clothed Adam and Eve in
tunics made of animal skins. How these hides were cut, sewn, or prepared,
he is not prepared to say, but he believes them to have been coarse. No serf
today, however, would deign to garb himself in such rude clothing. As in
Raoul Ardent's critique of aristocratic cooking, natural adornments are to
be preferred to artistry. Simple materials such as animal hides, sheep's
wool, hemp, and linen made from flax grown in the fields are acceptable,
but now there is a craze for the unnatural plumage of birds, which would
make a crow laugh, the offal of worms (evidently silk), and even thread
spun as fine as a spider's web. Turning to dyes, Pierre is willing to accept
natural colors, but human vanity has perverted them into bright red, rose,
green, saffron, and violet and mixed them together in such confusion that
they exceed the flowers of the fields that the Gospel says are greater than
Solomon's glory.[75] Without doubt the Chanter was responding to the ma-
nia for fine fabrics, brilliant dyes, and elaborate gold work displayed in the
romance literature. In a subsequent chapter, entitled "Against the Form of

Clothes," he considers the kaleidoscopic mixing of colors using different panels and other modes of tailoring. Modish long trains—the creation of tails (*caudandi*), as he phrases it—are his principal target here. What nature has denied humans, he complains, the tailor adds.[76] Criticism of extravagant trains on tunics and cloaks may be found as early as the preceding century, but the question in fact appears to have become moot by the Chanter's time. Although prostitutes may still have flaunted them, such trains were apparently no longer high fashion, and Chrétien, Jean, and Gerbert scarcely mention them.[77]

Jean's and Gerbert's absorption in the subject of festivities replete with lively entertainment, delicious victuals, and fashionable garb is simply a function of the jongleur's mission to celebrate court life. The mass of detail serves as resplendent decor, with little bearing on the central narratives of the romances. To contemporary audiences, this profusion offered verisimilitude for the pleasure of recognition; to modern historians, these "effets de réel" illuminate areas about which Latin chroniclers were reluctant to speak. These reality effects are not entirely faithful to life, however, but highly polished to celebrate the *éclat* of aristocratic society. No dishes are served cold, no robes are frayed at the sleeves, no fiddlers play off key. No one but the central characters is permitted a mournful face amid the festive rejoicing. Doubtless audiences understood this requirement, and by keeping the contemporary public's "horizon of expectations" in view, historians can perceive what lay beneath the brilliant veneer.

SEVEN

Aristocratic Religion

. ✂ .

FESTIVE tournaments, rental of lodgings, feminine beauty, courtly love, worldly entertainment, delicious food, and fine clothing were concerns that were either suspect or peripheral to the clergy, but religion was the speciality in which their competence was unquestioned and their jurisdiction exclusive.[1] Since the clergy expressed themselves in Latin on these matters, Latin texts resurface as an important vehicle in this chapter. Religion has always played a central role in the history of the Middle Ages because of the Church's dominant position in society. In recent decades, historians have returned to the relations between the clergy and the laity with special attention to negotiations forged between the monks and the lay aristocracy in the early Middle Ages. These histories are written from cartularies, obituaries, liturgical collections, and saints' lives, all composed exclusively in Latin. In other words, in a language written by and for the clergy, the monks kept the books on which these studies are based. These recent historians have been astute in coming to valid conclusions and detecting lay strategies, but for the most part they have not questioned how the monastic monopoly over the sources has affected their conclusions. The explanation is simple: because no other sources exist, the Latin documents are regarded as unproblematic.[2]

Conventional and Quotidian Religious Practice

Jean's and Gerbert's romances are so taken up with the laity's concerns that the authors tend to relegate the clergy to the periphery of their narratives. (This applies more to Gerbert's *Roman de la violette* than to his *Continuation*.) Although Jean's *Roman de la rose* is addressed to a high cleric, it takes even less notice of the clerical world. Jean's *Lai de l'ombre*, a tale of adultery, could have been appreciated only by the most worldly of

bishops-elect. The churchmen who do appear in the romances were limited, for the most part, to the great prelates who presided at solemn liturgical occasions. No churchman is identified by his baptismal name; a few of
Jean's prelates were identified by place-names to add geographic verisimilitude, but the vast majority are marked solely by the generic ranks of archbishop, bishop, and abbot.

The liturgical occasions that called for high churchmen are those that
figure in the life cycles of the heroes and heroines. Because these are romances of love, marriages are prominent in them. Guillaume and Aelis are
married at Rouen by the resident archbishop (*Escoufle* vv. 8329–33). The
archbishop of Cologne performs the same service for Conrad and Liënor
immediately before their coronation, after which other bishops join the
baronage at the festive banquet (*Rose* vv. 5380–81, 5395–96). Although
Gerbert mentions no clergy or churches in connection with Gerart and
Euriaut's wedding, Perceval and Blancheflor's marriage at Beaurepaire is
festively celebrated by the archbishop of Landemeure and the bishops of
Lumor and Lumeri, as well as by numerous unnamed bishops and abbots,
with their clerical entourages (*Continuation* vv. 6631–43).[3] The traditional
presence of clerics at the subsequent blessing of the nuptial chamber is
more prominent.[4] Although Jean neglects to mention clergy at Count
Richard's wedding to the lady of Genoa, a bishop spreads incense around
the nuptial bed, thus assuring the birth of the hero (*Escoufle* vv. 1740–43).
Gerbert does not omit the ceremony, when Perceval and Blancheflor contract a spiritual marriage, which, in effect, renders the blessing superfluous,
but assigns it to four archbishops and nine bishops (*Continuation* vv.
6773–89). Baptisms are likewise performed by bishops (*Escoufle* vv.
1758–67). Had Conrad been the lord of France, he would have elevated to
the see of Reims the priest who baptized and bestowed on Liënor her
beautiful name (*Rose* vv. 797–800). Burials occur less frequently, since few
die in Jean's and Gerbert's romances. The funeral services for Count
Richard are described in detail sufficient to indicate that he was interred
between the choir and altar by undesignated clerics (*Escoufle* vv. 2606–7).

Ecclesiastics also play a leading role at coronations. At Pentecost in
Rome, Guillaume and Aelis are led in solemn procession by innumerable
archbishops, bishops, and abbots to the church, where the pope bestows
the scepter, hat, and crown on the emperor and anoints the empress (*Escoufle* vv. 8944–65). Since Liënor's coronation is the constitutional consequence of her marriage, it is performed immediately after the wedding at

Mainz by the archbishop, who crowns the couple and intones chants to the Holy Spirit and the Trinity (*Rose* vv. 5374–85). Following Chrétien's well-established tradition, Gerbert occasionally evokes Arthur's festive courts. At Carlion, for example, vespers are attended by three archbishops and four bishops, all identified as being from the British Isles (*Continuation* vv. 3321–45).[5]

Medieval royalty attended Mass daily. Jean and Gerbert do not stress this, but the quotidian activities of royalty in the romances point to it. When the emperor and empress are thus occupied, for example, Guillaume and Aelis find opportunity to meet and to plot their elopement (*Escoufle* vv. 3561–62, 3622–29). Routine daily masses afford Conrad's courtiers the leisure to compare the gifts they have received (*Rose* vv. 1904–23). While the knights attend a special mass before the tournament at Montargis, King Louis hears the regular mass in his own chapel (*Violette* vv. 6127–29). Naturally, the religious obligations of royalty are more visible than those of the lower levels of society, but Jean also provides glimpses of popular devotion. When Lïenor encounters two bourgeois women on the street of Mainz, for example, they are returning from morning mass (*Rose* vv. 4215–18). (The coincidence is not fortuitous, however, since Jean makes it clear that it is in answer to Lïenor's prayer.)

The routinization of religious observances accords with Jean's less than respectful attitude toward piety in the *Rose*, even though the romance was addressed to a prominent clergyman. During the banter at the imperial table, Conrad would rather talk about his newfound love for Lïenor than about the usual subjects of roofing churches (*Rose* vv. 1636–41). In the opening scene on the spring hunt, when Conrad and his companions join the ladies under the sheets during their husbands' absence, Jean comments in a well-known passage: "They did not think of their souls; they had no church bells, ministers, or chaplains (for which they hardly had need); only birds [to awaken them from their pleasure]" (*Rose* vv. 224–27).

The lower clergy appear only in occasional vignettes, which illuminated their immersion in mundane affairs more than their religious duties. Aelis's shop at Montpellier, for example, becomes a rendezvous for both clerics and knights, who are lured there by her fine embroidery and luxury couture (*Escoufle* vv. 5944–45). After mass and breakfast, the illiterate knight Guillaume de Dole engages a cleric to write letters to procure his equipment for the upcoming tournament (*Rose* vv. 1924–26). When Guillaume's mother needs knights to entertain the seneschal at Dole, she finds them at the house of a priest in town, where they are playing chess (*Rose* vv. 1924–26). From the highest prelate to the lowest parish priest and simple cleric, the clergy are reduced, like other "effets de réel," to routine decor.

Pilgrimages to holy sites, one of the most traditional of religious practices, do figure prominently in Jean's *Escoufle*, serving to advance the narrative. We remember that after seven years of fruitless search, Guillaume finds employment in a pilgrim's hostel at Santiago de Compostela, doubtless hoping that the celebrity of the shrine will draw someone who might provide news of his *amie*. The monks who care for the saint's relics play no role in the episode, but the strategy pays off, because a pilgrim appears astride Aelis's mule (*Escoufle* vv. 6184–6351). The mule leads Guillaume back to Toul, where the trail grows cold again. Guillaume promises whatever saint will hear his prayer that he will make a pilgrimage to that saint's shrine. This time he chooses Saint-Gilles du Gard, whose shrine was that favored by the family of Hainaut to whom Jean addresses the romance.[6] Arriving before the altar, he makes his offering and repeats his vow with tears and supplications. The saint hears his prayer, directs him to employment in the service of a *hôtelier* (*Escoufle* vv. 6478–6523), and eventually brings about the lovers' reunion.

The highest form of pilgrimage was, of course, the crusade to liberate the Holy Land from the infidel. Only a decade or two before Jean Renart undertook his romances, the three leading monarchs of Europe, the emperor Frederick Barbarossa, King Philip Augustus of France, and King Richard of England, had undertaken the Third Crusade, which succeeded in capturing the seaport of Acre, but failed to win Jerusalem. When the great princes of the Empire implore the emperor Conrad to marry and produce an heir in the *Rose*, they warn him that he may die or go on a pilgrimage overseas (vv. 3063–67), doubtless with Barbarossa's death in 1190 en route to the Holy Land in mind. Jean opens his first romance with an extended account of Count Richard's crusade that, despite counterfactual features, patently evokes King Richard's recent exploits.[7] Throughout this enterprise, the clergy are prominently identified. After Richard decides "to go overseas to save his soul" (*Escoufle* v. 125), he summons his barons, who include not only the counts of Varenne and Eu but also his intimate friend the bishop of Lisieux (vv. 153–57). Mass is celebrated at the nunnery of Montivilliers, presided over by the archbishop of Rouen (vv. 202–14). Two of the abbess's most talented nuns lead the choir in a musical accom-

paniment to the service (vv. 225–30). After the count presents his magnificent gifts and the mass is finished, his pilgrim staff and wallet are blessed
and the nuns' prayers are solicited (vv. 247–56). In a protracted and tearful
farewell, the archbishop blesses the pilgrims and commends them to God
(vv. 345–48).

Arriving by sea at Acre, Richard proceeds to Jerusalem, which is threatened (not occupied) by the Muslims, where the king and populace receive
him festively and joyfully. Evoking the successful First Crusade, Jean
comments that "never since the time of Peter the Hermit was a French
knight received with such honor in the city of Jerusalem" (vv. 550–53).
(The historical Peter the Hermit in fact never arrived at Jerusalem.) The
count is led to the Temple and the Church of the Holy Sepulcher and lays
the gold cup on the altar, to the admiration of the church wardens (vv.
576–79, 623–33). The festivities are cut short, however, by a new Muslim
incursion. Joining with the king, local barons, the patriarch of Jerusalem,
and the Knights Templar, the Norman knights repulse the Muslim forces.
To embellish the crusaders' prowess, Jean borrows allusions from romances and the chansons de gestes: "Everyone said that Arthur and Gauvain were alive again [vv. 988–89] . . . . More [of the] enemy perished than
those killed at Roncevaux by Roland and the companions whom Charles
chose for the rear guard" (vv. 1282–87). Faced with such opposition, the
Muslims settle for a three-year truce, and Richard starts the journey home
(vv. 1314–29).[8]

The crusade served purposes other than fighting for God and displaying chivalric glory. When the seneschal is finally exposed of perfidy, Lïenor refuses to sentence him to death but imposes a long penance, which
consists of exile from Germany and France and service overseas as a Templar (vv. 5579–90). Bearing a cross prominently on his garment (*to₃ croi-
sie₃*), certifying his vow, the unhappy seneschal is brought before the empress to render thanks for her grace (*Rose* vv. 5617–20). In comparable
circumstances, Gauvain offers to go overseas for three years to do penance
for the soul of a knight whom he has slain in combat (*Continuation* vv.
12825–27). Crusades were a means of clearing the realm of undesirable
characters and offering propitiation for sin.[9]

If crusades were unequivocal channels for belligerent behavior, tournaments were not. Although ecclesiastics attempted to excommunicate participants and to refuse them burial in sacred soil, we have seen that Jean
and Gerbert always provide their romance knights with clergy willing to

say Mass for those entering the field. At the tournament of Saint-Trond, Jean parades knights—like monks bearing relics in a procession—to a church outside the walls, where the chaplain of an abbess celebrates the office of the Holy Spirit (*Rose* vv. 2432–45). It is significant that it was not the abbot of the great Benedictine abbey of Saint-Trond but the abbess of the less influential nunnery of Sainte-Catherine who possessed a chapel outside the walls at the Stapelpoort.[10] Masses are likewise provided at the tournaments of Montargis and Lancien. Just why Jean and Gerbert specify that the priests at Saint-Trond and Montargis celebrate the office of the Holy Spirit is not yet apparent. As votive and *specialis*, it may have been instituted for particular intentions. At Innocent III's consecration as pope in 1198, for example, the new pontiff celebrated a Mass of the Holy Spirit to beseech divine aid to overcome his insufficiencies.[11]

Underlying these routine religious services was the theological concept that God is everywhere present in human affairs and able and willing to intervene whenever called upon. Like preceding writers, Jean and Gerbert punctuate their verse with numerous invocations of the names of God and his saints. Although frequently introduced to supply the stylistic requirements of meter and rhyme, these phrases nonetheless convey an impression of the pervasive ubiquity—even the banality—of the divine presence. Beyond the conventional farewell or adieu, Jean seasons his lines in the *Rose* with "by God," "in God's name," "if God pleases," "God grant you," "thank God," "God help me," and numerous equivalents.[12] Such exclamations could be more explicitly theological, like Jean's "by the five wounds of God," or "since God was born without sin." Gerbert is particularly partial to such phrases in his *Continuation*, invoking, for example, "God born of the Virgin" and "God who made this world."[13]

Saints were invoked for similar purposes. Jean frequently names the Virgin Mary, the most popular of all, as well as the apostolic saints, Peter and Paul, whom Gerbert also invokes.[14] Gerbert invokes ten saints in the *Violette* and twenty-two, the highest number in the romances, in the *Continuation*. Because saints' names offered greater variety than the divine nomenclature, they were more useful for rhyming purposes, but the saint could also perform his characteristic attributes and duties. For example, the holy knight St. George is invoked during Count Richard's crusade (*Escoufle* v. 937), and his feast day (23 April) is thought an appropriate time for the tournament at Saint-Trond (*Rose* v. 2321).[15]

The romance penchant of interlarding conversation with the name of

God and his saints would appear to contravene the Second Commandment
(Exod. 20:7): "You shall not take the name of the Lord your God in vain."
It is not clear whether romance authors and their audiences considered
such speech habits as oaths, but contemporary theologians did classify
these locutions as *iuramenta*. Their definition of *iuramentum* was "the assertion of a certain proposition by the witness of a sacred or nonsacred
thing."[16] "Against Those Prone to Swearing" is the title of one chapter of
Pierre the Chanter's *Verbum abbreviatum*, and Robert of Courson and
Thomas of Chobham follow suit with sections in their writings devoted to
oaths or perjury.[17]

The Chanter opens with Jesus' injunction in the Sermon on the Mount:
"You have heard it said of old you shall not commit perjury but render to
the Lord your oaths . . . but I say to you that you shall not swear at all. . . .
Let your words be 'yes, yes' and 'no, no'; anything else is from the evil
one" (Matt. 5:33–34, 37). How was this to be understood in a world where
oaths were universal? Recognizing the Jewish tradition of verbal sobriety
fostered by the Second Commandment, Pierre asserts that oaths are uttered more easily and often in the Christian church than in the Jewish syn-
agogue. Today no king is anointed, no prelate is installed, no canon is
granted a prebend in his church without an oath. In the courts plaintiffs
and defendants swear oaths; no one testifies without an oath, procedures
enforced by popes and princes. Indeed, if one refuses to swear, one risks
being accounted a heretical Cathar.[18] Oaths invoking the name of God and
the saints are therefore essential to the functioning of law and society. In
his guide to confessors, Thomas of Chobham gives a sample: "By God!"
"By St. Peter!" "So help me God and St. ——!"—all oaths common in the
romances.[19]

For the Chanter, one way of interpreting the evangelical prohibition is
to limit it to oaths uttered for frivolous reasons and without necessity.
These cases of swearing may be considered as taking the Lord's name in
vain. For example, one might idly or in jest swear almost inadvertently by
saying, "By God!" Judging this a venial sin, Pierre nonetheless warns
against making it a habit. Invoking the names of saints, moreover, renders
one vulnerable to their displeasure.[20]

Uttering God's name casually is examined more fully by Robert of
Courson apropos of those who swear idly, rather than consciously for the
sake of deception. The prohibition of taking the Lord's name in vain applies not only in sacred contexts but also to ordinary speech, and if it is ob-

jected that habit and usage excuse such oaths, it may be countered that frequency in fact aggravates the sin, as with drunkenness and lust. Robert
agrees with the Chanter, however, that although such oaths may be mortal
sins in some cases, under normal conditions, they are only venial. If uttered when the mind is suddenly provoked during the course of speaking,
they are not mortal sins, because the tongue is the most difficult member to
control.[21] Chobham's conclusion is not as indulgent: "It is not good to
swear without cause," he insists. When the Lord said you should never
swear, he meant you should seek not to swear. It is not the oath that is prohibited but the urge or custom of swearing, and he who habitually swears
useless or idle oaths always sins venially, if not mortally.[22]

In contrast to idle, customary swearing of the kind that permeates romance discourse, theologians designated another category as *ignominiose*
and condemned it as gravely mortal. The Chanter identifies oaths uttered
knowingly and seriously on the eyes, tongue, or blood of God. Chobham
alludes to oaths on certain members of Christ that should not be mentioned, which Courson, who also mentions God's head or hair, identifies
as Christ's and his mother's genitals. The Chanter remarks that those who
swear on God's members are frequently punished in the same place on
their own bodies. Courson's solution is for bishops to depose them if they
are in ecclesiastical orders or to excommunicate them if laity.[23]

The Angevin kings of England were notably guilty of ignominious
oaths. Gerald of Wales reports their penchant for swearing on the members of God.[24] By contrast, Pierre the Chanter recalls that Philip Augustus
cleared his palace of those who swore ignominious oaths on God and the
saints. The rich were fined 5 sous, to be donated to the lepers, and the poor
were dunked in full clothing. Similar penalties were enacted at the courts
of other princes. The Chanter's recollections coincide with those of the
royal historiographer Rigord, who notes the king's antipathy to gamblers
accustomed to swearing in courts and taverns. When a knight who was
gaming in the king's presence let slip an inadvertent oath, he was immediately dumped into the river. The king published an interdict against
blasphemy invoking the head, stomach, or other parts of God, which became established Capetian policy. Instead, Philip's habitual oath was the
innocuous "By the lance of Saint James!"[25] The royal campaign for restraint of swearing was predictably unsuccessful. Pope Innocent III complained of recent abuses to the archbishop of Reims in 1213. Out of custom, anger, or mental levity, men of the realm employed wicked and

horrible oaths, in which they were not afraid to swear by the feet and hands, and even the more secret members, of Christ and the saints. Innocent urged the archbishop to exhort his suffragan bishops to enforce the sacred canons that they had neglected to apply.[26]

The ecclesiastical-royal campaign against ignominious oaths did not directly target the romance authors, because their invocations of God and the saints do not normally name the divine members; the closest is perhaps Jean's calling on the "five wounds of God" (*Rose* v. 3808). But the objections against widespread, customary, and idle oaths in common parlance did pertain to romance speech habits. Often such invocations are genuine requests for help, as when Aelis implores St. Julien to find her lodging at Toul (*Escoufle* vv. 4868–69), but many, if not most, could be heard as taking the Lord's name in vain, which remained a venial sin in the theologians' schema.

Making the sign of the cross—the evocation of Christ's redemptive death—is the symbolic gesture, par excellence, of Christianity.[27] Jean's and Gerbert's characters employ it in a variety of contexts: upon encountering great misfortune or terrifying news that produces profound consternation, as when Guillaume sees the buzzard steal Aelis's purse (*Escoufle* vv. 4560–61, 5084), when Conrad hears the seneschal boast that he has taken Lïenor's virginity (*Rose* v. 3590), and when Eurïaut learns of Lisïart's similar accusation (*Violette* v. 9760); when embarking upon crucial and decisive enterprises, as when Lïenor enters the imperial court at Mainz to plead her case (*Rose* vv. 4602–3); and simply when setting out on a journey, as when the messenger Nicole mounts his horse and passes through the gate to ride off to Dole (vv. 906–7).

By the time of Gerbert's *Continuation*, crossing oneself has become the nearly reflexive response to all threats of harm and evil. Confronted with mounting adventures and dangers, both Gerbert's heroes and lesser figures do so with accelerating frequency throughout the *Continuation*. Perceval, for example, thereby preserves his chastity from seductive maidens (*Continuation* vv. 2572–86), and challenging the terrifying Dragon Knight, he both crosses himself before doing battle and wields a white shield bearing a red cross, containing a piece of the True Cross, which protects him against the enemy's devastating fire (vv. 9449–50, 9556–68, 19616–19). Even when the less pious Gauvain forgets God and falls in love with the treacherous Bloiesine, the sacred gesture saves his life. Only when he crawls into bed does he remember to make the sign and thereby discovers the dagger with which the maiden intends to kill him concealed under the covers (vv. 12598–609). When Thomas of Chobham recommends making the sign of the cross before retiring at night, he is doubtless thinking of less melodramatic circumstances.[28]

God not only responds unfailingly to the ritual gesture but intervenes in human affairs in direct response to prayer. The crusade is, of course, the archetype of a holy enterprise for which it is legitimate to supplicate divine aid and expect victorious results, as has been abundantly seen in Count Richard's pilgrimage to the Holy Land. Before returning home, Richard does not neglect to offer prayers at the Church of the Holy Sepulcher in evident thanksgiving.

The crusade operated on an international scale, but God's help could be supplicated for more personal matters. It has been noted how St. Jacques and St. Gilles intervened in the *Escoufle*, but throughout the *Rose*, with one exception, Jean has little occasion to require divine assistance. In the *Violette*, however, Gerbert has his characters enlist God's intervention on individual adventures. When a lady who is about to be gang-raped by three knights calls upon the name of Jesus Christ, Gerart immediately appears on the scene (vv. 4494–4500). His rescue of the castle of Bien-Assis/Illes-Pertes from a giant is sustained by repeated invocations of divine help (vv. 4793–94, 4824–25, 4848). Gerart's own search for Eurïaut is facilitated by his prayer to be led to the place where he can see his *amie* (vv. 5110–11). For her part, when Eurïaut is bound to a stake to be burned for a murder she did not commit, she offers a long invocation to God. By its very length, the prayer allows the hero time to come to her rescue (vv. 5177–5331). Perceval's quest for the Grail throughout the *Continuation* is accompanied at crises by prayers for purification and guidance, which finally result in his return to the Grail Castle.

Ordeals: The Institutionalization of Divine Intervention

Although Jean largely ignores God's direct intervention in human affairs in the *Rose*, a cold-water ordeal is at the heart of his narrative. Lïenor's accusation against the seneschal is put to "the judgment of God." A legacy of Germanic and Christian traditions from the early Middle Ages, the ordeal regularized and institutionalized God's intervention within the realm of law.[29] By the twelfth century, ordeals were divided between the unilateral variety, consisting of hot-iron and hot- and cold-water proofs, and the

bilateral, which was most often limited to the judicial duel. I shall begin
with the unilateral and defer discussion of the bilateral until later. Ordeals
were central to medieval mentality. Designated "judgments of God," they
affirmed that God could and, in fact, did intrude directly into human affairs to resolve perplexing judicial decisions.[30] In practice they were resorted to in extreme cases where the normal means of proof through documents and witnesses were unavailable.[31] They functioned, in effect, as the
philosopher's stone of medieval justice. They constituted the legal equivalent to the saint, whose canonization required not only exemplary piety
but also the performance of clearly attested miracles.

In the late twelfth century, however, ordeals rapidly came under suspicion in the romances that provided the "horizon of expectations" for the
knights and ladies making up Jean's and Gerbert's audiences, who knew
the Tristan legend as recorded by Béroul, Thomas de Bretagne, and Gottfried von Strassburg, in which Iseut swears an equivocal oath, thus manipulating the hot-iron ordeal to cover up her lover's patent adultery. In Chrétien's *Charrete*, an equivocal oath likewise permits Lancelot to fight a
judicial duel to clear Queen Guenièvre and conceal his own complicity in
their adultery. The various branches of the *Roman de Renart* mercilessly
parody the judicial process by which the ordeal was perverted with false
oaths. Cynicism about the ability of the ordeal to render justice reached a
high point in Gottfried von Strassburg's often-quoted opinion: "Thus it
was made manifest and confirmed to all the world that Christ in his great
virtue is as pliant as a windblown sleeve. He falls into place and clings,
whichever way you try him. . . . He is at the beck and call of every heart for
honest deeds or fraud. . . . This was amply revealed in the facile queen. She
was saved by guile and by the doctored oath which went flying up to
God."[32]

Although Jean was fully conversant with the Tristan legend and the *Renart* stories, the ordeal he places at the center of the *Rose* is unlike those
preceding him, because it actually exposes falsehood and does justice in a
difficult legal case. It will be recalled that the imperial seneschal cites the
rose on her inner thigh in support of his claim to have debauched Lïenor.
Not to be outmaneuvered, Lïenor devises her own plan. Journeying to the
imperial court at Mainz, she sends the seneschal a belt, purse, and jewels,
purportedly as a *gage d'amour* from a châtelaine de Dijon, who requests
that the seneschal wear them next to his skin if he cares to enjoy her favors.
Appearing before the emperor's court, Lïenor then accuses the seneschal of

raping her and stealing her jewels. Having never seen Lïenor before, the seneschal quickly denies the charges, but his plea of innocence collapses when he is made to reveal the belt and purse under his tunic. His only recourse is to request the cold-water ordeal.[33] Taking an oath that he has not raped or deflowered the girl, he enters the ordeal basin, sinks, and is straightaway cleared. But so is Lïenor. Not only does the seneschal deny raping the girl, he also swears that he has not taken her virginity (vv. 4024–5101). The cold-water judgment, in effect, exposes a double falsehood—Lïenor's fabricated accusation of rape and the seneschal's calumny.

The seneschal's ordeal plays a central role in the narrative of the *Rose*. Since Jean has need of a reliable instrument for establishing the truth, he is scrupulous in following contemporary judicial procedure.[34] The ultimate grounds for the decision is the swearing of an oath.[35] At first the seneschal pays no attention to Lïenor's accusation. When the emperor advises him to take counsel, he summarily refuses, but after being forced to reveal the planted evidence, he turns to his barons for advice on framing an oath that precisely denies the charge of rape (vv. 4799–4801, 4980–24). "I shall make one hundred knights swear . . . that these misfortunes have come to me by magic. . . . By God, my upbringing, and my merits, . . . I declare that I have never seen her in all my days, nor have I sought her shame or harm, nor have I taken her virginity. May the emperor allow me to purge myself by a *juïse* [ordeal] as reward for my service" (vv. 4908–22). Since to offer such an oath was to take the awesome step of calling upon God and his saints to witness to the truth of one's declaration, such judgments had to be held in the presence of clergy. At Mainz, the water ordeal takes place in the church of St. Peter, as it did in cathedrals and large churches throughout western Christendom. The archbishop of Cologne administers the ceremony and blesses the water; the clergy chant praises and ring bells after the decision (vv. 4995–5051).[36]

Of equal note, Jean integrates this ordeal into the theology implicit in the romance oath invoking God and his saints. In devising her strategy, Lïenor calls upon the Holy Spirit to counsel her (vv. 4038–40). She expresses her confidence that Christ, who in the Gospels feeds his entourage with five loaves of bread and two fishes, will now produce an open miracle for her (vv. 4054–57). As she enters the imperial court, she crosses herself and addresses her complaint to the emperor, interspersed with banal oaths, now freighted with providential meaning: "Noble and honorable emperor, for God's sake, hear me now, and may God help me because I am in need. One day, not long ago, a man, your seneschal over there, came by chance to a place where I was sewing . . ." (vv. 4602–3, 4775–82). After the seneschal formulates an oath of denial, solicits numerous co-swearers, and proposes the ordeal, Lïenor prays once again to God "to perform an open miracle. All those present echo, Amen" (vv. 4988–91). In contrast to the response to Iseut's blasphemy, God does answer Lïenor's plea to reveal the truth.

Jean's deployment of the ordeal fits into a long tradition in hagiography that asserted that God had not only intervened directly in human affairs in the past but continued to perform miracles through his saints in the present. At the end of the twelfth century, saints' lives furnished the most powerful testimony to the ordeal's abiding efficacy. When Pope Innocent III came to the throne in 1198, an inquest into the canonization of Cunegunda of Luxemburg was already under way. Cunegunda was the wife of the last Ottonian emperor Henry II, who had died in 1024.[37] Since the imperial couple had produced no children, they were credited during their lifetimes with living a continent marriage like Joseph and Mary. Their lavish donations to churches enhanced their reputation for sanctity, especially at the cathedral of Bamberg, which Henry founded and Cunegunda endowed from her dowry. Before Pope Eugenius III canonized Henry in 1147, the legend of their celibate marriage was already reported by contemporary historians and included in a saint's life devoted to the emperor.[38] Added to the *vita* was a new story in which the Devil, unable to corrupt the couple, starts rumors that cast suspicion on the empress's virtue. To put a halt to the calumny, Cunegunda chooses to clear herself by the ordeal of glowing hot plowshares. Calling upon the Lord God as judge and witness, she declares before the emperor and his court that neither Henry nor any other man has had carnal knowledge of her. Then to the terror of all she treads with bare feet over the plowshares unharmed. Cunegunda's own canonization did not occur until 1200, but investigations were initiated in the 1190s under pressure from Bamberg. Of two versions drafted of her hagiography, one refers to her ordeal only briefly, but the other incorporates verbatim the account previously drafted in Henry's *vita*.[39] In the bull of canonization, Innocent III declared that full and careful investigation had confirmed in her the two qualities necessary for sainthood, the virtue of morals, or *merita*, and the virtue of signs, or *miracula*. Among the former, Innocent listed the endowments to Bamberg cathedral and the celibate marriage. Among the latter, he included not only the miracles at her tomb but also, that during her lifetime, as recorded in Henry's and her *vitae*, she had proved her innocence of diabolically inspired suspicions with her bare feet on glowing plowshares.[40]

Once Cunegunda was officially inscribed in the Roman calendar of saints, the account of her ordeal took on renewed life. Shortly after canonization, an addition was composed for the life of Saint Henry that transformed the whole story into a romance. Unable to disturb the love and continence of the imperial couple, the Devil assumes the likeness of a knight and exits the empress's chamber after Cunegunda has arisen at dawn. When this happens for three days in full view of the domestics, malicious rumors reach the emperor's ears. Cunegunda notices the change in her husband and requests that his princes and bishops be summoned so that they can hear the charges against her by judicial procedure. To the emperor's accusation that she has seduced another man in contempt of legitimate marriage, the empress replies: "Since the most prestigious of all women has been accused of the most infamous crime, it is necessary that she be tried by the harshest of judgments." Twelve glowing plowshares are brought to the basilica. The empress approaches them guided by two bishops on either side, like a sheep led to slaughter. Unable to endure the horrible sight, Henry concedes her innocence and beseeches her to cease, but Cunegunda raises her eyes to heaven and calls upon God to witness her oath. Although the emperor suffers as if he has lost his firstborn son, she walks across the smoking irons as if they were flowers. Having trod upon eleven, she pauses on the last to praise the supreme king through whom she has vanquished the Devil.[41] In an unmistakable challenge, Cunegunda has declared herself to be an anti-Iseut.[42] The ordeal was memorialized in contemporary sermons and in liturgies sung at Bamberg on the feast days of the two saints.[43] Its high drama was depicted in the manuscript illumination to the queen's life drawn for the church of Bamberg at the beginning of the century; by the late Middle Ages, it had become a popular iconographic motif throughout the Empire.[44]

When Innocent pronounced the empress's canonization in 1200, he had two reasons for hesitation. Bamberg was an imperial church traditionally loyal to the Staufen dynasty, whose claims to the Empire the popes contested.[45] Equally important, his bull, relying on information supplied by Bamberg, had nonetheless attested an ordeal among Cunegunda's miracles. As a canonist and theologian, the pope was well aware of the long-standing hostility to these so-called judgments of God.[46] From the early Middle Ages on, churchmen were of two minds. Although they could occasionally think of exceptions,[47] in general, they resisted use of these procedures, which they called *iudicia peregrina* (foreign judgments) or *purgationes vulgares,* to be distinguished from acceptable *purgationes canonice,* or purgations by oath. Throughout the second half of the century, canonists were engaged in lively discussion over the exceptions, but by the turn of the century, Huguccio, the foremost authority at Bologna, finally resolved all ambivalence. Addressing each specific exception, he concluded that ordeals should be totally eradicated from both ecclesiastical and secular courts.[48]

Among the theologians, the most strident voice against ordeals was that of Huguccio's contemporary Pierre the Chanter. His polemics may be reduced to three points.[49] First, ordeals are fundamentally immoral. By insisting that God intervene directly in the judicial process at the request of a human judge, the ordeal violates the Old and New Testament commandment, "You shall not tempt the Lord your God" (Deut. 6:16; Matt. 4:7). Second, ordeals frequently do not work, condemning the innocent and setting free the guilty. The hot iron merely tests the calluses on the proband's hand; the cold water functions according to the proband's specific gravity. To oppose the hagiographic literature recounting how God worked miracles in ordeals by means of saints, Pierre takes malicious delight in collecting stories about the failure of ordeals. His most noteworthy concerns two English pilgrims to Jerusalem. When one returns home while the other goes on to Santiago de Compostela, he is accused by the other's kinsmen of murder, put to the water test, fails, and is hanged—much to the sorrow of the companion, who shows up later.[50] In the third place, ordeals depend upon the priestly blessing of the iron and the water, and ecclesiastics should be unconditionally excluded from participation, because they are thereby implicated in judgments leading to the shedding of blood. Assuming a bold personal stance, the Chanter declares: "Even if the universal Church under the penalty of anathema commanded me as a priest to bewitch the iron or bless the water, I would quicker undergo the perpetual penalty than to perform such a thing." By removing the clergy, the Chanter hoped to lay an ax to the root of the practice. In addition to arguing passionately against ordeals throughout his biblical commentaries, theological questions, and popular treatises, Pierre carried his campaign personally to the cardinals at Rome.[51]

As the Chanter's pupil, Pope Innocent finally resolved his ambivalence over ordeals. Neither the pope nor the theologian ever doubted God's ability to intervene in human affairs, but ordeals were wrong because they purported to limit God's choice. After issuing decretals against the practice,[52] Innocent brought this legislation to a conclusion in canon 18 of the Fourth Lateran Council of 1215. Adopting the Chanter's suggestions, he framed ordeals in the context of blood judgments and forbade the clergy to consecrate the cold or hot water and the hot iron.[53] The pope's and the theologian's strategy was to discourage ordeals by unequivocally removing the clergy from the procedure. The effects of the legislation were remarkable. Deprived of clerical blessing, use of the iron and water of the unilateral ordeal underwent a marked decline. They were explicitly repudiated in English and Danish law and began to disappear from practice elsewhere.[54]

Trial by battle, the bilateral ordeal, to which I now turn, followed another trajectory. Associated with tournaments since the council of Clermont in 1130, it was prohibited with them by all the major French and Roman Church councils. Canon 18 of the Lateran Council of 1215 reminded the faithful that judicial duels in which blood was shed were forbidden, as in the past. Yet trial by battle continued to flourish as before throughout the thirteenth century. In France, it encountered little resistance from lay authority until the anti-dueling ordinances of Louis IX.[55]

Jean's and Gerbert's audiences were well accustomed to bilateral ordeals from previous romances, in which they are interspersed among the interminable single combats. Chrétien introduces three noteworthy examples. In the *Lion* (vv. 3598–3743, 4307–4569), Yvain rescues Lunette from burning on the charge of treason against her lady. In the same romance (vv. 5835–6439), Yvain and Gauvain each champions one of two sisters in a judicial battle to decide a dispute between them over the seizin of land. In the *Charrete* (vv. 4533–5033), as we have seen, Lancelot defends Queen Guenièvre against Méléagant's accusation that she has committed adultery with the seneschal Kay. Chretien's purpose, however, appears to be to poke gentle fun at, or even to undercut, the judicial institution. The first case obliges Yvain to face three adversaries, eventually with the aid of his pet lion. The second offers another unprecedented feature. Two evenly matched champions fight incognito. When they both fall exhausted, unable to reach a decision, King Arthur tricks the older girl into admitting her wrongful disseizin and recompenses the younger sister. In the last,

Lancelot, himself the actual adulterer, clears the queen through an equivocal oath.[56] Chrétien takes few pains to provide these judicial proceedings
with realistic features, except in the last case, where the decision results
from a combat that confirms the oaths sworn upon holy relics in accordance with customary practice.

Gerbert de Montreuil offers two further examples of trial by battle in
the *Violette*. Although susceptible to Chrétien's influence, he not only introduces historical personages but also strives to make them conform to
contemporary procedures. Like Jean, he needed a reliable means of deter-
mining the truth. When Gerart finally learns of Euriaut's innocence, he is
determined to "prove" Lisïart's treachery "body to body" ("cors a cors il
volra prouver," v. 1510) and thereby recover his inheritance. This terminology approximates the contemporary English practice of the king employing "approvers" (*probatores*) to serve as champions in judicial combats
in the royal courts.[57] Gerart finally catches up with Euriaut at Metz, where
he discovers that, like Chrétien's Lunette, she is about to be burned on a
charge of murder. After failing to rape Euriaut, the villainous Melïatir has
murdered the duke of Metz's sister and framed the heroine by placing the
dagger in her hand while she is asleep. Since the girl is found in flagrante
delicto, Melïatir argues for immediate execution at the stake. After consult-
ing his uncle the count of Bar-le-Duc, the duke of Metz declares that he
will respect judicial procedure. Twelve peers are summoned to give counsel, and they agree to hear two barons representing the two parties.
Against the arguments for immediate execution offered by the lord of
l'Ancy, kinsman of Melïatir, the lord of Apremont exposes the improbabil-
ity of the evidence and maintains that a formal accusation should be made.
If the accused denies the charge, Melïatir must prove it in battle, now that
Euriaut has a defender. Gerart defeats Melïatir in battle, forces him to confess, and the true murderer is immediately hanged (vv. 5331–5643).[58]

A second injustice, however, remained to be righted. After the tournament of Montargis, Gerart appears before King Louis's court and accuses
Lisïart of betrayal and unlawful dispossession. If Lisïart denies the charge,
"he is prepared to prove it body to body in battle" ("je suis pres de prouver
... cors a cors ... par bataille," vv. 6239–40). In need of a truth-revealing
instrument, Gerbert is again careful not to omit realistic details of current
judicial procedure. The king receives wagers from the two parties and demands pledges to guarantee their appearance on the Monday after Pentecost. Members of the court attempt to reconcile the adversaries through in-

quest or peaceful settlement. When these efforts fail, the two attend Mass on the appointed day; the king has the relics produced, and both swear their oaths. "You will not go further," proclaims Lisïart. "By St. Clement," replies Gerart, "he who doesn't tell the truth, lies" (vv. 6368–71). Once again, Gerart is victorious in battle, and Lisïart is condemned and hanged (vv. 6276–6563). Except for Normandy (under English influence), the customary procedures on trial by battle were not codified in France until the end of the thirteenth century in the *Coutumes de Beauvaisis* of Philippe de Beaumanoir. Already in the first third of the century, however, Gerbert creates fictional cases that appear to be following contemporary practice.

The effect of the Fourth Lateran Council on ordeals, both unilateral and bilateral, in the world of romance may now be assessed in Gerbert's *Violette*, composed at least a decade later (1227–29). Like the *Rose*, the *Violette* is a "wager" story that has need of a reliable truth-telling device. Following Jean, Gerbert has duplicated the function of the ordeal, but the *Violette* contains two, and written after the council, it has now substituted bilateral duels for the unilateral trial. The first echoes the Tristan legend, but concerns an accusation not of adultery but of murder (vv. 4008–32). Melïatir asserts that if Eurïaut does not offer the *juïse* to clear herself, and no one comes to her defense, he will demonstrate that she deserves death at the stake. When Gerart does arrive to defend her, Eurïaut proposes to clear herself by *juïse*, but her lover rejects this procedure as long as trial by battle is available (vv. 5361–5484).

Scrupulously mirroring judicial procedure after the Lateran Council, the unilateral ordeal proposed by Melïatir and Eurïaut is thus expressly rejected in favor of the bilateral duel. Equally significant, the clergy, their relics, and oaths are conspicuously absent from the scene. The decision that clears the heroine nonetheless rests on immanent justice explicitly guaranteed by God. While the flames of the stake creep up, Eurïaut offers a long prayer to Christ, followed by her profession of innocence and the Lord's Prayer. At the end of his legal brief, the lord of Apremont further affirms that God will acquit her if she is innocent, and Eurïaut once again calls upon Jesus as the battle begins (vv. 5177–5332, 5463–64, 5503).

Taken by itself, however, this one example does not reveal the full complexity of the judicial scene. The *Violette* contains a second trial by battle over the dispossession of Nevers. Appearing before the court of King Louis, Gerart accuses Lisïart of falsehood and unjust claims and is prepared to prove his case in battle (vv. 6216–72). Unlike in the case of the previous combat, however, the clergy and their accouterments make their appearance. Scripture is recited to confirm the clerical claim that treason is the worst of sins (vv. 5868–72, 6108–29, 6329–33, 6348–53). The outcome replicates the first battle. When the second duel is juxtaposed against the first, however, the Lateran Council's influence appears equivocal. A dispute over the possession of land required the return of the Mass and relics. The Lateran Council evidently did not succeed in excluding clerical mediation in all cases. Nor did it eliminate the choice of bilateral ordeals in cases of murder and disseizin. Faith in the operations of divine justice, however, remained as firm as it had been for centuries.

Like the conciliar legislation against tournaments, the difficulties of the Lateran Council in eliminating trial by battle were anticipated by the Paris theologians. Pierre the Chanter poses two problematic cases. The first concerns the custom of allowing hired champions to attend Mass but not to receive the Eucharist. If they die in a duel, however, they are to be refused burial in consecrated land. How could one reconcile the discrepancy of communicating with a malefactor before death but not afterward? The Chanter justifies the refusal of burial on the grounds that it discourages duels by means of terror. The second concerns a defendant who has to decide between waging battle or death. In this case, the Chanter is doubtful whether he should be given the Eucharist, because a fight to the death cannot be conducted without fraternal hatred, which is a sin against the Holy Spirit.[59]

Concurrent with the Lateran Council, Thomas of Chobham assembled his master's brief and hesitant suggestions into a coordinated discussion of champions selling their services to fight judicial duels (*pugiles, duelliones, monomachi*), concluding that their profession should be abolished because of fraternal hatred and the ecclesiastical prohibition of ordeals and single combats, although he acknowledges that secular princes prevent the Church from enforcing the prohibition. Thomas then turns to the dilemma of a defendant whose legitimate inheritance is challenged in a duel. Unlike the Chanter, Thomas allows battle to an innocent defendant, in the same manner that one has the right of defense against a robber, countering force with force. It is forbidden to a plaintiff, however, no matter the justice of his cause.[60] On the grounds of defense, therefore, the theologians accord moral justification to Chrétien's and Gerbert's heroes, who habitually defend victims who have been unjustly accused. The theologians limit their consideration to professional champions or parties directly implicated, however; they are silent about the knights of romance who undertake these services as their mission and without pay. The theologians' hesitancies nonetheless help to explain the secular resistance to the conciliar legislation against trial by battle.

A New Clergy: The Hermit

As in the *Escoufle, Rose,* and *Violette,* high-ranking clerics appear throughout Gerbert's *Continuation,* and priests say Mass on occasion, but another type, the solitary religious hermit, also makes his appearance in this romance. This personage is isolated deep in the forest, lodged in a hermitage with a chapel close by, and solitary except for a cleric and an occasional priest. Absent from the *Rose* and the *Violette,* the figure may be found sporadically in Béroul's *Tristan,* Marie de France's *Eliduc,* and Chrétien's *Lion* and *Charrete,* but he emerges as virtually the sole clergyman in Chrétien's *Conte de graal* and remains the chief representative of the clergy in Gerbert's *Continuation.*[61]

The historical phenomenon of the religious hermit was not new in western Europe around 1200. Modeled on the prophets Elijah and Elisha in the Old Testament and John the Baptist in the New, the hermit combined the attributes of solitude, hospitality, friendship, prayer, and asceticism. The solitary monk flourished in late antiquity in the movement known as the Desert Fathers, and the figure underwent a revival toward the end of the eleventh century in western France and England, the alleged setting of the Arthurian legends.[62]

Chrétien identifies his sole hermit as a *preudome* (*Graal* v. 6303), a term denoting chivalric excellence; later he is revealed to be the brother of Perceval's mother and therefore of royal/knightly origins. The continuations to Chrétien's story retain this social level whenever the family origins of hermits are mentioned.[63] Although Gerbert is rarely explicit, he appears to have adopted this pattern as well; two hermits of advanced age, for example, are likewise designated as *preudome* (v. 15748). Men predominate, but anchoresses also appear on occasion.

At times the hermits are depicted as occupied with mundane activities. One provides secretarial services (Béroul vv. 2428–32), another clears the forest (*Lion* v. 2833), and another provides a Psalter on which a defeated knight takes an oath (*Continuation* vv. 7362–65). A more pious service is that of burial. Marie de France's King Eliduc intends to bury his lover at a hermitage in a forest not far from his palace (*Eliduc* vv. 889–901), and Perceval also finds the grave of his mother in a forested hermitage (*Continuation* vv. 2707–9). After burying her knightly lover at the abbey of Saint-Sulpice, the maiden of Dras Envers seeks out a deserted chapel in the woods of Claradeure, where she becomes a hermitess to pray for the soul of her *ami* (vv. 10118–25, 10159–85). Defeated by Perceval, the knight Lugarel li Covoitiez becomes a hermit to propitiate for having killed other knights (vv. 14947–50).

The most characteristic service performed by hermits, however, is the daily celebration of the office, the *opus Dei* or divine *mestier*. Since the adventures of the knights in the romance world frequently take them on extended journeys through the forest, not only is their lodging supplied by sylvan hermits, but the liturgical offices are celebrated for them before their departure each morning. In Chrétien's version, both Perceval's mother and his mentor Gornemans urge the young neophyte to attend church to pray to the Lord and to hear masses and matins (*Graal* vv. 567–69, 592–94, 1666–67), but Perceval becomes so engrossed in his chivalric adventures that he does not think of God or enter a church for five years, until he is recalled to his senses on Good Friday (vv. 6217–23). With pangs of repentance, he discovers a hermitage in the woods where a hermit, a priest, and a cleric have begun the service in a small chapel (vv. 6337–47). Thereafter in Gerbert's *Continuation,* Perceval performs his obligation without fail, as do most Arthurian heroes throughout the Perceval continuations. No sooner has Perceval abandoned his wife, Blancheflor, on the morrow of their wedding, for example, than he plunges into the forest and comes upon a small chapel with a hermit's house close by, where he is offered hospitality. The next morning, he listens to the *preudom* singing matins, terce, prime, and nones before he takes his leave (*Continuation* vv. 7126–35). On five latter occasions, hermits provide this service according to the same formula.[64]

The devotion of Chrétien's and Gerbert's Perceval to the divine office contrasts with the careless and derisive attitudes of Jean's knights. The shift is best articulated by a hermit who interprets to Perceval the marvelous vision of the mother beast (*la beste glatissant*) who is devoured by her infants. The beast signifies Holy Church, the infants, those parishioners who disturb the priest as he begins to sing Mass. Like Jean's congregations, they are occupied with the sale of wheat, oats, and the harvest, which they discuss so noisily that the priest cannot continue. If the priest slackens, they shout, "Sing quickly! We're in a hurry to return to dinner" (*Continuation* vv. 8674–91).

Although a secular cleric oriented to a ministry in the world, Pierre the Chanter held hermits in high regard. In a chapter entitled "In Praise of Solitude of Place," he distinguishes between two kinds of solitary lives, those of the cenobites and the anchorites.[65] The first kind, practiced by monks in communities, better accommodates human imperfections and is the safer form, but the second is more excellent because it permits fuller expression of love (*caritas*) for God. Most of the chapter consists of encomia to the solitary life excerpted liberally from the letters of St. Jerome and Seneca. Of particular note, the Chanter recited Jerome's romantic vision of the natural habitat in which hermits enjoy the spring flowers and sweet psalmody of the birds, as well as the shade of trees against the summer heat and the temperate airs of autumn, in contrast to the urban pollutions of Rome. The prime examples of hermits are the Lord himself, who suffered temptation in the desert, and the solitary St. John the Baptist. Hermits of the early Church include St. Martin of Tours, St. Germain of Auxerre, and St. Remi of Reims. Martin was, in fact, a more effective thaumaturge as a hermit than as a bishop. The Chanter's catalogue does not extend to recent times, however, and he may have harbored doubts about the services demanded by the knights-errant of romance, who compromise the sanctity of his solitary heroes.

Christian Doctrine

In addition to saying daily masses, a further function of the hermit in Chrétien's *Graal* and Gerbert's *Continuation* is to instruct the laity in Christian doctrine such as that contained in the so-called Apostles' and Constantinopolitan creeds.[66] In the ancient Church, the creed was taught to catechumens in preparation for baptism, but during the twelfth century, when infant baptism was universal, such instruction became the responsibility of children's godparents.[67] To aid them, one version of the creed was recited after the reading of the Gospels on liturgical feast days on which the articles of faith were celebrated (Trinity Sunday, Christmas, Easter, etc.). In commenting on the liturgy, Jean Beleth specifies that the Constantinopolitan Creed could be said at masses for the instruction of neophytes. On Sundays after the sermon to the people, the priest could explain the Lord's Prayer and the Apostles' Creed in the vernacular.[68] Maurice de

Sully, bishop of Paris (d. 1196), preached sermons in French devoted to elucidating the creed and the Lord's Prayer and advising priests on how to perform the task.[69]

Apparently these provisions for imparting religious instruction were less than satisfactory to the theologians. "There is no virtue more lacking today than faith," complains Pierre the Chanter before the close of the twelfth century.[70] Thomas of Chobham notes that many are well versed in fatuous *chansons* and the vernacular deeds of Charlemagne and other princes but ignorant of right faith, the deeds of the Savior, and the saints. For that reason each parishioner seeking to confess his sins should be examined for even a superficial knowledge of the articles of the Apostles' Creed. Belief in the creed was prerequisite to receiving penance.[71]

In statutes drawn up for the diocese of Paris, Bishop Eudes de Sully (1199–1208) urged priests to exhort the people to say the Lord's Prayer, the Apostles' Creed, and the Ave Maria frequently. Priests were commanded to devote some part of their sermons on Sundays and feast days to teaching the creed to the faithful, as Bishop Maurice de Sully had urged for his priests and congregations.[72] This minimal requirement of teaching the creed, the Lord's Prayer, and the Ave Maria to the laity was repeated in the synodical statutes published in France and England into the thirteenth century.[73] In England the rudiments could be recited in the vernacular,[74] but in France this was inhibited for fear of heresy. On account of the heretics, Eudes de Sully urged priests to corroborate articles of faith with authorities and reasons from Scripture. Evidently the heretics were also circulating vernacular versions of the creed and the Lord's Prayer. When Pierre de Corbeil, archbishop of Sens, condemned the Amaurician heretics at Paris in 1210, he ordered that all theological texts in the romance vernacular, including creeds and the Lord's Prayer, be handed to the diocesan bishops for examination.[75]

The danger of heresy and of theological controversy encouraged Pope Innocent III to expand and elaborate the articles of faith in the opening canon of the Lateran Council of 1215, which the canonist Johannes Teutonicus calls the fourth *symbolum* of the Christian faith.[76] Drawing upon a century of theological discussion and debate in the French schools, the pope offered the Latin Church a reformulation of doctrine couched in the most recent and technical terminology of the theologians. The synodical statutes of councils held in England and France following 1215 took immediate notice of the new statement. Quoting the opening passage verbatim,

Bishop Richard Poore increased instruction in the articles of faith at the council of Salisbury (1217–19). The archdeacons were to explain the formulations of the general council to priests in simple words, so that they, in turn, could instruct their parishioners in the vernacular.[77] In France, the Statutes of Angers (1216–19) summarized the essential tenets of the Trinity and the Incarnation and reminded the laity that they were not to seek the reasons for the articles, which were so exalted that they could not be comprehended with the intellect. One should not subject the mystery of the Trinity, for example, to questioning about how or why, but simply believe; in the future one would understand fully.[78]

Like most romances composed before the Lateran Council, Jean's *Rose* is devoid of formal theology, except for an occasional oath, for example, "since God was born without sin" (v. 5308). In Chrétien's innovating *Graal*, however, the neophyte Perceval is instructed not only in the first tenets of chivalry but also in the rudiments of the faith by his mother, by his mentor, Gornemans de Gorhaut, by a group of knights and ladies, and by the hermit, his uncle. After his terrifying encounter with the knight-angels in the forest, the young boy throws himself to the ground and "recites the entire creed and all the prayers he knew, which his mother had taught him" (*Graal* vv. 155–58). This is less a profession of faith than a gesture of fear, comparable to crossing himself. After his amnesia of five years, a knight reproaches him for negligence: "My dear friend, do you not believe in Jesus Christ who wrote the new law and gave it to Christians?" (vv. 6255–57). Thereafter *novele loi* becomes the principal term for designating Christian doctrine in the continuations to Chrétien's *Graal*.[79] Occasioned by Good Friday, the knight proceeds to recite the principal articles of the creed relating to the doctrines of the Incarnation and the Atonement (vv. 6266–6300).

Gerbert de Montreuil offers the longest creedal statement after the Council of 1215 in his *Violette* (vv. 5182–5334). When the heroine Eurïaut is condemned to execution at the stake, as has been seen, she seeks to postpone her death by reciting the principal events of the biblical narrative of salvation. In 150 verses, she recounts the story from Creation to Pentecost. The entire narration is directed to God as a prayer and concludes with a Pater Noster (vv. 5181–62, 5532). The recitation of biblical-creedal statements in the form of prayers had precedents in Latin monastic collections of a century earlier,[80] but Gerbert's direct source was undoubtedly the chansons de geste, where heroes like Guillaume d'Orange offer such prayers at moments of danger. The *Couronnement de Louis,* for example, contains Guillaume's longest prayer (95 verses), spoken before he fights a Turk.[81] Whereas Eurïaut asks God to receive her soul, having abandoned her body to the stake, Guillaume prays that God will defend his body against death and keep him from disgracing his lineage. Despite these divergent goals, the two prayers are remarkably similar. Although exact verbal borrowings are rare, Guillaume covers the same biblical ground, including the two extrabiblical episodes of St. Anatasia of the Nativity and Longinus of the Crucifixion. The major difference lies in the exposition. Although two-thirds the size of the *Violette,* the *Couronnement* treats more scriptural episodes, but more concisely. In contrast, Gerbert chooses fewer events, but develops them more fully around the central doctrines of the Creation, Fall, Incarnation, and Atonement. To the creation of the world, for example, he adds that of the angels; to the expulsion from paradise, he includes the assignment of souls to hell with Lucifer. In other words, rather than simply reciting biblical events, Gerbert regroups the narrative according to major theological themes. Eurïaut's prayer fulfills the program of the statutes of Angers and Salisbury to formulate Christian belief for the laity *simpliciter* and unaccompanied by logical justification. In addition to Eurïaut's prayer, Gerbert repeatedly turns to discrete articles of faith throughout the *Continuation* and assigns their explication to hermits.

The articles of faith that the romance writers insert in their narratives extend beyond the individual tenets of the ancient creeds recited during the liturgy, but all are to be found in the contemporary statement with which Innocent III prefaced the canons of the Lateran Council of 1215. Whereas the council's declaration was orientated toward resolving questions of speculative theology, such as the nature of the Trinity and of Christ, and opposing heretical views on the Church's authority and the sanctity of marriage, the romance writers choose less controversial fundamental beliefs. Like Eurïaut's prayer, they may be grouped around the articles of Creation, Fall, Incarnation, and Atonement; two sacraments are added, the Eucharist and penance.

The romance writers ignore the theological formulations of the Trinity that opened the Lateran *symbolum,* but not the subject of the Creation. In the creeds, the work of creation is specifically assigned to God the Father. The formulation of "I believe in God the omnipotent Father, creator of heaven and earth" of the Apostles' Creed was expanded by the Lateran Council to "creator of all things visible and invisible, spiritual and corporal . . . angelical and mundane, and thereafter human, as if a common constitution from spirit and body." The council went on to specify that the Devil and other demons were also created by God with a good nature. In Chrétien's *Graal,* Perceval's mother identifies God as "he who made heaven and earth" and adds "who placed men and women there" (*Graal* vv. 574–76). In the *Continuation,* Gerbert reverts to the simple formula "God who made land and sea," but in Eurïaut's prayer, he embroiders the article of faith with details from the biblical narrative: "True God, who created the world and raised the air above the earth and placed the angels in heaven and made them spirits with great beauty. . . . And you made Adam with your hand and then his wife Eve and commanded them to keep watch over paradise" (vv. 5182–86, 5196–99).

Ignored in the ancient creeds, the doctrine of the Fall was inserted into the Lateran formulation, and particular responsibility was assigned to the Devil. Although the Devil and the demons had been created good, "they made themselves wicked," and "man sinned through the suggestion of the Devil." Once again, Gerbert elaborates on the statement with details from Scripture in the *Violette.* Although created good, Lucifer became enamored of his own beauty through pride. Because of this, God threw him into hell and remade the other angels more beautiful. In paradise, God gave everything to the first couple except the fruit of the apple tree, which he forbade them to eat. By the suggestion of wicked Satan, Eve made Adam eat of it. After that, when they looked at each other, they saw that they were naked. An angel arrived and expelled them from paradise with his sword. God provided them with a spade, distaff, and spindle with which to work. Thereafter hell was opened, where the wicked suffer great torments with Lucifer. Whenever souls depart from the body, they go straight to hell (vv. 5187–5215). When the hermit king Elyas Anais instructs Perceval in the *Continuation,* he summarizes the essentials of the *Violette,* to which he adds the detail that Adam was expelled from paradise not only naked but also poor and begging (vv. 8729–37). Later Perceval encounters Lucifer directly in the form of a serpent's body with the head of a man (vv. 14435–36). When the hero judges the beast to be hideous in body but with a sweet manner (vv. 14470–71), the Devil explains that he possessed the same form when he deceived Eve, who never perceived his body, however, because it was hidden. Had she seen it, he would have labored in vain (vv. 14474–82).

The incarnation of Christ the Son directly follows the article on God the Father. To the formula of the Apostles' Creed, "I believe in Jesus Christ, his only son, our Lord, who was conceived of the Holy Spirit, born of the Virgin Mary . . . ," the Lateran Council offered theological elaboration to deal with the dual nature of Christ: "the only-born son of God, Jesus Christ, commonly incarnate from the whole Trinity, conceived in Mary who remained always virgin through the cooperation of the Holy Spirit, he was made a true human [*homo*] composed of a rational soul and human flesh, one person in two natures."

Although the romance writers recognize Christ's duality as God and human, they emphasize the central tenet of the Incarnation that God became human flesh and the special role of the Virgin Mary. In Chrétien's *Graal,* for example, the knights declare that Jesus "became man for our sins. He was true God and man, a son born of the Virgin, conceived by the Holy Spirit in which God assumed flesh and blood and covered his deity with human flesh" (vv. 6274–85). In the *Violette,* Gerbert directly links the Incarnation and souls in hell, on whom God takes pity. Through the angel Gabriel, he announces to the Virgin that he will hide in her and assume human form. When Mary hears this, she is both joyous and frightened. She carries him for nine months until he is born on Christmas Day (vv. 5219–27). In the *Continuation,* Gerbert extolls Mary as "a gem above all others" (vv. 685–86), an example of the Marian hyperbole common in romance oaths. To answer the misogynous remarks of Dragoniaus li Cruels, Perceval equates Mary's role in the Incarnation with the redemptive act of the Harrowing of Hell: "A woman was the first bridge over which God passed to hell and through whom all his friends returned from hell and exited by the gate" (vv. 7232–38).

According to the creed, the son of God was born to die. Omitting Christ's life, the Apostles' Creed follows Christ's birth immediately with his death—"born of the Virgin Mary, suffered under Pontius Pilate, was crucified, dead and buried." The Lateran Council interpreted this formulation according to Christ's two natures: "Who was immortal and immune to suffering according to his divinity, was made subject of suffering and mortal according to his humanity; indeed, for the salvation of the human race he suffered on the wood of the cross and died." In the *Violette,* Gerbert merely elaborates the historical events of the Crucifixion with details from the Gospels. After Jesus enters Jerusalem in triumph on Palm Sunday, the felon Judas has him taken and sold to unbelievers. On the holy day of Friday he is hung on a cross, with his limbs spread and nailed. His head is encompassed with piercing thorns; because of his royal dignity, he is crowned on the cross (vv. 5264–83). Like the Lateran Council, Chrétien and his followers connect the historical events to the Atonement. In the *Graal*, Perceval's mother explains that Jesus "was tied to the stake, beaten and then crucified and bore a crown of thorns" (vv. 589–91) because "he was betrayed and wrongly judged and suffered the torments of death for men and women" (vv. 583–85). Later the knights repeat that one should worship the cross on Friday, because on that day he was sold for thirty deniers and was hung on the cross. Seeing the sins that ensnared and polluted everyone, he who was free of all sin became human for our sins' sake (vv. 6266–74).[82] In Gerbert's *Continuation*, the hermit king Elyas Anais reveals the significance of the hermit who beat the cross. He beat the wood for the grief and anguish that Jesus Christ suffered on the cross when he offered his body to death for us (vv. 8625–29). Later another hermit admonished Perceval to put his faith in God and remember that he suffered death for us when he offered himself on the cross (vv. 15835–38).

For the romance writers, the most vivid illustration of the Atonement is the corollary of the Harrowing of Hell, that is, Christ's descent into hell after his death. The Apostles' Creed declares succinctly: "He was crucified, dead and buried; he descended into hell; the third day he arose from the dead and ascended into heaven." The Lateran Council repeated the formula but added: "He descended in his soul, was resurrected in the body, and ascended in both," a clarification that addressed Pierre Abélard's doubts as to whether Jesus' soul descended truly into hell. According to Western tradition, the purpose of Christ's descent was to deliver the souls of the just from hell and to represent Christ's victory over the Devil. From late antiquity on, the Harrowing of Hell is portrayed in art and sculpture with Christ treading upon the Devil, hand outstretched to Adam and other souls, helping them leave hell, which is depicted as gaping jaws or the entrance of a cave. Often Christ is seen brandishing a cross.[83]

Once again the romance writers rehearse the declaration of Christian belief with little attention to theological interpretation or debate. In Chrétien's *Graal*, for example, Perceval's mother explains Jesus' redemption of the souls of men and women that went to hell after leaving the body (vv. 585–88). On Good Friday, the knights elaborate that when Jesus was placed on the cross, he drew all of his friends out of hell and brought the dead back to life (vv. 6287–91). Gerbert's longer recitation in the *Violette* supplies further details: "When souls depart from the body, they go straight to hell. For five hundred years all who had died suffered torment in hell" (vv. 5214–18). Reversing the temporal order of the creedal formulations, Gerbert continues: "On the third day you were resurrected, sweet Lord, and you went straight into hell where you broke the gates and brought out your friends whom the Devil had placed there" (vv. 5303–7). When the Dragon Knight sees the cross on Perceval's shield, he fears that same cross on which Jesus Christ won the battle and shattered hell, releasing his friends who had suffered torment (*Continuation* vv. 9556–64). Gerbert was doubtless recalling the prevailing iconography when he devised this imagery.

Among the seven sacraments, the Lateran Council singled out three that pertained directly to salvation: baptism, the Eucharist, and penance. Except for occasional mentions, the writers of romance pay little notice to baptism, but occupy themselves with the theology of the other two. Against the teaching of the heretics, the council took pains to define the doctrine of transubstantiation in the Eucharist: "Jesus Christ is both the priest and the sacrifice whose body and blood are truly contained in the sacrament of the altar under the form of bread and wine, that is, the bread is transubstantiated into the body and the wine into blood by divine power." Gerbert, following Chrétien, not only makes his heroes attend Mass frequently but accepts the implications of the orthodox teaching that Christ's body and blood are truly present in the bread and wine after they are consecrated on the altar during the Mass. In Chrétien's *Graal*, for example, Perceval's mother defines a church as a "beautiful and holy house where there are holy bodies and treasures and where the body of Jesus Christ, the holy prophet, is sacrificed" (vv. 577–81). Since only the bread was regularly communicated to the laity at this time, while the wine was reserved for priests, most attention is paid to Christ's body. Because the bread became the actual body of Christ at the moment the priest pronounced the words "Hoc est corpus meum," the custom arose in French churches of the priest elevating the host above his head so that all of the faithful could see Christ's true body. This practice was regulated by Bishop Eudes de Sully for the diocese of Paris in his synodical constitutions, which were widely followed in France and England. With his back to the congregation, the priest was required to keep the host at the level of his chest and out of sight until he pronounced the words of consecration. Only then could the miracle be displayed to the congregation.[84]

Gerbert testifies to the laity's desire to have the host elevated so that it could be seen. On one occasion Perceval watches through an iron grille as Mass is celebrated in a church in the presence of a wounded king lying on a bed near the altar. When the priest comes to the sacrament, he raises the body of God on high. The man responds immediately and lifts himself to a seated position (*Continuation* vv. 10285–91). The laity's desire to see the host raised a debate among contemporary theologians as to what one actually saw: the accidents of the bread or the substance of the body? Earlier theologians such as Pierre the Lombard had maintained that it was only the bread and wine that were visible; Christ's body was invisible. More recently, Pierre de Poitiers had argued that the body of Christ is seen as if it were a hand under a cloak. Although Pierre the Chanter concedes that the Lord's body is veiled under the form of bread, he rejects the negative conclusion that it cannot be seen. For him, it is like a hand veiled in a glove.[85] By this metaphor, the Chanter preserves the rationale of the idea that the laity were seeing God when the consecrated bread was elevated. In Gerbert's *Continuation,* Gornemans de Gorhaut insists on the visual nature of the Sacrament when he encourages Perceval to attend Mass willingly: "It is the body of Jesus Christ himself who can be seen with the eyes when the priest performs the Sacrament and holds it in his hands. He is neither more nor less than when he was born of the Virgin and hung on the cross" (vv. 5159–67). At Perceval's last attendance at Mass before his return to the Grail Castle, a hermit takes him to a chapel where the *le Dieu mestier* is performed. "Perceval listens attentively with a true heart, but when he *sees* the Sacrament, he joins his raised hands and prays to God that he be pardoned for his sins" (vv. 15797–805).

The New Sacrament of Penance

Chrétien de Troyes not only established the hermit in vernacular literature, he also supplied him with a new religious mission, that of promoting private penance.[86] The first two continuations of the *Graal* (Gauvain and Perceval) largely ignore the new practice, treating it only sporadically;[87] it remained for Gerbert to treat its theology and to integrate it into his narrative.

The principal features of personal penance—remorse for sin, avowal of specific faults, and efforts to make amends—are virtually absent in the early chansons de gestes and the first romances, even those of Chrétien himself.[88] Béroul's version of *Tristan* radically subverts the underlying propositions. Attributing their conduct to the magic potion, Tristan and

Iseut feel little remorse for their adultery. When they first approach the hermit Ogrin, he refuses them absolution because of their unwillingness to confess. Their acknowledgment of sin is only implied when they recognize their inability to bring to an end their love. Although Ogrin prays for their repentance, they do not consent to a separation until three years later. Rather than beseeching pardon, Tristan asks Ogrin to write a letter that will enable Iseut to return to court. Once again Ogrin urges repentance and penance, but he quickly compromises his exhortation with contrary advice. To remove shame and conceal evil they are permitted to lie (*par bel mentir*). The only tears are those of the hermit.[89] Jean Renart likewise takes little interest in sin or personal cleansing. Divine grace intervenes in the *Rose* only to vindicate Lïenor's good name. Similarly, in the *Violette,* Gerbert's heroine Eurïaut has no need for penance. Her confession at the stake is of faith, not of her shortcomings. Declaring her innocence, she expresses confidence that God will have mercy on her soul (vv. 5178–81, 5326–32).

Toward the end of the twelfth century, Pierre de Blois complained that the laity wept copiously over the tragedies of Arthur, Gauvain, and Tristan but were indifferent to the stories of God's love and shed no tears of repentance.[90] At the opening of Chrétien's *Graal,* neither Perceval's mother nor Gornemans include penance in the instruction they impart. After five years of oblivion, however, on Good Friday, Perceval meets a company of knights and ladies who not only remind him of the articles of faith, but also urge that all who believe in God should do penance on this day ("qui en lui ont creance / doivent estre hui en peneance," vv. 6298–99). They further explain that they have just returned from visiting a hermit, from whom they have asked advice concerning their sins and to whom they have confessed (*confesse*) their faults—the most important duty that a Christian wishing to return to God can perform (vv. 6308–14). In distress at his sins, Perceval follows their example, locates the hermit in a small chapel, tearfully falls at his feet, seeks counsel, confesses, and receives the Eucharist on Easter Day as a sign of forgiveness.[91]

In the opening verses of the *Continuation,* Gerbert has the Fisher King urge upon the young Perceval the remedies of the new penance: "If you continue in sin by which you anger God, make your confession, repent, abandon the sin, and do true penitence" (vv. 29–33). This teaching is reiterated on at least eight occasions, scattered throughout the narrative. At times Perceval recommends it to those whom he opposes in combat, but the most sustained treatment is offered by hermits. When the hero visits the last hermitage before obtaining the Grail vision, he prepares himself by kneeling, striking his breast, praying, repenting his sins, confessing, and hearing the divine service before he departs on his concluding adventures (vv. 15841–51).

By the time Chrétien had begun writing his *Graal* (the 1180s), theologians and canonists had been at work on the doctrine of penance for nearly a century.[92] Designed to treat sins committed by Christians after baptism, the new penance radically altered the ancient penitential system practiced into the eleventh century. In place of the severe penalties and humiliations imposed publicly and ceremoniously on sinners, the new penance was administered privately and secretly by confessors according to the circumstances of the individual sinner. Rather than establishing penalties through fixed and written schedules calibrated according to the severity of the crime, the confessors adapted the remedies to the penitents' personal needs.[93]

The basic elements of the new teaching were fashioned by Pierre Abélard at the beginning of the twelfth century and reformulated and promulgated in the theological and canonical collections of Pierre the Lombard and Gratian at mid-century. Along with baptism and the Eucharist, the Lombard defines penance as one of the seven sacraments. This schema was given final confirmation by the Lateran Council of 1215.[94] At the turn of the century, Pierre the Chanter and his school accepted the Lombard's formulation and proceeded to work on the practical application of the sacrament of penance.[95] This occupies the greater part of the Chanter's and Courson's voluminous *summae*. Their efforts, in turn, promoted the composition of handbooks for the instruction of priestly confessors, of which Thomas of Chobham's is noteworthy.

Abélard had divided penance into three constituent elements, *penitentia*, *confessio*, and *satisfactio*, which established the standard pattern for succeeding theologians.[96] At the end of the century, Pierre the Chanter identifies the three elements as contrition of heart, confession by mouth, and satisfaction of works, a classification adopted by Courson and Chobham as well.[97] In a sermon composed for the first Sunday in Lent, Bishop Maurice de Sully translated the three elements into the vernacular as *la repentance del corage*, *la confessions de la bouce*, and *la penitance*.[98] The tripartite formula penetrated the synodical legislation of the statutes of Angers by the second decade of the thirteenth century.[99] In Chrétien's *Graal*, the

hermit orders Perceval to say his *confession*, because he will not receive remission until he has confessed and is *repentans* (vv. 6360–63). Later the
hermit adds that if Perceval achieves true *repentance*, he will go to church
in the name of *penitance* (vv. 6441–43). Although the three elements are
present in the hermit's instruction, they are not yet as formulaic as in the
theologians' discussions. Not long after the Statutes of Angers, however,
Gerbert brings the constituent parts together, but not always in the same
order. "[C]onfessez . . . et repentenz . . . et faites vraie penitance," the
Fisher King exhorts Perceval (*Continuation* vv. 31–33). Perceval warns the
Dragon Knight that his soul is lost if he does not *confess*, do *penitance*, and
have *repentanche* toward God (vv. 9642–44). Later he urges his adversary
to believe holy "confession, repentance, et contrition de cuer" (vv.
9907–9).

Abelard had defined *penitentia* as the "sorrow of mind over what it has
done wrong"—what was later termed repentance or contrition. When
Chrétien's Perceval hears the invitation to penance, he begins to weep and
sets out to the hermitage sighing from the depths of his heart at sins of
which he greatly repents (vv. 6315–36). Tears coursing from his eyes, he
embraces the hermit's feet. What the romance writers call *repentance* is
simply the theologians' *contritio cordis*. Since mid-century, when the Lombard concurred with Abélard's suggestion, the theologians had been
agreed that contrition of heart, or interior penance, as they also called it,
was the foremost element of penitential doctrine. No sin could be forgiven
without it, and in extreme cases it was sufficient for the remission of sin.[100]
Although the theologians had long agreed on the supremacy of contrition,
it was Courson who applied this priority to a situation that faced the solitary knight-errant of romance literature: What if one died in a forest
where priests were unavailable for confession? Robert responds that oral
confession can be performed in two ways, at the tip of ones lips or with the
interior lips of the heart. There is no salvation without one or the other,
but if priests are lacking and one is contrite and confesses one's sins to God
alone, such a person will be saved.[101] The Chanter's school, holding contrition to be all-sufficient, likewise stresses the intensity of repentance. Pierre
expresses this in terms that could be understood by aristocratic families
whose survival depended on lineage. Repentance for a mortal sin should
equal the pain caused by the death of an only son.[102]

Agreeing on contrition, what engaged the theologians at the end of the
century was the place of confession by mouth and its relation to contrition

and satisfaction. Perceval's tears in Chrétien vividly illustrate the contri-
tionalism of the theologians of mid-century. If not as dramatically, Gerbert's sinners likewise experience remorse, but like the contemporary theologians, his characters are chiefly concerned with confession. For the
Chanter, confession by mouth, along with satisfaction, belongs to exterior
penance.[103] If contrition is necessary and sufficient to forgive sin, scriptural passages, such as James 5:6, nonetheless command all Christians to
confess their sins. Pierre defines confession as the process by which "we
confess to priests by mouth our sins nakedly, openly, and stripped of skin
with all their circumstances. . . . [including both] sins we have committed
and virtues we have omitted."[104] Both in his *questiones* and his *Verbum abbreviatum*, Pierre discusses a wide variety of issues relating to confession,
which were pursued by his disciples.

The romance writers are also preoccupied with the subject. *Confession*
lies at the center of Chrétien's and Gerbert's penitential system. I cannot
encompass here the full range of the theologians' discussions and merely
focus on those points echoed in Chrétien's *Graal* and in Gerbert's *Continuation*. In demanding that sins be revealed, Pierre the Chanter drew attention to the surrounding circumstances. His *Verbum abbreviatum* repeats
that "no circumstances be hidden, that sin not be garbed in robes, but revealed to the confessor as it was done."[105] This attention to *circumstantia*
became the hallmark of the Chanter's school and generated endless pages
of casuistical discussion of specific cases.[106] Adopting their terminology,
the Lateran Council's influential canon 21, *Omnis utriusque sexus*, urged
priests as physicians "to inquire diligently into the circumstances of the
sinner and sin" and to avail themselves of the advice of men skilled in the
medicine of the soul. Both before and after the general council, the synodical statutes in France and England overwhelmingly sought to implement this program.[107]

In applying penance, Chobham emphasizes that a priest cannot absolve
the penitent from one sin unless from all. Neither can the priest absolve
any sin that has not been confessed, because if a sin is hidden, there is no
confession and no absolution.[108] Gerbert's hermit further elaborates this
imperative to Perceval:

> My friend, in the name of penitence, I command you to say your sins without
> concealing any. . . . For you should know for certain that there is no hiding
> toward God. If, by chance, you received seven mortal injuries and were healed

of six, but left the seventh unattended without medicine, you would most surely die. . . . One mortal sin that you have concealed from confession and hoarded up in your heart will drag you down to death in hell. (vv. 14206–25)

After five years of forgetfulness, Chrétien's Perceval thus confronts his sins on Good Friday. He beweeps them to the hermit after the service is said (*Graal* vv. 6495–96) and on Easter Sunday partakes of communion most worthily (vv. 6512–13). This is in direct fulfillment of the hermit's command that he say his confession, because he will not receive *remission* (*comenion*, MS. Guiot v. 6150) until he has confessed and is repentant (vv. 6361–63). Apparently Perceval follows the practice of confession before taking the Eucharist on Easter Day. Around 1200, custom varied as to the number of times one should perform confession. In the synodical statutes of Paris, for example, Eudes de Sully instructs priests to enjoin their parishioners to confess frequently, but priests should explicitly urge confession at the beginning of Lent. Stephen Langton also prescribes the opening of Lent for the diocese of Canterbury, but if Christians fall into sin, they should confess more frequently. In particular, three times a year are appropriate, at Easter, Christmas, and Pentecost. Thomas of Chobham reports the opinion that it suffices to confess once a year, because it is the Church's custom to do this during Lent. In his vernacular Lenten sermon, Maurice de Sully concurs. Although practice varied, the minimum appears to have been once a year.[109]

Whatever the confusion, the Lateran Council officially mandated that "all believers of either sex after arriving at the age of discretion each should faithfully confess all of his or her sins to his or her own priest at least once a year and strive to fulfill the enjoined penance so that he or she can reverently receive the sacrament of the Eucharist at least at Easter." This requirement was repeated in subsequent synodical statutes.[110] Thomas of Chobham adds the qualification "unless sickness first intervenes." At whatever time one falls sick, therefore, a person should confess, lest one die without avowing one's sins and taking communion.[111] Accordingly, Gerbert's Perceval recommends confession to those whom he has severely wounded in battle. When he takes revenge against the knight who has harmed Gornemans and his sons, the opponent dies unshriven (vv. 5852–71), but the Dragon Knight heeds the hero's sermon. Before dying, he summons a priest and confesses his sins with tears and sighs from his heart.

His body prostrate, his soul thereupon departs (*Continuation* vv. 9892–
10009).

Whatever the minimal requirements, Gerbert's hermits nonetheless
urge confession without respect to seasons and frequency. Perceval himself
confesses at least twice before he achieves the Grail vision (vv. 14304–7,
15848–51). Chobham likewise wrestles with the problem of frequent practice, marshaling arguments for and against. Any Christian who has sinned
should repent in his heart with the firm intention that he will come to confession next Lent. But it is also good to rush to a priest immediately after
sin, because old sins, like old wounds, putrefy and fester and become more
difficult to cure. It is therefore foolish for one who has sinned mortally to
defer confession too long, but it is equally true that when a man repents in
his heart, his guilt and culpability are canceled. He can therefore await
confession with the confidence of a sick person awaiting medicine, knowing that the illness is contained. In the final analysis, Chobham decides for
the sufficiency of contrition over the practice of frequent confession.

In decreeing annual confession, the Lateran Council specified that each
person should perform this duty to his or her priest (*proprio sacerdoti*).[112]
Discussing the underlying rationale for confession, the Chanter elucidates
the importance of the priest. On confessing to a priest, the sinner receives
instruction as to the gravity of his misdeeds so that he can better know
how to do penance for those he has committed and how to avoid others in
the future. If, for example, he believes before confession that a certain sin
is venial, he may discover from his confessor that it is, in fact, mortal. Just
as Moses assigned the inspection of lepers to priests in the Old Testament
(Lev. 14), so Christian priests are to distinguish among sins. For that reason, the confessor is likened to a spiritual physician who has the skill to
prescribe medicine to the sick and to enjoin penance for healing.[113] "Like a
skilled physician who applies wine and oil to the wounds of the injured,"
the *Constitutiones* of the Lateran Council continue, "the priest should act
with discernment and caution to inquire carefully into the circumstances of
the sinner so that he can wisely understand the sins, how he should give
advice and what remedies he should apply, since different techniques can
be used for healing the sick." Chobham's *Summa confessorum* and the other
guides to confessors served simply as medical manuals for the treatment of
sin.[114] The medical analogy originated deep in Christian antiquity and continued to inform discussion throughout the Middle Ages. Gerbert echoes it

when Perceval urges the Dragon Knight to seek divine healing from the injuries of his sins. True confession is a doctor ("vraie confessions est mire") that heals without fire or iron those wounds for which one burns in hell (*Continuation* vv. 9960–75).

If, however, anyone has a just reason to confess his sins to "another priest" (*alieno sacerdoti*), the Lateran Council further decreed that he should first obtain permission from his own priest. This formula enacted the conclusions to extensive discussion among the Paris theologians.[115] Pierre the Chanter explains that we ought to confess to our own pastors first, because they see us frequently, are able to warn us if we backslide, and can best help us avoid both sin itself and its occasions. Confession should therefore follow the order of jurisdiction: the laity to their parish priests, priests to their bishops, and canons to their deans.[116] In Chrétien's *Graal* and Gerbert's *Continuation*, however, it is scarcely feasible for knights-errant to return to their parish priests, wherever they might be. The clergy most accessible to the itinerant Perceval are holy hermits isolated in the forest who have never seen the penitent before. Throughout the Chanter's wide-ranging discussions as to whom one should confess to, the theologian considers varied possibilities, including the laity, and even heretics and Jews in times of dire necessity.[117] Among the candidates discussed are monks and hermits. Because monks are secluded from the world, their voices are those of the dead, of weeping and groaning. A monk, moreover, is a *moniade*, that is, the guardian of a single person, but not one who has been commissioned to confess others. On the other hand, if one can go to a regular canon or a rural canon for confession, why not also to a monk? If a monk can be elected bishop, why can he not also be appointed to hear confessions? Just as ordained monks celebrate Mass, so they may also hear confessions at specified times and places.[118]

From these opposing arguments, Chobham arrives at an unequivocally negative conclusion: since cloistered monks and hermits have neither parishes nor pastoral responsibilities, they should be forbidden to hear confession.[119] The Chanter, however, opens a way for a resolution of the problem by introducing the distinction between the power to bind and loosen—that is, the priest's authority to assign penitential satisfaction and to grant absolution—and the ability simply to give advice (*ad consulendum*).[120] Courson applies this distinction to the non-parish "other priest" who does not have the jurisdiction to bind and loosen. His solution is to construct a threefold distinction: the offering of advice, the simple indicating of penance, and the obligatory enjoining of penance (*penitentiam iniungere*). It is appropriate for a knowledgeable person of any condition to offer advice to neighbors on the perplexities of sin. Anyone may likewise indicate appropriate penance to the dying, according to the quantity and quality of their sins, following the Church Fathers, as long as it is not imposed as penitential satisfaction. "Other priests" may therefore give counsel and indicate penance, but they may not enjoin without special permission of a superior.[121] The theologians' distinction between indicating and enjoining appears to have caught the notice of the compiler of the Statutes of Angers (1216–19). From the sick in danger of death, a pure confession should be requested, he urges, not the enjoining (*injungenda*) of penance but the acknowledging of sins. If the penitent regains health, he should, of course, seek a priest who will prescribe the appropriate penance.[122]

The discussions of the "other priest" undoubtedly arose from the exigencies of parochial jurisdiction, intensified by the Lateran legislation, but they were applicable to situations arising from literature as well. Courson's solution appears to have offered the romance hermit a justifiable role in the ministry of confession. Throughout Gerbert's *Continuation*, none of the hermits or priests who exhort or administer confession are recorded as explicitly enjoining penance. Their ministrations could apparently be considered as offering advice. In Chrétien's *Graal*, the lady whom Perceval meets on Good Friday declares that the holy hermit has offered her companions *conseil* along with confession (vv. 6309–11). In distress, Perceval himself seizes the hermit by the feet and also asks for *conseil*, of which he has urgent need (vv. 6356–59). But after Perceval has confessed and discovers that he is, in fact, the hermit's nephew, the uncle now replies that he wishes to enjoin and give penance ("enjoindre et doner penitence," vv. 6432–33). The hero is thereupon commanded to attend church and to fast in the name of penance (vv. 6442–44, 6476–79). Perhaps Chrétien was unaware of the anomaly of a hermit imposing satisfaction on a non-parishioner, but he may also have decided that once kinship was established, the hermit could legitimately impose penance.

After the Lateran Council, the synodical statutes regularly repeat the command to confess to one's parish priest,[123] but they also begin to acknowledge competition from monks. Reasserting that it is the priest who has the responsibility of hearing confessions and enjoining penance, the Statutes of Cambrai (1238–48), for example, forbid the priest to associate monks with these ministries without the bishop's or abbot's special permission. Statutes for an unspecified English diocese around 1225 face the problem directly. They admit that some parishioners refuse to go to their rectors or ordained priests but approach monks and other religious who lack jurisdiction. To remedy this situation, two qualified priests should be appointed in each archdeaconry to act in the place and with the authority of the parish priest. Monks, canons, anchorites, and hermits should henceforth stop imposing penance.[124] In strict terms, this legislation may not have affected the monks discussed by the theologians or the hermits created by the romance writers, who hear confessions and merely offer advice, but it did attempt to restrain a practice widely attested to in literature.

Exterior penance consisted not only of oral confession but also of satisfaction of works. After the repentant sinner had confessed his faults, the parish priest was assigned the task of enjoining the appropriate good works by which the misdeeds were to be expiated.[125] This was the *injunctam penitentiam* that the Lateran Council urged parishioners to perform between confession and communion,[126] called *penitance* in the vernacular. Bishop Maurice enumerates fasting, vigils, prayers, and the giving of alms as remedies that the priest might enjoin (*encarge*) in the name of *penitance*.[127] As a remedy for Perceval's forgetfulness in the *Graal*, the hermit commands his nephew in the name of *penitance* to attend church each day before setting off on his journeys. In addition, the hermit commands Perceval to aid any maiden, lady, or orphan who seeks help. As a final act, the nephew is asked to share the hermit's diet until he communicates at Easter (vv. 6440–6504). When Perceval (in Gerbert's *Continuation*) visits the hermitage where his mother is buried, a holy man exhorts him to endure the *afflictions* of fasting, prayer, and the wearing of a hair shirt, as the consequence of true repentance, confession, and *penitance* (vv. 2755–60). When the young knight confesses his neglect of Blancheflor, his former mentor Gornemans counsels him to attend Mass, where he resolves to seek God's pardon by fulfilling his promise to marry the lady (vv. 5128–73).

A final example is the Lugarel li Covoitiez, who seeks to avenge the death of his *amie* by killing knights in single combat. After he is defeated by Perceval, he promises to become a hermit to expiate his sins against those whom he has killed (*Continuation* vv. 14947–50). Although he dies before fulfilling his vow, his intention to do penance is sufficient, because an inscription "Pray for the soul of Lugarel le Covoitié . . ." appears miraculously on his tomb (vv. 14973–87).

Not all confession of sin is followed by satisfaction in Gerbert's *Continuation*. Neither Lugarel nor the Dragon Knight (vv. 9994–99) are able to expiate their sins before their deaths. Perceval's last two acts of confession before achieving his quest are not accompanied by penitential deeds. In the first case, after the hero confesses, the hermit immediately assuages his hunger by bringing him venison. Although the meal is accompanied by penitential water, venison was not a fasting regime (vv. 14307–13). In the other, his confession is followed immediately by his exiting the church, arming himself, and taking leave of the hermits (vv. 15849–54). The Chanter and Chobham argue that the first reason why oral confession is useful and necessary is because it produces shame. When anyone confesses his wickedness to a priest, the shame that results is sufficient penance for him. In fact, confession productive of shame is the great, even the greatest, part of satisfaction or exterior penance. Confession by mouth was introduced into the Church because it fostered humility, modesty (*verecundia*), and shame (*erubescentia*).[128] Béroul's Ogrin advises Tristan and Iseut to disguise their shame with lies (vv. 2353–54), but the hermit, who offers the fullest treatment of confession in Gerbert's *Continuation*, accepts the theologians' analysis. After warning Perceval against the dangers of unconfessed sin, the hermit proceeds to plead with the knight not to allow shame (*vergoigne = verecundia*) to prevent him from confessing. "When God, our lord, sees a soul in distress and sadness over his sins, and sweating in shame, God wipes clean its heart and remits the sins that have stained it and the misdeeds that have weakened it. Shame is the penitence [la vergoigne est la penitance] that greatly alleviates the soul" (*Continuation* vv. 14228–39). Chobham concludes that shame in confession is the sign of interior contrition, the essential element of penance. Whereas the unrepentant Brandin Dur Cuer (Hardhearted) is dispatched straight to the Devil (vv. 15134–51), Lugarel and the Dragon Knight are saved by the tears of confession, even though unable to perform satisfaction.

Following Pierre the Chanter, Chrétien and Gerbert are at heart contritionalists in whom the abundance of tears constitutes a central element of true penance. Before the Lateran Council, Eudes de Sully sought to transmit this attitude to the clergy of Paris by urging confessors not to terrify the confessee over individual sins. As if enticing a viper out of his hole, the confessor should persuade the penitent straightforwardly by the biblical examples of pure repentance expressed by David, Peter, Mary Magdalene, and the thief on the cross. But penance was also heir to a long tradition of fear conveyed by the judicial analogies of judgment and penalty for crime. After the institutionalization of the penitential regime by the Lateran Council, contritional motivation increasingly gave way to fear of punishment. The Statutes of Cambrai (1238–48), for example, instruct priests to warn their parishioners that they should diligently examine their hearts and painfully recall their sins, approaching confession with fear as if before the judgment of God.[129]

The Competition between Confession and the Ordeal

Confession and the ordeal sought to deal with crimes in different ways—the former touched the sinner's soul; the latter, his body. The two practices were effectively in competition with each other, however, and in the twenty years surrounding the Lateran Council of 1215, which abolished ordeals by eliminating the clergy's presence and institutionalized confession by mandating annual observance, the interaction between them was explicitly debated in the schools.

Thomas of Chobham reports a depraved custom in an unnamed region. If someone suddenly died, the cold-water ordeal might be resorted to by a friend to ascertain whether the deceased had been in a state of repentance and could therefore be interred in a consecrated cemetery; but the general prohibition of ordeals now banned this custom.[130] Robert of Courson questions the interaction between confession and the ordeal differently. Brought to the gallows in a certain city, a man accused of homicide is offered the choice of clearing himself by cold water or hot iron. The defendant has, however, admitted his guilt to a priest in confession. What advice should the priest give him? Courson does not confront the question of whether confession and absolution render the accused innocent and thereby capable of undergoing the ordeal unharmed. He simply adopts Chobham's solution. Under no circumstances should the defendant submit to the ordeal, which is prohibited in both the Old and New Testaments; rather, he should suffer execution as a martyr.[131]

The question that Courson neglects—the effect of confession on the ordeal—was extensively discussed by the Cistercians shortly before and after the Lateran Council. The manuscript Paris BN lat. 15912, most likely from the Cistercian abbey of Beaupré near Beauvais around 1200, contains several exempla exploring the interaction of confession with the ordeal, and the Cistercian Caesarius of Heisterbach includes a number of similar exempla in Distinction 3 of his *Dialogus miraculorum* (1224–25), which seeks to demonstrate the superiority of confession.[132]

Some argued forthrightly that true confession was capable of saving a guilty defendant from the condemnation of the ordeal. The Beaupré collection offers the case of a man accused of disbelief in the sacraments. Out of fear he agreed to submit to the hot iron. Before the appointed day, however, he repented of his disbelief, confessed it purely and sincerely to a priest, and received due penance. Carrying the iron before all the people without harm, he praised the power of confession to cleanse one of all disbelief.[133] In this case, prior confession intervened in the ordeal; in another from Caesarius of Heisterbach, confession was able to efface the verdict, even after it had taken place. Recently, several heretics had been taken at Cambrai. Although they denied their errors, they were nonetheless convicted by the hot iron. The examining cleric, however, persuaded one of the heretics, a nobleman, to repent of his crime and confess it to a priest. As he began to confess, the burns on his hand diminished. Half way through, they were half gone; when he had finished, the hand had returned to its pristine state. The nobleman was spared, but the others were burned.[134]

Others held that confession must be true and sincere, or it would not protect against relapses. An adulterous woman in the Beaupré collection confessed her guilt secretly to a priest and poured out tears before she carried the hot iron, which she performed without injury. Later, resuming her former habits, she by chance found the iron stuck between the masonry of the church portal. When she extracted it as a joke, the iron burned her hand and her entire body. In a similar case, Caesarius tells of a fornicating fisherman who was saved by confession from conviction by the hot iron. Returning to his boat and his former liaison, he was asked why he had not been burned, since his affair was widely known. Plunging his hand into the water, he replied: this is how much it hurt me, but at that instant the water became as hot as the iron, stripping the hand of its skin.[135]

Confession was equally effective in judicial battle. Caesarius reports a castellan who had rapaciously despoiled the Lombards during the reign of the emperor Henry VI. His victims sought justice in the imperial court by challenging him to a duel. When it appeared that the Lombards were to be championed by a virtual giant, the castellan's brother offered to fight in his place. Preparing himself through contrition, confession, and prayer and bearing Christ's sign on his hauberk and shield, the brother won against overwhelming odds. Thus the power of confession not only rendered a champion invincible, but, as the narrator comments, a man worthy of death escaped death.[136]

In these Cistercian exempla, the newly instituted practice of confession openly and directly challenged the authority of the traditional ordeal, obstructing its decisions, and undercutting its justice. In Caesarius's selection, confession does not produce results all the time and for everyone; nor does every true confession guarantee sinners against the consequences of sin. Only one individual from each of the heretical groups, for example, was saved. At the end of the section, the interlocutor asks a question the reader might pose: why do such benefits not follow every act of confession? The monk replies that it is not expedient, because then confession would become an excuse to sin. God wishes the miracles obtained through confession to serve as exempla to show the utility of confession as medicine for the soul.[137] Although the iron's fire operates by God's power, Caesarius considers the ordeal a *mirabile*, because it works against nature.[138] In a collection of exempla entitled *Dialogus miraculorum*, however, Caesarius's preferred term for the effects of confession is, to be sure, *miraculum*.[139]

Marvels

Unlike most romances, Jean Renart's *Escoufle* and *Rose* and Gerbert de Montreuil's *Violette* portray a world virtually free of the marvelous or supernatural in either Christian or secular guise.[140] Gerbert's *Continuation*, however, follows a romance fashion introduced by Marie de France in her Breton lays and popularized by Chrétien de Troyes, both of whom blend marvelous, fantastic, and supernatural elements into their narratives. Thus the term *la merveille* (n.) / *merveillos* (adj.) was introduced into vernacular literature to correspond to the Latin *mirabilia* (pl.), from *mirari* to wonder or marvel. Difficult to distinguish or to define with precision, the marvels of the romance writers parallel the *miracula* that ecclesiastics attribute to saints in Latin literature. The *irréel* is thereby juxtaposed with the *réel*.[141]

By interposing magic beds, rings, fountains, and giants with realistic features, Chrétien maintains a playful, detached attitude toward the marvelous. For example, when Gauvain recounts his adventures in the bed of marvels in the *Graal*, Guiromelans replies: "By God, I am amazed [*trop me merveil*] at the story you tell. It is delightful to listen to your fabrications. I would gladly hear any storyteller [*fableor*] like you. You are truly a jongleur [*jogleres*] whom I had believe to be a knight [worthy of] . . . feats of valor" (vv. 8674–83). Chrétien's chief contribution to the marvelous in romance literature was, however, to introduce the legend of the Grail, the appearance of which is soberly narrated:

> As they were speaking of one thing or another, a squire came forth from a chamber carrying a white lance by the middle of its shaft; he passed between the fire and those seated upon the bed. Everyone in the hall saw the white lance with its white point from whose tip there issued a drop of blood, and this red drop flowed down to the squire's hand. . . . The two other squires entered holding in their hands candelabra of pure gold, crafted with enamel inlays. . . . In each of the candelabra there were at least ten candles burning. A maiden accompanying the two young men was carrying a grail (*graal*) with her two hands; she was beautiful, noble, and richly attired. After she had entered the hall carrying the grail the room was so brightly illuminated that the candles lost their brilliance like stars and the moon when the sun arises. After her came another maiden carrying a silver carving platter (*tailleoir d'argent*). The grail, which was introduced first, was of fine pure gold. Set in the grail were precious stones of many kinds, the best and costliest to be found in earth or sea; the grail's stones were finer than any others in the world, without any doubt. The grail passed by like the lance; they passed in front of the bed and into another chamber. (*Graal* vv. 3190–3242, trans. William W. Kibler, 420–21)

There is no explanation of why the lance bleeds continuously, the Grail shines like the sun, and the castle is inexplicably emptied of its inhabitants the next morning, but years later, on Good Friday, Perceval's hermit uncle tells him that the Grail contained a single host (*oiste*), which nourished the Fisher King for twelve years (*Graal* vv. 6420–31).[142] The later verse continuations do not, however, pursue this association by Chrétien of the Grail with the Eucharist.

Chrétien's intentions aside, it was nonetheless a felicitous stroke that the *Conte de graal* was left unfinished, because its incomplete status made it wondrously fertile of continuations and interpretations. Robert de Boron and the author of the *Perlevaus* added expansions and contexts to the story in prose that accentuate its religious significance,[143] but more pertinent for my purposes are the verse continuations of Chrétien's own text. Since Chrétien breaks off in the middle of Gauvain's quest, the *First (Gauvain) Continuation* pursues the adventures of this hero, bringing him twice to the

Marvelous animals are another device for conveying religious significance. For example, we remember that after observing two hermits adoring and whipping a cross, Perceval encounters a large beast pregnant with yelping offspring (*la bête glatissant*), who breaks apart and is eaten alive by her emerging whelps (vv. 8379–8406). This prodigy is interpreted by Elyas Anais to signify (*senefie*) Holy Church, which is rent by parishioners who will not respect the divine offices (vv. 8674–8728).[151] Another monstrous beast is a worm, as long as a fathom, imprisoned within a red marble stone. When Perceval releases it, a terrifying storm is stirred up, and it reappears as a large serpent with a man's head. This time the prodigy is self-interpreting, claiming to be a demon whom Merlin incarcerated to prevent it from hindering the knight seeking the Grail. The great Enemy himself had used this form to deceive Eve in paradise (vv. 14347–495).[152]

These prodigies point to the Grail, the one marvel that demands explanation. Toward the end of Gerbert's account, the author remarks that Perceval did not yet know its truth or *senefïance,* although he had already seen it twice, but he was confident that if he could find it again, he would finally learn the truth (vv. 14085–97). Because the naive Perceval has asked silly questions of the knights in Chrétien's version, his mentor, Gornemans, advises him to refrain from speaking too much. Accordingly, the youth does not ask the Fisher King the questions on his mind while the Grail ceremony unfolds. Only afterward does he learn of the disastrous consequences to the king and the countryside of this silence (*Graal* vv. 3494–3611). Perceval's initial failure to ask the pertinent questions implicitly results in his exclusion from the *senefïance.* Subsequently, therefore, the knightly questers are quick to ask questions, but the answers are now contingent upon new conditions. When Gauvain arrives at the Grail Castle for the first time in the *First Continuation,* he is put to the sword test before he can receive answers. Failing to mend the broken sword, he falls asleep, apparently exhausted from his travels (vv. 1194–1509). When Gauvain again fails the sword test on his second visit, the Fisher King is nonetheless willing to identify the lance as the one with which the soldier Longinus pierced Christ's side on the cross. But when the king begins to explain the broken sword, he finds Gauvain asleep, again exhausted from his labors (vv. 13003–13602).

Perceval's second visit to the Grail Castle at the end of the *Second Continuation* is preceded by a series of preliminary marvels: a child climbs to the top of a tree and disappears (vv. 31432–505); an oak is illuminated with thousands of candles (vv. 32070–91); and there is a slain knight on the altar of a chapel in which the light is extinguished (vv. 32092–151).[153] At the castle, Perceval asks the king the meaning of the child, and after the ceremony he desires to know the truth about the Grail, the lance, and the broken sword. The king explains that the child climbing the tree signifies that Perceval should not face earthward but aspire upward to the Creator in heaven. The answers to the other questions are deferred until after dinner, when Perceval takes his turn at the sword test. Although fearing failure, the knight succeeds in mending the blade, except for a tiny remaining notch. The king praises Perceval as the most worthy knight alive, joyfully embraces him, and makes him lord over his house, but warns that he still has not done enough—presumably to merit an answer to the Grail. The sword is removed, but Perceval feels greatly comforted. At this point of high tension in the *Second Continuation*, the scribe of Paris BN fr. 12756 interpolates Gerbert's version.

Framed between Perceval's second and third visit to the Grail Castle, Gerbert must likewise face the Grail's *senefïance*. But the romancier once again deflects the answer, this time turning to the subject of sin and penance. Feeling himself a sinner and unworthy to know the truth about the Grail, Perceval nonetheless persists with questions:

> My friend, [the king replies] after dinner you shall hear things that will delight you, but I shall not speak about the grail or the lance, for you must not at this point know the secret. You have not fully served the one who will reveal the secrets to you, until the notch in this sword . . . has been repaired and joined by your hands. But listen! I will tell you this: I know of no man in this world who can ever know about these things but you; but make sure you do not lose that prize through sin. And if you do dwell in sin and anger God, then confess and repent and abandon sin and do thorough penance. . . . [I]f you can return here, it could well be that you'll repair the notch, and then you could ask about the grail and the lance; and truly then, you may be sure, you will know the profound truth, the secrets, and the divine mystery. (*Continuation* vv. 12–42; adapted from Bryant's translation, p. 194)

Alluded to at the opening of the text and closely linked to the Grail apparition, sin and penance now become Gerbert's preoccupation.

When Perceval wonders what past sins have prevented him from learning about the Grail, the king reminds him of his neglect of his mother, which caused her death (vv. 43–55). That night a voice summons him to

244 · ❧ ARISTOCRATIC LIFE IN MEDIEVAL FRANCE

Perceval finds the last a great marvel, he asks for elucidation (vv. 17005–9). Again, the king deflects his question until after he has eaten, but during the meal the Grail and lance reappear and the sword is placed on the table. Perceval reproaches the king for deferring his questions in the past, even after he has mended the sword. Granting that Perceval has suffered much, the king invites the knight to mend the sword for a second time. Perceval smoothes out the notch, tests the joint, and returns it to the joyful king, who responds: "Friend, you have been rewarded for your trouble when God has given you the honor to be worthy of knowing the truth of these matters" (vv. 17079–80). After evoking Perceval's great happiness, Gerbert ends his *Continuation*, like its predecessor, without further response.

To Gerbert's audience, the only *senefïance* accorded to Perceval concerns the lance from the *First Continuation* and the child in the tree from the *Second*. Gerbert himself has not supplied a single word of explanation to all of Perceval's queries about the mystery of the Grail. This absence no doubt explains why the scribe of manuscript Paris BN français 12756 added Manessier's *Continuation*, repeating the linking words of the *Second Continuation* (vv. 32581–94). Ignorant of Gerbert, Manessier does respond to the aborted question of the *Second Continuation*, but his lengthy continuation lies beyond the scope of my study.[157]

At the turn of the twelfth century, vernacular literature displayed a renewed interest in the marvelous. Whether or not these phenomena expressed the chthonic forces of paganism still latent in western Europe, they doubtless meant different things to different interpreters. Because these marvels were perceived as supernatural, they impinged upon religion and competed with the miracles of the Christian scriptures and saints' lives. Jean Renart and Gerbert in the *Violette* prefer to ignore the supernatural. Only the ordeal is labeled a *miracle aperte* (*Rose* vv. 4268, 4990). For the most part, Jean's use of the term *merveilles/mervelle* refers to Lïenor's beauty (*Rose* vv. 690, 1404, 4687, 4766), to the rose on her thigh (vv. 3363, 3366), or to the tall tales hunters tell about their game (v. 458), matters that avoid the supernatural.[158] Gerbert is receptive to the Perceval legend in his *Continuation*, however, where he attempts to adopt and christianize the marvelous. His technique is to attribute Christian *senefïance* to some marvels and to demonize others. Chrétien's Grail ceremony, nonetheless, remains the chief concern. Gerbert acknowledges the previous interpretations of the lance and the child in the tree, but refuses to pronounce upon the central image of the Grail itself. For him, the quest's underlying im-port is, above all, to motivate Christians to perfect themselves through the now formulaic means of contrition, confession, and satisfaction of the current theology of penance.

It is possible that Pierre the Chanter died (1197) before he perceived the impact of Chrétien's legacy on romance literature, but it is noteworthy that neither his students nor any other theologian of the thirteenth century have been found to comment on the legend of the Grail in Latin. At the turn of the century, Hélinand, abbot of Froidmont, a former trouvère turned Cistercian chronicler, refers to a "gradalis . . . et dicitur vulgari nomine graalz," but avers that he could not find a history of the Grail in Latin, only in numerous French writings. Rather, the theologians seem to have waged a war of silence against this foremost effort of vernacular authors to introduce a religious theme into romance literature.[159] The explanation may lie in the theologians' sharp ontological distinction between *miracula*, which lay within their purview as works of God, and *mirabilia*, which pertained to secular *scientia* as natural phenomena.[160] The Chanter's potential reaction to the marvelous may nonetheless be extrapolated from his assessment of ordeals, which he identifies as *miracula*, if not *mirabilia*, and which took place in the present.

As a biblical scholar, the Chanter was repeatedly obliged to account for the difference between Old Testament times, when miracles were permitted, and his own day, when they were to be avoided. In ancient times, the Lord desired that miracles be performed for the spreading of the faith—for example, Moses crossed the Red Sea, Daniel was protected in the lions' den, and the three boys were rescued from the furnace. Now that faith is widespread, he does not always perform miracles, but requires of the faithful that they perform good works.[161] Exorcists, to take another example, can no longer cast out demons as they did in the primitive Church.[162] The Chanter's most recent example had occurred at Reims within living memory. When a severe drought afflicted the city, the Jews of the city proposed a contest between their sacred scrolls and the holy relics of the Christians as to which could produce rain. Master Albéric, a theologian of the school of Reims, vigorously opposed the exposing of the Christian faith to the mercy of the marvelous, since because of our sins the Jews might, with God's permission, produce water from heaven through magical arts and the Devil's agency. It is often reported that the wicked have performed miracles.[163] Repeatedly the Chanter warns that modern miracles, although permitted by God because of sin, are performed by the

EIGHT

Audiences

. ✀ .

S INCE Jean Renart's and Gerbert de Montreuil's audiences have
never been large, they can be conveniently arranged in concentric
circles radiating out through time from the authors. Closest to the
authors themselves are the elusive contemporaries who heard the romances recited by the authors or by professional entertainers, or who read
manuscripts now lost. A second circle was formed at the end of the thirteenth century when a handful of rich patrons commissioned expensive
new copies. To what extent these manuscripts were consulted by their contemporaries cannot be known, but the romances were thereby saved from
extinction. In modern times the manuscripts were eventually set in type,
then edited critically, and sold in modest printings to an expanding reader-
ship that included literary critics and historians as well as those who savored the stories for pleasure.

The Contemporary Audience

The interest of historians in such literature is not aesthetic but social.
Rather than trying to analyze the literary merit of Jean's and Gerbert's
verse, historians are concerned with the contemporary audiences of the
early thirteenth century. Their questions are: how were the romances first
received, and what do they reveal about the original listeners/readers? If
more is known about these audiences than about the authors, it is still not
much.[1] All we have in the end is what the texts themselves divulge. Jean
announces that he has composed his works for the "courts of kings and
counts." While both romanciers include kings and emperors in their stories, the personages to whom they address their works were at the rank of
counts. Baudouin was count of Hainaut, Marie, countess of Ponthieu, and
Milon, provost of Reims, a high ecclesiastical dignitary. These three his-

torical figures provide the most reliable indications of the contemporary audiences. Two were of the high lay aristocracy, one a prelate; two were men, one a woman; although all were francophone and understood Francien, two were involved in the politics of the Empire against the Capetian party, while the other was married to a baron who rebelled against the Capetians. But it is important to remember that Jean addressed his romances not to high barons alone but to their courts—that is, to their entourages. Although these constituencies are not identified by name, Jean and Gerbert exhibit a singular interest in knights and demoiselles of the lower aristocracy. Guillaume de Dole and Perceval, who are of this class, are presented as exemplary heroes; good French knights are recruited from it for service in the Empire and exhibit their prowess in the lists of tournaments. The demoiselles Lïenor and Eurïaut share the same social status. Lïenor's dream of marrying an emperor—a fantasy to be sure—would certainly have appealed to her peers.

In addition to their social status, Jean and Gerbert reveal what culture was demanded of their audiences. Their listeners/readers were familiar with the canon of vernacular literature: the *Chanson de Roland* and other chansons de geste, the legend of Tristan and Iseut, the lais of Marie de France, and, most important, the Arthurian universe of Chrétien de Troyes. Equally required was an appreciation of the current repertory of lyric songs, not only of the southern troubadours of the previous generation, but also of the latest "hits" of the most popular trouvère of the day, Gace Brulé. This was the literary "horizon of expectations" in terms of which the audiences received Jean's and Gerbert's stories set in their own time and place.

The Audience a Century Later

Inextricable from the aesthetic qualities of literature is its capacity to survive. A recitation that failed to command an audience would not have been written down. A work that was not preserved in multiple manuscripts was likely to disappear, and even texts that were copied needed to appeal to later audiences, which might have different tastes and habits. Enduring literature must possess qualities that outlive its own day and continue to attract both new audiences and literary critics who will promote its success. Inherent in what is deemed to be literature is a certain transhistorical character.

Jean and Gerbert drew upon themes, such as the wager, and techniques, such as lyric insertions and contemporary awareness, that were adopted by

capitals were intended for the *Violette*, but only the lyric insertions were inscribed in red. The manuscript contains two sections from the same period that collect religious verse, chansons de geste, including the popular *Girart de Vienne*, and two romances, *Cligès* by Chrétien de Troyes and *Florimont* by Aimon de Varennes. Only the chanson de geste, *Parise la duchesse*, unique to this manuscript, bears affinities to the *Violette*. Belonging to a family of stories from the second quarter of the thirteenth century called the *Geste de Nanteuil*, it features a heroine named Parise, the wife of Raymond, duke of Saint-Gilles who has been wrongfully accused of murder and is finally vindicated in the manner of Gerbert's Euriaut. Also like the *Violette*, much of the action takes place at Cologne.

The second copy of the *Violette* is found in a deluxe collection of heteroclite pieces, Paris BN fr. 1553, copied by several scribes in the Picard dialect.[12] The scribe responsible for the *Violette* (fol. 288r–325va) dated his transcription to February 1285 (new style). Gerbert's romance joins five other major works: the *Roman de Troie* of Benoît de Saint-Maur, the *Ymage du monde*, a cosmological treatise by Gautier de Metz, the anonymous *Roman de Witasse [Eustace] le Moine*, and the *Fergus* of Guillaume le Clerc, none of which bears a readily discernible relationship to the *Violette*. The remaining some fifty pieces consist of religious works, fabliaux, and erotic lais, including Jean's *Lai de l'ombre* (MS. G). The manuscript is embellished throughout with elaborated capitals in red and blue. (As in Jean's *Rose*, they indicate the lyric insertions.) An illuminator has provided miniatures and historiated initials to the major titles of the collection.[13]

At the end of the thirteenth century, therefore, Jean's and Gerbert's romances were saved from extinction by wealthy aristocratic and bourgeois patrons. Indeed, it may be argued that the cost, artistry, and embellishments account for the survival of the manuscripts, because the collectors exhibit few traits of literary taste or connoisseurship in common. The most that these manuscripts tell us about the later audience is that Jean and Gerbert found their greatest market in northeastern France (with the sole exception of the southern manuscript). The collectors do not appear to have recognized the affinities between the two authors; nor did they judge these romances to be incompatible with the more popular Chrétien de Troyes.

The collectors not only rescued the romances from oblivion; the luxurious copies also suggest that the stories did command an audience, if only a modest one. The existence of this audience is remarkably confirmed by the clerics of the period who recorded in Latin two of Jean's and Gerbert's most distinctive *contes*. Since the early Middle Ages, preachers had enlivened their sermons with exempla, short but picturesque stories intended to teach religious or moral lessons. Pierre the Chanter thus embellished his theological lectures and encouraged his students to do likewise in their sermons. Among the most noteworthy was Jacques de Vitry, who seasoned his preaching with exempla and collected them for colleagues. Throughout the second half of the thirteenth century, the preachers of the Dominican Order pursued this practice most energetically. By the closing decades, one friar preacher in particular, the author of the *Compilacio singularis exemplorum,* had assembled a large number, as the preface explains, from previous collections or from those he heard narrated. The compiler offered them to preachers not only for moral edification but also for the solace (*ad solacium*) of the audiences. Two in particular rehearse the salient elements of the *contes* of the *Rose* and the *Violette*.[14]

Entitled "Guillermus Nivernensis," the first concerns a Guillaume and his sister, children of the deceased count of Nevers. When Guillaume, aged twenty, is unconcerned about marriage but prefers to live with his sister, evil tongues accuse the two of incest. To counter this reputation, the girl proposes to seclude herself with her maidens while the brother goes to Rome to gain chivalric renown at the emperor's court. A forthcoming tournament provides him with this opportunity, which he uses with such success that the emperor is entranced and offers to marry Guillaume's sister. Alarmed by the newcomer's ascendancy at court, an imperial marshal proposes to visit the girl—on the pretext of a pilgrimage to Saint-Denis— to ascertain her qualities. Bribing an old nurse (*nutrix, vetula*) with gold rings, he obtains the precious information that the girl is without blemish from head to toe except for a mark on her right thigh in the shape of a rose. With this proof, the marshal convinces the emperor and Guillaume that the sister has become a whore. When the sister hears of the calumny, she pours out her prayers to the blessed Virgin, assembles her knights, journeys to Rome, and accuses the marshal before the emperor of having raped her. The marshal swears on relics that he has never seen the girl and offers to defend his plea in battle. Then the maiden replies, "[T]he marshal has sworn truly; neither he nor any other has slept with me, because I am the sister of Guillaume who was defamed before you of a false crime just as has now been proved by oath." Admiring the girl's beauty and wisdom, the emperor takes her as his wife.[15]

mances because of their fanciful plots.[21] In 1904, doubtless impressed by what he read in the recent editions, the historian Charles-Victor Langlois published *La société française au XIIIe siècle d'après dix romans d'aventure,* in which the *Rose* and *Escoufle* are assigned separate chapters. Decrying the contemporary preoccupation with politics and administration, Langlois wished to recapture the society of the thirteenth century. For him there was no more trustworthy approach than to summarize and paraphrase these two texts, allowing them to speak for themselves as authentic documents of their times, without further commentary.[22]

Langlois's ultimate audience was the "grand public," but the first attempt to subject Jean to sustained scholarly scrutiny was Rita Lejeune's doctoral dissertation of 1935, *L'oeuvre de Jean Renart: Contribution à l'étude du genre romanesque au moyen âge.* Encompassing Jean's oeuvre as a whole and devoting attention to its multiple literary qualities, Lejeune's greatest contribution was, however, to uncover meticulously and exhaustively Jean's contemporary allusions and to situate them within a historical context. In a section devoted to his "réalisme," she concludes that Jean Renart "for the first time in the medieval production of romances [offered] a real and direct painting of French society, that of the time of Philip Augustus."[23] Anthime Fourrier, later defined "réaliste" as "a work of imagination that proposes to represent the reality of life without idealizing or caricaturing it."[24] In 1965, Faith Lyons devoted two chapters to Jean's techniques in describing contemporary life, concluding that his greatest originality lay in constructing a realistic framework for his stories.[25] The approach of Lejeune and her followers was later labeled "positivist" by its critics, who accused them of accepting without question Jean's literary language as unmediated "reflections" of his surroundings. Nonetheless, modern scholars have continued to uncover realistic observations in his romances.[26]

With the appearance of the new series of texts, Les classiques français du moyen âge and Textes littéraires français, Jean's works were assigned new editions. Félix Lecoy reedited the *Rose* in 1962; Franklin Sweetser, the *Escoufle* in 1974; and Lecoy, the *Lai* in 1979 (again based on MS. A).[27] This campaign to revise and reissue the texts was accompanied by a new era of critical interest in Jean's works, this time not as history but as literature. Previous literary interest in the romances had passed from the lyrics to the narratives, which literary historians such as Emile Littré and Gaston Paris found deficient according to their tastes.[28] The new era was opened by Michel Zink's influential *Roman rose et rose rouge: Le roman de la rose ou de*

Guillaume de Dole (Paris, 1979). With the inscription of Jean's *Rose* on the program of the French national *agrégation* (competitive examination for teachers in *lycées*), Zink had the opportunity to offer students a reading radically different from the historicizing of the positivist school. Paul Zumthor's *Essai de poétique médiévale* (Paris, 1972) offered him inspiration. Zumthor had subsumed medieval literature under the techniques of poetry. The literary text did not imitate reality but chose itself as its object. An underlying qualitative difference separated history from literature, which required the critic to be occupied with the creative processes of fiction, genre, style, rhyme, and language. History was thereby relegated beyond the text to peripheral darkness. Applying these themes to the *Rose*, Zink explores how Jean uses his poetic artistry to create a work of pure literary imagination, not of historical realism. In effect, Jean devoted his talents of imagination and invention to produce the illusion of reality. The true referent of his romances was not exterior, historical reality but the nature of the literary text itself. Geographic precision and the appearance of contemporary personages at Saint-Trond, for example, constitute the "incongruous presence of the real within the unreal."[29]

The poststructuralist climate that has animated literary studies since the appearance of Zink's book has reinforced his major themes. In the past two decades, numerous articles have recalled the reflexivity of Jean's authorial stance and the intertextuality of his oeuvre. Particular attention has been paid to the artistry of his language; what was formerly interpreted as ambiguity became masterful irony; former inconsistencies became purposeful contradictions that consciously undercut naive realism.[30] Jean has been hailed as "one of the cleverest writers of the Middle Ages," and the recognition of this virtuosity has added to the difficulties of his editors and translators.[31] These tendencies found their extremity in Roger Dragonetti's *Le mirage des sources: L'art du faux dans le roman médiéval* (Paris, 1987).[32] Where Zumthor sees all medieval literature as poetry, Dragonetti reduces it to the work of the *poeta mendax*, who writes only fictions and lies. The historical propaedeutic is now replaced by the craft of the forger. Just as medieval hagiography is dominated by deliberate and conventional fabrication, so literature is controlled by rhetorical artifice, which conceals through metaphors, symbols, and similitudes. Jean Renart joins those writers who evoke their sources only to deform them. A deconstructionist *avant la lettre*, Jean is purported to have seen all language as auto-referential, useful only to subvert and destroy itself. His words are polyvalent,

the literal-historical level. In other words, both their narratives and their realistic frameworks were meant to be heard and read equally at the surface of the text. Pierre the Chanter insists that the reading *ad litteram* (*historice*) of Scripture has to be firmly established before the figures of allegory and tropology can be understood, and I believe that Jean and Gerbert had comparable expectations of their audiences. As a historian, I do not suggest that the linguistic and rhetorical strategies can be excluded, but the literal interpretation is equally legitimate and sufficient for my purposes. This is the level at which I have entered the text. The chief obstacle to my superficial, "flat" reading is Jean's and Gerbert's employment of irony, which may subvert the apparent meaning. My solution has been to seek to take account of irony wherever I identify it, while resisting the proposition that the romances are entirely ironic and therefore subversive of the literal meaning.[43]

To help me negotiate Jean's and Gerbert's literary craft, I have brought to bear the hermeneutic tools of the horizon of expectation and *effets de réel*, outlined in Chapter 1. By relating the four romances to what Jean and Gerbert expected their audiences to know and thereby comparing their works with their predecessors', I have sought to distinguish the conventional and stereotypic from the original in the two authors' oeuvres. This has given me a literary horizon. By further comparing Jean and Gerbert with the Paris theologians, I have benefited from a clerical horizon to highlight their distinctive laicity and to identify the historically significant. My assumption here has been that those matters in which both lay and clerical authors engaged were of historical consequence. In the second place, my concentration on "reality effects," or self-authenticating details, has shifted my attention away from Jean's and Gerbert's central narratival concerns to the peripheries of their stories. Marginal episodes and details inserted to provide the audiences with the "pleasure of recognition" are less influenced by authorial strategies than the main narrative. Where elements that interest me do become involved in the central narratives, I have sought to read them in that light. My ultimate purpose in deploying these two techniques has been to uncover the historical realities embedded in Jean's and Gerbert's texts.

Romance and History

Still, the *Escoufle, Rose, Continuation,* and *Violette* are indubitably romances, and as fictions they contain what modern historians consider fantasy. Although careful to situate his stories in realistic frameworks, Jean Renart himself twice cites a *mervelle* in the *Rose*. After hearing of the glories of Guillaume de Dole, the emperor Conrad exclaims:

> Tels chevaliers fet l'en en faules:
> s'il est tels, dont est il faez!

> Such knights as these are made up in fables; / if he is such, he must be an enchanted sprite! (vv. 1431–32)

Lïenor's triumphal arrival at the imperial diet in Mainz provokes comparable amazement:

> "Tex puceles soelent venir
> ça en arrier, por esbauder,
> a la court le bon roi Artu,"
> font cil qui teinent a vertu
> ou a mout bel enchantement.
>
> .   .   .   .   .
>
> Puis cele heure que Dex fu nez,
> neïs au tens le roi Artu, . . .
> n'avint ausi bele aventure. . . .
> Quë il i a venu
> une mervelle tote droit,
> la plus bele et la plus adroite
> Ne sai se c'est ou fee ou fame. . . .

> "Such maidens were accustomed to come / long ago to astonish / the court of good King Arthur," / they all said, considering it a miracle / or a wonderful enchantment. / .   .   . / Not since that hour when God was born, / nor even in the time of King Arthur, . . . / has come about such a wonderful adventure. . . . / A genuine marvel / has arrived, the most beautiful and perfect person, / I don't know whether she is a fairy or a woman. . . . (vv. 4617–21, 4680–89)

Of the two central figures, Guillaume is a *faeȝ* of a type found only in fables,[44] and Lïenor, an *enchantement* or *mervelle*, a *fee* worthy of Arthur's court or of the Gospel, yet the former fights effectively with his lance at Saint-Trond and the latter demonstrates her skill with the needle in the

Countess Marie broke forth in song in public, or whether this is also just a pleasant jongleur fantasy. We recall that William Marshal, the historical knight we know best, provided the music for dancing at the tournament at Joigny by singing "with a clear voice and a sweet sound" (*Histoire de Guillaume le Maréchal*, 1: vv. 3477–80). It is not implausible, therefore, that all who danced were prepared to contribute to the music by singing. At the close of the Marshal's life, his biographer narrates a moving scene at the old baron's deathbed, where he is surrounded by his family. The Marshal confesses to a great urge to sing, but refrains, because people would think him deranged; nonetheless, he listens with pleasure to one daughter sing "with a clear voice and sweet sound"; another, who is timid, he teaches how to sing the words of a *rotruenge* (2: vv. 18528–580). This was a private family affair, to be sure, but the leading earl of England had evidently had frequent recourse to song throughout his life.

Since the trouvères wrote the lyrics and doubtless composed the melodies to the chansons attributed to them, it is likely that they performed the pieces as well. Although a few trouvères were non-noble, around 1200 many of the most celebrated, like Gace Brulé, were knights, and others, like the châtelain de Coucy, were at the middle range of the nobility. The next generation boasted a great baron, Thibaut IV, count of Champagne, who continued to write chansons after he became king of Navarre. Jean Renart and Gerbert de Montreuil anthologize the lyrics of the trouvères of their generation but omit the music. By the mid thirteenth century, however, the famous *chansonniers* begin to appear, including not only the words but also the musical scores to the repertory. These luxurious manuscripts, highly decorated with ornate illuminations, were even more costly than the first surviving manuscripts of Jean's and Gerbert's romances. The earliest and meanest of these texts, the *chansonnier* of Saint-German-des-Prés (1240–75), is not a jongleur's handbook but a more expensive creation. These manuscripts recorded the words and music of chansons for the high aristocracy of the second half of the thirteenth century. The miniatures in the manuscripts both emblematize the social status of the trouvères and picture them performing. Thibaut, king of Navarre, however, is represented only as listening to a fiddler playing one of the king's melodies.[45] More study is needed to evaluate the evidence of the *chansonniers* for performance, which, in any case, is later than the period of Jean and Gerbert, but they do suggest that the aristocracy participated more actively in music than we have heretofore imagined. It is not inconceivable that the knights and demoiselles of the historical entourages of Hainaut and Ponthieu sang in public. That emperors like Conrad performed in their courts may exceed the boundaries of historical actuality and pass into the prescriptive realm of the jongleur's imagination.

Closely allied to song was lyric poetry, one of the chief media for expressing the sentiments of love. Although the romanciers are fully cognizant of the ceremonies and regulations of the Church governing marriage, they also trace the parallel customs of *fin'amours*, which could function independently, whether within or without the boundaries of matrimony. Since, with few exceptions, the only evidence for these practices is found in romances, literary and social historians have long debated their historical reality. The question may never be satisfactorily resolved, but given the pervasive influence of literature on human emotions, with what assurance can we deny the existence of *fin'amours* in the aristocratic society of the Middle Ages? In matters of love, life has often sought to imitate art.

My conclusions about the historical status of romance have been couched in the subjunctive mood and range on a scale from "highly likely" to "not impossible." Most of the material culled from Jean's and Gerbert's efforts to create verisimilitude can, however, be accorded greater probability, if not full certainty. This can be argued because it is possible to fit the details into a historical context already established, or because they involve issues that also engaged the attention of clerics writing independently in another medium, or because the details are so marginal to the fictional strategies that few compelling reasons can be imagined to doubt them. The geographical precision with which Normandy, Provence, Lotharingia, and the Capetian domain are located can readily be ascertained from available documentation. The events in their narratives can also be fitted into a political context involving the contemporary crisis over the succession in the Empire, the rivalry between the Welf and Capetian parties in Lotharingia, and similar rivalries between the Capetians and the restive barons in France. The distrust of lowborn agents by the two emperors accords with the current institution of *ministeriales* in the Empire and a pervasive aristocratic suspicion of "men raised from the dust" in the French kingdom.

The romanciers' evident delight in elaborating on festivities, entertainments, fine food, and elegant clothing derives in the first place from their desire to embellish the *éclat* of aristocratic living, but framing their narratives with such details also gave their audiences the pleasure of recognition. That the Capetian wardrobe contained similar apparel, and that

Short Titles

TEXTS

Actes de Philippe Auguste
  Recueil des actes de Philippe Auguste, ed. Henri-François Delaborde, Charles
  Petit-Dutaillis, Jacques Boussard, and Michel Nortier, 4 vols. (Paris, 1916–79)
Anonyme de Béthune
  Extrait d'une chronique française des rois de France par un anonyme de Béthune,
  ed. Léopold Delisle, *RHF* 24: 750–75
Ardent, *Speculum*
  Raoul Ardent, *Speculum universale*, MS., Paris BN lat 3229 and 3240
Béroul
  Béroul: Le Roman de Tristan, ed. Ernest Muret and L. M. Defourques, Les
  classiques français du moyen âge ([1913] Paris, 1982); trans. Alan S. Frederick
  as *The Romance of Tristan by Béroul* (Harmondsworth, Eng., 1970)
Budget
  Le premier budget de la monarchie française: Le compte général de 1202–1203, ed.
  Ferdinand Lot and Robert Fawtier, Bibliothèque de l'Ecole des hautes études,
  Sciences historiques et philologiques, 259 (Paris, 1932)
Chanter, *Summa*
  Pierre le Chantre, *Summa de sacramentis et animae consiliis*, ed. Jean-Albert
  Dugauquier, Analecta mediaevalia Namurcensia, 5 vols., 4, 7, 11, 16, 21
  (Louvain, 1954–67)
Chanter, *Verbum abbreviatum*
  Petrus Cantor, *Verbum abbreviatum*, ed. J.-P. Migne (short version), *PL*, 205:
  23–554; MS. V (long version), Vatican Reg. lat. 106
Chobham, *Summa*
  Thomas de Chobham, *Summa confessorum*, ed. F. Broomfield, Analecta me-
  diaevalia Namurcensia, 25 (Louvain, 1968)

Chrétien, *Charrete*

Les romans de Chrétien de Troyes: Le chevalier de la charrete, ed. Mario Roques, Les classiques français du moyen âge (Paris, 1983); trans. William W. Kibler in *Chrétien de Troyes: Arthurian Romances* (Harmondsworth, Eng., 1991), 207–94

Chrétien, *Cligès*

Les romans de Chrétien de Troyes: Cligès, ed. Alexandre Micha, Les classiques français du moyen âge (Paris, 1982); trans. William W. Kibler in *Chrétien de Troyes: Arthurian Romances* (Harmondsworth, Eng., 1991), 123–205

Chrétien, *Erec*

Les romans de Chrétien de Troyes: Erec et Enide, ed. Mario Roques, Les classiques français du moyen âge (Paris, 1970); trans. Carleton W. Carroll in *Chrétien de Troyes: Arthurian Romances* (Harmondsworth, Eng., 1991), 37–122

Chrétien, *Graal*

Chrétien de Troyes: Le roman de Perceval ou le conte de graal, ed. William Roach, Textes littéraires français (Geneva, 1956); trans. William W. Kibler in *Chrétien de Troyes: Arthurian Romances* (Harmondsworth, Eng., 1991), 381–494

Chrétien, *Lion*

Les romans de Chrétien de Troyes: Le chevalier au lion, ed. Mario Roques, Les classiques français du moyen âge (Paris, 1982); trans. William W. Kibler in *Chrétien de Troyes: Arthurian Romances* (Harmondsworth, Eng., 1991), 295–380

Constitutiones, ed. García y García

Constitutiones concilii quarti Lateranensis una cum commentariis glossatorum, ed. Antonius García y García, Monumenta iuris canonici, ser. A, Corpus glossatorum, 2 (Vatican City, 1981)

Courson, *Summa*

Robert de Courson, *Summa,* MS., Paris BN lat. 14524

Decretum

Decretum Gratiani, in *Corpus iuris canonici,* ed. Emil Friedberg (Leipzig, 1879), 1

First Continuation

The Continuations of the Old French Perceval of Chrétien de Troyes, ed. William Roach (Philadelphia, 1949), 1

Gerbert, *Continuation*

Gerbert de Montreuil, *La continuation de Perceval,* ed. Mary Williams and Marguerite Oswald, Les classiques français du moyen âge, 3 vols. (Paris, 1922, 1925, 1975); trans. with synopsis by Nigel Bryant in *Perceval: The Story of the Grail,* Arthurian Studies, 5 (Cambridge, 1982), 194–270

Gerbert, *Violette*

Le roman de la violette ou de Gerart de Nevers par Gerbert de Montreuil, ed. Douglas L. Buffum, Société des anciens textes français (Paris, 1928); trans.

into modern French by Mireille Demaules in *Gerbert de Montreuil: Le roman de la violette*, "Moyen age" (Paris, 1992), 27–171

Gislebert de Mons, *Chronique*

Ed. Léon Vanderkindere, Commission royale d'histoire, Recueil de textes pour servir à l'étude de l'histoire de Belgique (Brussels, 1904)

Guillaume le Breton, *Gesta*

In *Oeuvres de Rigord et de Guillaume le Breton, historiens de Philippe-Auguste*, ed. Henri-François Delaborde, Société de l'histoire de France, 210 (Paris, 1882), 1: 168–333

Guillaume le Breton, *Philippidos*

In *Oeuvres de Rigord et de Guillaume le Breton, historiens de Philippe-Auguste*, ed. Henri-François Delaborde, Société de l'histoire de France, 224 (Paris, 1885), 2

Histoire de Guillaume le Maréchal

Ed. Paul Meyer, Société de l'histoire de France, 3 vols., 255, 268, 304 (Paris, 1891–1901)

Innocent III, *Regesta*

Ed. Vienna, *Die Register Innocenʒ' III*, ed. Othmar Hageneder, Anton Haidacher et al., Publikationen der Abteilung für historische Studien des Österreichischen Kulturinstituts in Rom, 5 vols. (Vienna, 1964–97)

Ed. *PL*, 214–16, 3 vols.

Potthast indicates the number assigned in *Regesta pontificum romanorum*, ed. August Potthast (Berlin, 1874), 1

Jean Renart, *Escoufle*

Jean Renart, *L'Escoufle: Roman d'aventure*, ed. Franklin Sweetser, Textes littéraires français (Geneva, 1974); trans. into modern French by Alexandre Micha as *L'Escoufle: Roman d'aventures*, Traductions des classiques français du moyen âge, 48 (Paris, 1992)

Jean Renart, *Lai*

Jean Renart, *Le lai de l'ombre*, ed. Félix Lecoy, Les classiques français du moyen âge (Paris, 1979); ed. Joseph Bédier, Anciens textes français (Paris, 1913), trans. Norma Lorre Goodrich in *The Ways of Love: Eleven Romances of Medieval France* (Boston, 1964), 253–74

Jean Renart, *Rose*

Jean Renart, *Le roman de la rose ou Guillaume de Dole*, ed. Félix Lecoy, Les classiques français du moyen âge (Paris, 1979); trans. into modern French by Jean Dufournet, Jacques Kooijman, René Menage, and Christine Tronc as *Guillaume de Dole ou le roman de la rose*, Traductions des classiques français du moyen âge (Paris, 1979); trans. Patricia Terry and Nancy Vine Durling as *The Romance of the Rose or Guillaume de Dole* (Philadelphia, 1993); ed. and trans.

Regina Psaki as *Jean Renart: The Romance of the Rose or Guillaume de Dole (Roman de la rose ou de Guillaume de Dole)*, Garland Library of Medieval Literature, 92A (New York, 1995)

Lombard, *Sententiarum*

Ed. Pierre the Lombard, *Sententiarum in IV libris distinctae* in *PL*, 192: 519–962

Mansi

Sacrorum conciliorum nova et amplissima collectio, ed. J. D. Mansi, 31 vols. (Florence and Venice, 1759–93)

MGH

Monumenta Germaniae historica

MGH SS

Monumenta Germaniae historica, Scriptores

PL

Patrologiae cursus completus . . . series latina, ed. J.-P. Migne, 221 vols. (Paris, 1857–1903)

Registres de Philippe Auguste

Ed. John W. Baldwin, Françoise Gasparri, Michel Nortier, and Elisabeth Lalou, *RHF*, Documents financiers et administratifs, 7 (Paris, 1992), 1

RHF

Recueil des historiens des Gaules et de la France, 24 vols. (Paris, 1734–1904)

Rigord

In *Oeuvres de Rigord et de Guillaume le Breton, historiens de Philippe-Auguste*, ed. Henri-François Delaborde, Société de l'histoire de France, 210 (Paris, 1882), 1: 1–167

RNI

Regestum Innocentii III papae super negotia Romani imperii, ed. Friedrich Kempf, Miscellanea historiae pontificiae, 12 (Rome, 1947)

RS

[Roll Series], Great Britain, Public Record Office, Rerum Britannicarum medii aevi scriptores

Second Continuation

The Continuations of the Old French Perceval of Chrétien de Troyes, ed. William Roach (Philadelphia, 1971), 4

Teulet

Layettes du Trésor des Chartes, ed. Alexandre Teulet, Henri-François Delaborde, and Elie Berger, 5 vols. (Paris 1863–1909)

STUDIES

Baldwin, *Government of Philip Augustus*

John W. Baldwin, *The Government of Philip Augustus: Foundations of French Royal Power in the Middle Ages* (Berkeley, 1986)

Baldwin, *Language of Sex*
    John W. Baldwin, *The Language of Sex: Five Voices from Northern France around 1200* (Chicago, 1994)
Baldwin, *Masters, Princes, and Merchants*
    John W. Baldwin, *Masters, Princes, and Merchants: The Social Views of Peter the Chanter and His Circle*, 2 vols. (Princeton, 1970)
Chênerie, *Le chevalier errant*
    Marie-Luce Chênerie, *Le chevalier errant dans les romans arthuriens en vers des XIIe et XIIIe siècles*, Publications romanes et françaises, 172 (Geneva, 1986)
Jean Renart, ed. Durling
    Jean Renart and the Art of Romance: Essays on Guillaume de Dole, ed. Nancy Vine Durling (Gainesville, Fla., 1997)
Lejeune, *"Guillaume de Dole"*
    Rita Lejeune, "Le *Roman de Guillaume de Dole* et la principauté de Liège," *Cahiers de civilisation médiévale* 17 (1974): 1–24
Lejeune, *L'oeuvre de Jean Renart*
    Rita Lejeune-Dehousse, *L'oeuvre de Jean Renart: Contribution à l'étude du genre romanesque au moyen âge*, Bibliothèque de la Faculté de philosophie et lettres de l'Université de Liège 61 (Liège, 1935)
Lyons, *Les éléments descriptifs*
    Faith Lyons, *Les éléments descriptifs dans le roman d'aventure au XIIIe siècle*, Publications romanes et françaises, 84 (Geneva, 1965)
Zink, *Roman rose*
    Michel Zink, *Roman rose et rose rouge: Le Roman de la rose ou de Guillaume de Dole de Jean Renart* (Paris, 1979)

Notes

PREFACE

1. Léon Gautier, *La chevalerie* (Paris, 1884); Sidney Painter, *French Chivalry: Chivalric Ideas and Practices in Medieval France* (Baltimore, 1940); Maurice Keen, *Chivalry* (New Haven, 1984); among Jean Flori's many books, see *L'idéologie du glaive: Préhistoire de la chevalerie* (Geneva, 1983); *L'essor de la chevalerie: XIe–XIIe siècles* (Geneva, 1986), and the forthcoming *La chevalerie dans la littérature française de Roland à Lancelot du Lac*. His *Chevaliers et chevalerie au moyen âge* (Paris, 1998) is an excellent introduction to the subject. Although based on German literature, Joachim Bumke's magisterial study *Höfische Kultur: Literatur und Gesellschaft im hohen Mittelalter*, 2 vols. (Munich, 1986), trans. Thomas Dunlap as *Courtly Culture: Literature and Society in the High Middle Ages* (Berkeley, 1991), deals with French chivalry as well.

2. Jean Renart also wrote the *Lai de l'ombre* (1200–1202), but because of its character and brevity, I only occasionally allude to it. The romance *Galeran de Bretagne*, the fabliaux *Aubérée*, and *Du plait Renart de Dammartin contre Vairon, son roncin* and *De Renart et de Piaudoue* have likewise been attributed to Jean. See Lejeune, *L'oeuvre de Jean Renart*, 24–34, 341–45, 379–442, and Charles Muller, "Les moyens statistiques et l'attribution des textes médiévaux anonymes: à propos d'une recherche sur Jean Renart," in *Actes du XIIIe congrès international de Linguistique et Philologie romane à Laval, 29 août–5 septembre 1971*, ed. Marcel Boudreault and Frankwalt Möhreu, 2: 632–41. Because objections to Jean's authorship of these works have been widely accepted, I have not included the works.

3. Philippe Walter, "Tout commence par des chansons . . . (Intertextualities lotharingiennes)," in *Styles et valeurs: Pour une histoire de l'art littéraire au moyen âge*, ed. Daniel Poirion (Paris, 1990).

4. Constance Brittain Bouchard, *Strong of Body, Brave, and Noble: Chivalry and Society in Medieval France* (Ithaca, N.Y., 1998) is the most recent introduction to modern work. The question of knighthood and nobility has been recently

treated by Theodore Evergates, "Nobles and Knights in Twelfth-Century France," in *Cultures of Power: Lordship, Status and Process in Twelfth-Century Europe*, ed. Thomas N. Bisson (Philadelphia, 1995), 11–35, and Flori, *Chevaliers et chevalerie*, 64–85.

5. Bouchard, *Strong of Body*, 172, urges this goal.

6. William the Marshal is not only the best-studied medieval knight but perhaps also the only one who can be known directly from historical sources, thanks to the *Histoire de Guillaume le Maréchal*. See the studies of Paul Meyer, in *Histoire*, 1: i–cvii; Sidney Painter, *William Marshal: Knight Errant, Baron, and Regent of England* (Baltimore, 1933); Georges Duby, *Guillaume le Maréchal ou le meilleur chevalier du monde* (Paris, 1984), trans. Richard Howard as *William Marshal: The Flower of Chivalry* (New York, 1985); and David Crouch, *William Marshal: Court, Career, and Chivalry in the Angevin Empire, 1147–1219* (London, 1990). The life of Baudouin de Guines is explored by Georges Duby in *Medieval Marriage: Two Models from Twelfth-Century France,* trans. Elborg Forster (Baltimore, 1978), 83–110, and *Le chevalier, la femme, et le pretre: Le marriage dans la France féodale* (Paris, 1981), 269–300, trans. Barbara Bray as *The Knight, the Lady, and the Priest: The Making of Modern Marriage in Medieval France* (New York, 1983), 253–84.

CHAPTER 1.
Literary Craft: Jean Renart, Gerbert de Montreuil, and Their Romances

1. For an earlier sketch of Jean Renart, see Baldwin, *Language of Sex*, 26–36.

2. For the two other anagrams in the *Escoufle*, see "fait par bien povre = povRE bienN pAR faiT" (v. 9100) and "povRE seurnonN corRT" (vv. 9100–9101). The anagram "Renart," however, may occur often. By such means *Floriant et Florete* has also been attributed to Jean Renart. Claude Levy, "Un nouveau texte de Jean Renart?" *Romania* 99 (1978): 405–6.

3. Charles François, *Etude sur le style de la Continuation du "Perceval" par Gerbert et du "Roman de la violette" by Gerbert de Montreuil*, Bibliothèque de la Faculté de philosophie et lettres de l'Université de Liège 50 (Liège and Paris, 1932).

4. For further discussion of the addressees, see Chapter 2.

5. Philippe of Flanders was dead by Gerbert's time. Manessier, who provided a continuation, perhaps later, but certainly independently of Gerbert, dedicated his version to Jeanne of Flanders, daughter of Count Baudouin IX.

6. See Chapter 8, "The Contemporary Audience," and also Baldwin, *Language of Sex*, 34–35.

7. On this narrative technique, see Pierre Gallais, "Recherches sur la mentalité des romanciers français du moyen âge," *Cahiers de civilisation médiévale* 13 (1970): 338–46.

8. Chrétien's *Erec* (vv. 9–22) similarly suggests that his source was a previously circulating tale, but an oral one, not written down.

9. Throughout his narrative, Jean occasionally reminds his listeners/readers of the preexisting book (*Escoufle* vv. 2652, 5046) or the tale (vv. 2686, 5586), and at the conclusion he confirms the two separate versions by declaring that it is right that the *romans* has the same name as the *contes* (vv. 9074–75).

10. *Estoire* does not appear in Chrétien's preface in this sense, but elsewhere at vv. 2807, 3262, 6217, and 7681.

11. *Roman du comte de Poitiers*, ed. V. F. Koenig (Paris, 1937).

12. For the repertory, see *Chanson de Roland: Escoufle* vv. 1282–87, *Rose* vv. 1746–48, 2755, 4509–10; *Guillaume d'Orange: Rose* v. 2304; *Gerbert de Metz: Rose* vv. 1335–67; *Roman de Troie: Escoufle* vv. 7674–75, *Rose* vv. 5324–51; *Roman d'Alexandre: Rose* vv. 2880–81, 5320–21; Perceval: *Rose* vv. 1746–48, 2880–81; Gauvain: *Escoufle* vv. 988–89, *Lai* v. 61; Keu: *Rose* vv. 3159–64; *Graelent Muer: Rose* v. 2546; *Lai de Lanval: Rose* vv. 5511–12; *Piramus et Tisbé: Escoufle* vv. 6360–87; *Roman de Renart: Rose* vv. 444, 5421.

13. On the influence of the Tristan legend and Chrétien on Jean, see Baldwin, *Language of Sex*, 30–33.

14. Hans Robert Jauss, "Literary History as a Challenge to Literary Theory," trans. Timothy Bahti, in *Toward an Aesthetic of Reception*, Theory and History of Literature 2 (Minneapolis, 1982), 3–45. Jauss's "aesthetic distance" refers to the space between the present work and its predecessors. For Peter Haidu, "aesthetic distance" refers to the space between the present work and its readers generated by author's use of irony or comedy. See his *Aesthetic Distance in Chrétien de Troyes: Irony and Comedy in Cligès and Perceval* (Geneva, 1968).

15. On prologues, see Gallais, "Recherches sur la mentalité," *Cahiers de civilisation médiévale* 7 (1964): 479–93; 13 (1970): 333–46. I am grateful to Stephen Nichols for help here.

16. Lyons, *Les eléménts descriptifs*, 85–86; Walter, *Mémoire du temps*, 114; id., "Tout commence par les chansons . . . ," 196–97.

17. However formally Jean and Gerbert sought to distance themselves from Chrétien, the differences may, in fact, have been more nuanced. It can be argued that Chrétien also attempted to explore the interaction between his historical context and his Arthurian narratives. This is a problem that Chrétien scholars can best address.

18. See further discussion in Chapter 2.

19. See further discussion in Chapter 2.

20. See the examples in Chapter 6.

21. Roland Barthes, "L'effet de réel," *Communications*, 1968: 84–89. In the same scene in "Un coeur simple," however, Flaubert notes eight mahogany chairs. When they are removed at the end of the story, they indicate the final

demise of the household. Lyons (*Les éléménts descriptifs*, 96) calls such reality effects "details pittoresques mais inutiles." Closely associated is also "l'effet *du réel*" or the "impact of the real" which is directly referential to the historical context. These two devices serve different literary functions, but both can be useful to the historian to inform him or her of the context. For the distinction, see Nancy Freeman Regalado, "Effet de réel, Effet du réel: Representation and Reference in Villon's Testament," in *Images of Power: Medieval History / Discourse / Literature*, ed. Kevin Brownlee and Stephen G. Nichols, Yale French Studies 70 (1986), 63–77.

22. See Jean's use elsewhere, *Rose* vv. 1816–18, and Chrétien's use in *Erec* v. 1336. For fuller discussion, see Chapter 6 at n. 61.

23. Lecoy has calendared them in his edition of Jean's *Rose*, xxii–xxix.

24. Buffum included forty in his edition and found four more in the manuscript variants. See Gerbert, *Violette*, lxxxii–xci, and Douglas L. Buffum, "The Songs of the *Roman de la Violette*," in *Studies in Honor of A. Marshall Elliott* (Baltimore, 1911), 1: 129–57.

25. Jean includes twenty-two rondeaux, or dance refrains, sixteen *grands chants* (twelve of whose authorship can be identified), five *chansons de toile*, and two *pastourelles*. Gerbert includes twenty-eight dance refrains, thirteen *grands chants* (nine can be identified), one *chanson de toile*, and two *pastourelles*. Categories of classification can differ.

26. See Chapter 8 at n. 36.

27. Although private reading is never excluded, public-oral performance is most always assumed in the prologues of the romances. See Gallais, "Recherches sur la mentalité," *Cahiers de civilisation médiévale* 7 (1964): 482–93. On the specific case of Jean and Gerbert, see the discussion of Margaret Switten, "Song Performance, Song as Quotation, Song Repertories in Renart's *Rose*," in *Jean Renart: The Romance of the Rose or of Guillaume de Dole*, ed. Margaret Switten, Booklet II to accompany videocassette (1993), 19–35, and of Michel Zink, "Suspension and Fall: The Fragmentation and Linkage of Lyric Insertions in *Le roman de la rose (Guillaume de Dole)* and *Le roman de la violette*," in *Jean Renart*, ed. Durling, 105–21.

28. For the range of meanings, see *Altfranzösiches Etymologisches Wörterbuch*, ed. A. Tobler and E. Lommatzsch (Tübingen, 1922–), s.v. *noter*; on the sense "to transcribe musical notation," see Jean Renart, *Rose*, ed. Lecoy, glossary, and Christopher Page, *The Owl and the Nightingale: Musical Life and Ideas in France, 1100–1300* (Berkeley, 1989), 107.

29. On *chansonniers*, see Mark Everist, *Polyphonic Music in Thirteenth-Century France: Aspects of Sources and Distribution* (New York, 1989), 187–201.

30. Zink, "Suspension and Fall," 110–19.

31. Maurice Accarie, "La fonction des chansons du *Guillaume de Dole*," in

Mélanges Larmat, Annales de la Faculté des Lettres et Sciences humaines de Nice, 39 (Paris, 1983), 13–29.

32. John W. Baldwin, "The Image of the Jongleur in Northern France around 1200," *Speculum* 72 (1997): 654–57.

33. I have treated the hermaneutic stance taken here at greater length in Baldwin, *Language of Sex*, xxiv–vii. On the question of irony, see Sarah Kay's review of *Language of Sex* in *Medium Aevum* 64 (1995): 299–300.

34. This section is derived from a more comprehensive version, Baldwin, "Image of the Jongleur," 635–63.

35. On the centrality of the theme of jongleurs in Jean's *Rose*, see Dufournet, "Guillaume de Dole ou la glorification des ménestrels" (see Chapter 8, n. 26), 115–49.

36. A sister of a jongleur performs at an imperial palace (*Rose* vv. 1332–67), but her existence rests on an ambiguity in the text.

37. *Jougleour: Escoufle* v. 8997, *Rose* v. 1333, *Violette* v. 1367, *Continuation* v. 6688; *vïelleors: Rose* v. 503; *menesterel: Rose* v. 2183, *Violette* v. 6578, *Continuation* v. 6709. On the wide semantic range surrounding *jougleur* and *menestrel*, see Raleigh Morgan Jr., "Old French *jogleor* and Kindred Terms: Studies in Mediaeval Romance Lexicology," *Romance Philology* 7 (1953–54): 279–325, and L. M. Wright, "Misconceptions concerning the Troubadours, Trouvères and Minstrels," *Music and Letters* 48 (1967): 35–39.

38. For sporadic glimpses of *joculatores*, see, e.g., Gislebert de Mons, *Chronique*, 155–56, and Benedict of Peterborough in *The Chronicles of the Reigns of Henry II and Richard I*, 2 vols., ed. William Stubbs, RS (London, 1867), 2: 216.

39. Chanter, *Verbum abbreviatum*, *PL*, 205: 153C; "Contra histriones, meretrices, mimos, ioculatores, alleatores, magos, tyrocinatores," MS. V, fol. 60vb. On the theological evaluation of the jongleur, see Baldwin, *Masters, Princes, and Merchants*, 1: 198–204, which has been further developed in Christopher Page, *The Owl and the Nightingale*, 15–33. See also Michael Richter, *The Formation of the Medieval West: Studies in the Oral Culture of the Barbarians* (Dublin, 1994), 106–11, 160–72.

40. Hermann Reich, *Der Mimus* (Berlin, 1903), 744–74.

41. *Glossa ordinaria* to Gratian, *Decretum* D. 86, c. 7 *Donare*.

42. Rufinus, *Summa decretorum*, ed. H. Singer (Paderborn, 1902), 176, to Gratian, *Decretum* D. 86, c. 7 *Donare*.

43. Chanter, *Verbum abbreviatum*, *PL*, 205: 155BCD. "Item martialis: ante iovis statuam crepuit satur histrio penam; iupiter instituit vivere de proprio. Item ieronymus: Paria sunt histrionibus dare et demonibus immolare. Item Jeronymus: Non solum tales sed etiam fautores eorum promoveri prohibet super illum locum apostuli in epistola ad thimot[heum]: Non neophitum id est rudem. Glossa: Heri catecuminus, hodie pontifex, heri in theatro hodie in ecclesia, heri in foro hodie in

choro, heri in circo hodie in altari, dudum fautor histrionum, nunc consecrator virginum." MS. V, fol. 61va. The source in Jerome has not yet been located.

44. Chobham, *Summa*, 293.

45. Rigord, 71–72. Pursuing this policy in 1212, Philip expelled mimes (*mimos*) from his court as an example to other princes. Vincent de Beauvais, *Speculum historiale* [*Speculum maius* 4] (Douai, 1624), 1238. At his wedding to Isabella of England in 1235, the emperor Frederick II warned princes against giving too much to actors. *Chronica regia Coloniensis*, ed. G. Waitz, *MGH SS*, rer. Germ. 18 (Hannover, 1880), 266.

46. *Budget*, clvi (1)–vii (2), clxxxiii (1, 2), cc (1)–cci (2). Robes were, however, provided for new knights at Pentecost.

47. Gace Brulé received an annual *fief-rente* of 24 livres from the *prévoté* of Mantes. *Registres de Philippe Auguste*, 1: 203, no. 120, "Gatho Brulet (variants: Gacho Brule, Reg. C., Gasco Brule, Reg. E.), XXIIII lb. ad Omnium sanctorum." Gace Brulé was recorded through Register E in 1220. On *fief-rentes*, see Baldwin, *Government of Philip Augustus*, 272–77. The household account of Prince Louis lists *Gatho Bruleʒ* as receiving 10 livres in February 1213, likewise from the *prévoté* of Mantes, and Tornebeffe (*istrio*) as receiving 20 sous. Robert Fawtier, "Un fragment du compte de l'hôtel du prince Louis de France pour le terme de la Purification 1213," *Moyen Age*, 3d ser., 4 (1933): 243, nos. 67, 77. Fawtier recognized the importance of this discovery in "Thibaut de Champagne et Gace Brulé," *Romania* 59 (1933): 83–92.

48. Guillaume le Breton, *Gesta*, 226. On Guillaume, see Baldwin, *Government of Philip Augustus*, 397–99.

49. Chanter, *Verbum abbreviatum*, *PL*, 205: 155D. "Ait enim quidam ex eis iactans: Ille prelatus singulis annis michi servit in tanta summa summorum quasi pro redditibus. Sic ille et ille et tercius in tanta. Quod sic fatebatur se habere annuatim centum libras de donis et promissis prelatorum gallie. Dicebat enim tot valet mihi illa civitas tot illa tot et tanta illa tercia. Deinde omnibus maxime divitibus clericis imprecatus est eo quod pessimis moribus eius suggessissent sumptus eis superfluos exhibendo rithmos fabulas et gestus eius laudando et non corripendo eum vel pena arcendo." MS. V, fol. 61vb.

50. Chanter, *Summa* 3 (2a): 239, 241.

51. Mansi, 22: 840, 919. C. 16, *Constitutiones*, ed. García y García 64; Mansi, 22: 1003–6.

52. The comprehensive study of Bishop Wolger and his financial accounts is Hedwig Heger, *Das Lebensʒeugnis Walthers von der Vogelweide: Die Reiserechnungen des Passauer Bischofs Wolger von Erla* (Vienna, 1970). Devoted to the imperial interests during the succession crisis, Wolger first supported Philip of Swabia of the Staufen party, but remained on good terms with Pope Innocent, and

later became, as patriarch of Aquileia, Otto of Braunschweig's agent in Italy. For his political career, see 27–56.

53. Mentions of entertainers are in the edition of the accounts, Heger, *Lebenszeugnis*, 80–106; of Walther, 81, 86. For commentary, see 222–25. Although Walther dispatched songs to both the Staufen and Welf parties, he wrote an *Otteton* for Otto of Braunschweig in which he described the heraldry on Otto's shield, just as Jean Renart had depicted it for Milon de Nanteuil. *Die Gedichte Walthers von der Vogelweide*, ed. K. Lachmann, C. von Kraus, and H. Kuhn (Berlin, 1965), 12, 18. See Chapter 2 at n. 53.

54. "Possumus tamen licite audire uersus iocundos de honesta materia, uel instrumenta musica ad recreationem sed nullomodo ad uoluptatem. Simile dicimus de omnibus magis et incantatoribus . . . funambulis et saltatoribus, ioculatoribus. . . . Quicumque ergo talibus dat, demonibus immolat. . . . Item. Distinguendum est modicum in superioribus circa ioculatores. Quidam enim cum ludibrio et turpitudine sui corporis acquirunt neccessaria, et deformant ymaginem Dei talibus uera sunt que diximus. Sed si cantent cum instrumentis, uel cantent de gestis rebus ad recreationem uel forte ad informationem, uicini sunt excusationi." Chanter, *Summa*, 3 (2a): 176–77.

"Sed notandum quod histrionum tria sunt genera. Quidam enim transformant et transfigurant corpora sua per turpes saltus vel per turpes gestus, vel denudando corpora turpiter, vel induendo horribiles loricas vel larvas, et omnes tales damnabiles sunt nisi relinquant officia sua . . . . Est enim tertium genus histrionum qui habent instrumenta musica ad delectandum homines, sed talium duo sunt genera. Quidam enim frequentant publicas potationes et lascivas congregationes ut cantent ibi lascivas cantilenas, ut moveant homines ad lasciviam, et tales sunt damnabiles sicut et alii. Sunt autem alii qui dicunt ioculatores qui cantant gesta principum et vitas sanctorum et faciunt solatia hominibus vel in egritudinibus suis vel in angustiis suis et non faciunt nimias turpitudines sicut faciunt saltatores et saltatrices et alii qui ludunt in imaginibus inhonestis et faciunt videri quasi quedam phantasmata per incantationes vel alio modo. Si autem non faciunt talia sed cantant instrumentis suis gesta principum et alia utilia ut faciant solatia hominibus sicut dictum est, bene possunt sustineri tales, sicut ait Alexander papa." Chobham, *Summa*, 291–92.

These opinions were anticipated earlier in the century at the school of Laon. See Odon Lottin, *Psychologie et morale aux XIIe et XIIIe siècles* (Gembloux, 1959), 5: 300–301. I am grateful to Philippe Buc for this reference.

55. "Hi similes sunt cantantibus fabulas et gesta. Qui videntes cantilenam de Langrico non placere auditoribus, statim incipiunt de Narciso cantare, quod si nec placuerit, cantant de alio." Chanter, *Verbum abbreviatum*, *PL*, 205: 101AB. "Hi tales sacerdotes similes sunt ioculatori vel fabulatori qui videns cantilenam de

landerico non placere auditoribus statim incipit cantare de antiocho. Quod si non placuerit de alexandro quod fastidio cantilenam permutat in appollonium vel karolum magnum vel quemlibet alium." MS. V, fol. 35ra.

56. "Ystriones dicuntur qui ludibria sui corporis exercent et gesticulatione et motu corporis et tranformatione vultus gestus aliorum representant. . . . Sed quod de citharistis et liricis et sidicinibus [siticinibus] et huiusmodi qui instrumenta musica tangunt et exercent? Numquid eis dare peccatum est aut audire eos vel tangere musica instrumenta, et quidem si quis utitur tali instrumento ad laudem dei vel ad salutem corporis sive anime vel ob neccessitatem ecclesie honestam. Non peccat vel si peccat veniale est. Nam David sic faciebat talia scilicet ad laudem dei et etiam causa ministerii et similiter audire talem ob eandem causam vel nullum peccatum est vel est veniale, et in tale casu licet dare talibus pro tali opere. Si vero talia ad voluptatem et luxuriam incitandam facit, peccat quia deum moribus stimulat qui populum vocibus delectat ut [Gratian, *Decretum*, D. 92, c. 2] *In sancta* et pro tali opere non licet alicui dare talibus. Similiter dico quod tales audire ad laudem dei vel ob salutem corporalem non est peccatum vel modicum est, si quod est ar. [ibid. D. 41, c. 1] *Quisquis* et *De con.* [D. 3, c. 12] *Pervenit.*" Huguccio, *Summa* to Gratian, *Decretum* D. 86, c. 7, *Donare*, in Vatican Arch. S. Petr. C 114, fol. 101ra and Paris, BN lat. 15396, fol. 87ra. The *glossa ordinaria* to *talibus*, Gratian, *Decretum* D. 86, c. 7, *Donare* recapitulates Huguccio.

57. "Vnde quidam talis dum accessisset ad papam Alexandrum, et quesisset ab eo utrum posset saluare animam suam, sic sibi uictum queritando cum aliter nesciret papa nec dedit licentiam, nisi quia per consequentiam illius concessio traheret ad ampliorem licentiam." Chanter, *Summa*, 3 (2a): 177. " . . . sicut ait Alexander papa cum quidam ioculator quereret ab eo utrum posset salvare animam suam in officio suo. Quesivit enim papa ab eo utrum aliquod aliud sciret opus unde vivere posset, et respondit ioculator quod non. Permisit igitur papa quod ipse viveret ex officio suo, dummodo abstineret a predictis lasciviis et turpitudinibus." Chobham, *Summa*, 292. Around 1220, Guillaume d'Auxerre adopted this position as well. *Summa aurea*, ed. Jean Ribaillier, Spicilegium Bonaventurianum 18A (Paris and Rome, 1986), 3 (1): 445–47.

58. At Gornemans's castle Perceval is put to sleep by another minstrel who sweetly plays the "Lai de Gorron" on his Cornish pipe. *Continuation* vv. 6117–19.

59. John Stevens, *Words and Music in the Middle Ages: Song, Narrative, Dance and Drama, 1050–1350* (Cambridge, 1986), 222–25.

60. See nn. 22–25 above.

61. See Chapter 8 at n. 14.

62. Gerbert, *Continuation* vv. 6984–87, 6997–7001. *The Didot Perceval*, ed. William Roach (Philadelphia, 1941), 220, ll. 1472–75. Huon de Méry, *Li tornoiemenz Antecrit'*, ed. Georg Wimmer, Ausgaben und Abhandlungen aus dem Gebiete der romanischen Philologie, 76 (Marburg, 1888), 36, 88.

Gautiers d'Arras qui fist d'Eracle . . .
Et Chrestiens qui molt belt dist
Quant Cleget et Percheval fist . . .
Et Beneois de Sainte Moire
De Troies translata l'estoire
Tout cil estoient menestrel. . . .

Gautiers d'Arras who wrote *Eracle* . . . / and Chrétien who spoke well / of the deeds of Cligès and Perceval . . . / and Benoît de Saint-Maure / who translated the history of Troie / all these were minstrels. . . .

Miracle to the Virgin, Paris, Arsenal MS. 3518, fol. 96rb, in *Französische Literarästhetik des 12. und 13. Jahrhunderts,* ed. Ulrich Mölk (Tübingen, 1969), 75. I am grateful to David Hult for indicating this passage.

63. This conclusion goes back to Edmond Faral, *Les jongleurs en France au moyen âge* (Paris, 1910), 79, 109. See also Dufournet, "*Guillaume de Dole* ou la glorification des ménestrels," 117, 145, and Marie-Claude Struyf, "Le personnage de Jouglet dans le *Guillaume de Dole:* Une figure de l'écrivain," *Figures de l'écrivain au moyen âge,* ed. Danièlle Buschinger, Actes du Colloque du Centre d'Etudes médiévales de l'Université de Picardie, Amiens, 18–20 March 1988, Göppinger Arbeiten zur Germanistik, 510 (Göppingen, 1991), 381–88.

CHAPTER 2.
Addressees and Their Politics

1. For the references to the addressees: "par devant rois, par devant contes," *Escoufle* vv. 21, 9076, *Lai* v. 49, *Rose* v. 5646; "gentil conte en Hainaut," *Escoufle* vv. 9060, 9079–80; "l'Eslit," *Lai* v. 41; "en Raincïen en Champaigne . . . li biaus Miles . . . de Nantuel," *Rose* vv. 5–7; Gerbert: "a contesse Marie de Pontiu," *Violette* vv. 58, 6643–44. Chrétien: "ma dame de Champagne," *Charrete* v. 1; "li quens Phelipes de Flandres," *Graal* v. 13. Marie de France had followed a similiar pattern in her dedications. The *Lais* were written for a *nobles reis* (probably King Henry II of England) and the *Fables* for a certain "cunte Willame" (perhaps William Longsword, d. 1226). A preliminary version of this chapter may be found in John W. Baldwin, "'Once There Was an Emperor': A Political Reading of the Romances of Jean Renart," in *Jean Renart,* ed. Durling, 45–82. After the research for this chapter was completed, I discovered William Mendel Newman's study of the family of Nanteuil-la-Fosse in his *Les seigneurs de Nesle en Picardie (XIIᵉ–XIIIᵉ siècle), leurs chartes et leur histoire,* Bibliothèque de la Société d'histoire du droit des pays flamands, picards, et wallons, 27, 2 vols. (Paris, 1971), 1: 193–96. His work confirms my own findings.

2. The most convenient summary of Baudouin's career is in Robert Lee Wolff, "Baldwin of Flanders and Hainaut, First Latin Emperor of Constantinople: His Life, Death and Resurrection," *Speculum* 27 (1952): 281–322. *De Oorkonden der Graven van Vlaanderen (1191–aanvang 1206),* ed. W. Prevenier, Commission royale d'histoire, Recueil des princes, 5 (Brussels, 1964), is the edition of his charters. Gislebert de Mons wrote his *Chronique* in Baudouin's behalf. Less likely candidates are Baudouin VI's father, Baudouin V (1171–95) of Hainaut (VIII of Flanders) and Ferrand (1212–33), the son of King Sancho of Portugal, who married Baudouin VI's daughter Jeanne, but was imprisoned by Philip Augustus from 1214 to 1226 after Bouvines. Baudouin V, father-in-law of Philip Augustus, remained generally favorable to the Capetians and made no alliances with Richard. Ferrand was count for only a tumultuous two years before his lengthy imprisonment.

3. Baudouin inherited Flanders from his mother. Gislebert de Mons, *Chronique* 229, tableaux 1, 4, 5.

4. Gislebert de Mons, *Chronique* 2, 60, 96.

5. Pilgrimages are recorded for Baudouin's mother and wife. Gislebert de Mons, *Chronique* 150, 332. On Saint-Gilles du Gard as a contemporary pilgrimage site, see Mary C. Mansfield, *The Humiliation of Sinners: Public Penance in Thirteenth-Century France* (Ithaca, N.Y., 1995), 111, 121, 125, 277.

6. Gislebert de Mons, *Chronique* 191–92. For Baudouin IV's and V's bastards, see tableaux IV and V. Marie's and Aliénor's theories were publicized by Andreas Capellanus, *De amore,* ed. P. G. Walsh (London, 1982), 154–157, 266, and reinforced by the adulterous leitmotiv of Chrétien's *Charrete,* dedicated to Marie. Whether or not the two women actually held the views in question, their reputation for doing so was established.

7. The dossier for the disputed election of 1202–4 consists of Innocent III, *Regesta,* VI, no. 9, Vienna ed., pp. 17–19, ed. *PL,* 215: 16; VI, no. 198 (200), Vienna ed., pp. 334–35, ed. *PL,* 215: 224; VII, no. 116, Vienna ed., pp.184–88, ed. *PL,* 215: 398; Potthast nos. 1841, 2085, 2269; *Chronicon Laudunensis canonici, RHF,* 18: 712, 713; and Aubry de Trois-Fontaines, *Chronica,* ed. P. Scheffer-Boichorst, *MGH SS,* 23: 884. Robert of Courson's text comes from his *Summa,* Paris, BN lat. 14524, fol. 38v: "Unde ecclesia Remensis repulit adolescentem nobilem et offerentem illi redditus trium milium marcuarum quos habebat iure hereditatis ut promoveretur in archiepiscopum." See Baldwin, *Masters, Princes, and Merchants,* 1: 19, and *Government of Philip Augustus,* 181. Milon is named only in the Laon chronicler, but his candidature is corroborated by Courson's testimony. According to the chronicler, he was rejected because of his youth. This may explain why his name does not appear in the reports of Innocent III. The editors of the Vienna edition (*Regesta,* VII, no. 116) raise the possibility that the provost was

Milon, but in 1204, the provost was clearly Baudouin, identified by his missing finger in both Innocent's letter and the Laon chronicler. I have found no evidence of Milon as provost before 1207.

8. Milon is listed as canon of Reims in 1206 in the cartulary of Saint Martin de Laon (Laon Bibl. mun. 532, fol. 61) along with his two brothers. His first appearance as provost was in October 1207. Teulet, 1: no. 827bis. Thereafter he is cited in numerous charters. In 1208, he was designated also as provost of Rozoy and Saint-Quirace at Provins. M. Veissière, *Une communauté canonicale au moyen âge: Saint-Quiriace de Provins (XI–XIIIe siècles)* (Provins, 1961), 141, 296, 297. On his career at Reims, see *Gallia christiana in provincias ecclesiasticas distributa* (Paris, 1739–1877), 9: 167–68, Guillaume Marlot, *Histoire de la ville, cité, et université de Reims* (Reims, 1843–46), 1: 651, and Pierre Desportes, *Reims et les rémois aux XIIIe et XIVe siècles* (Paris, 1979), 91 n. 185, 155. See also Lejeune, *L'oeuvre de Jean Renart*, 77–80. I am grateful to Pierre Desportes for confirmation on Milon's career at Reims.

9. His election to Beauvais was facilitated by his holding of an archdeaconry there. Newman, *Seigneurs de Nesle*, 1: 195, 247, 255. *M[ilo] Belvacensis electus vices domini Remensis gerentes* (June 1218), cartulary of the chapter of Laon, Arch. dép. Aisne G 1850, fol. 64r. *M[ilo] Belvacensis electus vicens gerens domini Rem[ensis]* (July 1218; the charter also includes his two brothers), cartulary B of the chapter of Reims, Arch. mun. fol. 345v–346. Cartulary G of the chapter of Reims, Arch. mun. fol. 69v, 101v. *M[ilo] Belvacensis electus . . . Actum Remis, vacante sede Remensi* (March [1219]), cartulary G of the chapter of Reims, Arch. mun. fol. 82r. Desportes, *Reims* 126 n. 216. For his departure on the crusade with his brother in 1219, see Aubry de Trois-Fontaines, 908.

10. On Milon's reputation: *Récits d'un ménestrel de Reims au treizième siècle*, ed. Natalis de Wailly, Société de l'histoire de France (Paris, 1876), 96–99. On his dispute with Louis IX: Odette Pontal, "Le differend entre Louis IX et les évêques de Beauvais et ses incidences sur les conciles (1232–1248)," *Bibliothèque de l'Ecole des Chartes* 123 (1965): 5–34. On his career at Beauvais and his contributions to the rebuilding of the cathedral, see Stephen Murray, *Beauvais Cathedral: Architecture of Transcendence* (Princeton, 1989), 29, 35–38, 61–62, 83. An account of his career after 1217 is found in Louis-André Vigneras, "Sur la date de 'Guillaume de Dole,'" *Romanic Review* 28 (1937): 113–15.

11. André Duchesne, *Histoire de la maison de Chastillon-sur-Marne* (Paris, 1621), 613–18. Numerous gifts are recorded in the documents of Igny in the Archives départmentales of Marne 19 H 1–67 and the cartulary of Igny, Paris BN lat. 9904, as well as in the cartulary of Longueau, Arch. dép. Marne 72 H 2. For the latter, see the inventory in Paul Pellot, "Le Cartulaire du prieuré de Longueau," *Revue de Champagne et de Brie*, 2d ser., 7 (1899): 19–39, 161–80, 279–

88, 337–50, and, separately, *Cartulaire du prieuré de Longueau* (Arcis-sur-Aube, 1895). In 1222, e.g., Milon's brother and wife gave Igny a rent from Nanteuil to buy fur cloaks for the nuns and tunics for lepers. These gifts of clothing are recorded in Arch. dép. Marne 19 H 49 (2), cartulary of Igny fol. 241v–242r. A similar gift was made to Longueau in May 1224, cartulary of Longueau, fol. 14r–v.

12. For a summary of the arguments for Milon de Nanteuil, see *Lai*, ed. Lecoy, xii–xiv. On Hugues de Pierrepont, see Chapter 2 at nn. 29–33. A nephew of the bishop of Liège appears in the *Rose* (v. 5185) in the role of a singer.

13. *Gesta episcoporum Leodiensium abbreviata, MGH SS*, 25:134.

14. The most recent, comprehensive, and authoritative study of the period is now Bernd Ulrich Hucker, *Kaiser Otto IV., MGH* Schriften, 34 (Hannover, 1990). Before its appearance the fundamental studies were Eduard Winkelmann, *König Philipp von Schwaben, 1197–1208*, and *Kaiser Otto IV. von Braunschweig, 1208–18*, Jahrbücher der deutschen Geschichte (Leipzig, 1873, 1878), 2 vols. The documentation has been calendared in *Regesta imperii:* 5 (1, 2), *Die Regesten des Kaiserreichs unter Philipp, Otto IV, Friedrich II . . . 1198–1272*, ed. J. F. Böhmer, J. Ficker, and E. Winkelmann (Innsbruck, 1879–94), and *Nachträge und Ergänzungen*, ed. Paul Zinsmaier, in *Regesta imperii*, ed. Böhmer (Cologne, 1983), 5: 4 (6). For another recent interpretation, see Theo Holzapfel, *Papst Innozenz III., Philipp II. August, König von Frankreich und die englisch-welfische Verbindung, 1198–1216*, Europäische Hochschulschriften, 3: 460 (Frankfurt am Main, 1991). Overviews of the cultural activities of Otto IV's court are Hans Martin Schaller, "Das geistige Leben am Hofe Kaiser Otto IV. von Braunschweig," *Deutsches Archiv für Erforschung des Mittelalters* 45 (1989): 54–82, and Bernd Ulrich Hucker, "Literatur im Umkreis Kaiser Ottos IV," in *Die Welfen und ihr Braunschweiger Hof im hohen Mittelalter*, ed. Bernd Schneidmüller, Wolfenbütteler Mittelalter-Studien, 7 (Wiesbaden, 1995), 377–406.

15. The pope was so preoccupied with the imperial election that he devoted a separate volume of chancery registers to its affairs, entitled *Regestum Innocentii III papae super negotia Romani imperii* (cited hereafter as *RNI*), ed. Friedrich Kempf, Miscellanea historiae pontificiae, 12 (Rome, 1947), which contains the principal documentation of interest to the papacy.

16. Lejeune, *L'oeuvre de Jean Renart*, 64–67, 355, and *"Guillaume de Dole,"* esp. 17–18. From her impressive historical scholarship, Lejeune assembled the suggestive data that constitute my point of departure.

17. Gislebert de Mons, *Chronique*, 234.

18. Only on rare occasions does Jean raise comparisons with the royal domain, citing Lendit (*Escoufle* vv. 6528–38), Lorris (v. 7138), and Sens (v. 7160).

19. For examples: Montivilliers (*Escoufle* v. 8593), Rouen (v. 8234), Caux (v. 60), Pont de l'Arche (v. 76), and Arques (v. 8089).

20. Bradford B. Broughton, *The Legends of King Richard I Coeur de Lion* (The Hague, 1966), 116–17, has discussed the evidence. The abbey of Montivilliers had long and strong ties to the ducal family. See the summary of Edwin Hall and James Ross Sweeney, "The 'Licentia of Nan' of the Abbess of Montivilliers and the Origins of the Port of Harfleur," *Bulletin of the Institute for Historical Research* 52 (1979): 1–2.

21. Jean further claims that the counts of Normandy and Saint-Gilles shared the same coat of arms because of friendship and lineage. *Escoufle* vv. 8445–49.

22. *Chronica magistri Rogeri de Houdene*, ed. William Stubbs, RS (London, 1870), 3: 234. *De Oorkonden der Graven van Vlaanderen*, ed. Prevenier, no. 66. *Foedera, conventiones, litterae*, ed. Thomas Rymer (London, 1816), 1 (1): 67. Gervase of Tillbury, an apologist for Otto of Brunswick, also recognized the matrimonial ties between the Welf emperor and the house of Toulouse. *Otia imperialia*, ed. G. W. Leibniz, *Scriptores rerum Brunsvicensium* (Hannover, 1707–10), 1: 947; ed. R. Pauli, *MGH SS*, 27, 383. Raymond VI also called upon Otto for help against Simon de Montfort in 1210 and 1213. Winkelmann, *Otto von Brauschweig*, 293–94. Hucker, *Otto IV.*, 209.

23. *Die Urkunden Heinrichs des Löwen, Herzogs von Sachsen und Bayern*, ed. K. Jordan, *MGH, Constitutiones*, 3, Laienfürsten- und Dynastenurkunden der Kaiserzeit, 1 (1941–49), 49. See Hans Eberhard Meyer, "Die Stiftung Herzog des Löwen für das Hl. Grab," in *Heinrich des Löwe*, ed. Wolf-Dieter Mohrmann (Göttingen, 1980), 307–30. The chief source was Arnold of Lübeck's *Chronica Slavorum*, ed. G. H. Pertz, *MGH*, Scriptores rerum Germanicarum in usum scholarum (Hannover, 1868), 22, completed around 1195 and probably an eyewitness account, but the story is also found in ten other chroniclers, including those from Normandy and Cologne. For a full study, see Einar Jorganson, "The Palestine Pilgrimage of Henry the Lion," in *Medieval and Historiographical Essays in Honor of James Westfall Thompson*, ed. James L. Cate and Eugene N. Anderson (Chicago, 1938), 146–92. Most attention devoted to Count Richard's gift has concerned the anomaly of the cup's decorations illustrating the Tristan and Iseut legend. See Linda Cooper, "L'ironie iconographique de la coupe de Tristan dans l'*Escoufle*," *Romania* 104 (1983): 157–76.

24. Mainz (*Rose* vv. 4146–5641), Cologne (vv. 2968 f.), Kaiserwerth (v. 632), and Maastricht (vv. 1975, 2018).

25. Dinant (*Rose* v. 2521), Huy (v. 5528), Nivelle (v. 4677), Looz (v. 2386), and Namur (v. 2100).

26. Lejeune, *L'oeuvre de Jean Renart*, 130–38, and "*Guillaume de Dole*," 1–16, has studied the geography of the romance.

27. A Fleming [*tyois*], e.g., impolitely suggests that the evening's festivities be prolonged (*Rose* vv. 2406–21). On this linguistic frontier, see Albert Henry, *Esquisse d'une histoire des mots wallon et wallonie*, 3d ed. (Mont-sur-Marchienne,

1990), 18–21 (I am grateful to Paul Maevert for this reference). Guillaume le Breton calls Lotharingia bilingual, *Lotharingi bilingue* (*Philippidos*, 296), and also records French disdain for "barbaric" Flemish (272–73).

28. Lejeune, *"Guillaume de Dole,"* 16–19.

29. Gislebert de Mons, *Chronique*, 12, 100, 189, 331.

30. On Hugues's career, see *Actes des princes-évêques de Liège, Hugues de Pierrepont, 1200–29*, ed. Edouard Poncelet, Commission royale d'histoire, Recueil des actes des princes belges, 3 (Brussels, 1941), vii–xiv. The Pierreponts were associated with the counts of Hainaut as early as 1184. In that year Guillaume de Pierrepont, Hugues's brother, received a *fief-rente* from Baudouin V. Gislebert de Mons, *Chronique*, 175. Hugues was related through his mother to the family of Albert de Rethel, who, as provost of the chapter, had long been influential in the affairs of Liège. See Jean-Louis Kupper, *Liège et l'église impériale. XIᵉ–XIIᵉ siècles*, Bibliothèque de la Faculté de philosophie et lettres de l'Université de Liège, 228 (Liège, 1981), 182, 301, 343–44.

31. *Reineri annales*, ed. G. H. Pertz, *MGH SS*, 16: 655. In 1203, Hugues dated a charter by referring to the reign of Otto. *Actes des princes-évêques de Liège* no. 13. This was a rare practice among Otto's partisans. Georg Schreibelreiter, "Der deutsche Thronstreit 1198–1208 im Spiegel der Datierung von Privaturkunden," *Mitteilungen des Instituts für Oesterreichische Geschichtsforschung* 85 (1977): 40, 72, 73.

32. It is also noteworthy that the bishop and chapter of Liège formed a confraternity (*societas*) with Hildesheim in 1204, when the bishopric of Hildesheim was occupied by Hartbert (1199–1216), a partisan of Otto's. Hucker, *Otto IV.*, 439. Liège had similar ties with Reims and Saint Gereon in Cologne, also churches favorable to Otto. *Actes de princes-évêques de Liège*, no. 29, and Schreibelreiter, "Der deutsche Tronstreit," 62.

33. *Reineri annales*, 671. *Gesta abbatum Trudonensium auctore anonymo saec. XIV* in *Chronique de l'abbaye de Saint-Trond*, ed. Camille Borman (Liège, 1877), 2: 180–84. For the complications of the situation, see Holzapfel, *Papst Innozenz III.*, 239–41.

34. On the provost of Speyer, see Hans-Eberhard Hilpert, "Zwei Briefe Kaiser Ottos IV. an Johann Ohneland," *Deutsches Archiv für Erforschung des Mittelalters* 38 (1982): 134–37, 140. Hucker, *Otto IV.*, 214. On Conrad of Scharfenberg, see Paul Zinsmaier, *Die Urkunden Philipps von Schwaben und Ottos IV. (1198–1212)*, Veröffentlichungen der Komission für geschichtliche Landeskunde in Baden-Württemberg, ser. B, Forschungen, vol. 53 (Stuttgart, 1969), 59. Hucker, *Otto IV.*, 415–16. On the count of Dagsburg, see Chapter 2 at n. 40.

35. Otto, count of Gueldre, was a vassal of the bishop of Liège's; see *Actes des*

princes-évêques de Liège, xxix–xxxii; *Regesta imperii,* 5 (1): 57, 67. His successor, Gerhardt, also participated with the Welfs in 1212 (ibid., 146).

36. Schreibelreiter, "Der deutsche Thronstreit," 347, 348. By 1212, however, Ludwig had made peace with Otto. *MGH, Constitutiones,* 2: 49–50, no. 40. Hucker, *Otto IV.,* 99, 644, 657.

37. Lejeune, *L'oeuvre de Jean Renart,* 88–107, modified in *"Guillaume de Dole,"* passim, was the first to identify these names, of which the French forms are: *li sires* de Ronqeroles, *li* Barrois, *cil* de Couci, Alains de Roussi, Gauchiers de Chastillon, *uns autres* Maulïon, Gautier de Joëgni, *li quens* Renaus de Boloigne, and Michiel de Harnes. They are all included in Philip Augustus's Register A (1204–8), and, except for Guillaume des Barres, twice. For the references, see *Registres de Philippe Auguste:* Ronquerolles, 318, 334; Barres, 319; Couci, 317, 329; Roucy, 318, 334; Châtillon (as *comes* Sancti Pauli), 316, 328; Mauléon, 313, 314, 329; Joigny, 320, 332; Boulogne, 315, 328; and Harnes, 315, 316, 333. Mauléon may be identified with the Guillaume of the Registers rather than the more noted Savari de Mauléon, who fits with difficulty into the present context.

38. Jean Renart states that a contingent of knights was led by the count of Champagne ("li quens de Champaigne i amaine," v. 2088). Count Thibaut III took the cross in 1199 and died prematurely in 1201. His successor, Thibaut IV, did not come of age until 1222. The Champenois may have been led by someone other than the count, as on the field of Bouvines, in the latter case, the count of Grandpré. Guillaume le Breton, *Gesta* 1: 276. Baldwin, *Government of Philip Augustus* 285.

39. Duke Heinrich of Saxony: "bon chevalier de Saissoigne et . . . duc." *RNI,* nos. 11, 40, 41, 121. *Regesta imperii,* 5 (1): 60, 136, 137. Schreibelreiter, "Der deutsche Thronstreit," 58, 59. Lejeune, *"Guillaume de Dole,"* 9. Along with Adolf of Cologne, Heinrich briefly defected from Otto in 1205–6. He owed his title as duke of Saxony to Otto. Hucker, *Otto IV.,* 40–46, 359–67.

40. Count Albert II of Dagsburg: "le conte d'Auborc." *RNI,* nos. 8, 11, 35, 45. Winkelmann, *Philipp von Schwaben,* 78, 79, 85, 86. Lejeune, *"Guillaume de Dole,"* 8. Hucker, *Otto IV.,* 24, 36.

41. Dukes Heinrich III and Walram III of Limburg: "le mor Galran de Lanborc et le duc son per." *RNI,* nos. 40, 59. *Regesta imperii,* 5 (1): 57, 59, 60, 67, 71, 72, 80, 136, 148. Guillaume le Breton, *Gesta,* 266, 287; *Philippidos,* 297. Lejeune, *"Guillaume de Dole,"* 7. Hucker, *Otto IV.,* 307, 318, 688.

42. Count Thibaut I of Bar[-le-Duc]: "li quens de Bar." *Oorkonden der Graven van Vlaanderen,* no. 114. Guillaume le Breton, *Gesta,* 243. Lejeune, *L'oeuvre de Jean Renart,* 110–12. Marcel Grosdidier de Matons, "Le comté de Bar des origines au traité de Bruges (950–1301)," *Mémoires de la Société des lettres, sciences et arts de Bar-le-Duc* 43 (1918–21): 203–39. Georges Poull, *La maison souveraine et ducale de*

Bar (Nancy, 1994), 129–57, esp. 133–34. Thibaut I died in 1214; he was succeeded by his son, Henri II, who fought at Bouvines on the side of Philip Augustus (161).

43. Duke Henri of Louvain and Brabant: "duc de Louvain." For evidence of his support of Otto: *RNI*, nos. 11, 40, 90. 121; *Regesta imperii*, 5(1): 57, 58, 60, 61, 64, 65, 136, 137, 142, 146–48; Guillaume le Breton, *Gesta*, 266, 287. Georges Smets, *Henri Ier, duc de Brabant (1190–1235)* (Brussels, 1908). Lejeune, "*Guillaume de Dole*," 7. Hucker, *Otto IV.*, 377–78.

44. Count Louis of Looz: "le conte de Los." *RNI*, no. 59. *Regesta imperii*, 5 (1): 142. Lejeune, "*Guillaume de Dole*," 7. On the complexities of his situation, see Holzapfel, *Papst Innozenz III.*, 124, 189, 202–3, 207–8.

45. Count Dietrich VI of Kleves: "li quens de Cleve." *Regesta imperii*, 5 (1): 57. Lejeune, "*Guillaume de Dole*," 9.

46. Josef Fleckenstein, "Friedrich Barbarossa und das Rittertum: Zur Bedeutung der grossen Mainzer Hoftage von 1184 und 1188," in *Festschrift für Hermann Heimpel zum 70. Geburtstag* (Göttingen, 1972), 2: 1023–41, and *Das Rittertum im Mittelalter*, ed. Arno Borst, Wege der Forschung, 349 (Darmstadt, 1976), 392–401.

47. Holzapfel, *Papst Innozenz III.*, 54. Hucker, *Otto III.*, 410–11.

48. An alternative explanation may simply be that Jean neglected to identify the new archbishop with the change in scene. The archbishop of Mainz is therefore meant. Such negligence is, however, uncharacteristic of Jean's careful attention to details.

49. *Regesta imperii*, 5 (1): 56; *RNI*, nos. 9–11, 16, 20, 26 . . . , 59. Holzapfel, *Papst Innozenz III.*, 21, 24. Hucker, *Otto IV.*, 437.

50. *Reinerii annales* (cited n. 31 above), 658, 659. Arnold of Lübeck, *Chronica*, 254, 255–64. *RNI*, nos. 113, 116. *Regesta imperii*, 5 (1): 57, 72. See also Schreibelreiter, "Der deutsche Thronstreit," 36–40, and Holzapfel, *Papst Innozenz III.*, 89, 117, 119. Hucker, *Otto IV.*, 447–48.

51. Holzapfel, *Papst Innozenz III.*, 128, 194. Hucker, *Otto IV.*, 441.

52. On Guillaume's name: Arnold of Lübeck, *Chronica*, 12. On Mathilda's residence at Argentan, where she met Bertran de Born: Benedict of Peterborough in *The Chronicle of the Reigns of Henry II and Richard I*, ed. William Stubbs, RS (London, 1867), 1: 288; Gérard Gouiran, *L'Amour et la guerre: L'oeuvre de Bertran de Born* (Aix-en-Provence, 1985), 1: lxxvii, lxxviii. The name Elena (Helen) had become familiar at Henry II's court after Benoît de Sainte-Maure dedicated his *Roman de Troie* to Queen Eleanor of Aquitaine.

53. Discussion of Conrad's heraldry begins with Anthime Fourrier, "Les armoiries de l'empereur dans *Guillaume de Dole*," in *Mélanges offerts à Rita Lejeune* (Gembloux, 1969), 2: 1211–26. The major elements of what follows are provided by an extant seal of the lords of Clermont, in Emile Boulet and René Wattiez, *Sceaux armoriés de Hesbaye*, Société des bibliophiles liégeois (Liège,

1985), 131–32, no. 540; drawings of Otto's heraldry in Matthew Paris, *Chronica majora*, ed. H. R. Luard, RS (London, 1857), 2: 457– 58; *Historia Anglorum*, ed. F. Madden, RS (London, 1866), 2: 65; Suzanne Lewis, *The Art of Matthew Paris in the Chronica Majora* (Berkeley, 1987), 255–56; Marie's seal in *Die Siegel der deutschen Kaiser und Könige von Pippin bis Ludwig den Bayern*, ed. Otto Posse (Dresden, 1909), 2: pl. 26, no. 3; Otto's coins in *Die Münzen der Welfen seit Heinrich dem Löwen*, ed. Gerhard Welter (Braunschweig, 1978), 18–29 (see no. 186 for the rampant lion and the *Reichsdoppeladler*); see also Arthur Suhle, *Deutsche Münz und Geldgeschichte von den Anfängen bis zum 15. Jahrhundert*, 2d ed. (Berlin, 1964), 92, 149, and Winkelmann, *Otto IV. von Braunschweig*, 498, 499. On Walther, see *Die Gedichte Walthers von der Vogelweide*, ed. K. Lachmann, C. von Kraus, and H. Kuhn (Berlin 1965), 12, 18.

Since Clermont-en-Hesbaye was held by the counts of Duras, the lords could also have been known as counts. *Actes de princes-évêques de Liège*, xxiv, xxvii. The most recent and complete discussion of Otto's heraldry is Hucker, *Otto IV.*, 578–87, which adds the evidence of the "Mauritius sword" and the Quedlinberger casket, as well as lesser testimony. Hucker is doubtful whether problems of heraldry can be resolved by numismatic evidence because of the great variety of Otto's coinage (579). Since the major evidence does not agree whether the three lions were to the right or the left (Matthew Paris and Marie's seal, to the left; "Mauritius sword" and Quedlinberger castet, to the right), it is pointless to try to determine how Jean and Walther saw the arrangement of their shields. Moreover, it is difficult to determine from the visual evidence whether the three beasts are fully grown lions or small lions/leopards. Matthew Paris's and the Quedlinberger casket's three lions are gold on a field of red; Jean Renart's single lion is gold on a field of azure. I am grateful to Brigitte Bedos-Rezak and Michel Pastoureau for help on these questions.

54. On the family, see Duchesne, *Histoire de la maison de Chastillon-sur-Marne*, 47–54. Gaucher's royal connections were also known to Aubry de Trois-Fontaines, 846. On Bouvines, see Guillaume le Breton, *Gesta*, 278–80 who, however, reports a rumor that Gaucher might favor the enemy (*Gesta*, 276). Robert de Châtillon, Gaucher's brother, was also at Bouvines as the bishop-elect of Laon.

55. *Registres de Philippe Auguste*, 322, 334. *Documents relatifs au comté de Champagne et de Brie, 1172–1361*, ed. Auguste Longnon (Paris, 1901), 1: 437. *Registres*, 201. In 1223, Gaucher II de Nantueil and Gaucher III de Châtillon both attended the royal judgment over the succession of Beaumont. *Registres*, 530–31. Newman, *Seigneurs de Nesle*, 1: 195–96.

56. "Ego Sophia, domina de Nantolio, notum facio, presentibus et futuris, quod ego, saluti propriae consulens, religiosorum hominum consilio, concessi ecclesiae de Longua Aqua, ut ipsa possideat pacifice, sive vivam, sive moriar,

elemosinam illam quae ipsi ecclesiae facta fuit mariti mei et meo assensu, quando ipse peregrinacionem adversus Albigenses hereticos [word missing]. Concessi quidam quantum ad me pertinet, attendens debilitatem corporis mei, et maxime aegritudinis eminens periculum, quoniam in prima concessione, quum dominus meus viam, sicut praedictum est, arripuit quandiu viverem, ipsa elemosina ad ecclesiam devenire non poterat, unde rogo dominum et maritum meum, ut amore dei et pauperis ecclesie istud sine molestacione ecclesie teneat. Actum postquam dominus meus recessit pro via Albigensium, anno domini MCCIX, mense julio." Cartulary of the Priory of Longueau, Arch. dép. Marne 72 H, fol. 13r–v.

In June 1209, Gaucher with the consent of his wife Sophie and his brothers Guillaume and André came to an agreement with and made donations to the poor house of Hautvilliers. Arch. dép. Marne 2 G 1099, fol. 1r. In a charter of May 1224, Sophie, then deceased, was designated "comitissa de Chiviniaco" (countess of Chevigny). Cartulary of the Priory of Longueau, Arch. dép Marne 72 H 2, fol. 13r. See Pellot, *Cartulaire du prieuré de Longueau*, 169, 338. Newman, *Seigneurs de Nesle*, 1: 193–94.

After the assassination of the papal legate Pierre de Castelnau in 1208, the pope called for a crusade against the Albigensian heretics. Meeting with his barons at Villeneuve-sur-Yvonne in May 1209 to discuss the matter, Philip Augustus decided to let them participate in the crusade, although he could not commit himself because of the threat of Otto and Jean. Among those barons at Villeneuve were Gaucher de Châtillon, who later proceeded south to Lyon with "many others too numerous to name." Gaucher de Nanteuil undoubtedly accompanied his cousin. Pierre des Vaux de Cernay, *Hystoria Albigensis*, ed. Pascal Guébin and Ernest Lyon, Société de l'histoire de France, 412 (Paris, 1926), 1: 73–74, 81–84. Anonyme de Béthune, 763. Teulet, 1: no. 875. Alexander Cartellieri, *Philipp II. August, König von Frankreich* (Leipzig, 1899–1921), 4: 266–70.

57. "*Testamentum domini Galcheri de Nantholio quondam mariti domine Aelidis de Betunia.* Galcherus de Nantolio univeris presentes litteris inspecturis in domino salutem. Noverint univeris quod ego laborans in extremis ordinavi testamentum meum in hunc modum: Legavi ecclesie Igniacensi omni prata que habebam. . . . Inde debitur pitancia cum vino conventui Igniacensi in anniversario meo et uxoris mee. . . . Hec supradicta legavi ecclesie Igniacensi salvo iure ecclesie de Longa Aqua super legato quod dicitur esse factum eidem ecclesie a prima uxor[e] mea. Actum anno domini M CC XIII, mense maio." Cartulary of Igny, Paris BN lat. 9904, fol. 242v–243.

The scribe of the cartulary added the rubric sometime after Gaucher's death; hence the notation *quondam mariti*. In 1214, Gaucher also bequeathed to Igny bedding, cooking utensils, and table vases except for gold and silver. "Aelidis quoque uxor mea ad maius robur et minime non coacte sed spontanea suum fecit apponit." Actum 1214. Arch. dép. Marne 19 H 52, no. 5. Newman, *Seigneurs de Nesle*, 1: 193–95.

58. "Ego Galterus de Nantolio et Aelidis uxor mea." May 1215. *Cartulaire de l'abbaye de Saint-Cornelle de Compiègne*, ed. E. Morel, Société historique de Compiègne (Montdidier, 1904), 1: 440–41. "Ego Galcherus dominus Nantholi. . . . et dilecta mea Aelidis." 1222. Arch. dép. Marne 49 (1), cartulary of Igny fol. 235r. "Galcherus dominus de Nantolio et Aelidis uxoris eius." 1222. Arch. dép Marne 19 H 49 (2), cartulary of Igny, fol. 241v–242r. "Ego Gaucherus de Nantolio notum facio . . . quod ego assensu et voluntate Aelidis dilectae uxoris mea et Galcheri dilecti filii mei dedi." May 1224. Longueau Arch. dép. Marne 72 H 2, fol. 14r–v.

The tomb effigy of Gaucher de Nantueil, dated 1229, was copied by Gaignières from the church of Nantueil. *Les tombeaux de la collection Gaignières: Dessins d'archéologie du XVIIe siècle*, ed. Jean Adhémar and Gertrude Dordor, Extrait de la Gazette des beaux-arts, July–September (Paris, 1974), no. 128. André Duchesne, *Histoire généalogique de la maison de Béthune* (Paris, 1693), preuves 13, reads an epitaph on the tombs of Gaucher, Helvide his mother, and Aleyde his wife at Igny:

> G. De Nantholio lapidi qui subiacet isti;
> In coeli solio requiescat munere Christi.
> Igniaci cineres, coeli sit spiritus haeres.
> Hic iacet Helwidis domina Nantholio, mater amborum.
> Hic iacet domina Aelidis de Nantholio.

59. "Ego Willelmus dominus de Bethune et Teneremunde et advocatus Attrebatensis. . . . Hanc elemosinam concessit uxor mea Mathildis, Daniel, Robertus et Balduinus filii meii. Item Aelidis et Mathildis filie mee. Actum anno dominice incarnationis M C nonagesimo quarto." Cartulary of Saint-Yved de Braine, Paris AN LL 1583, pp. 107–8. The principal genealogical studies of the family of Béthune are Duchesne, *Histoire généalogique de la maison de Béthune*, and E. Warlop, *Flemish Nobility before 1300* (Kortrijk, Bel., 1975), 2 (1): 660–63.

60. The collaboration between members of the Béthune family and the English is amply recorded by the anonymous chronicler of Béthune. For examples, see Anonyme de Béthune, 756–57, and esp. *Histoire des ducs de Normandie et des rois d'Angleterre*, ed. F. Michel, Société de l'histoire de France (Paris, 1840), 88, 92, 97, 99–100, 128–30, 140–41, 152–54. For Jean, bishop of Cambrai, see *Gallia christiana*, 3: 34, 35. Hucker, *Otto IV.*, 102, 128–29, 214, 340, 437–38. For his reputation as provost of Seclin, see Innocent III, *Regesta*, I, nos. 109, 110, Vienna ed., pp. 161–66, *PL*, 214: 96–101; *PL*, 211: 531–32; III: no. 41, ed. *PL*, 214: 927–29; Potthast nos. 115, 116, 1071, 1186. Cambrai under Bishop Jean had the reputation of haboring traitors. Anonyme de Béthune, 92. For Jean's

conflicts with the bourgeoisie of Cambrai, see Wilhelm Reinecke, *Geschichte der Stadt Cambrai bis zur Erteilung de Lex Godefri* (Marburg, 1896), 153–60; and Henri Dubrulle, *Cambrai à la fin du moyen âge* (Lille, 1903), 19–29. For a sample of evidence of Jean's support of Otto, see *RNI*, nos. 54, 124, 133, 138, 150, 172. At Otto's death in 1218, it was revealed that the emperor had secretly taken the cross from the bishop of Cambrai after the coronation at Rome in 1209. *Thesaurus novus anecdotorum . . .*, ed. Edmond Martène (Paris 1717), 3: 1375. For his peace mission, see *Registres de Philippe Auguste*, 509 and Holzapfel, *Papst Innozenz III.*, 140, 180–84.

61. *Rotuli chartarum in turri Londoniensi*, ed. Thomas D. Hardy (London, 1837), 1 (1): 133. Holzapfel, *Papst Innozenz III.*, 103–5. Hucker, *Otto IV.*, 212.

62. Baldwin, *Government of Philip Augustus* 284, 285. Milon was provost in 1207, when the chapter agreed to come to the defense of the crown and realm, like all other chapters in France, whenever summoned by the king. Teulet, 1: no. 827bis. *Reneri annales* 663 states that the fortifications were raised "ut credimus propter metum Ottonis imperatoris auxilium patruo suo regi Anglie ferre volentis."

In 1218 when Milon was guardian of Reims and the allies had been defeated, the citizens of Reims wrote to Pope Honorius III and complained that since Reims was on the marches between the kingdom and the empire, it was subjected to harassment by enemies both near and far. Marlot, *Histoire de Reims* 3: 785–86. At mid-century these troubles were still recalled. Varin, *Archives administratives de Reims*, 1 (2): 868–69.

63. In fact, the Nanteuils were distantly related to the Pierreponts. Aubry de Trois-Fontaines, 823, 824, was aware of distant connections between the house of Châtillon and the family of Hugues de Pierrepont. Milon's great-grandfather, Hugues de Cholet, was the grandfather of the wife of Hugues de Pierrepont's brother. (To be precise, Aubry knows of Gaucher, Milon's father, and Gaucher de Nanteuil, Milon's brother.) Duchesne, *Histoire de la maison de Chastillon-sur-Marne*, 614–18.

64. Aubry de Trois-Fontaines, 884. On the family of Perche, see Oeillet des Murs, *Histoire des comtes du Perche de la famille des Rotrou de 943 à 1231* (Nogent-le-Rotrou, 1856), 431, 451–52, 492.

65. On Guy's activities in behalf of Otto, see *Reineri annales*, 656, 657; Aubry de Trois-Fontaines, 877; *RNI*, nos. 30, 33; Winkelmann, *Philipp von Schwaben*, 205–23. Werner Maleczek, *Papst und Kardinalskolleg von 1191 bis 1216: Die Kardinäle unter Coelestin III. und Innocenz III.*, Publikation des historischen Instituts beim österreichischen Kulturinstitut in Rom, 1, 6 (Vienna, 1984), 133–34. Guy has been given the toponym "de Paredo," which is difficult to locate.

66. In 1201, Guy met Hugues at Montpellier and remitted the debts he incurred in the disputed election to Liège. *Reinerii annales*, 655, 657.

67. *RNI*, no. 61.

68. Baldwin, *Government of Philip Augustus*, 284–85.

69. Teulet, 1: no. 827bis, p. 567. In 1208, Milon was named along with the bishop of Paris in one of Thibaut de Perche's tiresome contestations of Albéric's election to Reims. Innocent III, *Regesta*, XI, no. 102, ed. *PL*, 215: 1421; Potthast no. 3429.

70. Hilpert, "Zwei Briefe," 137–40. *Registres de Philippe Auguste*, 509 (the text has been damaged). Holzapfel, *Papst Innoȥenȥ III.*, 137–40, 170–81. Pierre des Vaux de Cernay, *Hystoria Albigensis*, 1: 73–74.

71. C. 18 in *Constitutiones*, ed. García y García, 66, and Mansi 22: 1006–7. See John W. Baldwin, "The Intellectual Preparation for the Canon of 1215 against Ordeals," *Speculum* 36 (1961): 613–26.

72. That Jean Renart places Renaud, count of Boulogne, among the French also helps to clarify the dating. An author of a romance cannot be expected to follow specific political allegiances with accuracy, especially when many individuals vacillated, but the tergiversations of Renaud were well publicized in France. From 1201 to 1211, he was officially on friendly terms with Philip Augustus. After November 1211, however, he was judged forfeit of his fief of Mortain, and he was openly cooperating with the Welf allies by 1212, fought valiantly against the French at Bouvines, was captured, and was imprisoned at Péronne until his death in 1227. To place him among the French after 1214, or even 1211, would have violated all appearance of political verisimilitude. For a summary of his later career, see Baldwin, *Government of Philip Augustus*, 200–202, 207–8, 211–13, 215, 217–19.

73. At least until Otto's excommunication in November 1210. In a technical sense, Otto's position as king and later as emperor was uncontested from November 1208 (death of Philip of Swabia) and September 1212 (arrival of Frederick in Germany). Zinsmaier, *Die Urkunden Philipps von Schwaben und Ottos IV.*, 59. This concurs with Lejeune's conclusions of 1208–10, proposed in 1974 ("*Guillaume de Dole*," 22).

Most of previous discussion of the dating of Jean Renart's writings has proceeded by means of negative arguments that exposed the weaknesses of former hypotheses. It has been more difficult to advance a positive position. This has been the case with Félix Lecoy, Jean's principal editor, who has proposed the date 1227–28 for the *Roman de la rose*, which has enjoyed wide acceptance ("Sur la date du *Guillaume de Dole*," *Romania* 82 [1961]: 379–402). After attacking Rita Lejeune's hypothesis by demonstrating inconsistencies among the participants in the tournament of Saint-Trond (not a difficult task), Lecoy anchors his dating on two points: (1) a period of peace that Jean alleges took place (*Rose* vv. 1619–29), and (2) the fact that the *Rose* must follow the *Lai*, because Lecoy assumes that the anonymous *Eslit* must be Milon de Nanteuil (bishop-elect from 1217–22). I find both these propositions equally problematic and prefer to base my own arguments, not on internal evidence, but on the external careers of the addressees.

74. *RNI*, no. 29.

75. Noting bestowal of the scepter, mitre, and crown at the coronation of Aelis and Guillaume:

> Mais deu ceptre vous di jou bien,
> Et deu cor et de la corone
> Dont l'apostoiles le corone
> K'il n'[en] estoit nule si riche. (*Escoufle* vv. 8950–53)

At the coronation of 1209, Otto IV also wore a mitre (*cor*). Hucker, *Otto IV.*, 595–96.

76. Gold-embroidered garments compared with ruddy visages apropos of the consecration:

> Ses atours passoit sa biauté
> Et li ors qui ert el biface
> Respont al vermel de la face
> De celi qui la ert enointe (*Escoufle* vv. 8960-63)

77. Guillaume le Breton (*Philippidos*, 111–12) asserts that at the death of Frederick Barbarossa in 1191, Henry VI had not succeeded by hereditary right but by election of the clergy and princes.

78. *De glorioso rege Ludovico* in *Vie de Louis le Gros par Suger*, ed. Auguste Molinier (Paris, 1887), 147–49. On Capetian dynasticism, see Andrew W. Lewis, *Royal Succession in Capetian France: Studies of Familial Order and the State* (Cambridge, Mass., 1981).

79. Milon de Nanteuil, it may be noted, was also distantly related to the first Staufen. Conrad was therefore an imperial name that resonated in the memory of the Châtillon-Nanteuil family. The Champenois chronicler Aubry de Trois-Fontaines, 823, the sole contemporary to trace parentage of the family of Nanteuil, affirms (*ut dicitur*) that Milon's great-grandfather Hugues de Cholet, count of Roucy, had married the sister of the emperor Conrad III of the Staufen family. This connection was noticed by Louis-André Vigneras, "Sur la date de 'Guillaume de Dole,'" *Romanic Review* 28 (1937): 87. On the Welf aversion to the Staufen name Konrad, see Hucker, *Otto IV.*, 5.

80. At least one bastard claimed Richard as father. For the story of the warning of a hermit, see Roger de Hoveden, *Chronica*, 3: 288–89. John Gillingham, *Richard the Lionheart* (New York, 1978), 54, 161–63, 166, 282–83, sums up his marital history.

81. For Otto's matrimonial chronology, see Hansmartin Decker-Hauff, "Das Staufische Haus," in *Die Zeit der Staufer: Geschichte, Kunst, Kultur: Katalog der*

Austellung (Stuttgart, 1977–79), 3: 361 and Hucker, *Otto IV.*, 378–79, 386–87. *Thesaurus anecdotorum*, ed. Martène, 3: 1375. *MGH, Constitutiones*, 2: 52, no. 42.

82. The Chanter's biblical commentaries have been studied by Philippe Buc, *L'ambiguïté du livre: Prince, pouvoir, et peuple dans les commentaires de la bible au moyen âge*, Théologie historique, 95 (Paris, 1994), 312–22. Chanter, *Summa* 3 (2a): 101–2. Baldwin, *Masters, Princes, and Merchants*, 1: 173–74. The Chanter's position was still remembered at the end of the century in the *Compilation singularis exemplorum*, ed. Marc Vaisbrot (Ecole des Chartes, thesis, 1968), no. 542: "Imperator quidam, rogatus ab amicis ut filium quem habebat nominaret futurum imperatorem post se, noluit acquiescere, dicens quod non sanguini debetur principatus se meritis et virtuti. Quod fuit valde commendabile reputatum."

83. Louis had five marriageable daughters. See his complaint at the birth of Philip Augustus cited in Cartellieri, *Philipp II. August*, 1: Beilagen 49. Elsewhere, daughters from the royal houses of Scotland, Iceland (Ireland?), and England are offered as alternatives (*Rose* vv. 3530–31, 3575).

84. Jean Frappier, "Le motif du 'don contraignant' dans la littérature du moyen âge," *Travaux de linguistique et de littérature* 8.2 (1969): 7–46. Philippe Ménard, "Le don en blanc qui lie le donateur: Réflexions sur un motif de conte," in *An Arthurian Tapestry: Essays in Memory of Lewis Thorpe* (Glasgow, 1981), 37–53.

85. See the complaints in England and France cited in C. Warren Hollister and John W. Baldwin, "The Rise of Administrative Kingship: Henry I and Philip Augustus," *American Historical Review* 83 (1978): 889–90. Ralph V. Turner's *Men Raised from the Dust: Administrative Service and Upward Mobility in Angevin England* (Philadelphia, 1988) is devoted to this theme. Benoît de Sant-Maure states that Duke Richard of Normandy tolerated no villains at his court and admitted only sons of knights. *Chroniques des ducs de Normandie*, ed. C. Fahlin, Bibliotheca Ekmaniana 60 (Uppsala, 1951–54), 2: 196–97. This is also asserted by Partonopeus de Blois (before 1188). Lionel J. Friedman, "Jean Renart and an Attribute of Rulers," *Modern Language Notes* 71 (1956): 426–30.

86. The topic of *ministeriales* is one of the most studied subjects of German medieval history, with scores of monographs devoted to individual regions. Karl Bösl, *Die Reichsministerialität der Salier und Staufer: Ein Beitrag zur Geschichte des hochmittelalterlichen deutschen Volkes, Staates und Reiches*, MGH Schriften, 2 vols. (Stuttgart, 1950), is the fundamental study at the imperial level. Recent introductions to the subject in English are John B. Freed, "The Origins of the European Nobility: The Problem of the Ministerials," *Viator* 7 (1976): 211–41; id., "Reflections on the Medieval German Nobility," *American Historical Review* 91 (1986): 566–73; and Benjamin Arnold, *German Knighthood* (Oxford, 1985). On Hainaut, see W. H. Jackson, "Knighthood and Nobility in Gislebert of Mon's

'Chronicon Hanoniense' and in Twelfth-Century German Literature," *Modern Language Review* 75 (1980): 801, 805, 807. The differences between the Empire and France were investigated by Marc Bloch, "Un problème d'histoire comparée: La ministeralité en France et en Allemagne," *Revue historique de droit français et étranger*, 4th ser., 7 (1928): 46–91. I am grateful to John B. Freed for help on this issue.

87. Wilhelm Pötter, *Die Ministerialität der Erzbischöfe von Köln*, Studien zur Kölner Kirchengeschichte, 9 (Düsseldorf, 1967). Knut Schutz, "Die Ministerialität als Problem der Stadtgeschichte: Einige allgemeine Bemerkungen, erläteret am Beispiel der Stadt Worms," *Rheinische Vierteljahrsblätter* 32 (1968), 184–219; id., *Ministerialität und Bürgertum in Trier*, Rheinisches Archiv, 66 (1968). François-L. Ganshof, *Etude sur les ministeriales en Flandre et en Lotharingie*, Mémoires de l'Acadèmie royale de Belgique, Classe des lettres et des sciences morales et politiques, 2d ser., 20 (Brussels, 1927), Liège: 137–61; Brabant: 80–138, 304–6; Hainaut: 203–7; Flanders: 356–74; the Erembauds: 343–51. Ludwig Schmugge, "Ministerialität und Bürgertum in Reims: Untersuchungen zur Geschichte der Stadt im 12. und 13. Jahrhundert," *Francia* 2 (1974): 152–212. More closely related to the knightly and bourgeois families, the *ministeriales* in Reims were not as significant as in the Rhenish cities.

88. Gislebert de Mons, *Chronique*, 209–14. *MGH, Constitutiones*, ed. Weiland, 2: 35, no. 30.

89. Nor could it be easily overlooked that the historical King Richard on his return from the crusade in 1192 was imprisoned in a castle (Dürnstein) commanded by a *ministerialis*, Hadmar von Künring. Arnold, *German Knighthood*, 84, 85, 114, 115, 128, 129, 200, 239–41.

90. Brian Woledge, "Bons vavasseurs et mauvais sénéchaux," in *Mélanges offerts à Rita Lejeune* (Gembloux, 1969), 2: 1263–77.

91. One of his duties was to hold pleas at Besançon where *baillis* brought their complaints. This duty gave him the excuse to visit Lïenor at Dole. *Rose* vv. 3311–15.

92. Arnold, *German Knighthood*, 135, 136, 212, 214. Henry VI absolved Markward of his *ministerialis* status to allow him to assume the high dignity of his Italian offices. As the chief Staufen agent in Italy, he naturally attracted the animus of Innocent III, who called him "raised from the dust and the dung-heap." Innocent III, *Regesta*, III, no. 212 (221), Vienna ed., p. 413, ed. *PL*, 214: 781, Potthast no. 877; and II: no. 217 (226), Vienna ed., p. 422, ed. *PL*, 214: 787, Potthast no. 883. In 1196, he was given a fief in France by Philip Augustus. *Actes de Philippe Auguste*, 2: no. 543. For Otto's aulic *ministeriales*, see Hucker, *Otto IV.*, 387–406. On Gunzeln, 389–92.

93. Gislebert de Mons, *Chronique*, 333–43. The seneschal of Hainaut, e.g., was Gérard de Saint-Aubert, from the highest nobility of the county. The inventory

prescribes the court service in detail. Ganshof, *Etude sur les ministeriales*, 207–9. The seneschals of the archbishop of Reims came from the noble family of Thuisy. Schmugge, "Ministerialität," 168, 169.

94. Bösl, *Reichsministerialität*, 2: 618, 619. Klaus Schreiner, "Die Staufer als Herzöge von Schwaben," in *Die Zeit der Staufer*, 3: 14.

95. *RNI*, no. 136, p. 319.

96. *Die Chronik des Propstes Burchard von Ursberg*, ed. Oswald Holder-Egger and Bernhard von Simson, *MGH, Scriptores rerum Germanicarum in usum scholarum*, 2d ed. (Hannover and Leipzig, 1916), 91, 97.

97. After the flight of the serfs, Richard advises the emperor never again to allow serfs into his court as *baillis*, because the high man is dishonored who has a *vilain* for a master (*Escoufle* vv. 1624–29).

98. Baldwin, *Government of Philip Augustus*, 133.

99. On the contrast between the Empire and France, see Jean-Pierre Ritter, *Ministérialité et chevalerie: Dignité humaine et liberté dans le droit médiéval* (Lausanne, 1955), esp. 173–76.

100. *Actes de Philippe Auguste*, 2: no. 508. Alix's dowry consisted of Eu and Arques and a loan of 5,000 marks of silver. In 1196, they were replaced with Villiers, Rue, Abbeville, Saint-Valery and Saint-Riquier. Teulet, 1: no. 451.

101. *Actes de Philippe Auguste*, 3: no. 1043. *Recueil des actes des comtes de Ponthieu (1026–1279)*, ed. Clovis Brunel (Paris, 1930), no. 188. *Recueil de documents pour servir à l'histoire de Montreuil-sur-Mer, 1000–1464*, ed. Georges de Lhomel (Compiègne, 1907), 10–11. Guillaume, the father of Marie, heiress of the county of Ponthieu, provided a dowry of 300 livres of rents from Normandy, later increased to 500 livres. *Actes de Philippe Auguste*, 3: no. 1044. Teulet, 1: no. 854. It was nonetheless "un mariage, dont molt de gens s'emerveilliènt." Anonyme de Béthune, 763. Baldwin, *Government of Philip Augustus*, 200–201.

102. Teulet, 1: no. 1480. The king rather than Marie confirmed the charters to the major communes of Ponthieu. *Actes de Philippe Auguste*, 4: nos. 1743–53, 1755. In 1219, Philip had ignored Marie's rights to Alençon. Baldwin, *Government of Philip Augustus*, 342.

103. Teulet, 2: no. 1713. Louis VIII confirmed the settlement in Registre E, Paris AN JJ 26, fol. 187rb. Brunel no. 278. Louis also remitted the relief she owed in 1221 and granted her the sum of 2,000 livres *par.* and certain revenues from the county. Marie acknowledged receipt of the sum. Teulet, 2: no. 1733. Brunel, no 279. Charles Petit-Dutaillis, *Etude sur la vie et le règne de Louis VIII*, Bibliothèque de l'Ecole des Hautes-Etudes, Sciences historiques et philologiques 101 (Paris, 1894), 360–61.

104. Teulet, 2: no. 2121. Louis IX confirmed the settlement in Registre E, fols. 184ra and 342va. Brunel, no. 287. For Simon's pledges, see Teulet, 2: nos. 2090–2120, 2122–26. Before the final settlement, Simon was in England in 1230.

Patent Rolls, Henry III (London, 1903), 2: 322. Afterward, Marie traveled there in 1233, ostensibly to make a pilgrimage, but perhaps to negotiate for the marriage of her daughter Jeanne de Ponthieu to King Henry III. The project failed. *Calendar of Patent Rolls . . . Henry III, 1232–47* (London, 1906), 25, 74, 175. Thomas Rymer, *Foedera*, 1 (1): 216. Elie Berger, *Blanche de Castille, reine de France* (Paris, 1895), 201–2.

105. *Actes de Philippe Auguste*, 1: no. 106, 2: nos. 488, 612. Teulet, 1: no. 502. Baldwin, *Government of Philip Augustus*, 26, 99, 270. For the genealogy of the house of Nevers through Mathilda (d. 1257), see Constance Brittain Bouchard, *Sword, Miter, and Cloister: Nobility and the Church in Burgundy, 980–1198* (Ithaca, N.Y., 1987), 340–51. Hervé's rise also attracted opposition from Eudes, the neighboring duke of Burgundy, who demanded that the pope annul Hervé's marriage to Mathilde. Eudes claimed that the marriage was consanguineous within the fourth degree. Innocent III, *Regesta*, VIII, no. 112, ed. *PL*, 215: 679–80, *RHF*, 19: 477–78, Potthast no. 2559; IX: no. 61, ed. *PL*, 215: 873–74, Potthast no. 2771. In December 1213, Innocent finally removed the impediment for consanguinity by dispensation, since the couple had cohabited for thirteen years and had produced progeny. *Regesta*, XVI, no. 151, ed. *PL*, 216: 943, *RHF*, 19: 586, Potthast no. 4861.

106. Guillaume le Breton, *Gesta* 1: 294, 299; *Philippidos* 251, 285, 306. Rymer, *Foedera*, 1 (1): 124. Cartellieri, *Philipp II. August*, 4: 434–35, 484–85, 489–90.

107. Teulet, 1: nos. 1302, 1447. *Registres de Philippe Auguste*, 523–26. Aubry de Trois-Fontaines, 902.

108. René de Lespinasse, *Le Nivernais et les comtes de Nevers* (Paris, 1911), 2: 129. Jean-Marie de la Mure, *Histoire des ducs de Bourbon et des comtes de Forez* (Lyon, 1860), 1: 219–23. The marriage is also reported in Aubry de Trois-Fontaines, 906. In 1222, Mathilde had promised Philip Augustus not to marry without royal permission. Teulet, 1: nos. 1502–8.

109. After his death the affairs of the two counties were separated in a charter issued by Mathilde. *Chartes du Forez antérieures au XIVᵉ siècle*, ed. Georges Guichard, Le Comte de Neufbourg, Edouard Perroy, and J.-E. Dufour (Mâcon, 1933–80), 1: no. 71.

110. To be precise, Gerbert notes the money that the barons of the two counties expended on their lord (vv. 6606–9).

111. The castles of Monglai (*Violette* v. 4590) and Bien Asis / Illes Perts (v. 4797).

112. Douglas Buffum seeks to relate the itineraries in the romance to the established routes known to the jongleurs of the chansons de geste (*Violette* lxxiii–viii).

113. For the most recent of abundant studies on the two houses, see Georges Poull, *La maison . . . de Bar*, 171, and *La maison ducale de Lorraine devenue la*

maison impériale et royale d'Autriche, de Hongrie et de Bohême (Nancy, 1991), 64–72. Gerbert claims that Gerart was the nephew of the duke of Metz/Lorraine, the son of his sister (*Violette* vv. 5693–96). I have not been able to find a comparable relationship between the houses of Nevers and Lorraine.

114. Michel Parisse, *Noblesse et chevalerie en lorraine médievale: Les familles nobles du XIe au XIIIe siècle* (Nancy, 1982), 76, 143, 351. By Gobert's death in 1263, he had gained a reputation for sanctity.

115. Baldwin, *Government of Philip Augustus,* 40.

116. Buffum, *Roman de la violette,* lv–lxxiii, made a preliminary effort to identify them.

117. "quens fut et sires de Boulogne." Andrew W. Lewis, *Royal Succession in Capetian France: Studies on Familial Order and the State* (Cambridge, Mass., 1981), 158–60.

118. "cil de Bretaigne et cil de Brainne." Pierre's career is looked at by Sidney Painter, *The Scourge of the Clergy: Peter of Dreux, Duke of Brittany* (Baltimore, 1937); Robert's by Louis de Mas Latrie, *Trésor de chronologie pour l'étude et l'emploi des documents du moyen âge* (Paris, 1889), 3: 1593, and André Duchesne, *Histoire généalogique de la maison royale de Dreux* (Paris, 1631).

119. "le quens de Saint-Pol." Duchesne, *Histoire de la maison de Chastillon-sur-Marne,* 47–54. See n. 54 above.

120. On "li quens de Pontiu, cil de Bares, cil de Garlande," see Baldwin, *Government of Philip Augustus,* 113–14.

121. "cil de Rousi, li quens de Monfort." De Mas Latrie, *Trésor,* 3: 1670–71, 1642.

122. Baldwin, *Government of Philip Augustus,* 109–11. Petit-Dutaillis, *Etude sur la vie et le règne de Louis VIII,* 336–37. Gérard Sivery, *Saint-Louis et son siècle* (Paris, 1983), 24–33.

123. Berger, *Blanche de Castille,* 144–59. For an example of their collaboration, in 1226 the counts of Boulogne, Brittany, Dreux, and Saint-Pol urged Louis VIII to move against the Albigensians. Teulet, 2: no. 1742.

124. The five central characters are identified as "li sires de Bourbon, li sires de Biaujiu, li quens d'Auvergne, li daufins de Mont-Ferrant, li quens Forois." Max Fazy, *Les origines du bourbonnais: 2, Histoire des sires de Bourbon jusq'à la mort de Archembaud VIII (1249) et la formation térritoriale du Bourbonnais* (Moulins, 1924), 78–80, and G. Devailly, *Le Berry du Xe siècle au milieu du XIIIe: Etude politique, religieuse, sociale, et économique* (Paris, 1973), 366–70, for Bourbon. De Mas Latri, *Trésor,* 3: 1558, for Beaujeu. Etienne Baluze, *Histoire généalogique de la maison d'Auvergne* (Paris, 1708), 1: 83–85, 163, for Auvergne and Montferrand. De la Mure, *Histoire . . . de Forez,* 1: 203–46 for Forez.

125. Rigord, 17. Ralph de Diceto, *Ymagines historiarum,* 2: 6, 7. Baldwin, *Government of Philip Augustus* 26.

126. On Auvergne, Baluze, *Histoire . . . d'Auvergne*, 1: 83, and Baldwin, *Government of Philip Augustus*, 199–200. On Montferrand, Teulet, 1: no. 501, 2: no. 1749.

127. *Chartes du Forez*, 12: no. 1154. The disputes are still mentioned in a charter of 1219. Ibid. 1: no. 30. In 1205, Philip Augustus had attempted to arrange a marriage treaty between Forez and Bourbon, but it too was unsuccessful. Ibid., 22: no. 1311. *Actes de Philippe Auguste*, 2: no. 894.

128. *Chartes du Forez*, 1: no. 36. *Actes de Philippe Auguste*, 4: no. 1784. For the marriage, see *Chartes du Forez*, 23: no. 1611.

129. Baluze, *Histoire . . . d'Auvergne*, 1: 83, 2: 89–90.

130. The powerful count of Champagne, Thibaut IV (d. 1253) was missing, but his region was represented by the count of Sancerre ("li quens de Sansore," v. 5952) and Alain, count of Grand-Prés ("de Grant-Pré le conte Alain," v. 5958). De Mas Latrie, *Trésor*, 3: 1679. A. Barthélemy, "Notice historique sur la maison de Grandpré," *Revue de Champagne et de Brie* 8 (1880): 339–62; 9 (1880): 97–105, 214–24; 10 (1880): 33–41, 225–32, 393–400. The former would have been Louis II (d. 1268) of a collateral branch of the Troyes-Champagne family. The latter must be an error because the Champenois county of Grand-Prés did not use the name of Alain; the contemporary count was Henri VI (d. 1231). Gerbert also pairs the count of Chalon with the "count of beyond the Saone" ("li quens de Chalon . . . li quens d'outre Seonne," vv. 5945–46). The first would have been Jean (d. 1267), count of the disruptive family of Chalon-sur-Saone; the second would have been Etienne III (d. 125?), count of Auxonne, whose mother was from the family of Chalon, with whom the counts of Auxonne collaborated closely. De Mas Latrie, *Trésor*, 3: 158. *Dictionnaire de biographie française*, 8: 218–19, and P. Camp, *Histoire d'Auxonne au moyen âge* (Dijon, 1960), 25–26. (I am grateful to William C. Jordan for help here.) "Li chastelains l'Ysoudun" (v. 5954) probably indicates the castellans of Issoudun from the Berry. Devailly, *Berry*, 375–76.

CHAPTER 3.
Chivalric Prowess

1. The comprehensive study of this literary fiction is Chênerie, *Le chevalier errant*.

2. For the taxonomy, see Chênerie, *Le chevalier errant*, 282–96.

3. For representative studies of the development of prowess, see Peter Haidu, *The Subject of Violence: The "Song of Roland" and the Birth of the State* (Bloomington, Ind., 1993); 66, Glyn Sheridan Burgess, *Contribution à l'étude du vocabulaire pré-courtois*, Publications romanes et françaises, 110 (Geneva, 1970), 9–103; and Chênerie, *Le chevalier errant*, 277–80. For *preudefame*, see Chrétien, *Yvain* v. 786 and *Graal* v. 6460. For lexicographical studies, see Jean Flori, "La notion de chevalerie dans les chansons de geste du XIIe siècle: Etude historique de vocabulaire," *Le Moyen Age* 81 (1975): 218, 229, 444, and "La notion de chevalerie dans

les romans de Chrétien de Troyes," *Romania* 114 (1996): 294–95, 314–15. *Preus*, as bravery, should be distinguished from its less common homonym *preus*, as profit or success, derived from the Latin *prodere/prode*. For examples of the latter in Jean and Gerbert, see *Escoufle* vv. 755, 4958; *Violette* v. 5815. For the contrast between the two terms, see *Escoufle* vv. 4957–58; *Violette* vv. 3068–69.

4. For examples of *preus = hardi* or *vaillant*, see *Escoufle* vv. 106, 1043–44, 1165, 2769; *Rose* vv. 662, 686, 2127, 4631; *Violette* vv. 66; *Continuatio* vv. 10857, 13997. For examples of prowess in battle, *Escoufle* vv. 1022, 1261, 7464; *Rose* vv. 2491, 2545, 2908, 2939; *Violette* vv. 5811, 6355, 2784; *Continuation* vv. 3754–55, 4739, 10857, 16027.

5. Guillaume le Breton, *Philippidos*, 54–56. Gislebert de Mons, *Chronique*, 178–79. The romance gesture was also reinforced by examples from the chansons de geste, which Jean explicitly evokes when he recalls the number of Saracens the Frankish hero Roland killed while defending the rear guard at Roncevaux (*Escoufle* vv. 1282–87).

6. Among an abundant literature, see Jacques Boussard, "Les mercenaires au XIIe siècle: Henri II Plangegenêt et les origins de l'armée de métier," *Bibliothèque de l'Ecole des Chartes* 106 (1945–46): 189–224.

7. This section is expanded from my earlier study "Jean Renart et le tournoi de Saint-Trond: Une conjonction de l'histoire et de la littérature," *Annales: Economies, sociétés, civilisations* 45.3 (May–June 1990): 565–88. For a representative sample of the vast literature, see Léon Gautier, *La chevalerie* (Paris, 1884). For the studies of Meyer, Painter, and Duby on the *Histoire de Guillaume le Maréchal*, see n. 9 below. And see also Sidney Painter, *French Chivalry: Chivalric Ideas and Practices in Medieval France* (Baltimore, 1940); Maurice Keen, *Chivalry* (New Haven, 1984), 83–101; and Michel Parisse, "Le tournoi en France, des origines à la fin du XIIIe siècle," in *Das ritterliche Turnier im Mittelalter: Beiträge zu einer vergleichenden Formen- und Verhaltensgeschichte des Rittertums*, ed. Josef Fleckenstein, Veröffentlichungen des Max-Planck-Instituts für Geschichte, 80 (Göttingen, 1985), 175–211. Parisse's article exploits the major sources used in my treatment. Fleckenstein's collection is the most recent and comprehensive interpretation of medieval tournaments. See also Joachim Bumke, *Höfische Kultur: Literatur und Gesellschaft im hohen Mittelalter* (Munich, 1986), 1: 342–79, and Juliet R. V. Barker, *The Tournament in England, 1100–1400* (Woodbridge, Suffolk, 1986).

8. Gislebert de Mons, *Chronique*, 95–160. Baudouin was following traditions of the counts of Flanders exemplified by Charles the Good, *Histoire du meurtre de Charles le Bon, comte de Flandre (1127–1128) par Galbert de Bruges*, ed. Henri Pirenne, Collection des textes pour servir à l'étude et l'enseignement de l'histoire (Paris, 1891), 9.

9. *Histoire de Guillaume le Maréchal*, 1: vv. 1201–7238. The nearly anonymous author, a trouvère named Jean, bases his account on unusually reliable contempo-

rary sources, both written and eyewitness. He himself had personally attended at least two of the tournaments, and he incorporates lengthy firsthand testimony for others. The section on tournaments has been commented on successively by Paul Meyer, *Histoire*, 1: xxvi–xliii; Sidney Painter, *William Marshal, Knight-Errant, Baron, and Regent of England* (Baltimore, 1933), 37–49; Georges Duby, *Guillaume le Maréchal ou le meilleur chevalier du monde* (Paris, 1984), 111–39; and David Crouch, *William Marshal: Court, Career and Chivalry in the Angevin Empire, 1147–1219* (London, 1990), 174–78.

10. See Béroul v. 1155 ff. The name was most likely derived from Lanthien in Cornwall.

11. *Jostes de plaideïces* were held at Eu (v. 3214), Joigny (v. 3501), Maintenon (v. 3709), Gournay (v. 5517), Gournay (v. 6057), and Saint-Pierre-sur-Dives (vv. 7205-6), and there is also mention of them at Sainte-Jamme (v. 1310), Saint-Brice (v. 1472), and Gournay (v. 2502). A suggestion of preliminary jousts occurs in Chrétine's *Charrete*, vv. 5603–5, but they are not clearly distinguished from the main *asenblee*.

12. Yvain and Gauvain tourney together for a year in Chrétien's *Lion*, vv. 2672–82, but the author offers no details of their collaboration.

13. This, incidentally, is the only example of combat on foot in all of the tournaments under consideration. Erec uses a sword only briefly (*Erec* v. 2189). The entire tournament of Noauz is devoted to jousting with lances; only once is a sword mentioned in the *Charrete* (v. 5972). There are two mentions of a sword in the *Graal* (vv. 6397, 6404).

14. *Erec* v. 2198; *Cligès* vv. 5006–7; *Charrete* vv. 6023–26; *Graal* vv. 6965–66.

15. At Sainte-Brice and Bouere, *Histoire de Guillaume le Maréchal*, 1: v. 1500; at Pleurs, vv. 2997–3002; at Eu, vv. 3375–76; at Lagny, v. 4970; at Gournay, vv. 5589–92; at Gournay, vv. 6150–54, 6206.

16. *Cligès* v. 4951; on the Marshal, see Chapter 3 at n. 15, *Continuation* v. 4772, *Violette* vv. 6031–36, *Rose* vv. 2880–81.

17. J. F. Verbruggen, *The Art of Warfare in Western Europe during the Middle Ages*, trans. Sumner Willard and S. C. M. Southern (Amsterdam, 1977), 74. Cf. *Histoire de Guillaume le Maréchal*, 1: vv. 2735–36: "De poindre as premiers de la rote. / Fols est qui trop tost se desrote."

18. For a characteristic description, see *Histoire de Guillaume le Maréchal*, 1: vv. 1441–44:

> Li uns le fert, l'autre le frape,
> Et quant ce est qu'il lor eschape
> De granz coups estordiz lor done;
> Lur servise lor guerredone.

19. For examples, see *Violette* vv. 5967–68, 6011–12, 6019, 6022, 6026, 6046; *Continuation* vv. 4120–22, 4193, 4314.

20. Guillaume rents lodgings at Saint-Trond ample for fifty knights. *Rose* vv. 2000–2013.

21. Cf. similar phrases in the *Histoire de Guillaume le Maréchal,* 1: vv. 2959, 3852–54.

22. "Ego autem cepi illi ostendere quod VII criminalia peccata coritantur torneamenta. Non enim carent superbia, cum propter laudem hominum et gloriam inanem in circuito illo impii ambulant et vani. . . . Non carent quinto criminali peccato, id est avaricia vel rapina, dum unus alium capit et redimit, et equum quem cupiebat cum armis aufert illi contra quem pugnando prevaluit." Jacques LeGoff, "Réaltés sociales et codes idéologiques au début du XIIIe siècle: Un *exemplum* de Jacques de Vitry sur les tournois," in *L'imaginaire médiévale: Essais* (Paris, 1985), 258, 259.

23. It is true that Gauvain presents three horses to the wife of a vavasor, his host in the castle, and her two daughters, which suggests that he is repaying hospitality. It was not a contractual debt, however, but a gift. *Graal* vv. 6957–62.

24. Gislebert de Mons, *Chronique,* 107–9. Robert of Courson discusses the case of a knight who hires other knights to increase his entourage and win more glory in a tournament. Baldwin, *Masters, Princes, and Merchants,* 1: 130, 2: 88, 89, n, 92.

25. William foiled such a tactic at Lagny, where Herlin de Vanci, seneschal of Flanders, attempted to capture the Young King. *Histoire de Guillaume le Maréchal,* 1: vv. 4935–70.

26. Gislebert de Mons, *Chronique,* 123, 127.

27. Particularly detailed accounts are provided for the tournaments at Pleurs, Eu, Anet/Sorel, and Epernon.

28. Similar disavowals were offered at Saint-Brice and Bouere (*Histoire de Guillaume le Maréchal,* 1: v. 1501), Pleurs (vv. 3007–9), and Gournay (vv. 5561–62).

29. At the tournament of Noauz, crusaders refrained from combat along with prisoners. Chrétien, *Charrete* v. 5769.

30. This refrain was well known from Provençal poetry. See Paul Meyer, "Explication de la pièce de Peire Vidal: Drogoman seiner s'agues bon destrier," *Romania* 2 (1873): 425–26, 429.

31. *Histoire de Guillaume le Maréchal,* 1: vv. 5102–8, on the Marshal's landed poverty and his reputation for prowess, goodness, and generosity.

32. Cf. Chrétien, *Erec* v. 2214.

33. Cf. *Histoire de Guillaume le Maréchal,* 1: vv. 5561–65, 5584–88.

34. The same expression occurs in the *Histoire de Guillaume le Maréchal,* 1: vv. 6076–77. For another shared cliché: "Que renomée qui tost vole," cf. ibid. v. 3427 with *Rose* v. 938 and *Escoufle* v. 8516.

35. *Foedera, litterae, et acta publica*, ed. Thomas Rymer (London, 1818), 1 (1): 65. William of Newburgh, *Historia rerum Anglicarum*, in *Chronicles of the Reigns of Stephen, Henry II, and Richard I*, ed. Richard Howlett, RS (London, 1885), 2: 422–23. Juliet Barker and Maurice Keen, "The Medieval English Kings and the Tournament," *Das ritterliche Turnier im Mittelalter*, 213–15.

36. In Chrétien's *Erec* (vv. 2084–87), guimples and sleeves worn as emblems by knights in the tournament suggest ladyloves, but the feminine presence is not developed. In the *Lion* (vv. 2672–95), Yvain departs with Gauvain for a year of tourneying to escape Laudine and forgets his promise to return. The Arthurian tradition of introducing ladies as spectators goes back to the first half of the twelfth century in Geoffrey of Monmouth, *Historia regum Britanniae* IX, 14.

37. Jean de Joinville, *Histoire de Saint Louis*, ed. Natalis de Wailly (Paris, 1874), para. 242. A similar sentiment is expressed by Buridant de Furnes when he is captured at Bouvines: "Nunc quisque sue memor esto puelle." Guillaume le Breton, *Philippidos*, 323.

38. The theme *d'armes et d'amors* is later associated directly with the tournament. *Rose* vv. 1644–47.

39. There is, however, one minor connection. As the participants gather, Guillaume asks of those who stay at Ligny whether they expect the arrival of Gautier de Joigny, who is dying for love of his *amie*. "Yes, he's ready to joust, because God has revived him" is the reply (*Rose* vv. 2101–6). Indeed, the tournament was God's medicine! A Gaucher de Joigny appears in the list of bannerets and castellans in the *Registres de Philippe Auguste*, 314, 326. Joigny was the site where women were present in the *Histoire de Guillaume le Maréchal*.

40. Women also participate in the evening festivities before the tournament. *Rose* vv. 1799–1845.

41. Council of Clermont (1130), in Mansi, 21: 439; Council of Reims (1131), ibid., 460; Lateran II (1139), ibid., 530; Council of Reims (1148), ibid., 716–17; Lateran III (1179), ibid., 229; Lateran IV (1215), ibid., 1066. *Constitutiones*, ed. García y García, 116. For canonist discussion, see Sabine Krüger, "Das kirchliche Turnierverbot im Mittelalter," *Das ritterliche Turnier in Mittelalter*, 401–22. For the theologians, see Baldwin, *Masters, Princes, and Merchants*, 1: 224–26.

42. Chanter, *Summa*, 2: 252–53, 446; Courson, *Summa* IV, 3, fol. 26vb–27ra, in Baldwin, *Masters, Princes, and Merchants*, 2: 161 n. 137.

43. Chanter, *Summa*, 2: 446. Baldwin, *Masters, Princes, and Merchants*, 1: 226; 2: 161 n. 143 for Courson.

44. Chanter, *Summa*, 2: 352–53; 3 (2a): 276–77. See Chapter 7 at n. 59.

45. Rigord, 68–69. Guillaume le Breton, *Gesta*, 185; *Philippidos*, 59. Benedict of Peterborough, *Gesta regis Henrici secundi*, ed. William Stubbs, RS (London, 1867), 1: 350. Gerald of Wales, *De principis instructione* 2.10, ed. George F.

Warner, in *Opera*, RS (London, 1891), 8: 176. *Notre-Dame and Related Conductus: Opera omnia*, ed. Gordon A. Anderson (Henryville, Pa., 1978–81), 4: viii (music, 13–17), 6: xx–xxi (music, 22–23). *Actes de Philippe Auguste*, 1: no. 325, and 5: no. 1830 (volume still to be published). *Obituaires de la province de Sens*, ed. Auguste Molinier, *RHF* (Paris, 1902–23), 1 (1): 153, 169. Even the Chanter refers obliquely to the endowment in his *questiones*. *Summa*, 3 (2a): 62–63.

46. Chanter, *Summa*, 2: 446; 3 (2a): 276. Chobham, *Summa*, 261.

47. Actually, Gauvain has not yet decided to participate. At most Chrétien may be suggesting that a knight who performs his religious duties cannot refuse to take part in a tournament when requested by a lady.

48. Chanter, *Summa*, 2: 446.

49. "Quare ergo communicamus in perceptione eucaristie tirocinatoribus . . . cum omnes generaliter sint excommunicati. . . . Dicunt quidam quod per dissimulationem ecclesie et per tolerantiam absoluti sunt et recepti ad communionem." MS. Paris BN lat. 3477, fol. 48r.

50. Chanter, *Summa*, 3 (2a): 278–79. Chobham, *Summa*, 427–28. See Chapter 7 at nn. 59–60.

51. Villehardouin, *La conquête de Constantinople*, ed. Edmond Faral, Classiques de l'histoire de France au moyen âge (Paris, 1973), 1: 4–10.

52. Innocent III, *Regesta*, IX, no. 197, ed. *PL*, 215: 1035; X: no.74, ed. *PL*, 215: 1174; Potthast nos. 2927, 3127. See also *Regesta*, XIV, no. 32, ed. *PL*, 216: 827, Potthast no. 4711. C. 71 of Lateran IV, *Constitutiones*, ed. García y García, 116; Mansi, 22: 1066. Krüger, "Das kirchliche Turnierverbot," 417 n. 91a, 418–19.

53. In *William Marshal: Knight Errant, Baron and Regent of England* (Baltimore, 1933) 44–46, Sidney Painter conjectures that the great tournament at Lagny recorded in the *Histoire* (vv. 4457–4970) was held to celebrate Philip Augustus's coronation, but the connection is purely circumstantial, based on coincidences of time and place. In all events, it is extremely unlikely that the king attended. The author is meticulous about naming the participants, including the young King Henry, a duke, and nineteen counts. Had Philip been there, his presence would surely have been noted.

54. *Registres de Philippe Auguste*, 502, 533.

55. *Quia in futurorum* in Extravagantes Ioannis XXII in *Decretales* ed. A. Friedberg (Leipzig, 1881), 2: 1215. Krüger, "Das kirchliche Turnierverbot," 418–22. From among an abundant bibliography, see the recent studies of Juliet R. V. Barker, *The Tournament in England, 1100–1408*, 70–111, and Michel Stanesco, *Jeux d'errance du chevalier médiéval: Aspects ludiques de la fonction guerrière dans la littérature du moyen âge flamboyant*, Brill's Studies in Intellectual History, 9 (Leiden, 1988), 71–102.

56. "Five days" in Guillot's version.

57. Chênerie, *La chevalier errant,* 31–32. The relationship between knighthood and nobility has preoccupied modern historical scholarship. See the recent summations in Constance Brittain Bouchard, *Strong of Body, Brave and Noble: Chivalry and Society in Medieval France* (Ithaca, N.Y., 1998), 1–27, and Jean Flori, *Chevaliers et chevalerie au moyen âge* (Paris, 1998), 64–85.

58. Jean Flori, "La notion de chevalerie dans les chansons de gestes," 444, and "La notion de chevalerie dans Chrétien de Troyes . . . ," 294–95, 314. It is of interest that Chrétien may have privileged the martial virtue of bravery over that of birth, although both categories were highly esteemed.

59. See Chapter 2 at nn. 83–84. Before Guillaume's identity is revealed, the count of Saint-Gilles asks him whether his father was a *gentils hom.* Guillaume responds that he was a *chevaliers. Escoufle* vv. 7378–81.

60. For some examples, Lïenor: vv. 816, 4774, 5034, 5538 . . . , Guillaume: vv. 1371, 1819, 5158 . . . , Conrad: vv. 383, 1895. . . .

61. For the Latin literature, see Jean Flori, *L'essor de la chevalerie, XIᵉ–XIIᵉ siècles* (Geneva, 1986).

62. The comprehensive taxonomy for Chrétien de Troyes is provided by Jean Flori, "Pour une histoire de la chevalerie: L'adoubement dans les romans de Chrétien de Troyes," *Romania* 100 (1979): 21–53. See also Chênerie, *Le chevalier errant,* 39–51.

63. To prepare Guillaume's dismissal as Aelis's fiancé, the imperial advisors propose that the boy return to his mother. When he wishes to receive his arms, he can return to the emperor's court. *Escoufle* vv. 2734–37.

64. Gislebert de Mons, *Chronique,* 95, 237, 292, 305. Baudouin V objected to the knighting of Henri, perhaps because he counted on King Henry VI's promise to promote one of his sons to the archbishopric of either Cologne, Mainz, Treves, or Liège.

65. Roger de Hoveden (*Chronica,* 4: 94) situates the knighting in 1199. Rigord (152) and Guillaume le Breton (*Philippidos,* 2: 162) in 1202.

66. Guillaume le Breton, *Gesta,* 226; Roger of Wendover in Matthew Paris, *Chronica maiora,* 2: 524; Anonyme de Béthune, 763; *Registres de Philippe Auguste* 502. For further discussion, see Chapter 6 at n. 4.

67. *Budget* CCI (1).

68. On the secular nature of chivalry in Chrétien, see Flori, "La notion de chevalerie dans Chrétien de Troyes," 300–314. This secularism contrasts with the ritual of dubbing (*consecratio militis*) reported by the contemporary Hélinand, a jongleur turned Cistercian abbot of Froidmont, which consisted of prayerful vigils in a church the night before and the solemn placing of the sword on the altar. The knight swore to defend Holy Church, oppose unbelief, honor the priesthood, repel injuries to the poor, pacify the province, and shed blood for his brothers. *De bono regimine principis, PL,* 212: 743–44.

69. When Gauvain dubs five hundred new knights on Pentecost at Orcanie, they also go to church after matins and keep vigils without kneeling. *Graal* vv. 9171–88.

70. See the study of Jean Flori, *L'idéologie du glaive*, whose findings are summarized on 167–73. The metaphor also derives inspiration from Bernard de Clairvaux's treatise *Liber ad milites Templi: De laude nove militie*, I, ed. J. Leclercq and H. M. Rochais, *Sancti Bernardi opera* (Rome, 1963), 214, written a century earlier for the Templars.

71. Baldwin, *Government of Philip Augustus*, 374–75.

72. For other examples: *Rose* vv. 530, 3201, 3452. For comparable usage, see Flori, "La notion de chevalerie dans Chrétien de Troyes," 299–300.

73. For some examples, Gerbert, *Continuation* vv. 7106, 15748. In contrast, the hermit Ogrin in Béroul's *Tristan* is not called *preudomes* but *maistre* (v. 2281) or *beau sire* (v. 2411).

74. Chanter, *Verbum abbreviatum*, *PL*, 205: 305, 306. "Item. fortitudo est virtus qua vincis mundum, vincis diabolum, vincis te ipsum si bene pugnas. Fortitudo audacter quod provisum et electum est aggreditur, conservat, et tuetur." MS. V, fol. 139rb.

75. Chanter, *Verbum abbreviatum*, *PL*, 205: 316. "Maganimitas est mater fortitudinis, fortitudo patientie, paciencia omnium virtum nutrix. . . . Magnanimitas autem virtus est que peperit, ut ait Jeronimus, rosas martirum et victoriosas coronas confessorum." V. fol. 143rb, 144ra.

76. Joinville, *Histoire de Saint Louis*, 306. Joinville did not issue this account until nearly a century after the event, when the distinction between the two kinds of *preu* was well established, but his record is unusually reliable for Louis IX, who, in turn, retained vivid memories of his grandfather. Joinville's usage may also attest the conflation of the two senses of *preus* as bravery and profit/success. See n. 3 above.

CHAPTER 4.
The Economy of Romance: Largesse and Hospitality

1. Georges Duby, in *The Early Growth of the European Economy: Warriors and Peasants from the Seventh to the Twelfth Century*, trans. Howard B. Clarke (Ithaca, N.Y., 1984), offers the most cohesive statement of this particular interpretation of gift-giving in the early medieval economy.

2. Jean Flori, *L'idéologie du glaive: Préhistoire de la chevalerie*, Travaux d'histoire éthico-politique, 43 (Geneva, 1983), 108. Hans Hubert Anton, *Fürstenspiegel und Herrscherethos in der Karolingerzeit*, Bonner historische Forschungen, 32 (Bonn, 1968). Aaron Y. Gurevich, "Wealth and Gift-Bestowal among the Ancient Scandinavians," *Scandinavica* 7 (1968): 134-35.

3. Flori, *L'idéologie*, 136. Jean Flori, *L'essor de la chevalerie: XIe–XIIe siècles*, Travaux d'histoire éthico-politique, 46 (Geneva, 1986), 180, 310-14.

4. Erich Köhler, *L'aventure chevaleresque: Idéal et réalité dans le roman courtois*, Bibliothèque des idées (Paris, 1974), 26–43. Dominique Boutet, "Sur l'origine et le sens de la largesse Arthurienne," *Le Moyen Age* 89 (1983): 397–411. For a general study of the virtue of largesse in medieval literature, see Marian Parker Whitney, "Queen of Medieval Virtues: Largesse," in *Vassar Medieval Studies*, ed. C. F. Fiske (New Haven, 1923), 181–215.

5. Marcel Mauss, "Essai sur le don: Forme et raison de l'échange dans les sociétés archaïques," *Année sociologique* 1 (1923–24), reprinted in *Sociologie et anthropologie* (Paris, 1950): 145–53, 205–12. Gurevich, "Wealth," 128–29.

6. Flori, *L'essor*, 267, 273, 278–79, 294. The devolution of the royal ethos to that of the knights is the underlying thesis of Flori's *L'idéologie* and *L'essor*.

7. Chanter, *Verbum abbreviatum*, *PL*, 205: 286.

8. Ibid.: 288.

9. Ibid.: 290. More details culled from the long version may be found in Baldwin, *Masters, Princes, and Merchants*, 2: 182. Raoul Ardent includes this exemplum in his *Speculum* XI, 195, Paris BN lat. 3240, fol. 86v. On Thibaut's image in the Chanter's circle, see Baldwin, *Masters, Princes, and Merchants*, 1: 236–37, 254–55.

10. Chanter, *Verbum abbreviatum*, *PL*, 205: 261–62.

11. Ibid.: 150.

12. "Dum machedonum favorem captaret alexander pecuniarum largitione, scripsit ei pater in hec verba: Quis error te in hanc spem induxit ut eos tibi fideles putares quos peccunia corrupisses? Ad id tu agis ut machedones non te regem sed ministrum et prestitorem putent?" Ardent, *Speculum* XI, 86, Paris BN lat. 3240, fol. 82ra.

13. Chanter, *Verbum abbreviatum*, *PL*, 205: 151. For more details from the long version, see Baldwin, *Masters, Princes, and Merchants*, 2: 105. Ardent incuded this exemplum in his *Speculum* XI, 89, Paris BN lat. 3240, fol. 83va. On Anselm and the incident, see Baldwin, *Masters, Princes, and Merchants*, 1: 151–52.

14. "*Que virtus sit collateralis beneficencie sive largitatis*. Beneficencie sive largitatis collateralis virtus est parsimonia. Est aut[em] parsimonia virtus modeste dispensandi bona nobis commissa. Hec autem tam in utendo quam in largiendo custodienda est ut videlicet utamur nostris tantum ad necessitatem et largiamur aliis iuxta facultatem. Sic largiamur aliis quod nos non reliquamus. Et sic retineamus quod aliis tribuamus. Nobis retinentes sola necessaria, aliis tribuentes supervacua. . . . Itaque largitas sine parsimonia prodigalitas est. Parsimonia vero sine largitate avaricia est. Sed largitas parca et parcitas larga virtus est. Est autem religiosi sibi esse parciorem, indigentibus vero largiorem." Ardent, *Speculum* XI, 97, Paris BN lat. 3240, fol. 87vb.

15. The *Histoire de Guillaume le Maréchal* compares Philippe's largesse with

that of the young King Henry. When the young Henry arrived on the Continent for the first time in the company of William the Marshal, he was openly and lavishly received by the count of Flanders. Hearing of a tournament announced between Gournay and Ressons, the Young King expressed his desire to attend, if he could procure the necessary horses and arms. With largesse appropriate to an Arthurian host, Count Philippe equipped his guest and his retinue to their complete satisfaction (vv. 2461–96). As a patron of chivalry, however, even the count of Flanders envied the example of his guest, the young Henry (vv. 2667–71).

16. See Matt. 13:3–23; Mark 4:3–20; Luke 8:5–15; 2 Cor. 9:6.

17. On *dieu-donné*, see Baldwin, *Government of Philip Augustus*, 367–68. Jean de Joinville, *Histoire de Saint Louis*, 133, ed. Natalis de Wailly (Paris, 1874), 364.

18. Baldwin, *Government of Philip Augustus*, 186–87, 314–15, 376–77, 388–89.

19. Rigord, 132; Guillaume le Breton, *Gesta*, 197, 199.

20. Rigord, 150; Guillaume le Breton, *Gesta*, 206.

21. Guillaume le Breton, *Gesta*, 226. This passage is placed between the summary of Rigord and the beginning of Guillaume's original contribution.

22. *Budget* CCI (1).

23. Duby, *Early Growth of the European Economy*, 135, 178, 228; the fundamental study of *gîte* is Carlrichard Brühl, *Fodrum, Gistum et Servitium Regis: Studien zu den wirtschaftlichen Grundlagen des Königtums im Frankenreich und in den fränkischen Nachfolgestaaten Deutschland, Frankreich und Italien vom 6. bis zur Mitte des 14. Jahrhunderts* (Cologne, 1968). For a contemporary list of the *gîte* owed to Philip Augustus by the churches in his royal domain, see *Registres de Philippe Auguste*, 243–45.

24. On the knight's equipment, see Bernard S. Bachrach, "*Caballus et Caballarius* in Medieval Warfare," and Rosemary Ascherl, "The Technology of Chivalry in Reality and Romance," in *The Study of Chivalry*, ed. Howell Chickering and Thomas H. Seiler (Kalamazoo, Mich., 1988), 173–211, 263–311.

25. The literary topos of hospitality in romance has been studied by Matilda Tomaryn Bruckner, *Narrative Invention in Twelfth-Century French Romance: The Convention of Hospitality (1160–1200)*, French Forum Monographs, 17 (Lexington, Ky., 1980), and Marie-Luce Chênerie, *Le chevalier errant*, 503–91.

26. The alternative to Gerbert's procedure was for the host to offer hospitality before the need could be made known. Urpin de la Montaigne Irouse, e.g., offers Gauvain lodging and food immediately (*Continuation* vv. 13092–94), as does the abbess of Saint-Domain to Perceval and a maiden (*Continuation* v. 9117), although she regrets not having a fine supper to give them (vv. 9139–40).

27. Duby, *Early Growth of the European Economy*, 234–270.

28. When William the Marshal captured an unusual windfall at Saint-Pierre-sur-Dives, he used his prize to pay for his lunch at an inn. *Histoire de Guillaume le Maréchal*, 1: vv. 7223–26.

29. In the *Escoufle,* the count of Saint-Gilles offers to advance Guillaume 30 marks for two months to cover the contract for his wages (vv. 7412–41). William the Marshal's reputation for keeping his word made him indispensible to the inveterate prodigality of his patron, the young King Henry. When the bourgeois presented a bill of his expenditures to Henry, the Marshal was usually asked to serve as pledge. Although he had no money of his own, his good faith was accepted as guarantee. *Histoire de Guillaume le Maréchal* vv. 5084–94.

30. On royal policy toward merchants and Jews, see *Actes de Philippe Auguste,* 1: no. 135, Baldwin, *Government of Philip Augustus,* 156, 158–61, and Baldwin, *Masters, Princes, and Merchants,* 1: 298–300.

31. Bruckner, *Narrative Invention,* 118–21.

32. See Chapter 3 at n. 35.

33. Chanter, *Verbum abbreviatum, PL,* 205: 325B. Raoul Ardent, *Speculum universale* XI, 71, Paris BN lat. 3240, fol. 79rb reproduces the substance of the Chanter's discussion.

34. Eugene Vance, "Chrétien's *Yvain* and the Ideologies of Change and Exchange," *Yale French Studies* 70 (1986), 42–62, and in id., *Mervelous Signals: Poetics and Sign Theory in the Middle Ages* (Lincoln, Neb., 1986), 111–51. By comparison to Jean Renart's, however, the commercial vocabulary that Vance detects in Chrétien's *Lion* is exceedingly sparse and virtually unrelated to an explicit commercial context. Peter Haidu likewise detects commercial exchange in a semiotic analysis of the romance in "The Hermit's Potage: Deconstruction and History in *Yvain,*" in *The Sower and His Seed: Essays on Chrétien de Troyes,* ed. Rupert I. Pickens, French Forum Monographs, 44 (Lexington, Ky., 1987), 127–45.

35. The gift here may be, in fact, a disguise for interest (*usure*), which was previously mentioned (*Rose* v. 1875). See the discussion of the canonists and the Chanter in Baldwin, *Masters, Princes, and Merchants,* 1: 281–82.

CHAPTER 5.
Women and Love

1. This traditional relationship is the focus of Sarah Kay's *The Chanson de geste in the Age of Romance* (Oxford, 1995). Her examination of the genre rightfully nuances and explodes many of the received axioms (see 14–15, 25–48). See also Simon Gaunt, *Gender and Genre in Medieval French Literature,* Cambridge Studies in French, 53 (Cambridge, 1995), chs. 1 and 2.

2. Roberta L. Krueger, *Women Readers and the Ideology of Gender in Old French Romance,* Cambridge Studies in French, 43 (Cambridge, 1993), 253–58.

3. "It's true that woman is a frail thing" ("Voirs est que feme est feble chose"), Bloiesine's brother replies (*Continuation* v. 12855). Moreover, after Aiglente has overcome Gerart's resistance with a magic potion, Gerbert comments:

Et c'est coustume par usage
A femme de legier corage,
Quant ele voit l'omme souspris,
Et il est de s'amour espris,
Tant fait vers lui plus le mescointe,
Et tant plus a envis s'acointe.

It is entirely customary / for a fickle woman / seeing a man head over
heels in love with her / to become indifferent to him / and avoid him.
(*Violette* vv. 3580–85)

Another example is offered by the treacherous demoiselle Felisse (*feleness*) de la
Blanclose, who provokes Perceval to utter a thought that is often on his mind: "So
much wickedness comes through women!" ("Tant malisse par feme vient!" *Continuation* v. 15380).

4. Gerbert's choice of Absolom is perplexing, because, although Scripture
characterizes David's son as beautiful (*pulcher*, 1 Sam. 14:25) and without blemish, his death is not attributed to a woman (1 Sam. 18). St. Jerome alludes to the
sensuality of Samson (*Adversus Jovianum* 1.23; *PL*, 23: 252–53), David, Solomon
(1.24, 2.4; *PL*, 23: 254–55, 301), and Adam (1.27; *PL*, 23: 260), but does not attribute their downfall to specific women. This conclusion appears in Abelard's *Theologia christiana*, 2, *PL*, 178: 1195–96; his *Planctus* for Samson, ed. Peter Dronke
in *Poetic Individuality in the Middle Ages: New Departures in Poetry, 1000–1150*
(Oxford, 1970), 121–23; and in Heloise's *Letter 2*, ed. J. T. Muckle, *Mediaeval
Studies* 15 (1953): 79, *PL*, 178: 195. For discussion of the topos, see Dronke,
119–45. See also Philippe Delhaye, "Le dossier anti-matrimonial de l'*Adversus Jovianum* et son influence sur quelques écrits latins du XIIᵉ siècle," *Mediaeval Studies* 13 (1951): 65–86.

5. With this operating assumption, I adopt the position of Barbara Newman,
From Virile Woman to WomanChrist: Studies in Medieval Religion and Literature
(Philadelphia, 1995). R. Howard Bloch, however, interprets medieval misogyny
as twofold: (1) all generalizations about women, whether positive or negative, are
misogynistic, because they reduce women to an essence; (2) in medieval misogyny, women are caught in a double bind, being both "Brides of Christ" and the
"Devil's gateway," perfect Marys and damnable Eves. That they are necessarily
both at the same time results in perpetual overdetermination and is worse than being simply vilified. See Bloch, *Medieval Misogyny and the Invention of Western Romantic Love* (Chicago, 1991), esp. 5, 90–91, 164, 191. I find these formulations too
comprehensive to be of historical use. The double evaluations are not necessarily
connected, and they obscure intermediary positions that can be perceived in the
historical evidence.

6. On a practical level, I cannot deal with all of the some fifty women whose appearances are sufficiently distinct, as well as the more numerous generalized characters. After classifying them, I hope to deal with a large enough sample so that the few omissions will not affect my conclusion.

7. *Registres de Philippe Auguste*, 327–35.

8. On *mésalliance*, see Chapter 2 at nn. 83–84.

9. Mathieu de Vendôme, *Ars versificatoria*, in *Les arts poétiques du XIIe et du XIIe siècle*, ed. Edmond Faral, Bibliothèque de l'Ecole des Hautes-Etudes, Sciences historiques et philologiques, 238 (Paris, 1924), 1: 56, 57. Geoffroi de Vinsauf, *Poetria nova*, in ibid., 773–75, vv. 563–97; id., *Documentum*, in ibid., 2: 2, 3. See, too, Alice M. Colby, *The Portrait in Twelfth-Century French Literature* (Geneva, 1965), 89–96, and Baldwin, *Language of Sex*, 97–99.

10. Ovid, *Amores* 1.5, ed. E. J. Kenney (Oxford, 1961).

11. The ladies on the hunt offer opportunity for a prior sketch (*Rose* vv. 194–207).

12. Marie de France, *Lanval* vv. 547–93, in *Lais*, ed. Alfred Ewert (Oxford, 1976).

13. Colby, *Portrait*, 59–60; Baldwin, *Language of Sex*, 100–106.

14. When Blancheflor hears of Perceval's arrival, her first thought is to prepare her wardrobe (*Continuation* vv. 6304–7).

15. The romance *Galeran de Bretagne* also contains a singular story of the education of two children, of whom the girl is taught to sew. See David Herlihy, *Opera muliebria: Women and Work in Medieval Europe* (New York, 1990), 55–59.

16. See also the *orfois d'Engleterre* in *Rose* v. 2197. On the *opus anglicanum*, see Raymond van Uytven, "Cloth in Medieval Literature of Western Europe," in *Cloth and Clothing in Medieval Europe: Essays in Memory of Professor E. M. Carus-Wilson*, ed. N. B. Harte and K. G. Pointing, Pasold Studies in Textile History, 2 (London, 1983), 161.

17. The daughter of the Persian king had embroidered a sleeve as a *gage d'amour* for her Turkish champion. *Escoufle* vv. 1141–55.

18. The sweatshop of three hundred girls who sew silk at the castle of Pireadventure in Chrétien's *Lion*, vv. 5178–5340, appears to have little precedent in romance literature.

19. For examples, see Chrétien's *Erec* vv. 707–16; *Charrete* vv. 430–58, 602–26; and *Lion* vv. 222–53, 970–1005, 1881–95.

20. On Gauvain's second visit, the Graal and lance perform their tasks without any human agency (vv. 13281–347).

21. See, e.g., Keith Busby, *Gauvain in Old French Literature* (Amsterdam, 1980), 394–96.

22. Penelope D. Johnson, *Equal in Monastic Profession: Religious Women in Medieval France* (Chicago, 1991), 18–41.

23. Subjects of this section have been treated at greater length in Baldwin, *Language of Sex.*

24. Echoing the ecclesiastical teaching on sodomy, Gerbert provides three expressions of homophobia among men: *Violette* vv. 3521–23; *Continuation* vv. 1554–61; and ibid. vv. 5715–19. See Baldwin, *Language of Sex*, 43–47. It is difficult to read homoeroticism in the scattered relations sustained between women (e.g., Aelis and Ysabel).

25. Sacrament: Lombard, *Sententiarum* 4.2.1; 4.26.6, *PL*, 192: 841–42, 909–10. Baldwin, *Language of Sex*, 63. For the debate between Gratian and the Lombard, see James Brundage, *Law, Sex, and Christian Society in Medieval Europe* (Chicago, 1987), 187–89, 235–37, 263–68, 331–41, and Baldwin, *Language of Sex*, 6–7.

26. "[Q]uod probatur auctoritate Augustini qui dicit quod quatuor de causis\ cognoscitur uxor, scilicet, causa prolis, vel causa reddendi debiti, vel causa incontinentie refrenande, vel causa libidinis explende. Duos priores modi, ut idem testatur Augustinus, nullius sunt criminis sed tercius semper habet culpam tamen venialem, sed quartus semper culpam mortalem." Courson, *Summa*, XLII, 31, fol. 154ra. Further discussion in Baldwin, *Language of Sex*, 119–25.

27. "Sequitur de causa finali matrimonii illa scilicet propter quam contrahitur matrimonium que multiplex est. Una est prolis susceptio, alia fornicationis evitatio, tercia caritatis dilatatio, quarta inimicorum reconcilatio, v. pacis et federis confirmatio." Courson, *Summa* XLII, 5, fol 132va. For discussion, see Baldwin, *Language of Sex*, 220, 321 n. 35.

28. James A. Brundage, "Implied Consent to Intercourse," *Consent and Coercion to Sex and Marriage in Ancient and Medieval Societies*, ed. Angeliki E. Laiou (Washington, D.C., 1993), 245–56.

29. See Dyan Elliott, *Spiritual Marriage: Sexual Abstinence and Medieval Wedlock* (Princeton, 1993), appendices 1, 3, and 5, for catalogues of historical examples.

30. Another example is the demoiselle des Illes Pertes, who resists a giant (*Violette* vv. 4765–74).

31. Kathryn Gravdal, *Ravishing Maidens: Writing Rape in Medieval French Literature and Law* (Philadelphia, 1991), and Baldwin, *Language of Sex*, 202–5.

32. Baldwin, *Language of Sex*, 80–84.

33. He repeats it throughout the mêlée (*Violette* vv. 6028–30).

34. On lovesickness, see Mary Frances Wack, *Lovesickness in the Middle Ages: The Viaticum and Its Commentaries* (Philadelphia, 1990), 3–176, and Baldwin, *Language of Sex*, 130–34, 142, 144–58.

35. Formerly preserved only in the German version of Gottfried von Strassburg, *Tristan und Isolde*, ed. Friedrich Ranke (12th ed., Zürich, 1967), vv. 11982–12019, Thomas's original passage has been recently recovered. Michael Benskin, Tony Hunt, and Ian Short, "Un nouveau fragment de Tristan de Thomas," *Romania* 113 (1992–95): 302–3, vv. 46–70.

36. See, e.g., *Andreas Capellanus on Love*, ed. and trans. P. G. Walsh (London, 1982), 147–57.

37. Within the abundant literature over this debate, see *The Meaning of Courtly Love*, ed. F. X. Newman (Albany, N.Y., 1967). The chapter by Benton (19–42) has exercised wide influence.

38. Baldwin, *Language of Sex*, 24–25, 251.

39. Chobham, *Summa*, 389–90. Baldwin, *Language of Sex*, 133–34.

40. Arch. dép. Calvados H 668, edited in *Registres de Philippe Auguste*, 465–66. Baldwin, *Language of Sex*, 70.

41. The critical literature on preceding authors is immense, but applied to Jean Renart this approach has been adopted by the Freudians Henri Rey-Flaud, *La névrose courtoise* (Paris, 1983), 77–104, and Jean-Charles Huchet, *Littérature médiévale et psychanalyse: Pour une clinique littéraire* (Paris, 1990), 174–75, as well as by Helen Solterer, "At the Bottom of Mirage, a Woman's Body: *Le Roman de la rose* of Jean Renart," in *Feminist Approaches to the Body in Medieval Literature*, ed. Linda Lomperis and Sarah Stanbury (Philadelphia, 1993), 213–33.

42. This is the concern apropos of Jean Renart and Gerbert de Montreuil of Roberta Krueger, "Double Jeopardy: The Appropriation of Women in Four Romances from the *Cycle de gageure*," in id., *Women Readers and the Ideology of Gender in Old French Verse Romance*, Cambridge Studies in French, 43 (Cambridge, 1993), 128–55.

43. See Rita Lejeune, "Le personnage d'Aelis dans le 'Roman de l'Escoufle' de Jean Renart," in *Mélanges de littérature du moyen âge au XXᵉ siècle offerts à Mademoiselle Jeanne Lods* (Paris, 1978), 378–92.

44. See Baldwin, *Language of Sex*, 151–58.

45. Solterer, "At the Bottom of Mirage," 226–30, and Krueger, "Double Jeopardy," 145–50.

46. Claude Lachet, "Présence de Liénor dans le *Roman de la Rose* de Jean Renart," in *"Et c'est la fin pour quoy nous sommes ensemble": Hommage à Jean Dufournet* (Paris, 1993), 2: 813–25. Lachet also proposes a number of anagrams for Liënor's name in the text, 822–23.

47. Gislebert de Mons, *Chronique*, 191–92.

48. Krueger, "Double Jeopardy," 129–30. As noted earlier, R. Howard Bloch argues in *Medieval Misogyny* that both positive and negative generalizations about women essentialize their qualities and constitute misogyny.

49. Krueger, "Double Jeopardy," 137–40, 154.

CHAPTER 6.
Embellishments: Festivities, Entertainment, Food, and Clothing

1. Rigord, 12–13. Ralph de Diceto (*Ymagines historiarum*, in *Historical Works*, ed. William Stubbs, RS [London, 1876], 1: 438) notes that Philip, count of

Flanders, carried the king's sword and claimed the *ministerialem* of serving the *regiis dapibus*, which implied that he was the seneschal who presided over the banquet.

2. Rigord, 20–22. Gislebert de Mons, the chronicler of Isabelle's father Baudouin V, count of Hainaut, provides a parallel account limited to the constitutional and religious ceremony (*Chronique*, 130).

3. Rigord, 150. The reticence about celebrations was shared by the other Latin chroniclers: Robert d'Auxerre, *Chronicon*, ed. O. Holder-Egger, *MGH SS*, 26: 260; Roger of Hovden, *Chronica*, ed. William Stubbs, RS (London, 1871), 4: 164; Gervase of Canterbury, in *The Chronicles of the Reigns of Stephen, Henry II, and Richard I*, ed. William Stubbs, RS (London, 1880), 2:93. The vernacular Anonyme de Béthune, 760, states merely: "et l'onera quan qu'il pot," but notes that later at Fontainebleau the French found it amusing that the English had drunk all the bad wine, leaving the good to the French.

4. Guillaume le Breton, *Gesta*, 226; Roger of Wendover, *Chronica*, in Matthew of Paris, *Chronica majora*, ed. H. R. Luard, RS (London, 1872), 2: 524. Anonyme de Béthune, 763. Charles Petit-Dutaillis, *Etude sur la vie et le règne de Louis VIII*, Bibliothèque de l'Ecole des hautes études, Sciences historiques et philologiques, 101 (Paris, 1894), 11; Alexander Cartellieri, *Philipp II. August, König von Frankreich* (Leipzig, 1922), 4: 285. On Pentecost 1203, Philip Augustus had given robes to youths who were newly knighted. *Budget* CCI (1).

5. See also "la feste et l'onor et l'afaire" at Count Richard's entry to Benevento (*Escoufle* v. 1441); "la grant feste l'onor, la joie" at Count Guillaume's entry to Rouen (*Escoufle* v. 8274); "grant joie et grant feste" at the tournament of Lancien (*Continuation* v. 4735). On the romance precedents for such festivities, see the comprehensive study of Philippe Walter, *La mémoire du temps: Fêtes et calendriers de Chrétien de Troyes à la Mort Artu*, Nouvelle bibliothèque du moyen âge, 13 (Paris, 1989).

6. Rigord, 10–12; Cartellieri, *Philipp II. August*, 1: 32–34.

7. See also *Rose* vv. 2182–83, 2295–96, 2462–63, 2554–55; *Violette* v. 5887.

8. Singing: *Rose* vv. 844–52, 1579–84, 1843–51, 2023–35, 2512–18; stories: vv. 657–74, 1764–68; playing the viol: vv. 637–42, 1799–1801, 1841–51, 2224–25.

9. On the nomenclature of string instruments, see Christopher Page, *Voices and Instruments of the Middle Ages: Instrumental Practice and Songs in France, 1100–1300* (Berkeley, 1986), 139–50.

10. Chrétien includes the *arpe*, *rote*, and *vïele* as illustrations of the liberal art of music on Erec's robe (*Erec* v. 6711).

11. See also *Continuation* v. 157: "orgues et harpes et vïeles." At Gorneman's residence, a minstrel plays the lai de Corran on a Cornish pipe ("estive de Cornoaille," *Continuation* vv. 6117–19).

12. Maria V. Coldwell, "*Guillaume de Dole* and Medieval Romances with Mu-

sical Interpolations," *Musica disciplina* 34 (1984): 55–86, esp. 66; Sylvia Huot, "Voices and Instruments in Medieval French Secular Music: On the Use of Literary Texts as Evidence for Performance Practice," *Musica disciplina* 43 (1989): 87–92, 98–103.

13. *Vallet: Rose* vv. 509, 520, 2386, 4122–24; *bachelers:* vv. 2231, 5230; *damoiseau:* v. 4163; sons: vv. 529, 2376; nephews: vv. 2521, 5183; *pucele:* vv. 301, 509, 1841.

14. On the dance songs, see Friedrich Gennrich, *Rondeaux, Virelais und Balladen aus dem Ende des XII., dem XIII. und dem ersten drittel des XIV. Jahrhunderts mit den überlieferten Melodien*, Gesellschaft für romanische Literatur, 43, 47 (Dresden, 1921, 1927), 1: 310, 2: 1–12; Margrit Sahlin, *Etude sur la carole médiévale: L'origine du mot et de rapports avec l'Eglise* (Uppsala, 1940), 1–36; and Robert Mullally, "Cançon de Carole," *Acta Musicological* 58 (1986): 224–31.

15. See also *Rose* v. 2527.

16. Working with materials supplied by Thomas de Bretagne, Gottfried von Strassburg stresses Tristan's attainments in languages, string instruments, chivalric arts, athletic prowess, and hunting. See C. Stephen Jaeger, *The Origins of Courtliness: Civilizing Trends and the Formation of Courtly Ideals, 939–1210* (Philadelphia, 1985), 237–40.

17. In *Les jeux au royaume de France du XIIe au début du XVIe siècle* (Paris, 1990), Jean-Michel Mehl seeks to assemble medieval evidence: 13–25 (in general), 76–90 (dice), 97 (*la mine*), 113–34 (chess), 135–48 (*tables*). See also Richard Eales, "The Game of Chess: An Aspect of Medieval Knightly Culture," in *The Ideal and Practice of Medieval Knighthood*, ed. Christopher Harper-Bill and Ruth Harvey (Woodbridge, Suffolk, 1986), 12–34.

18. Baudouin van den Abeele, *La fauconnerie dans les lettres françaises du XIIe au XIVe siècle*, Mediaevalia Lovaniensia, 1st ser., Studia, 18 (Louvain, 1990), 2, 41, introduces the abundant literature to the subject.

19. In *Erec* (vv. 351–54), Chrétien reviews the basic terminology for falcons: *espreviers* (sparrow hawk), *faucons de müés* (moulted falcons), *terciax* (tercels), *estors müez et sors* (goshawks moulted and red).

20. Van den Abeele, *Fauconnerie*, 60–62, analyzes the realism of Jean's and Gerbert's treatment of falconry.

21. Guillaume le Breton, *Gesta*, 1: 226.

22. See the catalogue of clichés in Grégoire Lozinski, *La bataille de caresme et de charnage*, Bibliothèque de l'Ecole des hautes études, Sciences historiques et philologiques, 262 (Paris, 1933), 71–84. This study is indispensable on the subject of medieval French alimentary practices and vocabulary, supplemented by Bridget Ann Henisch, *Fast and Feast: Food in Medieval Society* (University Park, Pa., 1976), and Odile Redon, Françoise Sabban, and Silvano Serventi, *La gastronomie au moyen âge: 150 recettes de France et d'Italie* (Paris, 1991). The most comprehen-

sive study is Terence Scully, *The Art of Cookery in the Middle Ages* (Woodbridge, Suffolk, 1995), but it is based on sources from the late Middle Ages.

23. Jacques LeGoff, "Codes vestimentaires et alimentaires dans *Erec et Enide*," in id., *L'imaginaire médiéval: Essais* (Paris, 1985), 188–207. Anita Guerreau-Jalabert, "Aliments symboliques et symbolique de la table dans les romans arthuriens (XIIᵉ–XIIIᵉ siècles)," *Annales: Economies, Sociétés, Civilisations* 47.3 (May–June 1992): 561-94.

24. See Emily Gowers, *The Loaded Table: Representations of Food in Roman Literature* (Oxford, 1993), 2–19.

25. On the cliché, see Lozinski, *La bataille*, 66–70.

26. Contrary to the observations of Guerreau-Jalabert, "Aliments symboliques," 572. For examples: *Escoufle* vv. 713, 4262; *Rose* vv. 1036, 1980; *Violette* vv. 494, 2525, 5096; *Continuation* vv. 1336, 4981, 6097, 9266, 16,653.

27. *Escoufle* vv. 678–88, 4438–45; *Rose* vv. 343–46, 465–70, 1260–63, 2900–907, 5481–84; *Violette* vv. 531–32, 3086–87; *Continuation* vv. 1122–25, 6441, 17014–15.

28. Anonyme de Béthune, 763. Jean de Joinville, an avowed witness, remembered in greater detail those who served and sliced at Louis IX's banquet at Saumur in 1241, where newly knighted sons were also honored. Jean de Joinville, *Histoire de Saint Louis,* ch. 21, ed. Natalis de Wailly (Paris, 1874), 54–57. Service at the court of Hainaut as described in the *Ministeria* (Gislebert de Mons, *Chronique,* 333–43) involved procurement of provisions more than honorific table service at high feasts.

29. A medical potion for Perceval shares many of these ingredients. *Continuation* vv. 11514–16.

30. Massimo Montanari, *The Culture of Food* (Oxford, 1994), 46–80.

31. The siege of Aigline's castle reduces provisions to the last five loaves of bread, three gâteaux, three peacocks, four plovers, and a barrel of wine (*Violette* vv. 1604–7).

32. Guerreau-Jalabert, "Aliments symboliques," 565–66.

33. "Habet autem nabuzaradan, id est venter, quatuor satellites, scilicit, quid, quantum, quale, quando. Quid: ad su[b]tanciam, quantum ad quantitatem, quale ad qualitatem, quando ad tempus. Quid consistit et attenditur in genere edulii ut scilicet delicatum sit. Quantum: ut se ingurgitet et ventrem vertat in saccum. Quale: multipliciter: quo ad preparationem ut elixa vel assa vel trixa, quo ad salsamentorum varietatem, quo ad condumentum, quo ad sectionem. In sumptione etiam frigidorum vel tempidorum, vel calidorum consistit qualitas et etiam in utilitate. Quando: ante vel post alia cibaria vel in temporis maturitate ut mane vel alia hora et etiam in frequentia." Chanter, *Verbum abbreviatum*, MS. V, fol. 150vb–151ra. *PL*, 205: 330AB.

34. "Tercia pars est a delictiosis lautioribus . . . cibis abstinere. . . . Hoc vicio laborant precipue potentes et magnates huius mundi qui communia respuentes et

expuentes deliciosa cara raraque disquirent pulmenta. Hii in cibo non querunt solum cibum sed vel saporem vel precium vel raritatem. Saporem: quia non fame
trahuntur sed sapore, esse ingluvies. Precium: quia placet eis non quia cibus XXX
sed quia preciosus, esse vana gloria. Raritatem quia super deliciis gaudent non
quia habent sed quia soli habent, esse superbia." Ardent, *Speculum*, Paris, BN lat.
3240 fol. 189ra. Raoul's definition of *abstinentia* is restricted to alimentary practices and not applied to sexual matters. "Hiis satellitibus ad majorem irritationem
gulae additur pretium, quia magis illa juvant, quae pluris emuntur," the Chanter
adds to his fourfold analysis. *Verbum abbreviatum, PL,* 205: 330B.

35. "Decima pars est a multorum varietate ferculorum abstinere. . . . Hoc est
contra eos quorum fastidiosa et insociabilis gula scrutatur per venatores terras,
per aucupes aera, per piscatores maria ut uni stomacho satisfacere queat." Ardent,
Speculum, Paris, BN lat. 3240, fol. 190vb.

36. "Deliciosi enim plus habent cibi laboris et sollicitudinis in acquirendo
quam voluptatis in utendo. Pretereo multos monachorum, multos reclusorum,
multos heremitarum, qui vel tantum pane et aqua victitabant vel etiam tantum
crudelibus radicibus herbis fructibus sese sustentabant." Ardent, *Speculum*, Paris,
BN lat. 3240, fol. 189va.

37. "Undecima pars est mensuram refectionis non excedere. Propter hoc vicium corruunt sodomite in ignominiosam luxuriam dicente domino per proph-
etam: Peccatum tuum sodoma habundantia panis et superbia vite. Sane cibaria
capienda sunt ut medicamenta et sic sumpta vivant aliter nocent. Ceterum sunt
quidem qui usque ad guttur se ingurgitant qui cibum capiunt non quantum satis
est sed quantum possunt. Qui manducare non desinunt usque quo amplius non
possunt, quibus finem manducandi imponit non modum sed necessitas." Ardent,
Speculum, Paris, BN lat. 3240, fol. 191ra.

38. "Quarta pars est a nimia causa in apparandis cibis abstinere. Possunt enim
etiam viles cibi cum nimia accuratione preparari. Porro sicut vitium est deliciosos
cibos querere sic et vicium est viles deliciose preparare. Immo pene maius. In de-
liciosis enim deliciositas est naturalis, in vilibus adulterina. Illis deus dedit ut essent deliciosi. Istis gestit conferre gulosus ex causa quod non habent ex natura.
Sane hoc modo gullositas arcem adinvenit coquinariam et coquos effecit mag-
istros qui cum summa studio ingenia exercerunt sua deservire gulositati vicio non
virtuti addiscendo diversa et inveniendo farcimenta, diversos sapores, diversa sal-
samenta, diversas mixturas, diversas frixuras, diversas assaturas, infinita quia gule
irritamenta." Ardent, *Speculum*, Paris, BN lat. 3240, fol. 189vb.

39. "Sexta pars est ab illis cum quibus vivitur in cibariis dissentire. Certe tur-
pissimum est gulositatis vicium cum singuli contubernalium singula sibi expec-
tunt cibaria cum singuli singulos coquos singulas ollas singula querunt salsa-
menta. Aut si eiusdem generis ciborum sunt contenti, diversi diverso modo illud

sibi volunt preparari. Ova alius vult sibi dare frexa, alius elixa, alius subcinericia, alius mollia, alius dura." Ardent, *Speculum*, Paris BN lat. 3240, fol. 190ra.

40. "Porro cum licitum videatur ter vel quater in die comedare, honesti viri est etiam die tantum semel et secundo comedere; si vero fuerit ieunium semel in die tantum." Ardent, *Speculum*, Paris, BN lat. 3240, fol. 188va. "Quinta pars est horam comedendi non prevenire. Approbata si quid consuetudo est in diebus ieuniorum non comedere ante nonam nec in aliis ante terciam." Ibid., fol. 189va.

41. "Duodecima pars est ad mensam brevius residere. Enim vero nonnulli convivium tam longius protendunt quod maiorem diei partem in conviviis expendunt. Ceterum melius esset sepius comedere continue. Hii putant se natos esse ad commedendum; vivunt enim ut comedant, non comedunt ut vivant. Horum studium est non rationari non servire deo sed ventri. In quibus enim quis plus delectatur in his plus moratur ut apostolus: deus venter est. . . . (Phil. 3:19) Templum eorum est quoquina, altare mensa, varia fericula, diverse hostie sacrificia, diversa vina diversa libamina." Ardent, *Speculum*, Paris, BN lat. 3240, fol. 191rb–va.

42. "*Propter que relaxanda est abstenencia.* . . . et propter solempnitates et propter infirmitatem et senectutem et propter hospites advenientes. Quod vero propter sollempnitates abstinentia sit relaxanda probatur et sanctorum auctoritate et ratione. Sanctorum auctoritate. . . . Ratione quoniam dies sollempnes temporalium festivitatum significant celestes et perpetuas sollempnitates ubi erit perpes requies, perpes gaudium, perpes habundantia, in quorum figura et hic quoque in sollempnitatibus quiecius iocundius habundantis debemus nos habere. . . . Quod vero propter hospites non solum abstinentia sit relaxanda sed etiam ieiunium frangendum; triplex causa nos ortatur: karitas fratrum, occultatio abstinentie nostre, evitatio scandali." Ardent, *Speculum*, Paris, BN lat. 3240, fol. 191vb–192ra.

43. LeGoff, "Code vestimentaire," 188–201.

44. See Chapter 6, first paragraph. For an exploration of this theme, see Caroline Jewers, "Fabric and Fabrication: Lyric and Narrative in Jean Renart's *Roman de la Rose*," *Speculum* 71 (1996): 907–24.

45. *Budget*, CLVI (1)–CLVII (2), CLXXXIII (1–2), CC (2)–CCI (1).

46. On clothing, see Eunice Rathbone Goddard, *Women's Costume in French Texts of the Eleventh and Twelfth Centuries*, Johns Hopkins Studies in Romance Literatures and Languages, 7 (Baltimore, 1927); Mireille Madou, *Le costume civil*, Typologie des sources du Moyen Age occidental, 47 (Turnhout, Bel., 1986); Yvonne Deslandres, *Le costume image de l'homme* (Paris, 1976), and Françoise Piponnier and Perrine Mane, *Dress in the Middle Ages*, trans. Caroline Beamish (New Haven, 1997). A glossary is found in Jean Renart, *The Romance of the Rose or Guillaume de Dole*, trans. Patricia Terry and Nancy Vine Durling (Philadelphia, 1993), 105–8.

47. Erec wears silk stockings at his first introduction (*Erec* vv. 99).

48. *Budget,* CLVI (2), CLXXXIII (2), CCI (1–2).

49. *Budget,* CCI (2).

50. See the comments by Terry and Durling in Jean Renart, *Romance of the Rose,* 101 n. 82.

51. Chrétien, *Graal* vv. 7912–13. On the *sorcot,* see Goddard, *Women's Costume,* p. 204–8.

52. Guillaume also gives a *sorcot* to a chamberlain (*Rose* v. 1816).

53. See also the *peliçons frais* in Chrétien *Cligès* v. 6874.

54. The appearance of a *supertunicalis ad manicas* (*sorcot* with sleeves) appears to confirm the identification. *Budget,* CLVI (2).

55. *Budget,* CLVII (1), CCI (1).

56. See the overview of Raymond van Uytven, "Cloth in Medieval Literature of Western Europe," in *Cloth and Clothing in Medieval Europe: Essays in Memory of Professor E. M. Carus-Wilson,* ed. N. B. Harte and K. G. Ponting, Pasold Studies in Textile History, 2 (London, 1983), 151–62.

57. For examples of *escarlate* in Chrétien, see *Erec* v. 2061, *Lion* v. 1885; for *porpre: Erec* v. 1598, *Graal* v. 1799. The important study on scarlat is John H. Munro, "The Medieval Scarlat and the Economics of Sartorial Splendour," in *Cloth and Clothing,* ed. Harte and Ponting, 13–70, esp. 13–15.

58. *Porpre: Continuation* v. 6618; *escarlate: Escoufle* v. 5766, *Rose* vv. 1530, 3282, 4344, *Violette* vv. 3464, 4980, *Continuation* v. 6586.

59. The *escarlate* of Lincoln was well reputed. Van Uytven, "Cloth in Medieval Literature," 162. Andreas Capellanus testifies that at the Capetian court, the tint of scarlet red appeared better in English wool than in that of Champagne or Italy. *On Love,* ed. P. G. Walsh (London, 1982), 88.

60. *Budget,* CLXXXIII (1) and CI (1).

61. Monro, "Medieval Scarlet," 1, 39.

62. Ibid., 17–18.

63. Anonyme de Béthune, 766.

64. *Budget* CLVI (2), CLVIII (1), CCI (1). Despite Guérin's pun, it is unlikely that the cloth took its name from the town of Steenvoorde. See Guy de Poerck, *La draperie médiévale en Flandre et en Artois: Technique et terminologie,* Rijksuniversiteit te Gent: Werken uitgegeven door de Faculteit van de Wijsbegeerte en Letteren, 110, 111 (Bruges, 1951), 1: 214–16, 2: 80. Two theories about the etymology of *estainfort* are now current. The first is that it took its name from the English textile center of Stanford. See E. M. Carus-Wilson, "The English Cloth Industry in the Late Twelfth and Early Thirteenth Centuries," in *Medieval Merchant Venturers: Collected Studies* (London, 1954), 211–12, 219, 238, and Natalie Fryde von Stromer, "Stamford Cloth and Its Imitations in the Low Countries and Northern France during the Thirteenth Century," in *Textiles of the Low Countries*

in European Economic History, ed. Eric Aerts and John Monro (Louvain, 1990), 8–13.

The second theory is that it originated from the Latin *stamen forte,* meaning "of a strong warp thread," as in worsted cloth. *Estain* in Old French means warp. See Patrick Chorley, "The Cloth Exports of Flanders and Northern France during the Thirteenth Century: A Luxury Trade?" *Economic History Review,* 2d ser., 40 (1987): 349–79; John Monro, "Industrial Transformations in the North-West European Textile Trades, c. 1290–c. 1340: Economic Progress or Economic Crisis?" in *Before the Black Death: Studies in the "Crisis" of the Early Fourteenth Century,* ed. Bruce M. S. Campbell (Manchester, Eng., 1991), 110–14; and John Monro, "The Origins of the English 'New Draperies': The Resurrection of an Old Flemish Industry, 1270–1570," in *The New Draperies,* ed. Negley Harte and Donald Coleman, Pasold Studies in Textile History (Oxford, 1997), 53–57. I am grateful to John Monro for generous help on this subject.

65. *Budget,* CLXXXIII (1).

66. *Budget,* CLVI (2), CLXXXIII (2).

67. Baldwin, *Language of Sex,* 104–5.

68. *Budget,* CLVI (2).

69. *Budget,* CLVI (2), CLVII (1).

70. *Registres de Philippe Auguste,* 229–37. The countess of Blois, e.g., received a clasp with rubies and emeralds that had formerly belonged to the queen mother, Adèle de Champagne. Ibid., 235, no. 73.

71. As a sidelight, it is interesting to compare the wardrobe accounts with Ingeborg's letter to Innocent III in May 1203. Innocent III, *Regesta,* VI, no. 85, Vienna ed., p. 133, *PL,* 215: 87. Amid complaints that the king had abused her royal dignity, Ingeborg specified that her clothing was neither abundant nor of the quality that befitted a queen. One year earlier, the accounts do not contradict the quantity but cast suspicion on her complaint about the quality. Philip spent considerably more on the queen's robes than his own. *Budget* CLVII (1) and p. 127. Ingeborg also complained about the availability of religious services. The accounts reveal, however, that the king was maintaining a chaplain in her behalf. *Budget,* CXLIV (2), CLXIX (2).

72. These figures are drawn from the entire *Budget* (see n. 45) resumed on p. 127. The cost of horses may be found on CLV (2), CLXXXIII (2), and CII (2). See also Baldwin, *Government of Philip Augustus,* 165 and 133 for wages.

73. Robert Fawtier, "Un fragment du compte de l'hôtel du prince Louis de France pour le terme de la Purification 1213," *Le Moyen Age,* 3d ser., 4 (1933): 243. Except for 420 sous for an old robe at Pentecost to Groignetus, the other items ranged between 24 and 40 sous (ibid., 240–43).

74. Ovid, *Remedia,* ed. E. J. Kenney (Oxford, 1961), vv. 343–44 quoted by

Chanter in *Verbum abbreviatum, PL*, 205: 26. Geoffroi de Vinsauf, *Poetria nova*, in Edmond Faral, *Les arts poétiques du XIIe et du XIIIe siècle*, Bibliothèque de l'Ecole des Hautes Etudes, Sciences historiques et philologiques, 238 (Paris, 1924), 197–262, vv. 600–621.

75. "Exceditur hodie in vestis materia, in tinctura, in forma, in composicione, in diversificacione, in materie mutacione. Quia hodie erubesceret etiam servus tegere nuditatem suam illa veste quam primis omnium inventium parentibus in paradiso preparavit et post lapsum eis compatiens dedit. Nempe illis ad tegendam erubescibilem nuditatem et turpitudinem suam dominus tunicas fecit pelliceas unde in Genesi [3:21]. . . . Si fuerint consuti vel forsipe cese vel arte pelliparii parate non querens a me quia nescio. Credo tamen eas rudes fuisse. Ecce rudis et simplex materia vestis a qua per humanum vel potius vanum curiositatem ventum est non solum ad corium animalium vel animantium, ad lanum ovium, ad linum vel canabrum agrorum. Tolerabilia essent si in naturali colore [*ms:* calore] subsisterent quia omnia illa profert nobis tellus et naturalia sunt, sed nec hic subsistere volumus imo processum est usque ad plumas avium ut moveat cornicula risum, ad stercora vermium quorum delicias pannus bobianus urit usque etiam ad aurifrigium nendo filum ex auro. Nec ultra possunt nisi ad telas aranearum procedere velit hominis inconstantia. Attende etiam quantus excelsus sit in colorum varietate. Naturalem enim colorem corrumpit vanitas hominum nunc pervertendo in rubeum, nunc in subrubeum, nunc in viridem, nunc in croceum, nunc in violaceum, nunc in quamlibet alium mixtum et confusum ut tria solo colore vestium perstringentur oculi intuentium et in admirationem rapiantur cum natura singulis rebus et maxime floribus innatum adeoque pulcrum colorem dederit quali non poterat operari Salomon in omni gloria sua [Mat. 6:29]." Chanter, *Verbum abbreviatum*, MS. V, fol. 111ra–rb. See also the short version in *PL*, 205: 251. Baldwin, *Language of Sex*, 296 n. 63.

76. "*Contra formam vestium*. Suggillavimus superfluitatem et luxum vestium, quo ad materiam et colorem. Suggillandus est luxus earum, quo ad formam. Formam attendimus in duobus: in colorum diversificacione et in modo composicionis. In colorum diversificacione ut in veste bipertita, tripertita, quadripertita, vel multipertita; bicolore vel multicolore quod ad diversorum variata pictacia. In modo composicionis, ut in modo cedendi, scindendi, consuendi, eligandi, fraccillandi, caudandi. Cuius in composicio in composicionem mentalem innuit. Cum enim natura hominem a bruto insigni et honesto caractere distinxerit, quod natura homini negavit, scilicet caudam, ipse per artificium illud in veste caudata. . . .Unde Tornacensis episcopus in sermone suo: non decet, inquit, matronas christianas vestes habere subtalares et post se trahentes quibus verrant sordes pavimenti et viarum." Chanter, *Verbum abbreviatum*, MSS. Paris Ste.-Gen. 250, 137rb, va. V, fols. 111vb–112ra. Short version *PL*, 205: 252. See also id., *Summa*, 2: 239–43. Baldwin, *Language of Sex*, 296 n. 64.

77. H. Platelle, "Le problème du scandale: Les nouvelles modes masculines aux XIᵉ et XIIᵉ siècles," *Revue belge de philologie et d'histoire* 53 (1975): 1071–78. Goddard, *Women's Costume*, 98–99, 215. For a prostitute, see *Richeut*, ed. Philippe Vernay, Romanica Helvetica, 103 (Berne, 1988), vv. 469–86. In Jean's *Lai* vv. 314–17, the lady wears a *chainse* with a train over a fathom long.

CHAPTER 7.
Aristocratic Religion

1. A shorter version of this chapter may be found in John W. Baldwin, "From Ordeal to Confession: In Search of Lay Religion in Early Thirteenth-Century France," in *Handling Sin: Confession in the Middle Ages*, ed. Peter Biller and A. J. Minnis, York Studies in Medieval Theology 2 (York, 1998), 191–209.

2. For historiographic introductions to this recent work, see Constance B. Bouchard, "Community: Society and Church in Medieval France," *French Historical Studies* 17 (1992): 1035–47, and Megan McLaughlin, *Consorting with Saints: Prayer for the Dead in Early Medieval France* (Ithaca, N.Y., 1994), 2–20.

3. These prelates are difficult to identify but appear to carry Celtic associations. See Amida Stanton, "Gerbert de Montreuil as a Writer of Grail Romance: An Investigation of the Date and the More Immediate Sources of the Continuation of *Perceval*" (diss., University of Chicago, 1942), 40–41. At the forced marriage between Faradieu and Ysmaine, a priest proclaims the marriage bans (*Continuation* vv. 2057, 2066).

4. See Baldwin, *Language of Sex*, 224.

5. See Stanton, "Gerbert de Montreuil," 33–35. Another example in Gerbert is Arthur's court in Dublin (*Continuation* vv. 16667–69).

6. Gislebert de Mons, *Chronique*, 150, 332.

7. D. A. Trotter, *Medieval French Literature and the Crusades (1100–1300)* (Geneva, 1987), 132–34, has treated the literary perspectives of this passage.

8. Although the historical Richard had also obtained a truce from the Muslim general Saladin, he did not succeed in liberating Jerusalem from Muslim control. At least two decades later, Gerbert's *Continuation* devises a prophecy about Perceval's lineage on the patently incongruous occasion of his spiritual marriage to Blancheflor. Gerbert foretells that three sons will spring from the hero's family who will conquer Jerusalem and recover the Holy Sepulcher and the True Cross. *Continuation* (vv. 6931–33).

9. That there was continual public penance in the thirteenth century is argued by Mary C. Mansfield, *The Humiliation of Sinners: Public Penance in Thirteenth-Century France* (Ithaca, N.Y., 1995); see 110–12 for examples of pilgrimages and crusades.

10. J. F. Charles, *La ville de Saint-Trond au moyen âge: Des origines à la fin du*

XIIe siècle, Bibliothèque de la Faculté de philosophie et lettres de l'Université de Liège, fasc. 123 (Paris, 1965), 197, 279–80.

11. For the liturgy, see Jean Deshusses, "Les messes d'Alcuin," *Archiv für Liturgiewissenschaft* 14 (1972): 24–25; *Le sacramentaire grégorien,* ed. Jean Deshusses, Spicilegium Friburgense 24 (Fribourg, 1988), 2: 42–43; and Arnold Angenendt, "*Missa specialis:* Zugleich ein Beitrag zur Entstehung der Privatmessen," *Frühmittelalterliche Studien* 17 (1983): 208–12. Innocent III, *Regesta,* I, no. 1, Vienna ed., 4, *PL,* 214: 1, Potthast no. 1. *Gesta Innocentii III, PL,* 214: xix.

12. Examples: "a Dex": *Escoufle* vv. 319, 327, *Rose* v. 1280; "por Deu": *Rose* v. 687; "e non Deu": *Rose* v. 291; "se Deu plest": *Rose* v. 3017; "vos doint hui Dex": *Rose* v. 1588; "por dieu, merci": *Rose* v. 4747; "m'ait Dex": *Rose* v. 4775.

13. Examples: "por les .v. plaies Deu": *Rose* v. 3808; "puis que Dex fut nez sanz pechié": *Rose* v. 5308; "Dieus qui nasqui de la pucele": *Continuation* v. 1732; "Dieu qui fist le mont": *Continuation* v. 4440.

14. St. Mary: *Escoufle* v. 5377, *Rose* v. 3936, *Violette* vv. 972, 2057, 3922, *Continuation* vv. 4074, 5954, 7062, 7174, 7558, 8960, 9384, 9714, 13498. St. Peter: *Escoufle* vv. 4482, 4955, *Rose* v. 3384, *Continuation* vv. 7251, 8866, 13940, 14373, 14868. St. Paul: *Rose* vv. 2562, 4728, *Continuation* vv. 2109, 7193.

15. E.g., "Saint Pol," rhymes with *col* (*Rose* vv. 2561–62), and St. Paul appeared to the crusaders besieging Jerusalem, according to Jacques de Voragine, *Golden Legend,* trans. Granger Ryan and Helmut Ripperger (New York, 1969), 237–38. See also ibid., 128, on St. Julien. And see index for examples of Sts. Julien, Jacques, and Gilles.

16. "Iuramentum est assertio alicuius rei cum attestatione rei sacre vel non sacre." Chobham, *Summa,* 548. "Est autem iuramentum alicuius rei confirmatio sub attestatione rei sacre vel non sacre adiuncta vel non adiuncta sollemnitate." Courson, *Summa,* XXVII, 1, fol. 94va. On perjury as a verbal sin, see most recently Carla Casagranda and Silvana Vecchio, *Les péchés de la langue* (Paris, 1991), 201–12.

17. Chanter, *Verbum abbreviatum,* "Contra pronos adiurandum," MS. V, fol. 146rb–147ra; "De vitando juramento," *PL,* 205: 322–23. See also Chanter, *Summa,* 3 (2a), 229–30. Courson, *Summa,* XXVII, fol. 94va–98vb. Chobham, *Summa,* 548–58.

18. Chanter, *Verbum abbreviatum, PL,* 205: 322A. "Nonne facilius et sepius iuratur in ecclesia quam in sinagoga? . . . Immo econtra ad imperfectionem nostram sub euvangelio multo pluries et frequentius et in minoribus causis iuratur quam sub lege. Hodie enim non ungitur rex vel imperator vel prelatus ecclesiasticus vel non canonizatur vel quilibet in ecclesia nisi prius iuret. In lege non iurabant in causis decidendis. Hodie iurant actor et reus in initio cause iuramentum de calumpnia. Hodie non sunt testes nisi iurati quod non exigebatur in lege. . . . Quare cogar a domino papa perhibere testimonium veritatis? Mihi vero non credetur nisi

iuravero. Ergo si cogar ad principale, videtur quod ad accessorium. Item, si iurare nolueris, catharus esse iudicaberis." MS. V, fol. 146–rb–vb.

19. Chobham, *Summa*, 550.

20. "Non falsum testimonium dices vel si dicatur quod prohibitum est in evangelio ne quis iuret pro levi causa vel non nisi in necessitate vel quod assiduitas ut frequentia iurandi in evangelio prohibetur, et hoc idem lex prohibet ut ibi [Exod. 20:7] 'Non assumes nomen dei tui in vanum . . .' Quod notandum quod si ex obreptione in simplici sermone iuras dicendo 'per deum'," ita est quasi occosum est verbum vel iocosum, et magis videtur veniale. . . . Iurationi non assuescat os tuum. Multi enim casus et ruine in illa. Nominatio vero dei non sit assidua in ore tuo. Et nominibus sanctorum non admisceatis quoniam non eris immunis ab eis." Chanter, *Verbum abbreviatum*, MS. V, fol. 146rb, vb.

21. "De illis autem qui passim iurant et non aliqua causa decipiendi disquisitus, obicitur sic: Iheronimos dicit [*Decretum* C. 22 q. 1 c. 12] in illo capitulo: 'Habemus in lege dei scriptum [Lev. 19:12] Non peierabis in nomine meo nec polluas nomen dei tui in vanum. Ideoque ammondendi sunt omnes ut diligenter caveant periurium non solum in altari in reliquiis sanctorum sed in communi loquela.' Hec sunt verbi iheronimi quibus consonant illam ex deo: [Exod. 20:7] 'Non assumes nomen dei tui in vanum,' id est, non iurabis pro nichilo nomen dei tui, vel aliter non assumes nomen dei etc., id est, ad mendatiam affirmandum, ne falisitati nomen dei associes. Sic ergo videtur quod vana et ociosa iuramenta et in communi loquela non fiant sine mortali peccato quia fiunt contra illam prohibitionem, non assumes nomen dei tui in vanum, id est, non iurabis pro nichilo. Si dicas quod assuefactio vel usus communis excusat talia iuramenta. Contra. In aliis peccatis usus vel assiduitas auget peccatum sicut in ebrietate, luxuria, et in aliis peccatis. Eadem ratione et hic aggravat peccatum. Non enim quod a multis vel consuetudine peccatur multum est apud deum.

Solutio. Credimus quod talia iuramenta in casu, scilicet, aut ex occasione scandali aut propter imitationem pravi exempli aut aliis ingruentibus circumstanciis possunt esse mortalia. Sed si fiant ex aliqua obreptione vel subito animi motu in communi cursu loquendi non sunt mortalia, et quia difficilius est cohibere linguam quam aliud membrum ut testatur iacobus [James 3:2] quia qui in langua non offendit, hic perfectus est vir. Non iudicamus ita de consuetudine circa ebrietatem vel luxuriam sicut de consuetudine circa iuramenta. Unde dicitur [Ps. 140:3] Pone domine custodiam ori meo etc." Courson, *Summa*, XXVII, 17, fol. 97rb–va.

22. Chobham, *Summa*, 549.

23. "Videtur, tamen, quod iuramentum ei additum facit illud esse plus quam ociosum vel iocosum, sed si serio et scienter ex deliberatione iuretur vel ignominiose ut quidam qui quasi caracter et iuramento proprio et execrabili ab aliis distinguntur qui, scilicet, specialia habent iuramenta. Alii per oculos dei iurant, alii per sanguinem, alii per linguam et huiusmodi. Gravissime peccatur sic iurando. Et

frequenter contingit quod quicumque iurat per aliquid dei membrum ante mortem in proprio membro consimili puniatur." Chanter, *Verbum abbreviatum*, MS. V, fol. 146vb. Chobham, *Summa*, 551.

"Item ut dicit canon 'Si quis per capillum dei vel per caput iuraverit vel alio modo blasphemia contra deum usitus fuerit, si in ecclesiastico ordine est, deponatur, si laicus est anathematizetur, et si per creaturas iuraverit, asperime castigetur.' Hoc habetur [*Decretum*, C. 22 q. 1 c. 10] Si quis per capillum. Ex hoc decreto elicitur quod clerici hodie iurantes per quecumque membra dei degradandi sunt et laici excommunicandi et episcopi si eos corripere neglexerint a crimine puniendi sunt sicut habetur in eodem decreto. Quid ergo de illis qui pudenda christi et gloriose virginis iurant et tamen nec ab episcopo ne ab ecclesia puniuntur?" Courson, *Summa*, XXVII, 17, fol. 97rb–va.

24. Gerald of Wales, *Gemma ecclesiastica* 1.54, ed. J. S. Brewer, in *Opera*, RS (London, 1862), 2: 161. Elsewhere, he contrasts Capetian sobriety with the behavior of other princes who swore on the death, eyes, feet, teeth, throat, and *strumellos* (?) of God (*De principis instructione* 3.30, ed. George F. Warner, in *Opera*, 8: 318–19).

25. "In hoc valde commendandus est rex noster philippus qui ignominiosa iuramenta de deo vel de sanctis ab aula sua eliminat puniendo divites in v solidos, unde solvant; non habent, in aquam vestitos proiciendo. Sic forsan est prohibitum in curiis quorundam aliorum principum sub consimili pena." Chanter, *Verbum abbreviatum*, MS. V, fol. 146vb–147ra, *PL*, 205: 322D. Rigord, 14. Guillaume le Breton, *Gesta*, 181. For examples of Philip's oath: Léopold Delisle, "Etienne de Gallardon, clerc de la chancellerie de Philippe Auguste, chanoine de Bourges," *Bibliothèque de l'Ecole de Chartes* 60 (1899): 23; Richer de Senones, *Gesta Senonensis ecclesie. MGH SS*, 25: 290; Ralph of Coggeshall, *Chronicon Anglicanum*, ed. Joseph Stevenson, RS (London, 1875) 199; *Compilacio singularis*, ed. Marc Vaisbrot (thesis, Ecole des Chartes, 1968), no. 560; *Istoire et chroniques de Flandre* ed. Kervyn de Lettenhove (Brussels, 1879), 1: 122. For Louis IX's subsequent legislation on swearing, see *Ordonnances des roys de France de la troisième race*, ed. E. de Laurière (Paris, 1723) 1: 99; Jean de Joinville, *Histoire de Saint Louis*, ed. Natalis de Wailly (Paris, 1874), 378, 384, 402; Philippe de Beaumanoir, *Coutumes de Beauvaisis*, ed. A. Salmon, Collection de textes pour servir à l'étude et à l'enseignement de l'histoire, 24 (Paris, 1899), 39–41.

26. Innocent III, *Regesta*, XVI, no. 3, ed. *PL*, 216: 786–87, Potthast no. 4678.

27. Jean-Claude Schmitt, *La raison des gestes dans l'Occident médiéval* (Paris, 1990), 62–63.

28. Chobham, *Summa*, 261.

29. For two preparatory but broader studies, see John W. Baldwin, "The Intellectual Preparation for the Canon of 1215 against Ordeals," *Speculum* 36 (1961): 613–36, and "The Crisis of the Ordeal: Literature, Law and Religion around

1200," *Journal of Medieval and Renaissance Studies* 24 (1994): 327–53. For a comprehensive survey, see Robert Bartlett, *Trial by Fire and Water: The Medieval Judicial Ordeal* (Oxford, 1986).

30. Paul Rousset, "La croyance en la justice immanente à l'époque féodale," *Le Moyen Age*, 4th ser., 3 (1948): 225–48, esp. 235–41.

31. The extent to which ordeals were practiced remains under debate. In addition to Bartlett, *Trial by Fire*, see Peter Brown, "Society and the Supernatural: A Medieval Change," *Daedalus* 104 (1975): 133–51; Paul R. Hyams, "Trial by Ordeal: The Key to Proof in Early Common Law," in *On the Laws and Customs of England: Essays in Honor of Samuel E. Thorne*, ed. Morris S. Arnold et al. (Chapel Hill, N.C., 1981), 90–126; Margaret H. Kerr, Richard D. Forsyth, and Michel J. Plyley, "Cold Water and Hot Iron: Trial by Ordeal in England," *Journal of Interdisciplinary History* 22 (1992): 573–97; and Stephen D. White, "Proposing the Ordeal and Avoiding It: Strategy and Power in Western French Litigation, 1050–1110," in *Cultures of Power: Lordship, Status, and Process in Twelfth-Century Europe*, ed. Thomas N. Bisson (Philadelphia, 1995), 89–123. White argues that ordeals were frequently transmuted to compromises in the Loire Valley in the late eleventh century. While this may be true for an area of weak political authority, it may not apply equally to regions of stronger royal or princely power, where, as in the case of England, the ordeal appears to have been imposed with greater effectiveness.

32. Béroul vv. 643–903, 3228–4231. Gottfried von Strassburg, *Tristan*, trans. A. T. Hatto (Harmondsworth, Middlesex, 1960), 240–48; quotation, 248. Chrétien, *Charrete* vv. 4533–5043. For fuller discussion of these examples, particularly the *Roman de Renard*, see Baldwin, "Crisis of the Ordeal," 330–40. On the equivocal oath, see Helaine Newstead, "The Equivocal Oath in the Tristan Legend," in *Mélanges offerts à Rita Lejeune, professeur à l'Université de Liège* (Gembloux, Bel., 1969), 2: 1077–85, and Ralph J. Hexter, *Equivocal Oaths and Ordeals in Medieval Literature* (Cambridge, Mass., 1975).

33. Jean Renart probably chose the cold-water ordeal for dramatic purposes, because it rendered an immediate verdict. See Bartlett, *Trial* 23.

34. Two studies on the legal practice of ordeals in medieval France are Yvonne Bongert, *Recherches sur les cours laïques du Xᵉ au XIIIᵉ siècle* (Paris, 1949), 205–51, and Marguerite Boulet-Sautel, "Aperçus sur les systèmes des preuves dans la France coutumière," in *La preuve*, Recueil de la Société Jean Bodin pour l'histoire comparative des institutions, 17 (1965), 2: 278–303. On the religious context, see Bongert, *Recherches*, 223–25; Boulet-Sautel, "Aperçus," 281.

35. Bartlett, *Trial by Fire* 30, 50; Bongert, *Recherches*, 205–10, 240; Boulet-Sautel, "Aperçus," 284, 286–87.

36. For ordeal basins in churches, see Bartlett, *Trial*, 51–52, 88–89, 93; and Bongert, *Recherches*, 216, 225. In Normandy, one basin was 12 feet deep and 20 feet in diameter.

37. The principal studies of St. Henry and St. Cunegunda are Robert Folz, *Les saints rois du moyen âge en occident (VIe –XIIIe siècles)*, Subsidia hagiographica, 68 (Brussels, 1984), 84–91; id., *Les saintes reines du moyen âge en occident (VIe –XIIIe siècles)*, Subsidia hagiographica, 76 (Brussels, 1992), 82–93; Renata Klauser, *Der Heinrichs- und Kunigundenkult im mittelalterlichem Bistum Bamberg* (Bamberg, 1957); and Klaus Guth, *Die heiligen Heinrich und Kunigunde: Leben, Legende, Kult, und Kunst* (Bamberg, 1986). On the development of the saints' lives, see *Bibliotheca hagiographica latina*, Subsidia hagiographica, 6 (Brussels, 1898–99), 1: 302–3, 568–69; Klauser, *Der Heinrichs- und Kunigundenkult*, 70–100, 108–13; Guth, *Die heilige Heinrich und Kunigunde*, 68–79.

38. *Adalberti Vita Henrici II imperatoris*, ed. G. Waitz, *MGH SS*, 4: 805, 810. A second version was made around 1170, which added passages relating to Henry's foundation of the church of Bamberg. One manuscript of the second version was copied by a deacon of Bambert named Adalbert (1170–84), but it is unlikely that he is the author of this version, although his name has been attached to the *vita*. Klauser, *Der Heinrichs- und Kunigundenkult*, 83–84.

39. *Vita sanctae Cunegundis*, ed. G. Waitz, *MGH SS*, 4: 821. *De S. Cunigunde imperatorice. Vita. Acta sanctorum* (Paris, 1865), Martii 1: 271–72.

40. *PL*, 140: 219–22, Potthast no. 1000. Two copies were produced by the papal chancery. For a full discussion and a critical edition, see Jürgen Petersohn, "Die Litterae Papst Innocenz III. zur Heiligsprechung der Kaiserin Kunigunde (1200)," *Jahrbuch für fränkische Landesforschung* 27 (1977): 1–25; text, 21–25.

41. *Vitae sancti Henrici addimentum*, ed. G. Waitz, *MGH SS*, IV, 819–20.

42. Cunegunda's legend may well have inspired a similar account (c. 1200) attached to the personage of Queen Emma, the mother of Edward the Confessor, by the *Annales de Wintonia* in *Annales monastici*, ed. Henry R. Luard, RS (London, 1865), 2: 20–25.

43. For closely contemporaneous sermons: *De semine scripturarum* (1201–4; later attributed to Joachim of Fiore), ed. Franz Pelster, "Ein Elogium Joachims von Fiore auf Kaiser Heinrich II. und seine Gemahlin, die heilige Kunigunde," in *Liber floridus: Mittellateinische Studien. Paul Lehmann zum 65. Geburtstag am 13. Juli 1949 gewidmet von Freunden, Kollegen and Schülern*, ed. Bernhard Bischoff and Suso Brechter (St. Ottilien, 1950), 351; *Sermo de sancta Chunigunda* (1200–1204), ed. in Klauser, *Der Heinrichs- und Kundigundenkult*, 195–96, and *Sermo magistri Conradi* (before 1208), ed. in id., 189. For the liturgy, see id., 143–48, and Robert Folz, "La légende liturgique de Saint Henri II, empereur et confesseur," *Clio et son regard: Mélanges . . . Jacques Stiennon*, ed. Rita Lejeune and Joseph Deckers (Liège, 1982), 253–54.

44. The titlepage of the *Vita S. Cunegundis*, MS. Bamberg Staatsbibliothek, R.B. Msc. 120, fol. 32v, reproduced in Guth, *Die heilige Heinrich und Kunigunde*, 70.

45. In 1201, Duke Philip of Swabia, the Staufen candidate for the imperial throne, whom Innocent had personally excommunicated, called his supporters to a Reichstag at Bamberg. On 8 September, the third anniversary of his own coronation, he had Cunegunda's body translated to a new burial site near the altar of the choir, thus associating the saint with his political fortunes. Klauser, *Der Heinrichs- und Kunigundenkult*, 67–68. Guth, *Die heiligen Heinrich und Kunigunde*, 74.

46. For the canonists, see John W. Baldwin, "Intellectual Preparation," 613–26.

47. See, eg., in the case of adultery, Gratian, *Decretum* C. 2 q. 5 c. 25, *Statuit*, and the use of bitter waters for adulterers, C. 2 q. 5 c. 20, *Consuluisti;* c. 21, *In libro*. The biblical authority is found in Num. 5:11–31. On the proof by bitter waters, see Bartlett, *Trial*, 84.

48. For Huguccio's texts, see Baldwin, "Intellectual Preparation," 624–26.

49. Ibid., 626–37. See also Baldwin, *Masters, Princes, and Merchants*, 1: 323–32.

50. Chanter, *Verbum abbreviatum*, *PL*, 205: 230D, 231A, 547A.

51. Ibid., 543A. Baldwin, *Masters, Princes, and Merchants*, 2: 233, n. 238.

52. E.g., Innocent III, *Regesta*, XIV, no. 138, ed. *PL*, 216: 502, Potthast no. 4358; *PL*, 217: 214; *Regesta*, XI, no. 46, ed. *PL*, 215: 1372, Potthast no. 3343.

53. C. 18, *Constitutiones*, ed. García y García 66; Mansi, 22: 1006–7.

54. *Foedera, conventiones, litterae*, ed. Thomas Rymer (London, 1816), 1: 154; *Diplomatarium Danicum, 1211–1223*, ed. Niels Skyum-Nielsen (Copenhagen, 1957), 1 (5) 141. In Norman customary law, ordeals are frequently mentioned before 1200 in the *Très ancien coutumier* 38, 51, and 71, in *Coutumiers de Normandie*, ed. J. Tardif (Rouen, 1881), 1: 33, 42, and 67. In the later *Summa de legibus* 76, in *Coutumiers de Normandie*, ed. J. Tardif (Rouen, 1896), 2: 109–91, they were declared to be abrogated by the Church. Bartlett, *Trial* 127–28.

55. For the councils, see Chapter 3 n. 41. Boulet-Sautel, "Aperçus," 278–298, 315–16. Bongert, *Recherches*, 234–37, traces Capetian resistance to battle back to Louis VII in 1174.

56. For the taxonomy of the judicial combat in romance and Chrétien's treatment, see Chênerie, *Le chevalier errant*, 351–77. See also Ross G. Arthur, "The Judicium Dei in the *Yvain* of Chrétien de Troyes," *Romance Notes* 28 (1987): 3–12. For a preliminary study of judical combat, see John W. Baldwin, "The Crisis of the Ordeal: Literature, Law, and Religion around 1200," *Journal of Medieval and Renaissance Studies* 24 (1994): 333–38, 348–51.

57. Richard fitz Nigel, *Dialogus de Scaccario*, ed. Charles Johnson, F. E. L. Carter, and E. E. Greenway (Oxford, 1983), 87, 88. Chobham, *Summa*, 428, accurately reports the English practice. The chief difference between the romance and English examples is that the latter were confessed criminals who accused and challenged others to battle in behalf of royal justice. Their successful prosecutions might, but did not always, mitigate their own sentences. Baldwin, *Masters, Princes, and Merchants*, 1: 329–30.

58. See the discussion of Frederick Carl Riedel, *Crime and Punishment in the Old French Romances* (New York, 1938), 70–73.

59. Chanter, *Summa*, 3 (2a): 278–79. In an unpublished *questio* (MS. Paris BN lat 3477, fol. 128ra), the Chanter reports a recent case of two hired champions who fought on an island, circumstances that bring to mind literary parallels. The moral question was whether the parish priest should permit burial of the dead champion. The Chanter's response is negative, although he admits that monks and other *religiosi* take the bodies away secretly and bury them.

60. Chobham, *Summa*, 293–94. In a subsequent section, Chobham discusses the difficulties facing a third party who has innocently bought stolen goods and is accused of theft in a duel. Thomas reports two lines of advice: (1) The defendent should declare himself innocent but refuse to participate in the duel because of the danger of fraternal hatred. In this case bishops or other prelates of the Church should be prepared to intercede with the prince in his behalf. (2) If the seller and true thief intends to implicate the buyer and to kill him, the latter is permitted to defend himself, but not to kill the accuser, who will be hanged unless he wins. Ibid., 427–28.

61. The most comprehensive introduction to the figure of the hermit is Angus J. Kennedy, "The Hermits' Role in French Arthurian Romance," *Romania* 95 (1974): 54–83.

62. On the historical phenomenon of hermits, see Settimana internazionale di studio, 1962, *L'eremitismo in occidente nei secoli XI e XII*, Università cattolica del Sacro Cuore, Pubblicazioni contributi, 3d ser., Miscellanea del Centro di studi medioevali, 4 (Milan, 1965). On western France, see Jean Becquet, 182–211; on England, Hubert Dauphin, 271–310. Giles Constable, *The Reformation of the Twelfth Century* (Cambridge, 1996), 10–11, 60–63.

63. Jean Frappier, "Le graal et la chevalerie," *Romania* 75 (1954): 165–210.

64. Gerbert, *Continuation* vv. 7382–87, 8828–31, 10252–54, 14184–89, 15746–801.

65. An intermediate stage was that of the Carthusians. Chanter, *Verbum abbreviatum, PL*, 205: 213–17; MS. V, fol. 90vb–92va; alternate version *PL*, 205: 535–38.

66. The three creeds that prevailed in the twelfth century were the Credo in Deum (the so-called Apostles' Creed), the Credo in unum Deum (the Constantinopolitan Creed), and Quicumque vult (the pseudo-Athanasian Creed), each divided into articles of faith. In 1208, e.g., Pope Innocent III proposed these three orthodox creeds to the Waldensians. See *Enchiridion symbolum*, ed. H. Denzinger (Barcelona, 1976), no. 700. The three are nos. 301, 150, and 74. See also Jean Beleth, *De ecclesiasticis officiis*, ed. J. Douteil, Corpus christianorum, Continuatio medievalis 41A (Turnhout, Bel., 1976), 2:75.

67. On the teaching of the creed, see Jean-Claude Schmitt, "Du bon usage du 'Credo,'" in *Faire croire: Modalités de la diffusion et de la réception des messages re-*

ligieux du XIIe au XVe siècle, Collection de l'Ecole française de Rome, 51 (Rome, 1981), 337–55. The Chanter discusses the practical questions of how the godparents are to discharge their responsibilities. *Summa,* 3 (2b): 500–503. See also Thomas of Chobham, *Summa de arte praedicandi,* ed. Franco Morenzoni, Corpus christianorum, Continuatio mediaevalis 82 (Turnhout, Bel., 1988), 170–71.

68. Jean Beleth, *Summa de ecclesiasticis officiis* 2:73–75, 214, 218.

69. C. A. Robson, *Maurice of Sully and the Medieval Vernacular Homily* (Oxford, 1952), 18–21, 82–87.

70. Chanter, *Verbum abbreviatum, PL,* 205:268.

71. Chobham, *Summa,* 242–44. See also *Summa de arte praedicandi,* ed. Morenzoni, 171. Chobham's advice was in accordance with subsequent synodical statutes: c. 51, Winchester (1224), and c. 8, Worcester (1229), in *Councils and Synods,* ed. F. M. Powicke and C. R. Cheney (Oxford, 1964), 2 (1): 134, 172.

72. C. 62, 84, Statutes of Paris (1199–1208), in *Les statuts synodaux français du XIIIe siècle,* ed. Odette Pontal, Collection de documents inédits sur l'histoire de France, Section de philologie et d'histoire jusquà 1610, ser. in 8°, vol. 9 (Paris, 1971), 1: 74, 84.

73. C. 16, Statutes of Cambrai, in *Les statuts synodaux français du XIIIe siècle,* ed. Joseph Avril, Collection de documents inédits sur l'histoire de France, Section d'histoire médiévale et de philologie, ser. in 8°, vol. 23 (Paris, 1995), 4: 32, made it the responsibility of the parents and godparents.

74. Statutes of Westminster (1200): "in lingua moderna," c. 1, in *Councils and Synods,* ed. D. Whitelock et al. (Oxford, 1981), 1 (2): 1070; Statutes of Salisbury (1217–19): "domestico ydiomate," c. 3, in *Councils and Synods,* ed. Powicke and Cheney, 2 (1): 61; Statutes of Winchester (1224): "in materna lingua," c. 51, in ibid., 134; Statutes of Worcester (1229), "sub lingua ei nota," c. 8, in ibid., 172. On English efforts to instruct the laity, see Franco Morenzoni, *Des écoles aux paroisses: Thomas de Chobham et la promotion de la prédication au début du XIIIe siècle,* Collection des études Augustiniennes, Moyen-âge et temps modernes, 30 (Paris, 1995), 124, 133.

75. Any such work found after a fixed date (except for saints' lives) was presumed to be heretical. *Chartularium universitatis Parisiensis,* ed. H. Denifle and Emile Châtelain (Paris, 1889), 1: 70.

76. C. 1, *Constitutiones,* ed. García y García, 41–43; Mansi, 22: 981–82.

77. C. 3, 4, Statutes of Salisbury, ed. Powicke and Cheney, 2 (1): 61.

78. Statutes of Angers, c. 123, 124, and 132, in *Les statuts synodaux français du XIIIe siècle,* ed. Pontal, 1: 226–34.

79. Although it echoed the New Testament terminology of *novum testamentum* (Matt. 26:28), *novum mandatum* (John 13:34), or *novus homo* (Eph. 4:24), *novele loi* also skirted the *nova lex* of the heretic Amaury de Bène, which was condemned at the Council of Sens in 1210. Guillaume le Breton, *Gesta,* 232.

80. Examples may be found in the earlier *orationes sive meditationes* of Jean de Fécamp and Anselm of Canterbury and the contemporary Englishman Alexander of Ashby. See André Wilmart, "La prière du symbol de foi," in *Auteurs spirituels et textes dévots du moyen âge latin: Etudes d'histoire littéraire* (Paris, 1932), 56–63, and Thomas H. Bestul, "The *Meditationes* of Alexander of Ashby: An Edition," *Mediaeval Studies* 52 (1990): 24–81.

81. *Le couronnement de Louis,* vv. 695–789, ed. Ernest Langlois, Les classiques français du moyen âge (Paris, 1925); *Guillaume d'Orange: Four Twelfth-Century Epics,* trans. Joan M. Ferrante (New York, 1974), 83–85 (see 32–33 on the occurrence of such prayers in the chansons de geste). The *Couronnement* belongs to the cycle of Guillaume d'Orange, which also contains the *Aliscans* that Gerbert quotes earlier (*Violette* vv. 1407–29). The closest verbal correspondence between the two narratives involves the burial and resurrection (cf. *Couronnement* vv. 778–80 with *Violette* vv. 5302).

82. Chrétien's assertion that Jews should be killed like dogs for their complicity (*Graal* vv. 6292–95) is not followed by Gerbert.

83. For comprehensive summaries of the Harrowing of Hell, see H. Quilliet, "Descente de Jésus aux enfers," in *Dictionnaire de théologie catholique,* 4: 565–619, and Ralph Turner, "*Descendit ad inferos:* Medieval Views of Christ's Descent into Hell and the Salvation of the Ancient Just," *Journal of the History of Ideas* 27 (1966): 173–94.

84. Statutes of Paris (1199–1208), c. 80, and Statutes of Angers (1216–19), c. 8, in *Les statuts synodaux français du XIIIe siècle,* ed. Pontal, 1: 82, 144. Statutes of Canterbury (1213–14), c. 45, Statutes of Salisbury (1217–19), and Statutes for an English diocese (1222–27), in *Councils and Synods,* ed. Powicke and Cheney, 2 (1): 33, 79, 143.

The elevation of the host during the Mass also prompted a debate among contemporary theologians over the question of at what precise moment the bread and wine were transubstantiated into the body and blood of Christ. Pierre the Chanter and Robert of Courson argued that the miraculous transformation did not occur until both bread and wine had been consecrated. This would have prevented the elevation of the bread after the words "Hoc est corpus meum" had been pronounced, because it was not then the true body of Christ. Other theologians such as Pierre de Poitiers and Stephen Langton countered that the bread and wine were transformed separately after the pronouncement of the specific consecrating formula, which would permit the elevation of the host before the consecration of the wine. The popular tradition of the elevation of the host confirmed and regulated by the Synod of Paris (before 1208) facilitated the acceptance of the latter view. For a discussion of this question, see V. L. Kennedy, "The Moment of Consecration and Elevation of the Host," *Mediaeval Studies* 6 (1944): 121–50, and Edouard Dumoutet, "La théologie de l'eucharistie à la fin du

XIIe siècle: Le témoignage de Pierre le Chantre d'après la 'Summa de sacramentis,'" *Archives d'histoire doctrinale et littéraire du moyen âge* 14 (1943–45): 179–262.

85. Chanter, *Summa*, 1: 166–67. Dumoutet, "La théologie de l'eucharistie," 215–18, 248–52.

86. The chief study of penance in vernacular French is Jean-Charles Payen, *Le motif du repentir dans la littérature française médiévale (des origines à 1230)* (Geneva, 1967). Although this work is comprehensive in its coverage of the subject, particularly with respect to Chrétien, it does not treat the verse continuations of Perceval, including Gerbert of Montreuil's (see 481 n. 59). Payen's conclusions are thus more equivocal than mine about the influence of the theologians, his "grands clercs," on the romance authors (591).

87. Before battle in the *First Continuation* (ed. Roach, 1, vv. 509–26) Gauvain repents of his sins and confesses them to a Bishop Salemon, from whom he receives communion. In the *Second Continuation* (ed. Roach, 4, vv. 24087–24129), as later in Gerbert's version, Perceval visits the hermitage where his mother is buried. The hermit, his uncle, preaches a sermon on penance, including the steps of repentance and confession. Perceval declares that he believes in the Sacrament of penance, but is not shown as performing it. The practice of penance is also depicted in Robert de Boron, *Joseph of Arimathea: A Romance of the Grail*, trans. Jean Rogers (London, 1991), 4; in *The High Book of the Grail: A Translation of the Thirteenth-Century Romance of Perlevaus*, trans. Nigel Bryant (Cambridge, 1978), 23, 54, 75, 144–45; and in the *The Romance of Perceval in Prose: A Translation of the E. Manuscript of the Didot-Perceval*, trans. Dell Skeels (Washington, D.C., 1961), 27, 55, 87.

88. Payen, *Le motif du repentir*, 108, 138, 278, 365–85.

89. Béroul vv. 1360–1422, 2289–2358. Payen, *Le motif de repentir*, 335–54.

90. Pierre de Blois, *Liber de confessione, PL*, 207: 1088–89.

91. One other incident of penance occurs in Chrétien's *Graal* (vv. 6964–76, 7053–74), this time involving Gauvain when he finds a knight who is nearly dead. When Gauvain enables the knight to speak, the latter requests a chaplain to whom he can confess and from whom he can receive communion, but this is only a ruse to steal Gauvain's horse.

92. The comprehensive study is Paul Anciaux, *La théologie du sacrement de pénitence au XIIe siècle*, Universitas catholica Lovaniensis, Dissertationes ad gradum magistri in Facultate Theologica vel in Facultate Iuris Canonici consequendum conscriptae, 2 (41) (Louvain, 1949).

93. As was characteristic of medieval reform, the new private penance did not eliminate the older public penance, but was added to it. On the relations of the two forms of penance and the survival of public penance in thirteenth-century France, see Mansfield, *Humiliation of Sinners*.

94. C. 2, *Constititutiones*, ed. García y García, 43; Mansi, 22: 981–82.

95. Chanter, *Summa*, 2: 3.

96. *Peter Abelard's Ethics*, ed. D. E. Luscombe (Oxford, 1971), 76.

97. Chanter, *Verbum abbreviatum, PL*, 205: 339A. "Robert Courson on Penance," ed. V. L. Kennedy, in *Mediaeval Studies* 7 (1945): 295. Chobham, *Summa*, 7. The Chanter prefaces the three elements with the Augustinian concept of "infusion of divine grace" without which the other three are useless. This prompts him to discuss the relations between penance and divine charity in his *Summa*, 2: 3–13.

98. Robson, *Maurice of Sully*, 98.

99. C. 127, Statutes of Angers, in *Les statuts synodaux français du XIIIᵉ siècle*, ed. Pontal, 1: 232.

100. See the conclusions in Anciaux, *La théologie de pénitence*, 463–64, 605.

101. "Robert Courson on Penance," ed. Kennedy, 300–301. Anciaux, *La théologie de pénitence*, 427–28.

102. Chanter, *Summa*, 2: 143. Anciaux, *La théologie de pénitence* 470.

103. Chanter, *Summa*, 2: 163, 279.

104. Ibid., 279.

105. Ibid., 279, 306, 420; Chanter, *Verbum abbreviatum*, 343C.

106. The fundamental study on circumstances is Johannes Gründel, *Die Lehre von den Umständen der menschlichen Handlung im Mittelalter*, Beiträge zur Geschichte der Philosophie und Theologie des Mittelalters, 39 (5) (1963).

107. C. 21, *Constitutiones*, ed. García y García, 68; Mansi, 22: 1007–10. Statutes of Paris (1199–1208), c. 26, 31, 37, and Statutes of Angers (1216–19), c. 76, in *Les statuts synodaux français du XIIIᵉ siècle*, ed. Pontal, 1: 62, 64, 190. Statutes of Westminster (c. 1200), c. 4, in *Councils and Synods*, ed. Whitelock et al., 1 (2): 1062. Statutes of Salisbury (1217–19), c. 33, 40, 74, Statutes of an English diocese (1222–25), c. 26, and Statutes of Worcester (1229), c. 8, in *Councils and Synods*, ed. Powicke and Cheney, 2 (1): 71, 73–74, 144, 172.

108. Chobham, *Summa*, 264–65.

109. Statutes of Paris, c. 36, in *Les statuts synodaux français du XIIIᵉ siècle*, ed. Pontal, 1: 64. Statutes of Canterbury (1213–14), c. 43, in *Councils and Synods*, ed. Powicke and Cheney, 2 (1): 32. Chobham, *Summa*, 236–37. Robson, *Maurice of Sully*, 98–99. See Broomfield in Chobham, *Summa*, xli–ii, for a discussion of confessional practice.

110. C. 21, *Constitutiones*, ed. García y García, 67–68; Mansi, 22:1007–1010 Statutes of Angers (1216–19), c. 75, in *Les statuts synodaux français du XIIIᵉ siècle*, ed. Pontal, 1: 190. Statutes of Cambrai (1238–48), c. 42, in *Les statuts synodaux français du XIIIᵉ siècle*, ed. Avril, 4: 36. Statutes of Salisbury (1217–19), c. 38, and Statutes of Worcester (1229), c. 13, in *Councils and Synods*, ed. Powicke and Cheney, 2 (1): 72, 173.

111. Chobham further elaborates that according to the decree of the general

council, a physician should not attempt to cure or administer medicine to the sick until they have first confessed, because many illnesses arise from God's punishment, or even from the devil, without natural causes. Such illnesses caused by sin cannot be cured without prior confession and penance. Chobham, *Summa*, 236. This is an explicit reference to c. 22 of the Lateran Council (*Constitutiones*, ed. García y García, 69; Mansi, 22: 1010–11), which Chobham may have added to his *Summa* after 1215. See Broomfield in Chobham, *Summa*, xli–ii.

112. C. 21, *Constitutiones*, ed. García y García, 68; Mansi, 22: 1010.

113. Chanter, *Summa*, 2: 283; *Verbum abbreviatum*, 342D–343A, 344B.

114. Chobham, *Summa*, 8.

115. Anciaux, *La théologie de pénitence*, 582–97.

116. The Chanter's clearest text is found in Anciaux, *La théologie de pénitence*, 591–92. See also *Summa*, 2: 429; 3 (2b): 693.

117. Chanter, *Summa*, 2: 312–15, 322–25, 425–26, 428–33, 439–40.

118. Anciaux, *La théologie de pénitence*, 592, Chanter, *Summa*, 2: 324, 430–31, 439.

119. Chobham, *Summa*, 200.

120. Chanter, *Summa*, 2: 324, 432.

121. "Robert Courson on Penance," ed. Kennedy, 326.

122. C. 72, Statutes of Angers, ed. Pontal, 1: 188.

123. Statutes of Angers (1216–19), c. 75, in *Les statuts synodaux français du XIIIe siècle*, ed. Pontal, 1: 190. Statutes of Cambrai (1238–48), c. 27, in *Les statuts synodaux français du XIIIe siècle*, ed. Avril, 4: 33. Statutes of Salisbury (1217–19), c. 38, in *Councils and Synods*, ed. Powicke and Cheney, 2 (1): 72–73. The Statutes of Paris (1199–1208), c. 104, ed. Pontal, 1: 90, prohibit deacons from hearing confessions, except in extreme emergencies, and they are never to offer absolution.

124. Statutes of Cambrai, c. 45, in *Les statuts synodaux français du XIIIe siècle*, ed. Avril, 4: 36; Statutes of an English diocese, c. 34, in *Councils and Synods*, ed. Powicke and Cheney, 2 (1): 145–46.

125. "Robert Courson on Penance, " ed. Kennedy, 295, 326

126. C. 21, *Constitutiones*, ed. García y García, 67–68; Mansi, 22: 1010.

127. Robson, *Maurice of Sully*, 98.

128. Chanter, *Summa*, 2: 282; id., *Verbum abbreviatum*, *PL*, 342D–343A, 345B. Chobham, *Summa*, 8–9, 203.

129. Statutes of Paris (1199–1208), c. 73, in *Les statuts synodaux français du XIIIe siècle*, ed. Pontal, 1: 94; Statutes of Cambrai, c. 26, in id., ed. Avril, 4: 33. For the later development, see Nicole Bériou, "La confession dans les écrits théologiques et pastoraux du XIIIe siècle: Médication de l'âme ou démarche judiciare?" in *L'aveu: Antiquité et moyen âge*, Collection de l'Ecole française de Rome, 88 (Rome, 1986), 261-82.

130. Chobham, *Summa*, 260-61.

338 · ❦ NOTES TO PAGES 234-236

131. "Robert Courson on Penance," ed. Kennedy, 303.

132. Jacques Berlioz, "Les ordalies dans les *exempla* de la confession (XIIIᵉ–XIVᵉ siècles)," in *L'aveu*, 315-40 has discovered this genre of exempla and collected those I discuss here. Brian Patrick McGuire, "The Cistercians and the Rise of the Exemplum in Early Thirteenth-Century France: A reevaluation of Paris BN MS lat. 15912," *Classica et mediaevalia* 34 (1983): 211–67, has identified, dated, and located this early collection.

133. Paris BN lat. 15912, fol. 37d–38a. Text in Berlioz, "Les ordalies," 323 n. 20. Although not involving the ordeal proper, confession also saved an adulterous woman from burning at the stake (Paris BN lat. 15912, fol. 37c–d; text in Berlioz, 330 n. 37). When a cleric and his sister were caught in the murder of a silversmith, the unrepentant cleric was burned at the stake, but the confession of the sister saved her from the flames. *Caesarii Heisterbacensis monachi ordinis Cisterciensis Dialogus miraculorum* 3.15, ed. Joseph Strange (Cologne, 1851), 1: 130–31.

134. *Caesarii Heisterbacensis . . . Dialogus* 3.16, ed. Strange, 1: 132.

135. Paris BN lat. 15912, fol. 37c–b. Text in Berlioz, "Les ordalies," 325 n. 26. *Caesarii Heisterbacensis . . . Dialogus* 10.35, ed. Strange, 2: 243. Of ten heretics charged at Strasbourg, one saved himself from conviction through confession. When he returned home, he was reproached by his wife for his inconstancy. When he reverted to his former beliefs, the couple suffered such terrible fire that they fled to the forest howling like wolves. Thus exposed, they were captured and burned with the others. *Caesarii Heisterbacensis . . . Dialogus* 3.17, ed. Strange, 1: 133–34.

136. *Caesarii Heisterbacensis . . . Dialogus* 3.18, ed. Strange, 1: 134–35.

137. Ibid. 3.19, ed. Strange, 1: 135.

138. His actual term is the comparative *mirabilius*. Ibid. 10.35, ed. Strange, 2: 243.

139. The first example is explicitly called a miracle, setting the pattern for the following stories. Ibid. 3.14, ed. Strange, 1: 131; Berlioz, "Les ordalies," 334–35. The story of the peccant fisherman in *Caesarii Heisterbacensis . . . Dialogus* 10.35 is likewise set within a group of miracles.

140. This lack of marvels is what attracted the attention of the first modern critics. Two exceptions in the *Violette* are the incidents of the dragon and the giant.

141. For a selection among the many studies on medieval marvels, see Mortimer J. Donovan, *The Breton Lay: A Guide to Varieties* (Notre Dame, Ind., 1969), 31; Daniel Poirion, *Le merveilleux dans la littérature française du moyen âge* (Paris, 1982); Jacques Le Goff, "Le merveilleux dans l'Occident médiéval," *L'imaginaire médiéval: Essais* (Paris, 1985), 17-39; Francis Dubost, *Aspects fantastiques de la littérature narrative médiéval (XIIᵉᵐᵉ–XIIIᵉᵐᵉ siècles): L'autre, l'ailleurs, l'autrefois*, Nouvelle Bibliothèque du moyen âge 15 (Paris, 1991); Chênerie, *Le chevalier errant*, 593-679. In "Wonder," *American Historical Review* 102 (1997): 1–26, Car-

oline Walker Bynum offers a comprehensive schema for understanding the role of the marvelous in medieval society. Although she excludes romance from her purview, her conclusions are nonetheless relevant to literary marvels as well. She identifies three different approaches in the Middle Ages: (1) the university scholars who insisted on an ontological difference between miracles and marvels and considered the latter as susceptible to further study and clarification; (2) preachers and hagiographers who insisted that the marvelous was not to be imitated, and (3) writers of travel accounts and fables who considered each marvelous phenomenon according to its singularity and individual perspective.

142. For an analysis of the marvel in Chrétien, see Lucienne Carasso-Bulow, *The Merveilleux in Chrétien de Troyes' Romances* (Geneva, 1976).

143. Robert de Boron, *Roman de l'Estoire dou Graal*, ed. W. A. Nitz (Paris, 1927), trans. by Jean Rogers as *Joseph of Arimathea: A Romance of the Grail* (London, 1990); Robert de Boron, *Merlin: Roman de XIIIe siècle*, ed. Alexandre Micha (Paris, 1980), trans. into modern French by Emmanuèle Baumgartner as *Merlin le prophète ou le livre du graal* (Paris, 1980); *Le haut livre du graal Perlevaus*, ed. William Nitze and T. Atkinson Jenkins (Chicago, 1932, 1937), 2 vols; trans. as *The High Book of the Grail: A Translation of the Thirteenth-Century Romance of Perlevaus* (Cambridge, 1978).

144. *The Didot Perceval According to the Manuscripts of Modena and Paris*, ed. William Roach (Philadelphia, 1941), trans. by Dell Skeels as *The Romance of Perceval in Prose: A Translation of the E Manuscript of the Didot Perceval* (Seattle, 1961).

145. Although Gerbert includes episodes that approximate those of Robert de Boron, *Perlevaus*, and the *Didot Perceval*, the exact relationship is difficult to determine. These prose accounts, however, contain numerous features and episodes of which the verse continuations appear to be ignorant.

146. For the editions of the verse continuations, see list of Short Titles.

147. For other examples: two terrifying serpents that guard a bridge (v. 573), a magic pillar made by Merlin on Mont Dolerous (vv. 963–67), and a bed covering at Beaurepaire made by the fairy Blanchemal that prevents sickness.

148. Sara Sturm-Maddox deals with this problem in *"Tout est par senefïance:* Gerbert's *Perceval,"* in *Arthurian Yearbook*, ed. Keith Busby, 2 (1992): 191–207.

149. See, e.g., the interpretations in Chênerie, *Le chevalier errant*, 593–679.

150. The Joseph of Arimathea legend was introduced into the Grail legend by Robert de Boron in the *Joseph* and is alluded to in the *Perlevaus*. Gerbert's version of King Mordrain is close to the prose *La quête de Saint Graal* (ed. Albert Pauphilet [Paris, 1984], 33, 84–86), but the exact relationship between the two versions is not clear.

151. See nn. 64–65 above. The images of the two monks before the cross and the *bête glatissant* were most likely taken from the prose *Perlevaus* (ed. Nitze, 240

and 257). See Dubost, *Aspects fantastiques*, 501–3; William A. Nitze, "The Beste Glatissant in Arthurian Romance," *Zeitschrift für romanische Philologie* 66 (1936): 409–18; Edina Bozoky, "La 'Bête glatissant' et le graal: Les transformations d'un thème allégorique dans quelques romans arthuriens," *Revue de l'histoire des religions* 186 (1974): 127-148; Claude Roussel, "Le jeu des formes et des couleurs: Observations sur 'la beste glatissant,'" *Romania* 104 (1982): 49–82; Janina P. Traxler, "Observations on the Beste Glatissant in the *Tristan en prose*," *Neophilogus* 74 (1990): 499–509; and Christine Ferlampin-Acher, "Le monstre dans les romans des XIIIᵉ et XIVᵉ siècles," in *Ecritures et modes de pensée au moyen âge (VIIIᵉ–XVᵉ siècles)*, ed. Dominique Boutet and Laurence Hart-Lancner (Paris, 1993), 69–83.

152. See Chapter 7, "Christian Doctrine."

153. The child in the tree also occurs in the *Didot-Perceval* (ed. Roach, vv. 203–4). For the pagan and Christian antecedents to the image, see Eleanor Simmons Greenhill, "The Child in the Tree: A Study of the Cosmological Tree in Christian Tradition," *Traditio* 10 (1954): 323–71. Gauwain also visits the chapel (*First Continuation* vv. 13018–55).

154. See Dubost, *Aspects fantastiques*, 703–5.

155. Carasso-Bulow, *Merveilleux*, 22.

156. See the discussion in Chênerie, *Le chevalier errant*, 650-74.

157. Other manuscripts attach Manessier directly to the *Second Continuation* (ed. Roach, 5: xviii–xix).

158. Only on one occasion does Jean appear to conflate miracles and marvels. The seneschal does not know whether it is by *miracles* or *mervelle* that the châtelaine remembers him (*Rose* vv. 4413-16).

159. *Chronicon*, *PL*, 212:815. In "La prédication effective à Paris au 13ᵉᵐᵉ siècle" (thesis, Paris, 1996; 6 vols.), an exhaustive treatment of the hundreds of sermons preached by university scholars at Paris in the last quarter of the thirteenth century, Nicole Bériou has not found references to the Grail.

160. Bynum, "Wonder," 6–9, draws this distinction based on a discussion of Thomas Aquinas, but claims that it had appeared by 1200. Further exploration of this issue would be useful.

161. Chanter, *Verbum abbreviatum, PL,* 205: 227C–D. "Antiquitus autem loco et tempore fieri dominus voluit miracula ad dilatandum fidem. Nunc autem dilatata fide, vult suos hic tribulari nec faci semper miracula." MS. V, fol. 97ra.

162. Chanter, *Verbum abbreviatum, PL,* 205: 228C–D. "Non enim exorcista potest hodie eicere demonia sicut in primitiva ecclesia, nec etiam omnes sacerdotes unius regni omnibus exorcismis salomonis, vel etiam suis possent virtute illorm liberare unum demonicum." MS. V, fol. 98rb.

163. "Item aliud exemplum ad hoc probandum quod dicimus. Accidit quon-

dam remis intolerabilis ariditas et aeris intemperies noxia. Extractis reliquiis et capsulis fecerunt per triduum fideles cuiuslibet sexus vel officii vel meriti arumambalia vel amburbalia, nec apparuit modica nubecula. Videns tantam afflictionem, iudeus quidam archisinagogus ait: Concedo ut omnes sumus christiani si infra triduum non dedero pluvias copiosas si rotulum nostrum et torach permiseritis nobis circumferre. Dixeruntque plerique fideles: Bonum est. Tandem ait magister albericus: Absit quod fides christi mittatur in periculum si iudeus de celo aquas eliceret arte magica, domino permittente propter peccata nostra vel diabolio procurante, quia mali etiam leguntur fecisse miracula. Et ita fides christi omnino posset exsufflari quia omnes ad iudaismum converti vellent, nec ausi sunt fidem nostram pro lucro tot iudeorum periculo exponere." Chanter, *Verbum abbreviatum* MS. V, fol. 99va.

164. Chanter, *Verbum abbreviatum* MS. V, fols. 96vb–97ra.

165. Chanter, *Verbum abbreviatum PL*, 205: 226D. "Item. Dominus ut in matheo legitur repondit diabolo suggerenti ei ut iuberet lapides panes fieri: Scriptum est, inquit, non in solo pane vivit homo sed in omni verbo quod procedit de ore dei. Glosa: Non utitur potestate sed scripturarum auctoritate docens nos magis doctrina pugnare quam miraculis." MS. V, fol. 96vb. *PL*, 205: 228B. "Noli ergo tu sacerdos peccator inniti hodie miraculis sed operibus bonis quia non invenitur dignus pro cuius merito operetur deus miracula." MS. V, fol. 97va. "Modo enim ecclesia magis innititur bonis operibus quam miraculis." MS. V, fol. 97vb.

166. Chanter, *Verbum abbreviatum*, Gloss to Ps. 59:14. "Item in psalmo: In deo faciemus virtutem. Glossa: Non in gladis non in miraculis sed in deo. In fide scilicet eius et bonis operibus vincendo diabolum." MS. V, fol. 98va.

CHAPTER 8.
Audiences

1. For fuller discussion, see Chapter 1 at nn. 4–6 and Chapter 2.

2. Gaston Paris, "Le cycle de la gageure," *Romania* 32 (1903): 487–526; Maureen Barry McGann Boulton, *The Song in the Story: Lyric Insertions in French Narrative Fiction, 1200–1400* (Philadelphia, 1993), 295–97; Lejeune, *L'oeuvre de Jean Renart*, 372–75.

3. MS. A, fol.40r–44v. Joseph Bédier's edition of this version in 1913 became the focal point for subsequent discussion of editing all Old French texts. Bédier casts doubt on the validity of constructing a "critical" and original text from so many manuscripts and argues for the selection of a "good" manuscript to be published in its place. Jean Renart, *Le lai de l'ombre*, ed. Joseph Bédier, Anciens textes français (Paris, 1913), xxiii–xlv. For a critical assessment of Bédier's edition, see F. Whitehead and C. E. Pickford, "The Introduction of the *Lai de l'ombre*: Sixty Years Later," *Romania* 94 (1973): 145–56. Félix Lecoy also made MS. A his base

text (Jean, *Lai*, v–viii). MS. E (Paris BN nouv. acq. fr. 1104, fol. 54v–61v), the other important text, has most recently been edited in Jean Renart, *The Lai de l'Ombre*, ed. Margaret E. Winters (Birmingham, Ala., 1986).

4. Brussels KBR II 139. Other than its transcription by Paul Meyer, *Bulletin de la Société des anciens textes français* 24 (1898): 85, and its inclusion in Sweeter's edition, it has not been studied.

5. Fol. 1r–76v, *L'Escoufle, roman d'aventure*, ed. H. Michelant and P. Meyer, Anciens textes français (Paris, 1894), liv–lix.

6. Fol. 168va–98vb. The fullest description of the manuscript is by Terry Nixon in *Les manuscrits de Chrétien de Troyes*, ed. Keith Busby, Terry Nixon, Alison Stones, and Lori Walters (Atlanta, Ga., 1993), 2: 62–63.

7. *Graal* fol. 1–37r, *First Continuation* fol. 37r–90r, *Second Continuation* fol. 98r–152v, Gerbert fol. 152v–220v, and Manessier fol. 220v–261r. For editions by William Roach, see *First Continuation* and *Second Continuation* in list of Short Titles; also Manessier, *The Third Continuation*, in *The Continuations of the Old French Perceval of Chrétien de Troyes*, ed. William Roach, vol. 5 (Philadelphia, 1983). For a description of the manuscript by Terry Nixon, see *Manuscrits de Chrétien de Troyes*, 2: 49–50; for discussion of the sections after Perceval by Roger Middleton, ibid., 2: 216–24.

8. The miniatures are calendered in *Manuscrits de Chrétien de Troyes*, 2: 275–77; reproduced in 2, nos. 103–36; and discussed by Alison Stones in 1: 236–43 and by Lorri Walters in 1: 333–35. Art historians may be able to detect iconographical programs in these miniatures, but these do not exclude the artist's intention merely to illustrate the various episodes of the complete story that the copyist selected for him. Sandra Hindman interprets the entire iconographic cycle as the transformation of Perceval from a knight to a cleric. *Sealed in Parchment: Rereadings of Knighthood in the Illuminated Manuscripts of Chrétien de Troyes* (Chicago, 1994), 11–48. It should nonetheless be noted that the miniatures of Gerbert's *Continuation*, which is the most clerical of all the versions and transforms the Grail quest into penitential purification, consistently omit all clerical imagery. See also Keith Busby's conclusions in *Manuscrits de Chrétien de Troyes*, 1: 354–59, 374–75.

9. Description by Terry Nixon in *Manuscrits de Chrétien de Troyes*, 2: 51–53. Comparison of scribal hands of MSS. T and V by Keith Busby in ibid., 2: 49–65.

10. Roger Middleton in *Manuscrits de Chrétien de Troyes* 2:216–24.

11. Description of the manuscript in *Manuscrits de Chrétien de Troyes* by Steward Gregory and Claude Luttrell, 1: 81–83; by Terry Nixon, 2: 41–43; and by Roger Middleton, 2: 189–93.

12. Yvain G. Lepage, "Un recueil français de la fin du XIIIe siècle (Paris, Bibliothèque nationale fr. 1553)," *Scriptorum* 29 (1975): 23–46. There are three systems of pagination: roman numerals contemporary with the medieval scribes and

two systems of modern arabic numerals, in ink and pencil. I have used the system in ink.

13. Gerbert's *Violette* received a historiated "S," but subsequent wear or defacement has made the image difficult to interpret. It consists of two seated figures dressed in red against a blue background under a triangulated red canopy. One figure is a male robed in fur, with legs crossed and his arm around the second figure, who may be a female. Two copies, one a deluxe illustrated manuscript, were made of the *Violette* in the fifteenth century: St. Petersburg, Bibl. publ. fr. F. r. XIV, no. 3, fol. 1–45, and New York, J. P. Morgan MS. 36. Two copies of a prose version also survive from the fifteenth century: Paris BN fr. 24378 and Brussels, Bibl. roy. 9631.

14. On the collection, see J.-Th. Welter, *L'exemplum dans la littérature religieuse et didactique au moyen âge* (Paris, 1927), 236–44. On jongleurs, see Chapter 1, "Jongleurs."

15. Text edited by V. Frederic Koenig ("Guillaume de Dole and Guillaume de Nevers," *Modern Philology* 45 [1948]: 149–51) from MS. Tours 468, fol. 33v. I am grateful to Marc Vaisbrot for providing a transcription from MS. Uppsala, University Library C523, fol. 29r.–31r.

16. See the discussion of Lejeune, *L'oeuvre de Jean Renart*, 54–57, and Koenig, "Guillaume de Dole," 145–49.

17. "Domina quedam famosa erat de magno valore; et cum coram rege milites loquerentur de mulieribus in malis, domina illa proposita est in medium. Tunc ait unus: 'Ego ponam meam terram quod infra quindenam faciam de ea quicquid voluero, et per bona indicia hoc probabo.' Maritus ejus contradixit, et terram suam posuit. Alius, vadens ad castrum, intrare non poutuit, et per fraudem domicellam domine seduxit. Que ei annulum quem maritus ejus ei dederat furata tradidit, et signum unum quod in coxa habebat revelavit. Et veniens ad hec signa se fecesse dixit. Maritus audiens et confusus, et nimis credulus recedens, et eam ad quoddam manerium ducens, in equam projecit. Que evadens, de veste sua vestem virilem faciens, ad abbaciam monachorum declinans, conversum se fecit. Et optime se habens, per abbatem est traditus regi pro elemosinario. Que optime et graciose officium illud fecit. Tandem elemosinam erogans et maritum qui fugerat inter alios considerans, ad partem trahens recreavit et factum suum peciit. Qui sibi omnia revelavit, et inter alia se dolere dixit quod circa sociam suam sic se habuerat. Que ei similiter factus suum dixit. Tunc ipsa repatriandi a rege licenciam accepit, et equum et arma querans in decenti muliebri habitu rediit, et militem illum de proditione appellavit, et quod eam violenter oppressit. Qui juravit et negavit se nunquam vidisse. Tunc ipsa: 'Rex, faciatis ergo michi justiciam, cum hoc michi imposuerit et per eum maritus meus terram amiserit, et ego exulata fuerim.' Judicatus fuit ad suspendium, et terra ei restituta; et rediit cum marito ad propria." *Compila-*

cio singularis exemplorm, MS. Tours 468, fol. 165v, MS. Uppsala, University Library C523, fol. 139r–v, ed. Marc Vaisbrot (thesis, Ecole des Chartes, 1968), no. 897; French trans. by Mireille Demaules in Gerbert de Montreuil, *Le roman de la violette* (Paris, 1992), 208–9. (I am grateful to Marc Vaisbrot for providing me the Latin text from his edition.)

18. The unique manuscript of Jean's *Rose* was collected and commented on by the antiquarian scholar Claude Fauchet in the sixteenth century. After his library was dispersed, the *Rose* was acquired by Queen Christina of Sweden in the seventeenth century and passed to the Vatican collections, where it remains today. In the mid nineteenth century, it attracted attention from German and French scholars interested in lyric poetry. *Jean Renart*, ed. Durling, 3–4.

19. *Le lai de l'ombre par Jean Renart*, ed. Joseph Bédier, Société des anciens textes français (Paris, 1913), vii–xxii.

20. In his edition, Gustave Servois surveys this scholarship. *Le roman de la rose ou Guillaume de Dole*, Anciens textes français (Paris, 1893), ii–iii, xv–xxvii. Gaston Paris treats the lyrics in the Servois edition, lxxxix–cxxi.

21. Léon Gautier, *La chevalerie* (Paris, 1884), xiii–xiv, 674, 677. He had originally intended his book to be entitled "La chevalerie d'après les chansons de geste."

22. The success of *La société française au XIIIᵉ siècle d'après dix romans d'aventure* (Paris, 1904) encouraged Langlois to add three volumes devoted to other genres: *La vie en France au moyen âge d'après quelques moralistes du temps* (Paris, 1908); *La vie en France au moyen âge: La connaissance de la nature et du monde d'après des écrits français à l'usage des laïcs* (Paris, 1927); and *La vie en France au moyen âge: La Vie spirituelle, enseignements, méditations et controverses d'après des écrits en français à l'usage des laïcs* (Paris, 1928). Earlier volumes were reprinted under the general title, *La vie en France au moyen âge du XIIᵉ au milieu du XIVᵉ siècle*. The first volume was reissued with an introduction by Jacques Le Goff (Paris, 1981). In the nineteenth century, German doctoral dissertations established a tradition of pursuing historical themes in romance literature. See, e.g., Carl August Hinstorff, *Kulturgeschichtliches im "Roman de l'Escoufle" und im "Roman de la Rose ou de Guillaume de Dole": Ein Beitrag zur Erklärung der beiden Romane* (Darmstadt, 1896).

23. Lejeune, *L'oeuvre de Jean Renart*, 332. Lejeune continued to develop this theme throughout her career, notably in "Jean Renart et le roman réaliste au XIIIᵉ siècle," in *Grundriss der romanischen Literaturen des Mittelalters*, ed. Hans Robert Jauss and Erich Köhler (Heidelberg, 1978), 4: 400–418; Lejeune, "*Guillaume de Dole*," 1–24; "L'ésprit 'clerical' et les curiosités intellectuelles de Jean Renart dans le 'Roman de Guillaume de Dole,'" *Mélanges de linguistique française et de philologie et littérature médiévales offerts à Monsieur Paul Imbs*, Travaux de linguistique et de littérature, 2 (Strasbourg, 1973), 2: 589–601; and *Du nouveau sur Jean Renart* (Liège, 1997).

24. Anthime Fourrier, *Le courant réaliste dans le roman courtois en France au moyen âge: 1: Les débuts (XIIᵉ siècle)* (Paris, 1960), 9.

25. Lyons, *Les éléments descriptifs,* ch. 4 and ch. 5, 170, with particular emphasis on the *Rose.*

26. G. E. Brereton, "Une règle d'étiquette royale au moyen âge," *Moyen Age* 64 (1958): 395–97; Anthime Fourrier, "Les armoiries de l'empereur dans *Guillaume de Dole,*" in *Mélanges offerts à Rita Lejeune, Professeur à l'Université de Liège* (Gembloux, Bel., 1969), 2: 1211–26; Marie-Luce Chênerie, "L'épisode du tournoi dans *Guillaume de Dole,* Etude littéraire," *Revue des langues romanes* 83 (1979): 41–62; Jean Larmat, "L'enfant dans l'*Escoufle* de Jean Renart," in *L'enfant au moyen âge, Sénéfiance* 9 (1980): 269–83; Jean Dufournet, "*Guillaume de Dole* ou la glorification des ménestrels," in Jean Renart, *Guillaume de Dole ou le Roman de la rose,* trans. Jean Dufournet et al., 2d ed. (Paris, 1988), 115–49; Maurice Accarie, "La fonction des chansons du *Guillaume de Dole,*" in *Mélanges Larmat,* Annales de la Faculté des Lettres et Sciences humaines de Nice, 39 (Paris, 1982). 13–29; Nathan Leroy Love, "The Polite Speech of Direct Discourse in Jean Renart's 'Guillaume de Dole,'" *Studi francesi* 33 (1989): 71–77; John W. Baldwin, "Jean Renart et le tournoi de Saint-Trond: Une conjonction de l'histoire et de la littérature," *Annales: Economies, sociétés, civilisations* 45.3 (May–June 1990): 565–88; "'Once There Was an Emperor': A Political Reading of the Romances of Jean Renart," in *Jean Renart,* ed. Durling, 45–82; and "The Image of the Jongleur in Northern France around 1200," *Speculum* 72 (1997): 635–63.

27. For the editions, see list of Short Titles under "Jean Renart."

28. In *Histoire littéraire de la France* (Paris, 1852), 22: 807–17, Emile Littré objects, for example, to the delayed introduction of the buzzard in the *Escoufle.* In "Le cycle de la gageur," 489–90, Gaston Paris pronounces the tournament in the *Rose* too long and unnecessary. For more recent appraisals of the narrative structure, see Jean-Charles Payen, "Structure et sens de *Guillaume de Dole,*" in *Etudes de langue et de littérature du moyen âge offertes à Félix Lecoy* (Paris, 1973), 483–98; Minnette Grunmann, "Narrative Voices in the Old French Epic and Romance, Exemplified by *La Chanson de Guillaume, Galeran,* and *Guillaume de Dole,*" *Romance Philology* 29 (1975): 201–9; Norris J. Lacy, "The Composition of *L'Escoufle,*" *Res publica litterarum* 1 (1978): 151–58.

29. Zink, *Roman rose,* 40, 120–21. Zink further elaborates this theme in *La subjectivité littéraire: Autour du siècle de saint Louis* (Paris, 1985), 42.

30. For some examples: George T. Diller, "Remarques sur la structure esthetique de *Guillaume de Dole,*" *Romania* 98 (1977): 390–98; "Techniques de contraste dans *Guillaume de Dole,*" *Romania* 99 (1978): 538–49; "*L'Escoufle:* Une aventurière dans le roman courtois," *Moyen Age* 85 (1979): 33–43; Marc René Jung, "L'empereur Conrad, chanteur de poèsie lyrique: Fiction et vérité dans le *Roman de la rose* de Jean Renart," *Romania* 101 (1980): 35–50; Daniel Poirion,

"Fonction de l'imaginaire dans l'*Escoufle*," in *Mélanges de langue et littéraire française du moyen âge et de la renaissance offerts à Charles Foulon* (Rennes, 1980), 1: 287–93; Sarah Kay, "Two Readings of the *Lai de l'ombre*," *Modern Language Review* 75 (1980): 515–27; id., *Subjectivity in Troubadour Poetry* (Cambridge, 1990), 183–98; Norris J. Lacy, "'Amer par oïr dire': *Guillaume de Dole* and the Drama of Language," *French Review* 54 (1981): 779–87; Linda F. Cooper, "The Literary Reflectiveness of Jean Renart's *Lai de l'ombre*," *Romance Philology* 35 (1981–82): 250–60; 'L'ironie iconographique de la coupe de Tristan dans l'*Escoufle*," *Romania* 104 (1983): 157–76; Nancy Vine Durling, "The Seal and the Rose: Erotic Exchange in *Guillaume de Dole*," *Neophilologus* 77 (1993): 31–40; Nancy A. Jones, "The Uses of Embroidery in the Romances of Jean Renart: Gender, History, Textuality," in *Jean Renart*, ed. Durling, 13–44.

31. Kay, *Subjectivity*, 196. On the difficulties of editing and translating, see Félix Lecoy, "Sur quelques passages difficiles de *Guillaume de Dole*," *Romania* 82 (1961): 244–60, and Patricia Terry, "On the Untranslatable Surface of *Guillaume de Dole*," in *Jean Renart*, ed. Durling, 142–53.

32. Roger Dragonetti, *Le mirage des sources: L'art du faux dans le roman médiéval* (Paris, 1987), 59–224.

33. Ibid., 7.

34. Gaston Paris in *Guillaume de Dole*, ed. Servois, xci–xcvi. Zink, *Roman rose*, 29.

35. Maurice Delbouille, "Sur les traces de 'Bele Aëlis,'" in *Mélanges de philologie romane dédiées à la mémoire de Jean Boutière (1899–1967)* (Liège, 1971), 1: 199–18; Marc René Jung, "L'empereur Conrad, chanteur de poèsie lyrique" (see n. 30 above); Emmanuèle Baumgartner, "Les citations lyriques dans le *Roman de la rose* de Jean Renart," *Romance Philology* 35 (1981–82): 260–66; Maurice Accarie, "La fonction des chansons du *Guillaume de Dole*" (see n. 26 above); Maria V. Coldwell, "*Guillaume de Dole* and Medieval Romances with Musical Interpolations," *Musica disciplina* 34 (1984): 55–86; Christopher Page, *Voices and Instruments of the Middle Ages: Instrumental Practice and Songs in France, 1100–1300* (Berkeley, 1986), 31–39; Sylvia Huot, *From Song to Book: The Poetics of Writing in Old French Lyric and Lyrical Narrative Poetics* (Ithaca, N.Y., 1987), 108–16; "The Lyric Insertions in Jean Renart, *Roman de la Rose*," in Jean Renart, *Romance of the Rose*, ed. Switten (see Chapter 1, n. 27, above), 7–17; Boulton, *Song in the Story* (see n. 2 above), 24–35; Margaret Switten, "Song Performance," in Jean Renart, *Romance of the Rose*, ed. Switten (see Chapter 1, n. 27, above), 19–36; Danièle Duport, "Les chansons dans *Guillaume de Dole*," in *"Et c'est la fin pour quoy nous somme ensemble": Hommage à Jean Dufournet* (Paris, 1993), 2: 513–23; Maureen Barry McCann Boulton, "Lyric Insertions and the Reversal of Romance Conventions in Jean Renart's *Roman de la Rose* or *Guillaume de Dole*," in *Jean Renart*, ed. Durling, 85–104; Michel Zink, "Suspension and Fall: The Fragmentation and

Linkage of Lyric Insertions in *Le roman de la rose (Guillaume de Dole)* and *Le roman de la violette*," in *Jean Renart*, ed. Durling, 105–21; Regina Psaki, "Jean Renart's Expanded Text: Lïenor and the Lyrics of *Guillaume de Dole*," in *Jean Renart*, ed. Durling, 122–41; Henrik van der Werf, "Jean Renart and Medieval Song," in *Jean Renart*, ed. Durling, 157–87.

36. Tournaments: Chênerie, "L'épisode du tournoi dans *Guillaume de Dole*" (see n. 26 above); Michel Parisse, "Le tournoi en France, des origines à la fin du XIIIe siècle," in *Das ritterliche Turnier im Mittelalter: Beiträge ƶur einer vergleichenden Formen- und Verhaltensgeschichte des Rittertums*, ed. Josef Fleckenstein, Veröffentlichungen des Max-Planck-Instituts für Geschichte, 80 (Göttingen, 1985), 175–211; Baldwin, "Jean Renart et le tournoi de Saint-Trond" (see n. 26 above). Jongleurs: Dufournet, "*Guillaume de Dole* ou la glorification des ménestrels" (see n. 26 above); Baldwin, "Image of the Jongleur" (see n. 26 above). Textiles: Caroline Jewers, "Fabric and Fabrication: Lyric and Narrative in Jean Renart's *Roman de la Rose*," *Speculum* 71 (1996): 907–24; Nancy Jones, "Uses of Embroidery" (see n. 30 above). Towns: Jean Larmat, "La ville dans l'*Escoufle*," *Razo: Cahiers du Centre d'Etudes médiévales de Nice* 1 (1979), 47–54; Marie-Claude Struyf, "Symbolique des villes et de demeures dans les romans de Jean Renart," *Cahiers de civilisation médiévale* 30 (1987): 245–61. Jean Larmat, "L'enfant dans l'*Escoufle*" (see n. 26 above).

37. Rita Lejeune, "Le personnage d'Aelis dans le 'Roman de l'Escoufle' de Jean Renart," in *Mélanges de littérature du moyen âge au XXe siècle offerts à Mademoiselle Jeanne Lods* (Paris, 1978), 378–92; George T. Diller, "*L'Escoufle*: Une aventurière" (see n. 30 above); Henri Rey-Flaud, *La névrose courtoise* (Paris, 1983), 77–104; Roberta L. Krueger, "Double Jeopardy: The Appropriation of Women in Four Old French Romances of the 'Cycle de la Gageure,'" in *Seeking the Woman in Late Medieval and Renaissance Writings: Essays in Feminist Contextual Criticism*, ed. Sheiler Fisher and Janet E. Halley (Knoxville, Tenn., 1989), 21–50; Kay, *Subjectivity* (see n. 30 above), 183–98; Laurence de Looze, "The Gender of Fiction: Womenly Poetics in Jean Renart's *Guillaume de Dole*," *French Review* 64 (1991): 596–606; Helen Solterer, "At the Bottom of Mirage, a Woman's Body: *Le Roman de la rose* of Jean Renart," in *Feminist Approaches to the Body in Medieval Literature*, ed. Linda Lomperis and Sarah Stanbury (Philadelphia, 1993), 213–33; Claude Lachet, "Présence de Liénor dans le *Roman de la Rose* de Jean Renart," in *"Et c'est la fin pour quoy nous sommes ensemble": Hommage à Jean Dufournet* (Paris, 1993), 813–25; Nancy Jones, "Uses of Embroidery" (see n. 30 above); Regine Psaki, "Jean Renart's Expanded Text" (see n. 35 above).

38. For examples of the symbolic approach based on structural anthropology, see the studies of Marie-Claude Struyf inspired by Gilbert Durand (see n. 36 above) and of Anita Guerreau-Jalabert (see Chapter 6 at n. 23).

39. Philippe Walter, *Le mémoir du temps: Fêtes et calendriers de Chrétien de*

Troyes à la Mort Artu, Nouvelle bibliothèque du moyen âge, 13 (Paris, 1989), 4, 89, 114–15. With this triple interaction, Walter sets about investigating feasts and festivities in medieval French literature from 1170 to 1235. See also Walter, "Tout commence par des chansons . . ." (see Preface, n. 3, above), 188. A similar approach is taken by Laurence de Looze, "Gender of Fiction" (see n. 37 above), 596–97; and Regina Psaki, "Expanded Text" (see n. 35 above), 137.

40. In 1871, Charles Potvin published a synopsis with extensive extracts at the end of his edition of the MS. Mons, Bibl. pub. 331/206, *Perceval le Gallois ou le Conte du graal publié d'après les manuscrits originaux*, 6 vols., Publications de la Société des bibliophiles Belges séant à Mons, 21 (Mons, 1866–71), 6: 161–259. Francisque Michel had published an earlier edition, *Roman de la Violette ou de Gérard de Nevers, en vers, du XIIIᵉ siècle, par Girbert de Montreuil; publié pour la première fois, d'après deux manuscrits de la Bibliothèque Royale* (Paris, 1834).

41. Charles François, *Etude sur le style* (see Chapter 1, n. 3, above); Amida Stanton, *Gerbert de Montreuil as a Writer of Grail Romance: An Investigation of the Date and the More Immediate Sources of the Continuation of Perceval* (diss., University of Chicago, 1939; extract published, Chicago, 1942); Jean Larmat, "Le peché de Perceval dans la *Continuation* de Gerbert," in *Mélanges d'histoire littéraire, de linguistique, et de philologie romane offerts à Charles Rostaing*, ed. J. De Caluwé et al. (Liège, 1974), 1: 541–57; Sara Sturm-Maddox, "*Tout est par s<i>enfi</i>ance:* Gerbert's *Perceval*," in *Arthurian Yearbook*, ed. Keith Busby, 2 (1992): 191–207.

42. Friedrich Kraus, *Über Girbert de Montreuil und seine Werke* (diss., Würzburg, 1896) (Erlangen, 1897); Maurice Wilmotte, "Gerbert de Montreuil et les écrits qui lui sont attribués," *Bulletin de l'Académie royale de Belgique, Classe des lettres, et des sciences morales et politiques et la classe des beaux-arts* (Brussels, 1900), 166–89; Douglas L. Buffum, *Le roman de la Violette: A Study of the Manuscripts and the Original Dialect* (diss., Johns Hopkins University, 1904) (Baltimore, 1904); id., "The Songs of the *Roman de la Violette*," in *Studies in Honor of A. Marshall Elliott* (Baltimore, 1911), 1: 129–57; Boulton, *Song in the Story* (see n. 2 above), 35–42; John W. Baldwin, "Crisis of the Ordeal: Literature, Law, and Religion around 1200," *Journal of Medieval and Renaissance Studies* 24 (1994): 348–51; Zink, "Suspension and Fall" (see n. 35 above), esp. 110–19.

43. See Chapter 1, "Hermeneutic Propositions," and Baldwin, *Language of Sex*, xxiv–vii.

44. The equation of Guillaume with *faeȝ* is an implicit reference to Benoît de Saint-Maure, *Roman de Troie* vv. 1423–28. Lyons, *Eléments descriptifs*, 109.

45. For examples of the luxurious *chansonniers:* (A) Chansonnier d'Arras. Arras 657 (1278); (K) Chansonnier de l'Arsenal, Paris Arsenal 5198 (fol. 1r, fiddler playing before the king and queen of Navarre); (M) le manuscrit du roi, Paris BN fr. 844; (O) Chansonnier Cangé, Paris BN fr. 846 (1287); (U) Chansonnier de

Saint-Germain-des-Prés Paris BN fr. 20050 (1240–75). Alison Stones (in *Les manuscrits de Chrétien de Troyes,* 1: 241, 256–57) has dated A and O. For the date and character of U, see Madeleine Tyssens, "Les copistes du chansonnier français U," in *Lyrique romane médiévale: La tradition des chansonniers,* Bibliothèque de la Faculté de Philosophie et Lettres de l'Université de Liège, 258 (Liège, 1991), 379–95. For a recent introduction to the manuscripts of the chansonniers, see Sylvia Huot, *From Song to Book: The Poetics of Writing in Old French Lyric and Lyrical Narrative Poetry* (Ithaca, N.Y., 1987), 46–80.

46. Baldwin, *Government of Philip Augustus,* 257–305. Susan Reynolds, *Fiefs and Vassals: The Medieval Evidence Reinterpreted* (Oxford, 1994), 276–78, 288, 309, 320. For an example of land exchanged for service, see *Rose* vv. 100–103.

Index

The fictional characters in the romances of Jean Renart and Gerbert de Montreuil are not included in the index, with the exception of some thinly disguised historical personages. For Jean's and Gerbert's views on particular subjects, see under those subject headings.

Isabel de Clare, countess, 81
Isabelle of Hainaut, queen of France, 164

Jacques d'Avesnes, 71
Jacques de Vitry, 79–80, 253
Jaufré Rudel, 158
Jauss, Hans Robert, 11–12
Jean de Betefort, master of the wardrobe, 183, 191
Jean de Béthune, bishop of Cambrai, 45–48
Jean de Jeanville, 96, 309n. 76, 319n. 28
Jean Renart, xii; as deconstructionist, 257; as jongleur, 30; name of, 1–2, 276n. 2
Jerome, church father, *Adversus Jovianum*, 125
Jerusalem, 38, 166; Church of the Holy Sepulchre, 105, 198
Jews, 116, 334n. 82
John, king of England, 36, 61; imperial politics of, 45–48; reception at Paris, 164, 167
John XXII, pope, 90
jongleurs, 6, 121, 168–70, 263, 266; economic support of, 23–26; profession of, 21–30; robes of, 21, 23
Joseph of Arimathea, 239, 339n. 150
Juglet: eponymous jongleur, 22–23; storyteller, 29

Keen, Maurice, xii
knights, xiv, 4, 7; creation of, 90–93, 165, 308n. 68; equipment of, 109–10; fighting in groups, 77–79; French, 6; German, 6; lineage of, 90–92, 262; mercenary, 266; order of chivalry, 93–95; prowess of, 69–70, 95–97; in single combat, 68–69, 75–77

Lagny-sur-Marne, 77, 307n. 53
Lai de l'ombre (Jean Renart), 1, 2, 6, 29, 194, 275n. 2; dedication of, 33; manuscripts of, 250, 252, 341n. 3; plot of, 5
La March-sur-Loire, 63
Langlois, Charles-Victor, 256, 259
largesse, 98–104
Lateran Council, Fourth (1215). *See* Innocent III, pope
Lecoy, Félix, 256, 295n. 73
Lejeune, Rita, 36, 39, 256, 259, 344n. 23
Liège, 13, 39, 82, 116
literal reading, 20–21, 259–60
Littré, Emile, 256
Longueau, nunnery, 44
Lord's prayer, 215–16
Lorraine, 5. *See also* Dole, Lorraine; Toul
Lotharingia, 13, 265
Louis, count of Looz, 41
Louis, king of France (fictional), 60, 63, 170, 196, 210–11, 263; *preu*, 70; without spouse, 127. *See also* Montargis; Pont de l'Arche
Louis, prince (future Louis VIII), 25; feasting at knighting, 109, 174; knighting of, 26, 90, 93, 164–65; patron of Gace Brulé, 25, 280n. 47; wardrobe of, 191–92
Louis VII, king of France, daughters of, 54, 143, 297n. 83
Louis VIII, king of France, 59–60. *See also* Louis, prince
Louis IX, king of France, 9, 60, 63, 263; anti-dueling ordinances of, 209; at banquet at Saumer, 319n. 28; against swearing, 328n. 25
lovesickness, 150–53
Ludwig I, duke of Bavaria, 40
lyrics, 29, 249, 258, 263; anthologies of, 14–19

Library of Congress Cataloging-in-Publication Data
Baldwin, John W.
    Aristocratic life in medieval France : the romances of
Jean Renart and Gerbert de Montreuil, 1190–1230 /
John W. Baldwin.
        p.   cm.
    Includes bibliographical references and index.
    ISBN 0-8018-6188-8 (alk. paper)
    1. Jean Renart, 12th/13th cent.—Political and social
views. 2. Gerbert, de Montreuil, 13th cent.—Political and
social views. 3. Aristocracy (Social class)—France—
History—To 1500. 4. Literature and society—France—
History—To 1500. 5. Aristocracy (Social class) in litera-
ture. 6. Romances—History and criticism. I. Title.
PQ1486.J7Z57   2000
841'.109—dc21   99-29030
                                                    CIP